Propaganda

The book is a modern primer on propaganda—aspects like disinformation, trolls, bots, information influence, psychological operations, information operations, and information warfare. *Propaganda: From Disinformation and Influence to Operations and Information Warfare* offers a contemporary model for thinking about the subject.

The first two decades of the 21st century have brought qualitative and quantitative technological and societal changes, and the subject of information influence needs to be re-ordered. Now is the time.

The book explains the origins of the meaning and phenomenon of propaganda—where it came from and how it has changed over the centuries. The book also covers modern methods, including artificial intelligence (AI) and advertising technologies. Legal, political, diplomatic, and military considerations ensure that the material is covered in depth.

The book is recommended for security and cybersecurity professionals (both technical and non-technical), government officials, politicians, corporate executives, academics, and students of technical and social sciences. Adepts with an interest in the subject will read it with interest.

Lukasz Olejnik, Ph.D., LL.M. (LukaszOlejnik.com) is an independent cybersecurity and privacy researcher and consultant.

He holds a Computer Science Ph.D. (INRIA, the French Institute for Research in Computer Science and Automation) and an LL.M. in Information Technology Law (University of Edinburgh). He worked at CERN (The European Organisation for Nuclear Research) and was a research associate at University College London. He was associated with Princeton's Center for Information Technology Policy, Oxford's Centre for Technology and Global Affairs, and Geneva Academy of International Humanitarian Law and Human Rights, and was elected a Member of the World Wide Web Consortium's (W3C) Technical Architecture Group. Former cyberwarfare advisor at the International Committee of the Red Cross in Geneva, where he worked on the humanitarian consequences of cyberwarfare, he advised on science and new technologies at the European Data Protection Supervisor.

A thorough primer on a complex, modern problem with ancient roots. *Propaganda* is an excellent resource for anyone who wants to better understand the fight for influence.

— **John Hultquist,** *Chief Analyst, Google Mandiant*

Lukasz Olejnik has written a comprehensive, dispassionate and sweeping study of propaganda, one that reflects deeply and eclectically on the nature of modern information technology and how it is woven into society, politics and international relations. He argues persuasively that while propaganda has a long history, it is now possible on an unprecedented scale and with new precision, with implications for state sovereignty, free speech and democracy.

— **Shashank Joshi,** defense editor, *The Economist*

Lukasz Olejnik's *Propaganda* is a treasure trove of information on influence operations ranging from the 17th Century Catholic Church to AI bot armies and everything in between. Appropriately, the book sticks to the facts and provides a historical, technical, geopolitical, and legal perspective but without offering value judgments. Olejnik makes serious and complex subject matter approachable and entertaining.

— **Arvind Narayanan,** professor of computer science at Princeton University, author of *AI Snake Oil: What Artificial Intelligence Can Do, What It Can't, and How to Tell the Difference*

In today's global society, where streams of information flow constantly and easily, distinguishing truth from falsehood is challenging. This book uncovers the subtle games of propaganda, information operations, disinformation and cyber operations, showing how these powerful tools are used to manipulate society. Analyzing the various techniques of propaganda and information operations, the author refers to both historical events and contemporary case studies. Can you tell the difference between real information and fabricated narratives? How do states use propaganda to shape the perception of internal and external visions? Are we vulnerable to the invasion of disinformation in an era of digital chaos? These questions become crucial in the face of today's challenges and technological developments, where the boundaries between fact and fiction are blurring on our screens and in our minds.

— **Maj Gen Karol Molenda,** first Commander of the Cyberspace Defense Forces of the Polish Armed Forces

Lukasz Olejnik's new book offers an invaluable categorization - and dissection - of propaganda in an age of information warfare. Packed full of both technical detail and historical context, Olejnik deepens and expands our understanding of how propaganda can work. From online trolling to psychological deception, one of Europe's premier experts shows the dangers emerging from authoritarian aggressors like Russia - and offers ways to counter them. For anyone interested in the battlefields of the 21st century, this book is essential reading.

— **James Palmer,** deputy editor, *Foreign Policy*

Propaganda

From Disinformation and Influence to Operations and Information Warfare

Lukasz Olejnik

CRC Press
Taylor & Francis Group
Boca Raton London New York

CRC Press is an imprint of the
Taylor & Francis Group, an **informa** business

Designed cover image: © Agnieszka Konkolewska

First edition published 2025
by CRC Press
2385 NW Executive Center Drive, Suite 320, Boca Raton FL 33431

and by CRC Press
4 Park Square, Milton Park, Abingdon, Oxon, OX14 4RN

CRC Press is an imprint of Taylor & Francis Group, LLC

Library of Congress Cataloging-in-Publication Data
Names: Olejnik, Lukasz, author.
Title: Propaganda : from disinformation and influence to operations and information warfare / Lukasz Olejnik.
Description: First edition. | Boca Raton, FL : CRC Press, 2025. | Includes bibliographical references and index.
Identifiers: LCCN 2024013220 (print) | LCCN 2024013221 (ebook) | ISBN 9781032802251 (hbk) | ISBN 9781032813721 (pbk) | ISBN 9781003499497 (ebk)
Subjects: LCSH: Propaganda. | Social change. | Artificial intelligence.
Classification: LCC HM1231 .O48 2025 (print) | LCC HM1231 (ebook) | DDC 303.3/75--dc23/eng/20240430
LC record available at https://lccn.loc.gov/2024013220
LC ebook record available at https://lccn.loc.gov/2024013221

ISBN: 978-1-032-80225-1 (hbk)
ISBN: 978-1-032-81372-1 (pbk)
ISBN: 978-1-003-49949-7 (ebk)

DOI: 10.1201/9781003499497

Typeset in Sabon
by SPi Technologies India Pvt Ltd (Straive)

Contents

Preface

Facing a complex issue is not easy. Hearing the word "propaganda," almost everyone intuitively recalls some understanding of it and has some associations linked to it. In this book, the term is used in a neutral and technical sense. I clearly mark the origin and evolution of the meaning of the term and present its historical background. It is not my goal to impose any view on the Reader, and I refrain from doing so. This approach is intended to clarify the basics for the purpose of discussing the many issues of contemporary importance in the information age.

This book is dedicated to the subject of propaganda. It covers elements such as information operations, influence operations, spread of false information (misinformation), disinformation, information war, various types of abuse, influence, and psychological operations, including even information methods that in the past led to the outbreak of wars and to commitment of crimes against humanity and of genocide. This may sound serious and complicated (some of it perhaps even not exactly related—read on!), but I strived to lay out this content accessibly. By its very nature, I could not reduce the topic to uniquely contemporary slice, for example, the use of methods such as bots and trolls on the Internet and in social media, to which a lot of space has been devoted (or reduced) in various analyses in 2016–2024. The whole issue is much broader. I also face contemporary stereotypes like "information bubbles" and "echo chambers." I do this on the basis of sound scientific research, not journalistic or anecdotal reports or personal views. The accepted premise of relying on reliable sources helps dispel misunderstandings and find the correct understanding of the issues.

In Chapter 1, I explain what is propaganda, including the origins of the phrase. Where did it come from? How did its meaning evolve over decades? What influenced this change? How is it perceived today? Is propaganda a negative thing, or is it a positive thing? These are questions of informational influence. Today, we refer to certain elements of the formerly understood meanings from this area as public relations, public affairs, and even public education.

In Chapter 2, I introduce the important concept of information environment. This is a useful analytical model that defines a certain system within which social groups, relationships, and interactions take place. The components of this environment can be people, digital platforms, traditional and electronic media, governments, NGOs, companies, and their advertising and lobbying campaigns (and more). The information environment is not a static creation. It is subject to evolution and dynamism. The informational influence of the various actors listed makes up this entire ecosystem. Learning about these concepts will facilitate an understanding of the possibilities of information modulation of this environment and how information campaigns are designed.

Technology plays an important role everywhere in this book. Chapter 3 is devoted entirely to it. It considers important fundamentals from digital platforms, social media, through methods of creating bot networks, to using AI (LLM) methods to create information payloads and propagate them through various channels. The chapter treats the topic holistically.

Thus, it talks about the printing press, radio, and more to the point—contemporary technical methods, as well as persuasion techniques. These are tools that are helpful and sometimes indispensable in the practical generation of information campaigns (and to defuse them).

In Chapter 4, I expound on the issues of the so-called commercial propaganda, understood as the propagation of information. This is a collective term for PR, advertising, and various types of campaigns, with different ethical qualities (I leave the evaluation to the Reader). I show how, referring to changes, topics, and social issues, it is possible to convey some content and information, doing so for profit.

Chapter 5 is devoted to legal issues—national laws but also international law and its evolution in historical perspective. I mention the failed attempts to legally curb propaganda and disinformation, if only to inform any contemporary or future approaches to similar intentions. States have tried to counter the informational influence of foreign States since the early 19th century. Increased interest in the subject came after World War I, when initiatives were created to regulate such practices. It didn't work then, but the topic was revisited after World War II. Nowadays—due to technological developments—there is a renaissance of concerns and, at the same time, of efforts made to stabilize informational influence. The Reader will decide for himself or herself whether contemporarily conditions exist that allow reaching better results compared to the situation before World War II.

Chapter 6 is devoted to political propaganda. This is both the exertion of influence in particular countries (inward, domestically) but also toward, against, and on other countries and entities (outward, externally). To fully appreciate these phenomena, it is necessary to assimilate the information that appears earlier in the book. In this chapter, I demonstrate how new media can be used to create information diversion, as well as to coordinate the actions of actors inside States and on the international stage. It's not merely about sowing confusion. The range of possibilities is broader and also includes information tools that initiate or support such activities as, for example, the instigation of coups d'etat, revolutions, and the overthrow of governments. The role of information cannot be overlooked in such affairs. New technologies make it possible to more effectively create information illusions that influence public perception.

Chapter 7 talks about the military and strictly warfare aspects. I explain what information warfare is and what it is not—how to understand the term strictly, without leaving any space for *grey areas*. I explain how States have used and continue to use propaganda during wars. In the third decade of the 21st century, we can see this with our own eyes, but it is not always simple or possible to discern these procedures in action. Perhaps it will become easier after reading this chapter. But be warned, it is not necessary to look for, and see, potential propaganda everywhere. Such a mode of reading the world leads to paranoia. In Chapter 7, I analyze the information and propaganda background during the war in Ukraine (as of 2022–2024). I also point out the need for States to rethink issues such as strategic communications, cyber warfare, decoding capability, disarmament, and the execution of information operations. I outline the role of psychological operations, sometimes with details such as psychological effects, and physical events, not just information messages.

This is a book about security, and even about strategy. It combines information from many fields: technical (computer science), social (psychology, sociology, etc.), legal (national, European, international Laws), as well as interaction in the digital environment (digital platforms and their privileged role). Only in this comprehensive way can such a complex issue be covered.

I strived to write this book concisely and accessibly so that it provides a solid introduction to these issues—relevant to our times. It, therefore, provides a good foundation and substructure, useful for the student as well as the expert, scholar, and public official. Or simply someone desiring to get familiar with the domain, not necessarily to use in practice any of the methods or techniques.

Author

Lukasz Olejnik, Ph.D., LL.M. (LukaszOlejnik.com) is an independent cybersecurity and privacy researcher and consultant.

He holds a Computer Science PhD (INRIA, the French Institute for Research in Computer Science and Automation) and an LL.M. in Information Technology Law (University of Edinburgh). He worked at CERN (European Organisation for Nuclear Research) and was a research associate at University College London. He was associated with Princeton's Center for Information Technology Policy, with Oxford's Centre for Technology and Global Affairs, Geneva Academy of International Humanitarian Law and Human Rights, and was elected a Member of the World Wide Web Consortium's (W3C) Technical Architecture Group. Former cyberwarfare advisor at the International Committee of the Red Cross in Geneva, where he worked on the humanitarian consequences of cyberwarfare, he advised on science and new technologies at the European Data Protection Supervisor.

He helps various companies and organizations, including with cybersecurity, privacy and data protection, and technology policy.

He is the author of the book *Philosophy of Cybersecurity*. His comments appeared in places such as *Financial Times*, *Washington Post*, *New York Times*, *Wall Street Journal*, *Sueddeutsche Zeitung*, *El Pais*, or *Le Monde*. He authored scientific papers, reports, and opinion articles in venues like *Wired* or *Foreign Policy*.

Chapter 1

The concept of propaganda—the evolution of meaning

A journey through the topics of propaganda—influence, information operations, information warfare, disinformation, psychological operations—has to start somewhere. We start from the beginning, including historical background. Laying out the subject in this way is not necessary to acquire an awareness of contemporary operations, or even to be able to apply techniques and technologies. However, it is definitely advisable. In this way, knowledge and awareness of the subject will be more complete. It will also help develop a sense of responsibility.

Then, what is propaganda?

1.1 THE PROBLEM FROM THE BEGINNING

Let me start by saying that the word "propaganda" does not have the best connotation today. Or actually, it has very, very bad associations. With something foul, dishonest, perhaps even demonic, evil, harmful, fraudulent, etc. This has not always been the case, but consideration of this subject must begin systematically and gradually.

This chapter is an introduction to the issue. The information in it is laid out coherently and outlined quite generally. It might not always be straightforward why specific topics are covered. Everything will come together after reading the book. If some of the information in this chapter seems particularly difficult for the Reader to digest (even though references are provided, for example), I still encourage you to persevere in order to properly understand the key fundamentals useful for further reading. Early on, I grapple with an enormous challenge stemming from the fact that the very word "propaganda" is today commonly perceived as something with a negative connotation. I realize that I won't win against this perception of the word—after all, the tradition of the nefarious meaning is almost 100 years old. That much is clear. It is not my intention or the purpose of this book. Moreover, I do not intend to express opinions (or force them on the Reader), that is not the point—that is a task for the Reader.

So, the purpose of this chapter is something else. It's about demonstrating how things happened, where it all came from, and why we perceive certain meanings, contents, and terms in particular ways, and not others. This may be of interest to the Reader, because of the presentation of information, its influence, its manipulation, and its modulation—this is something important in each chapter of this book.

After all, the essential subject of this book is precisely the issue of informational influence. Thus also is its importance to our lives, society, civilization, and State—the impact on individuals, as well as on entire populations. Information and communication circulation is a key issue in the information age. This is due to the significant acceleration of technology and, thus, the impact on societies, as well as States.

DOI: 10.1201/9781003499497-1

These are issues that affect many entities—companies, state institutions, organizations, militaries—because these things do not happen in a vacuum. These are also issues touching people (citizens) individually, collectively, and, more broadly, population-wise. This book is intended to provide a comprehensive picture of the issue. And thus we begin.

1.2 WE DO NOT VALUATE

Important Note for the Reader. In this book I try not to valuate. Except in places where it is unquestionable, I do not prejudge whether something is bad or good. Therefore, I do not necessarily express my views here. Rather, my goal is for this book to contain unbiased, well-reasoned, and useful information and content. The question of what they may be useful for is left to the Reader.

Some elements—even the mere mention of certain sources, references, events, processes, stories, anecdotes, people, or cited data—may be considered by some as inappropriate, controversial, or surprising. Perhaps, dear Reader, you will not agree with this; however, there is a method in it. It is necessary for the content of the book to be complete. Again, this is not a book of the so-called views, which—especially in places—may not necessarily be interesting to the Reader. That is not the point. And in such places—let's call them backdrops—the Reader does not have to agree with everything. It suffices to accept that something is or that something was (in the past, perhaps distant). The Readers should judge for themselves, and decide, or choose, what is relevant. This also applies to this chapter. The matter will be somewhat different in the later parts of the book, where strictly expert, technical, and scientific things are discussed.

1.3 NATURE OF CHANGE IN THE INFORMATION SPACE

A fundamental element that affects the whole issue discussed in this book is the phenomenon of rapid change. These are the rapid social and civilizational changes occurring as a result of the development of science and technology. Technology has a huge impact on the world today. Development in this regard has greatly accelerated. Some of the reasons for these processes are well known and even obvious. One of the elements of these changes and their manifestations, dear Reader, you probably often carry in your pocket or have close at hand. I am talking about the smartphone—a symbol of technological change in this century. People usually carry it with them, and it provides them with instant access to information and communication—for work and for entertainment. Smartphones, computers, and the so-called computerization and networking are, in fact, at the center of the current changes and are responsible for this acceleration. This is what proves that we are in the information age. This is also why the framing of the issue of propaganda 100 years ago must have been quite different from its conception today.

We can mention specific examples of mediums or tools: websites; apps, new information, and media channels. Instagram; Facebook; TikTok; Google's search engine; computers; smartphones; smart devices like watches, glasses, and even fitness devices; and variants and equivalents of these solutions in 5, 10, 20, and 50 years. Also of increasing importance are the foundational elements that in "higher layers" provide or otherwise act on data—the various models of information processing: generative AI (artificial intelligence), GPT-likes (generative pre-trained transformer, or artificial intelligence language model engine), LLM (large language models, which generate content based on a "learned" model describing knowledge).

The development of technology and science leading to these boons of civilization has occurred in the last 60 years, although they themselves directly appeared 5, 10, and 20 years ago. So, let's conventionally assume that the key timeframe is the first 20 years of the 21st century. It is a truism and an obvious fact that today we have information of all kinds at our fingertips: national and world events; the latest sports, economic, financial, and social news; and even entertainment gossip in various industries. This data influences our minds, it is consumed, processed, and shared. However, someone or something is responsible for creating this content. At the same time, we have governments with various centers responsible for social communication. We have various companies helping with communications. We have centers responsible for creating advertising and public relations (PR). We have radio, television, digital media, social media, and even various state or even military units operating in these or related areas. We also have education systems—schools. Many entities interact. Sometimes they compete (if only for our attention). Such information filling makes up (creates, builds, complements) a certain environment in which the modern human revolves. As this book shows, these things also affect our understanding of things, our individual development. They affect how we think, what actions we will take, who we are, or who we will become. Technical and informational goods are invaluable aids; they definitely improve our lives. But with these changes also come the risks, and good things can also lead to abuse. They enable some influence, some effects. Both as a result of chance, coincidence, and deliberate and systematic action.

To appreciate and properly understand this aspect, and the information space issue in general, it is necessary to begin from the start. The problem of changes in the information space, or information security, is a complex issue. In fact, it has existed since time immemorial, thanks to the gradual achievements of civilization. If it is to be from the start, then so be it.

1.4 IT'S THE "P" WORD

In fact, it is true that *in the beginning was the Word.*

Much was changed just by the development of formalized modes of communication—a language that enabled communication through messages, rumors, and gossip. Since then, information was in circulation, and events and stories could be spread more efficiently, exchanged, and passed on to others (including between generations). Information was contained in myths, in poems. And even in those dating back to the ancient era.

1.4.1 Propaganda in Antiquity

The first records of potential propaganda targets date precisely to Antiquity. I don't intend this to feel like a history lesson, but these are the facts.

Poems and elegies, for example, *On Virtue* (Gr. *Areté*) by Tyrtaios[1] have unmistakable propaganda overtones. Besides, poems and songs very often had such overtones also much later. How else to evaluate military marches or songs? They have a certain purpose, such as incitement to fight and building morale in the army or in society. Thus, they may be part of exerting influence, an information operation, or even information warfare (in this chapter, I am still using these phrases without providing definitions—in the intuitive understanding of them, details will start from Chapter 2). Tyrtaios knew his stuff. He was an expert in art. He was also a skilled Spartan propagandist, even if he merely expressed opinions or feelings shared by many of his fellow citizens. It is worth noting that similar or identical ideas to those expressed in Tyrtaios' work—sacrifice (of life) for the fatherland—also resonated much later, including in the history of other countries. These are beautiful literary adaptations. Beautiful art, there is no doubt about it. But the spread of such attitudes may have had very specific political and military goals, and, even if not necessarily goals, they had such effects. Although it must be admitted that Tyrtaios' very idea of "fighting to the end,"[2] that is, not retreating, even at the cost of one's life, does not necessarily make military or operational sense. This was an example of messages through channels known in Antiquity. It was the propagation through writing but primarily through spoken communication. The repetition of verses and transmission from one person to another.

From here, it is close to the records in books. Because the systematic use of writing—on paper—improved this process of propagating information carrying certain values and ideas, although even pictorial information was also spread on other elements important to civilization. An example would be the images of Roman emperors on coins. Here, in turn, we have a different picture of propaganda products. Coins are something that is mass-produced. Coins are minted in large quantities and used by everyone widely and constantly. Texts, on the other hand, were transcribed in medieval orders. This is the perpetuation of the message. However, such reproductions were limited because there were not many educated or trained monks (who initially were responsible for transcriptions), for example—their capabilities were limited in practical terms—such work was also time-consuming, which limited the range. Until, thanks to Gutenberg, the printing press was developed, which tremendously improved the copying of content, text, exchange, and circulation of information. Mechanical and repetitive reproduction of content also improved education, leading to the reduction of illiteracy and to the spread of knowledge. Since then, the number of reproductions has been able to increase significantly, thanks to the fact that they were done quickly and at a lower cost. Let alone today, when reproduction takes milliseconds. All it takes is a simple copy-and-paste on a computer or smartphone, and sending the content forward.

Such changes enable competition on the ground of information.

1.5 THE POWER OF WORDS

Are these considerations theoretical? By any means, no! In fact, this book touches on important issues of information (informational) security. The issue of terminology and words used is important, even crucial, and we must appreciate it. Words have great power, and used in the right way, they can have a great impact. Therefore, we start with words, for example—with a specific word. Because an important part of the techniques that make up this issue is the art of handling words in such a way as to have an impact. Examples here include rhetoric (speech), eristics (the art of argument), as well as persuasion (influence), to which you, the Reader, may often be subjected, sometimes in a non-obvious way; that is, you don't realize it. If only because you don't pay attention to it, because something else occupies you.

1.5.1 Pamphlets versus spreading the word

Sometimes, the mere propagation of information through some channels may suffice. This was the case in the 16th century in Germany, where, through the circulated pamphlets, some people wanted to get the authorities involved in the prosecution of so-called witches.[3] These messages were about women who were accused of conducting harmful activities, such as "magic," which often meant a situation where someone disliked someone but found it difficult to explain a person's behavior. These were "awareness" actions (e.g., about the "danger"), but city authorities were seriously concerned about the possibility of this leading to riots or upheaval by frightened city populations. And this was already a matter of stability, security, and public order. In Nuremberg, there was even censorship enacted (a ban on the spread of such information) because of fears of social destabilization, such as riots and frenzied crowds.[4] Such was the power of the pamphlets: convince groups of people to take action.

Elsewhere in Protestant society, however, the action led to the execution of women suspected of "witchcraft," and the method of spreading this information had the hallmarks of today's viral and moral panics on digital and social media. The content spread quickly, leading to panic, *infecting* wide territories with information—eventually leading to 20,000 executions over the years, a peculiarity of German Protestantism of the time.[5] The study from which we draw this information cites examples of elements of such written and shared text content, including authentic charges against witches:

> Her confession is
> That she should have frozen
> Grain and the grape-vine this year
> "In order to honor the devil".[6]

We are less concerned with how suspected individuals were "induced" to make such confessions, such as forcing them through violent means such as torture, for example. We are not getting into demonological considerations either, but one can imagine that in 16th-century society, with a low level of education, the propagation of such content could have had serious consequences. Most importantly, however, it led to the destabilization of society, risking the undermining of the public order. Therefore, such destabilizing propaganda was fought against. Printers creating such content were prosecuted.[7] After all, the stability of the city or the State was at stake.

We have already used the phrase "propaganda" several times, but have we done that in the right way? Not quite, for in the past, the word did not exist, and even if it did, it would not mean what it does today. It would not be perceived in the way it is today. But first things first.

A fundamental feature of language is that the meaning of words is subject to change. This is not a book about the specifics and evolution of word formation; however, these are facts. Such evolution can also be seen in the changes in the perception of the word "propaganda." When you see it today, you, the Reader, probably associate it with something bad, nefarious, or at least suspicious. Today, the phrase has a strongly pejorative character. It may even constitute an insult.

This was not always the case. In the past, the word "propaganda" had a more functional and descriptive meaning.

Information about the origin of the word "propaganda" may be surprising to some today. As I have already pointed out, according to the Gospel of St. John, "in the beginning was the Word." Indeed, in the case of the word "propaganda," we owe it to the Catholic Church.

1.6 THE ORIGIN OF "PROPAGANDA" IS DUE TO THE CATHOLIC CHURCH

In the 17th century, or more precisely in 1622, Pope Gregory XV established the Sacred Congregation for the Propagation of the Faith (*Sacra Congregatio de Propaganda Fide*), later known as the Congregation for the Evangelization of Peoples, and dissolved in 2022.[8]

This is the first use of the word—its creation.[9] So, paradoxically, when talking about propaganda, every time, as it were, we refer to the Catholic heritage. But here, propaganda is more about *propagation* of things, such as faith or views on it. It's about spreading of information about concepts. It's about education, or dissemination, including, for example, about the education of clerics. All this in a rather neutral, although from the point of view of the Church certainly desirable, that is, looking from this side—positive—sense. This, in a way, was a response to the clerical crisis of the time, but it was also the culmination of

Counter-Reformation activities, those directed against Reformation movements, such as Protestant ones. It was also a tool created in response to the needs of the times, arising from communication with new lands in the so-called New World. Reaching North America, South America, and other continents, from a European point of view, was "discovering new lands" (associated with desire to the spread religion or influence). It is also about the challenges created in Europe precisely by the development of other denominational (i.e., Reformation) currents, such as the aforementioned Protestantism. Reformation, an anti-Catholic activity (including in the sphere of information), was then a fact. Anti-Catholic pamphlets and other types of messages were created; anticlerical movements were organized. Thus, modern ways of influencing people's opinions were created.[10] It was then that the contribution of people skilled in the use of words, including writers,[11] was especially important. From this point of view, these circles also used propaganda methods, although without using the name.

With the rise of Protestantism, new structures and goals were created. And they sought space, followers, adherents, and people who could be persuaded. This clearly created a challenge to the existing order—in this case, to the Catholic Church. Whether the Reader of this book is a believer (and if so, in what or how) or a non-believer (and if so, how) is irrelevant here. The explanation of this phenomenon and process is not an issue of belief or disbelief. For it is simple. A new institution, an ideology (here: Protestant currents), appears, and it "pushes in," creating competition for the stagnant, established order (here: the Catholic Church). The existing institutions then face a choice. They can do nothing, quietly surrender, give up, and, say, fade from history. Or they can do something, counteract. It would be naïve to think that in the event of a challenge to a large and important institution, and the Catholic Church at the time was undoubtedly such, it would meet no resistance or even a fight. What to do then? Counter. That's what happened, and that's why the structure of the Sacra Congregatio de Propaganda Fide was created. Simply translated: the *congregation of propaganda*. To this, we owe this word "propaganda." So, the word "propaganda" comes from the Latin *propagare* (to spread), and you can find many definitions of it today.[12]

1.6.1 Revolutionary propaganda—the French Revolution

Only later did the word "propaganda" acquire the meaning of spreading certain other ideologies, values, and views, such as political ones. For example, during the French Revolution, when propaganda methods were used systematically. Different types of methods of forming opinions, conveying information, and methods of influence—propaganda, we would say—were definitely used during the French Revolution and it was revolutionary, political propaganda—contained in songs, in poems, in official speeches, in proclamations, and in actions.

1.6.2 Caricature, guillotining, heads on a stick

Significantly, at that time, the State's strategy harnessed multiple channels, which also dovetailed with these state and military activities.

Especially from today's perspective, it may be interesting to see how groups of people (often illiterate, uneducated) spread ideas about the change of the political system (overthrow the old monarchy, etc.), using art, for example. In particular, caricature—targeting political enemies (politicians, aristocrats, clergy, etc.)—gained importance.[13] But it is one thing to create caricature depictions of enemies' heads impaled on poles and quite another to depict actual actions (just as such). And I don't mean the famous guillotining, but the actual event when, in the French parliament (1975), the head of a Jean Féraud (deputy to the National Convention, the French parliament back then) ended up on a pike and was prodded at the

Speaker of the French Parliament. This not-so-savory and shocking example shows how a load of social unrest (due to hunger, in this case), also channeled by information, propaganda messages, can lead to real consequences.

1.6.3 The effects of propaganda—can future events be predicted?

It is the consequences that are important here. Because, after all, spreading information and trying to exert "influence" is not just about spreading something for the sake of spreading it. Those doing it are likely concerned with some concrete effects, with actions taken, like getting the audience to take action. And not merely to assimilate information.

In contrast, the notion that events happen "suddenly" makes limited sense. Wars have their causes, as did the French Revolution and everything that happened after it. Events such as sudden political or military eruptions are often preceded by publicly available information, such as those published in the press. This was the case before World War I, before World War II, before the war in Ukraine in 2022, and before—from today's perspective a distant event— the French Revolution.[14] Hence, analysis of the information environment is very important, including the study of the so-called open-source intelligence (OSINT). Of course, the stakes are not always as high as in the case of a World War. But already here we have a clear conclusion: it is always worth paying attention, or tracking, especially the work of selected individuals, institutions, and groups. At that time in France, these may have been people associated with the various so-called "salons," social groups bringing together "friends," sometimes political groups, creative groups, etc. They may have been aware of the processes going on, at least some of them (another thing is that timely insight, or access to such sources, is not always easy).

Why is this important to us? Because when observing and analyzing the information environment, even today, several approaches can be taken: analyzing communities (groups), from those of significant size to smaller ones, as well as analyzing individual people with potentially greater influence on communities (today sometimes called influencers). This boils down to studying information, including propaganda.

1.6.4 Lenin and social media propaganda

Propaganda methods were also used by another revolutionary—Lenin.[15] He understood the necessity of the propaganda struggle in a much more offensive, political sense.[16]

Some remnants of this evolution, developed also by the Soviet, communist system and those techniques, are felt even today. If only in the form of disinformation and propaganda messages through various types of media, social media channels. More grippingly, for example, in the actions of those proverbial "Russian bots and trolls" on social media, in meddling in the electoral processes of other countries. This is just a certain element. However, this will be discussed in later chapters. In this case, we touched on the important topic of the harmfulness of propaganda. Propaganda can undoubtedly be malicious, harmful.

But the meaning of the word itself has evolved strongly, and not so long ago, it was not treated as something unequivocally "bad." Let's examine a positive example.

1.6.5 Propaganda at the United Nations

The UN General Assembly is an international structure where words and expressed positions in a diplomatic and legal context matter. Back in 1947, the phrase "propaganda" was used in the resolution, basically routinely, as if it was a certain political process, or perhaps a mechanical one. As if propaganda was a tool.

The thing took place shortly after the end of World War II. Everyone was fed up with the war. Where was the place for propaganda? This came about through Resolution 110 "Measures to be taken against propaganda and the inciters of a new war,"[17] which called on UN member states to use "all channels of propaganda available to states" to spread peaceful relations between States, while condemning "propaganda that promotes acts of armed aggression." So, propaganda can be bad and good? Let's decode it!

The phrase "all forms" suggests that there are or can be many forms, methods, and means available. The resolution condemns propaganda that calls for and incites war. That is, some use of it, not at all arbitrary, because it is very specific—for some specific purpose. It refers critically to all forms of propaganda, "conducted in any country, the purpose or probable consequence of which is to provoke, encourage and threaten peace, a breach of the peace or an act of aggression" (point 1). From this, it is clear that propaganda is a bad, harmful thing here. Let's agree that wars are bad; after all, people are killed then; property is destroyed. It seems that we can take this for granted, although probably not everyone must agree with this statement.

Returning to the UN resolution, in the same resolution, we also have the phrase: "to promote, by all available means of publicity and propaganda, friendly relations between nations." Here, the word "propaganda" appears to be used in a completely different sense than before (or is it?). Suddenly, the meaning is not negative but more like neutral. Given its purpose. Perhaps even a positive meaning? It is even a somewhat technical formulation, not characterized by values ("evil" or "good"). It is about achieving something, a goal ("friendly relations between nations"). This prompts us to revise our understanding of the term "propaganda" in the first point of this resolution as something with an "evil" meaning. Moreover, it refers to "means"! Hence, to the technical methods used to propagate propaganda.

So, we have a purely technical formulation, not a journalistic or publicist one. This is how the term "propaganda" was used back in 1947. But perhaps this is an accident at work, an isolated example of something niche? Well, not exactly, because the resolution was adopted unanimously—by all members of the UN at the time, that is, representatives of 57 countries. All of these representatives accepted that propaganda is a measure—and not necessarily an issue of valuation (good/bad). As for the substance, it obviously referred to the theme of condemning warmongering—something understandable a few years after the hecatomb of World War II.

However, indirectly, we were also given a testimony of the time—the fine detail and concreteness that interest us, that is, the use of the word "propaganda" in a function and in a purely technical sense, not characterized as such by any general valuation. Such a conclusion is clear from the fact that in the same document, the same word refers to something negative (incitement to war, especially to an aggression war, an act of aggression), as well as to something positive (popularization of peaceful relations between States).

1.6.6 Propagation of ideas? We decode further

The word "propaganda," as we know it, is itself a borrowing from Latin. The *Oxford English Dictionary* dated 1679 provides several meanings of it. It is, for example, "an organization, scheme or movement to promote some doctrine or practice," but also "the systematic dissemination of information, especially in a biased or misleading manner, to promote a political cause or point of view.[18]"

Historically, it was about spreading ideas, views, information. Today, however, "propaganda" is reduced to something demonized, sometimes evil, negatively characterized. When the phrase "propaganda" is used, the instinct may be to apply it in the sense of something nefarious, perhaps to treat it as an insult, even—someone may be called a "propagandist."

Today, we developed and use different terms for these activities of a different nature (or identical but with a non-charged end goal): "public education," "public relations," "public communication," "corporate communication," even if the solutions used are similar and even if, therefore, it would be an euphemistic use of these words (it doesn't have to; it can be assumed that public education is, in principle, something positive, although some may consider that it depends on the specific educational content and who influences it).

Here, we often expect honesty: that the views or ideas presented will be objective, that they will not lean in any particular direction, and that they will be based on scientific standards, for example. Today, on the other hand, some consider propaganda to be the use of methods of propagating and spreading lies, or information in a loaded, biased way, such as selecting content in a dishonest or cynical way. And such a division of meaning has been created, although the details can always be debated. We do that here.

In this book, it is more about mechanics, technique. So, again, by definition we do not valuate the method of propaganda. In classical terms, propaganda had no exclusively bad connotations. That said, however, we must appreciate that today the meaning of the word *is* demonized, and this is due to wars in the 20th and 21st centuries. It is impossible not to be aware of this.

However, since we want to learn about such methods, it is necessary to understand the full picture. On the other hand, in general, there is no escaping the fact that the term "propaganda" is today pejoratively characterized. This change seems to be permanent.

1.6.7 What does Cardinal Richelieu teach about propaganda, and what do Napoleon and De Gaulle teach?

States are concerned with organizing the rules of life within their own frameworks, domestically, as well as in the area of relations with other States. An important part of this is communicating actions to the public and to people on a broad scale. States, therefore, conduct information activities and have information policies. Often, so do information obligations.

Cardinal Richelieu in the 17th century supported (financially),[19] so to speak, an official media outlet, to which he also wrote regularly. This is the "Gazette de France," promoting and explaining the goals of state policy. Such an institution simply had to be established. Such was the need of the times.

Napoleon also used propaganda methods, issuing state proclamations, also aimed at conquered populations. Propaganda methods were used on a daily basis during World War I and World War II. General de Gaulle used them to reach the French in occupied France via radio—but also, when he was the president of France, when responding to the crisis in Algeria.

More contemporarily, the methods of opinion formation were relevant during the 2020–2022 coronavirus pandemic. At that time, the importance of having some kind of reference, some source of truth, was emphasized. This, of course, refers to state or government centers, because they are the ones who shape population security and health policies. These information were often understood as based on input from scientific works or circles, although this was not necessarily always communicated directly to the public. For instance, it was considered that, like several hundred years ago, the so-called lockdowns and social isolation were an adequate solution. Such measures may make sense in protection against infectious disease spread (and if it serves something, such as preparation, and not just locking societies up). Still, it is a major intrusion into civil rights and freedoms. If the alternative was the possible collapse of the healthcare system, then States had difficult decisions to make. Crucially, any such decisions should be clearly communicated to the population, in an understandable way.

However, it was also inevitable for information to spread through informal channels, such as rumors, gossip.[20] This already poses a risk of destabilization, because who knows where such rumors come from, what their motivations may be, what they are based on, what their intended outcome is. Another thing is that looking at things in hindsight can affect the assessment of earlier decisions (here: those in 2020 and 2021). And back then, decisions had to be made "here and now," even at short notice and with the risk of making mistakes.

1.6.8 Attention paid to the rumors

Rumors and gossip can never be gotten rid of. The more ambiguous and subject to interpretation a situation is, the more susceptible people are to receiving such content with some *alternative* explanations. With new communication technologies, messages can quickly reach multiple audiences so there are additional risks involved (e.g., the need for immediate). This can create challenges for entire countries to take action in such a situation.

Now that it is clear that the meaning of words is evolving, we can move on.

1.7 WHY DO WE TREAT PROPAGANDA AS A BAD THING?

The evolution of the word "propaganda" is due to the uses and abuses and the effects this led to before, during, and after World War II. It is about the techniques used before and during World War II. Techniques coming straight from the repertoire of Dr. Goebbels and Adolf Hitler. Their "political projects" ended in a widespread death, extermination, and destruction. Genocide on a massive scale, carried out on an industrial scale. This is also why today the reception of the word "propaganda" is so strongly negative. This is understandable, natural.

Earlier, however, I laid out the ambiguous nature of the word "propaganda." Or perhaps even neutral, technical nature—since the "good-or-evil" valuation refers to the use of methods?

1.8 "PROPAGANDA" CLOSER TO US

As recently as 100 years ago, the term "propaganda" may also have been (still) somewhat synonymous even with advertising, public relations, etc.[21] As recently as 1992, a Swedish parliamentarian requested "propaganda works at schools, catering establishments, and fairs, to promote increased fish consumption."[22] Juxtaposing this with the form in which the term "propaganda" often functions today, the contrast is huge. Today, when an analyst, journalist, commentator, or a politician uses the phrase, it typically has negative connotations. At the same time, this is understandable: the meanings of words evolve, and indeed the term "propaganda" took on a grim meaning after World War II and the years of communism. There is no point in discussing this, because these are the facts.

1.8.1 Engaged poetry

While conclusions about the motivations are an exercise for the Reader, the communist, party agitation is not in question here—as it is quite a straightforward a fact. The following poem is a vehicle of propaganda supporting the communist system. To quote the poem penned by Bertolt Brecht titled "*Cantata on Lenin's Death Day*" *(1938)*, depicting the story of a soldier refusing to believe in Lenin's death *(cited verbatim below*[23]*)*:

The day Lenin passed away
A soldier of the death watch, so runs the story, told his comrades: I did not want to
Believe it. I went inside, and
Shouted in his ear: 'Ilyich
The exploiters are on their way!' He did not move. Now
I knew that he has expired.

When a good man wants to leave
How can you hold him back?
Tell him why he is needed.
That holds him.

What could hold Lenin back?

The soldier thought
When hears, the exploiters are coming
He may be ever so ill, he will still get up
Perhaps he will come on crutches
Perhaps he will let himself be carried, but
He will get up and come
In order to confront the exploiters.

The soldier knew, that is to say, that Lenin
Throughout his life, had carried on a struggle
Against the exploiters.

And the soldier who had taken part
In the storming of the Winter Palace wanted to return home, because there
The landed estates were being distributed
Then Lenin had told him: stay on!
The exploiters are still there.
And so long there is exploitation
One must struggle against it.
So long as you exist
You must struggle against it.

The weak do not fight. The stronger
Fight on perhaps for an hour.
Those who are stronger still fight for many years
The strongest fight on all their lives.
These are indispensable.

I don't know, Reader, if you are a fan of political engaged poetry. However, it is hard not to notice that the above poem is in strong praise of the communist system, and, more specifically, it is part of the cult of Lenin.[24] Such creations in communist times (and there were plenty of them in the Communist Block!) carry worldview-forming content to the audience of readers, perhaps unaware of anything, perhaps young people. Perhaps, because, after all, we have no insight into the decision-making process and conditions of the time. However, language and words can have great power.[25] Regardless of whether they are used to propagate ideas that are true or false. What matters is how they are used, applied. It's about impact, about influence, if that's the purpose of spreading content, then it's about achieving some effect. In this sense, it is worth considering the different nature of words. Referring to the purely linguistic issue, Orwell claimed that the phrase "fascism" reached a point of being stripped of its content, losing its value at a certain stage. That at some point it no longer meant anything concrete except "something unwanted."[26] Moreover, Orwell also claimed that even words such as "democracy," "socialism," "freedom," "patriotism," "realism," and "justice" each have several different meanings that cannot be reconciled with each other."[27]

Similar may be true of words referring to terrorism. Who is a terrorist? What does he or she do? According to one of the classic definitions, it is someone who wants to achieve political goals (some kind of influence on affairs, policies, or politics), using the threat of violence or violence itself. But as it happened, States were often found to refer to groups of people who acted against them (whether combatants or other opponents) or disagreed with them in some way—as terrorists. In this sense, soldiers of resistance movements during World War II (like Polish, or French) could also be (and were) labeled terrorists from the point of view of the German Third Reich. Although today, of course, such people would not be called by that name, under any circumstances. Words have great power, especially for those who know how to use them and have the means, monetary or technical, to do so. To refer to legitimate resistance movements as "terrorists" would rightly be considered slanderous; for it is not a proper term! Also because the word "terrorism" is all too often—by virtue of the times—associated by our generations with those taking militant combat action in the Middle East (even if the actual phrase itself is much broader and has been used in the past) or on the streets of Western European cities. And that's what the information space was filled with for years, that's the kind of content people absorbed for years, so the meaning got attached. However, by stewarding and abusing phrases like "fascism," "terrorism," or even "meat," one can end up overloading them and actually changing the perception. But where did *meat* suddenly come from? Over the centuries, meat has been equated with a food product of animal origin, but it turns out that nowadays it can also be acceptable to refer to products of plant origin by a similar term. This is not a criticism but rather a statement of fact: words can change their meaning. Also in a commercial context, not just limited to political, social, or military dimensions. One can disagree with this, of course.

Let's return to the word "propaganda" itself, a concept in this book, which, however, until relatively recently meant spreading information, even for educational purposes, or raising awareness, and it did not have a pejorative, demonic, evil resonance.

1.9 "PROPAGANDA" AS SOCIAL CAMPAIGNING AND EDUCATING?

We will now review some necessary concepts of propaganda and information campaigns, equally important in operations, even in conflict, combat, or information warfare.

As explained, until about 100 years ago, the word "propaganda" was used in a different way than it is used today. Like, for example, in a scientific publication from 1926 with the charming (from today's perspective) title *Cancer Propaganda*.[28] This scientific paper does not talk about some nefarious spreading of harmful or deceitful content or ideas, for example, political or extremist. On the contrary! It talks about "difficulties of cancer propaganda"[29] in a very positive and commendable sense. It is about the difficulties of disseminating information (informing) about this medical problem—about the problems of reaching the right audience with the right message. After all, it is also true today that "if only patients would come earlier for medical advice, cancer would be a much easier disease to treat – to a large extent even curable."[30] It is, therefore, a matter of life or death, because early detection and early treatment is critical. The goal of this campaign ("cancer propaganda") is, therefore, to achieve the effect of regular health screening. But to achieve this effect, it is necessary to shape public awareness—to disseminate information.

How to raise awareness of the problem? According to this scientific article from 1926, this can be achieved precisely with "propaganda." Because in 1926, the word did not have such a demonic meaning as it does today. Today, we would talk about a social or educational campaign. However, the more classic formulation turns out to be precisely "propaganda."

Moreover, speaking of "cancer propaganda," the author points out that the need for such propaganda can face many challenges and that not every method ("propaganda methods"!) is advisable for use against different populations, societies (and, therefore, different audiences). This is due to a number of considerations, such as the intellectual or mental composition of the audience. The message must be tailored to a particular country, to a particular society or a part of it. To groups of recipients, and not necessarily to people individually (which can be difficult, and certainly was so in 1926), which, in turn, can only be "determined locally."[31] This will be discussed further: how to direct information messages or propaganda, messages, information to achieve some effect, influence. It will also allow you to understand how to defend yourself if necessary. Because, after all, not every use of these methods is as positive as spreading information about cancer, oncology, and health problems.

Here, I just want the Reader to appreciate that propaganda really could and can have various uses. I don't think anyone will say that spreading information about serious health problems is undesirable. I know for a fact that it is not. As a person with experience of medical issues, I have absolutely no problem with the use of "propaganda" to disseminate information about such issues. Although, as I said, today exactly the same activities would be defined, called, differently, for example, as "dissemination of information," "social, educational information campaign," or with similar terms, although the goals would be (!) exactly the same as the said goals of "cancer propaganda" from 1926.

The Reader should, or at least can if he/she wishes, draw a number of conclusions now. First, propaganda in itself is not necessarily exclusively bad. Second, we commonly deal with such processes. Whole departments work on the creation of information messages and their propagation, only, of course, the word "propaganda" is not used in reference to them (e.g., because it has bad connotations). It is not necessarily a matter of pressure to bring about "involuntary decisions" in the audience, manipulation, or some unholy goals. The fact is that words change meaning, and today we would talk about "health communication" (or "outreach") rather than "propaganda,"[32] although in the past, these very methods—propaganda—were used to disseminate health information.

An interim conclusion comes to mind: we are subjected to information stimuli, coming from a variety of sources. This is natural, should be expected, and some of such information streams may also be valuable. The question is, which of them may not be fully valuable, desirable, or may even be harmful or malicious? How to determine this? How to evaluate? What to do then? That will be discussed in the following chapters.

1.9.1 An approach to defining propaganda

Here, it is also worth emphasizing the role of keywords in reaching (the audience) with information content (messages), in order to achieve results. Such information messages must be tailored to specific audiences. This may be a concise and true definition of propaganda.

1.9.2 Commercial information campaigns

From information campaigns, it is very close to commercial, advertising issues. Before 1945, it was not pejoratively characterized. The word "propaganda" simply described a certain process of identifying audiences and reaching them, by some means. Public relations and advertising have their place in the social and economic system. Societies dealt with advertising early on, and certainly as early as the 19th century.

These techniques were then adapted and developed for wartime use, during World War I. Civilian, and commercial, applications were found for them after the end of the war. Close to that time, "propaganda" may have begun to gain a bad name, there was an evolution in the meaning of it.[33] The understanding that state structures and governments influenced the public through it began to penetrate the public consciousness: "Government publicity, throughout the war, was like the beating of drums; except that they were silent drums, and the beating was not on parchment but on consciences."[34] The British government, for example, "modulated" the public understanding of war needs through informational, propaganda methods. Not always directly but in accordance with state goals, political goals, as well as war needs.

In the interwar period, former wartime American propagandist, Edward Bernays, built the foundations of modern PR, speaking plainly about the need to reach out to groups of audiences.[35] And if one can popularize the image or brand (positive, negative) of this or that country or nation, after all, one can do the same with the make or model of a car,[36] a television, a brand of yogurt, and perhaps the name or the face of a politician (candidate in an election). So, this is something that involves social engineering techniques. The issues of technique and methods will be discussed further in this book.

Concerns about "ubiquitous" and "open" propaganda, however, were expressed even then, understanding[37] that "propaganda as the great art of influencing public opinion seems to be a permanent addition to our social and political commitments."[38] It was noted that one of the earliest uses of propaganda was religious, but since then its methods have permeated politics, business, and advertising, that is, they have found themselves widely in social use. The method is one thing (often in the matters of the methodology itself, there may be no differences), the field of application (e.g., goals) is another. For us and for the purposes of this book, however, the key quote from the work mentioned here is this one: "it is difficult to draw any clear-cut line between advertising and propaganda on the one side, and between propaganda and education on the other."[39]

That's just the way it is. After all, it is about spreading information, somehow consistent, with a certain structure. Information that has been decided that it is worth (or even necessary) of dissemination, and even shaping minds with it.

1.9.3 Does 2 + 2 = 5?

We have all been taught that 2 + 2 = 4. This is information that everyone receives during universal education, at school. The same may be true of information from other areas of knowledge, such as that related to the number of primary colors, to biological sex, to chemical elements, to the political system. Not all information, and not at all times, is necessarily equally glorious, if only because times change, and views do so too. And sometimes things related precisely to political systems or regimes. Certain things are said differently in a communist State, for example, and differently when that State changes its structure to a different system. In view of this, is propaganda "the art of making up the other man's mind for him,"[40] or is it the "of gaining adherents to principles, of gaining support for an opinion or a course of action"?[41]

As with the 2 + 2 = 5 equation (false, in this case), I don't think anyone doubts that, for example, physical, mathematical, or literary education is some kind of pernicious problem or that it leads to doom. We don't wonder, even in a quasi-conspiratorial way, "who intends that we think 2 + 2 = 5" (a conspiracy of mathematicians, or perhaps the Tax System services?) or "in whose interest it is." This would be an absurdity. If we see any problems, it is in some other dimensions. Perhaps in response to something, in line with or against our personal (or someone else's) views. However, this is unlikely to apply to arithmetic.

The issue of propaganda stems from the fact that today it is somewhat a fuzzy term. Intuitively, however, we feel the difference between spreading information about the fact that the result of the mathematical operation 2 + 2 is (or is not) 5, and what we should think about international, political, commercial, or some other topics.

1.9.4 Who has determined that we think that 2 + 2 = 4?

These are important statements: who, in what way, wants to convince us to think something about a certain topic? Or do emotions (ours, of others) matter in a similar situation?

- How might one's knowledge or worldview influence such actions?
- Are any tricks, methods, or techniques used?
- Are things happening directly, or maybe indirectly, and not everything is clear and transparent?
- Maybe the processes are multi-layered?
- Are there attempts to exert a negative or positive influence?
- Or is there only obfuscation of the situation, contributing to us wasting time, wasting mental cycles?
- Are the messages directed to an individual recipient, or perhaps to entire groups?
- Does the dynamics of large groups even matter (processes occur differently in groups than individually)?
- Are psychological considerations important?

If so, is there an attempt to play up the views, perhaps the prejudices of individuals or groups of people, such as entire nations?

This is what will need to be decoded and demystified. We will do this systematically in the following chapters. The guide for us will be science, technology, and the so-called common sense.

1.10 EMERGING TERMINOLOGY

To summarize these considerations—in directing information messages, basic parameters are important:

- **What**—what resources we have at our disposal;
- **Payload**—what kind of message, idea, or concept one wants to spread;
- **Who**—who sends the message, and, most importantly, who the recipient is (to correctly select the payload, the message, you need to identify the nature of the recipient groups);
- **When**—timing is important for the success of an information (propaganda) campaign, certain events can either favor the messages or work against them;
- **Purpose**—for what purpose actions are taken, what is to be the end result.

These are the technical and organizational basics that will be developed later in the book.

1.11 SOCIAL OR PERHAPS SCIENTIFIC PROBLEMS

Sometimes, things are not said directly. This doesn't have to be about supporting this or that political option, a government or a State, or whatever. Sometimes, it can be about the importance of a social concept. Then what we speak of are "*issues*."

For example, it is worth noting that different Russian institutions promote different meanings of LGBT to different audiences.[42] For example, internally in Russia, skepticism and anti-LGBT attitudes are promoted, and the so-called LGBT propaganda is banned. In contrast, different, even opposing, views are promoted abroad—both anti-LGBT and pro-LGBT, and in different streams, depending on the intended audience. This is obviously about attempts at social engineering and creating divisions, polarization using (some) controversial topic. Thus, there is no hypocrisy of individuals or institutions taking such actions, as all of these actions are deliberate and done by professionals for professional purposes. It's not a matter of views or double thinking. This is their job. This suggestion by ideologues, such as those linked to the Kremlin, is a deliberate action to play up geopolitical objectives. The technical means of spreading such communication and propagation of this content are, for example, advertising channels.[43] Various techniques can be used: textual and visual (images, videos). Sometimes crude terms, juxtapositions, and comparisons are used.

Sharp, offensive, and threatening caricatures and juxtapositions always appeared in situations of strong political dispute, coups, political, or military upheaval. In Nazi Germany, calls were made to kill Jews, comparing them to rats spreading germs; the Stalinist regime referred to its enemies as parasites to be exterminated. The euphemism "purge" was also used to call these actions, perhaps adopted from the French Revolution.[44] The trend of spreading offensive content describing enemies through the prism of various kinds of secretions, obscene content, is also known from much earlier times—from the Renaissance, and its heyday was during the French Revolution. For example, the Pope was referred to as a "defecator," as were aristocrats and monarchs—European kings, queens, their entourages, etc.[45] Leftist deputies to the National Assembly of the French Republic were particularly fond of using such terms.[46] I will spare the Reader and myself from quoting more detailed descriptions and pictorial content.

1.12 COUNTERING PROPAGANDA?

The problem of propaganda was very quickly recognized by States. At some point, it began to be treated as unauthorized meddling in internal state affairs. From around the 19th century, States even created international treaties to limit interstate propaganda,[47] understood as something destabilizing to them. Such an agreement was, for example, the 1801 treaty between France and Russia, which stipulated that the parties

> mutually oblige themselves not to permit any of their subjects to carry on any correspondence whatever, direct or indirect, with the internal enemies of the existing government of the two states, to propagate there principles contrary to their respective constitutions, or to incite disorders.[48]

Today, we would consider this an interference with freedom of expression, or with freedom of thought. Censorship would be the term used. There have been more such agreements between different States. A good example is the agreement to avoid the use of propaganda methods via radio because it highlights that methods have always corresponded to the times. After all, it can't be otherwise, because it's all about efficiency, about actually reaching the audience with the informational messages.

As you can see, this problem was recognized early on. The problem from the decades 2000–2020 of the so-called bots and trolls in social media is not some complete novelty, at least conceptually. Reports or scholarly publications "revealingly" or dutifully writing that "disinformation is nothing new" are so frequent that it's fraught why post such obvious sentences at all; although it must be admitted that the world sort of rediscovered this issue around 2016 (the disinformation and influence issues covered after the US presidential election, and cognitive dissonances in many people), and since then many experts on the subject have emerged.

The only way to fully cover the issues of the subject is through a comprehensive approach. Therefore, there will be more, including international legal aspects (does propaganda breach any rules?), in the following chapters and in Chapter 5, which is devoted entirely to this topic. At the same time, let us immediately acknowledge that it is understood that States may be interested in maintaining internal order, as well as *the status quo*. This is why periodic subversive events of the revolution type worry many States. Of note, one of the official goals of the French State during the French Revolution was to spread its ideals—subversive, revolutionary—to other States, such as Great Britain.[49] As we know, the Bolshevik USSR had similar methods of operation, with the goal of propagating communist ideology and revolutionary content. Even today, the so-called state actors may be interested in spreading certain kinds of ideas, ideologies, and messages in other countries. They do so using modern channels, techniques, and methods.

1.12.1 Censorship

Since propaganda and public affairs are supposed to reach people and shape views or raise awareness, what about the situation of informational isolation? Indeed, States may consider imposing various types of censorship: shutting down the telecommunications network (the Internet), blocking communications, information, prohibiting the propagation of content, or truncating it. Over the centuries, this phenomenon has evolved in different ways. In 2022, 2023, and 2024 a kind of culmination is discernible. Western countries blocked certain content, such as that coming from Russia. Similarly, in Russia, information blockades, censorship, and a ban on calling certain things by their names were imposed, laws were introduced.

1.13 INFORMATIONAL USE OF ANTI-SCIENCE

One can hope that in countries where societies are mature, stability can be maintained. This need not be the case. For example, we currently have a renaissance of knowledge based on research, the achievements of science. Some phenomena are proven beyond reasonable doubt (and others disproven). And yet it is not difficult to identify groups of "enthusiasts" with the so-called "contrarian" attitudes, that is, attitude to the contrary to accepted norms and recognized knowledge. Perhaps by the very fact that it is commonly accepted knowledge? And so, views may spread that the Earth is flat, that biological viruses can be propagated by means of telecommunications networks (i.e., 5G), various facets of vaccinations. The circles responsible for this may be an element of risk if such influence is exerted by unfriendly external state actors, such as those preparing for war or even conducting hostilities.

It should be noted, to be perfectly fair, that sometimes even recognized research methods do not necessarily prove the truth of hypotheses or theses.[50] An interesting safeguard against the situation where "all experts" support a point of view is the Talmudic law requiring that in every situation there be at least one expert with a contrary opinion; the absence of such a person is supposed to mean that something is not right, and this is perhaps even socially rational (if the process is to be fair, it is certainly possible to find someone with a contrary view).[51] It's a rejection of unanimity and a promotion of pluralism. It's an encouragement to tolerate dissenting opinions (if not just as a facade). For us, this will not be a particular issue, because in modern propaganda methods, where techno-social and cyber-political methods are used, it is necessary to combine purely scientific and social approaches.

Anyway, very often assessments of whether something constitutes an influence campaign are based on confidence levels, on probabilities. Certainty is difficult to ascertain or is rare. And it cannot be determined by asking, for example, three randomly selected (or substituted) "experts" for their opinions. Sometimes, things may indeed be too good to be true.

1.14 HOW DO WE UNDERSTAND INFORMATION SECURITY, CYBER SECURITY?

In this chapter, it is necessary to build some distinctions. Cyber security can be understood as ensuring the confidentiality, integrity, and availability of information (IT) systems. Something broader is the information security (implicitly: including that of the State). It is something broader as it may also refer to the circulation of information, its impact, its use: what is being done with information, and how. It is, therefore, also an impact on the cognitive elements of societies. At the same time, as a curiosity, it is already worth noting here that the Russian Federation, for example, does not so strictly distinguish between information security and cyber security. Therefore, information operations and activities can often include elements of cyber attack. Or perhaps then it doesn't even make sense to conduct cyber operations or cyber attacks if it doesn't involve an impact on the information environment?

The effects of information activities are measurable. They can be positive (e.g., spreading education on some socially important topics). They can also be negative (e.g., war propaganda, demonizing groups of people, spreading false information). Ultimately, we live in an environment filled with information. Today, a certain dose of information stability is very important, especially during crises, when events happen quickly and the stakes can be high. It is also not surprising that there are centers or individuals who care about influencing opinions, influencing actions, or destabilization.

1.15 PRINCIPLES OF OPERATION AND THE ROLE OF TECHNOLOGY

One can look at propaganda as a social issue, an issue of social sciences, with all sorts of backgrounds. One can look at and analyze this issue from the point of view of sociology, psychology, anthropology, and even religion. In this book, special emphasis is placed on issues of science and technology. In this view, propaganda is a matter of technology (and its impact on security) and not necessarily an issue of expression, so it is not a journalistic issue, and therefore reserved for the media, or a sociological, anthropological, or psychological one. These areas are important in a holistic view of propaganda. However, none of them is sufficient to fully describe the phenomenon and its consequences. That would be an oversimplification.

Today, the role of technology is so significant; it exerts so much influence on how propaganda is shaped (how it is "made"), that the take must be broad. A different view would lead us astray—to analytical errors, potentially of great consequence. In matters of security and strategy, it would lead to wrong conclusions and even decisions.

In this sense, it will be a well-informed analysis but a technical, practical, factual one. The results of sociology and psychology, or the media play the role of a component in such a view. That is, they are a component, a substructure, although, still very important. Propaganda can be about commercial things but also political and military affairs, and warfare. Depending on the field, the problem can be looked at in different ways. It's always a matter of shaping the information environment, the information space. Sometimes it may be about actions that prevent others from accessing information. An example of such actions were the purchases made by the U.S. army.

1.15.1 Satellite imagery

Satellite imagery can provide a great deal of information about the humanitarian situation or activities during an armed conflict. We learned many things through satellite imagery prior to or during the escalation of the war in Ukraine in 2022. This includes massacres of civilians, such as in the Ukrainian town of Bucha in March 2022. This means that the aggressor State was unable to cover up such actions. They, the unfortunate effects, were clearly visible from Earth's orbit. The Soviet Union failed in the 1970s and later to impose norms and convince the United States to conclude a treaty banning "external" reconnaissance from space of States' territories. As a result, reconnaissance satellites provide a wealth of information. Satellite imagery is a matter of state information security. The United States, for example, understands this well.

1.15.2 Censorship of satellite imaging

It is worth noting that the United States realized early on the risks of imaging capabilities from space. In 2001, during operations in Afghanistan, there was a potential concern (whether rightly so depends on one's point of view) about how images of the effects and realities of combat might be interpreted. Consequently, the United States bought all the satellite images from that area of the Earth made available by the IKONOS satellite within a few months. They made an exclusive buyout, at a cost of nearly $2 million and $20 for each kilometer of territory imaged, committing to acquire images equivalent to a minimum of 10,000 kilometers. The contract covered three months.[52] This means that no one else could acquire the data. That is, no one had access to the information. Today, such an information blockade could be somewhat more difficult due to the fact that the number of satellites has increased significantly. Their accuracy is much greater, too.

Understandably, during crises, countries use commercial satellite imaging providers. A lot of information is needed, and, in addition, the technical capabilities of the military's own secret satellites cannot always be disclosed (which is also part of information security). This is where commercial services come to the rescue. One buys data and processes it or makes it available. In the specific case of IKONOS data, however, doubts arose as to whether this was not simply an action intended for censorship purposes to prevent others from acquiring such data. This highlights close relationships between technical censorship and propaganda and information security in general. Sometimes, moreover, such solutions are introduced into the legislation of countries. The flagship example is the Kyl and Bingaman Amendment (KBA),[53] which prohibits U.S. institutions from licensing the acquisition (from commercial companies) and dissemination of satellite images of the State of Israel if such images are of high resolution (higher than those available from "other commercial providers," non-U.S. companies).[54] However, it seems that since the late 2020s, the importance of such rights will become increasingly limited and heavily outdated. Very high resolution (10-centimeter) commercial images will be available.

We can clearly see how much things are changing, as it is hard to imagine that in the 16th century or even in the first half of the 20th century, space activities would have been something necessary when considering informational security or propaganda issues.

And I have just demonstrated that this is the case today.

1.16 CULTURAL CENSORSHIP, OR COMMERCIAL CENSORSHIP?

In general, we can also consider the issue of censorship of cultural goods, commercial censorship, perhaps motivated by the worldview. In 2022, Penguin House released Roald Dahl's classics for children in a censored version. The idea was to make sure that no one would accidentally and unintentionally be offended by the content in the original.

After criticism, the publishing house backed down and will continue to publish the original, although the screen rights to the "processed" version have been sold to Netflix (so there may be screen adaptations "based on the novel"). In this version of the book, the content on obesity, gender, race, etc., containing wording that could offend, stigmatize someone, was changed. Content was trimmed in several books, such as the famous "Charlie and the Chocolate Factory," where one character, instead of being described as "extremely fat" as in the original, is now "huge" in the new version. With that said, we are less interested in what specifically was done. What matters is that it was done.

1.17 A BRIEF SUMMARY AND LET'S MOVE ON

As I have already indicated, I refrain from advocating *for or against*. Given the subject matter covered, it will be better this way. I also hope that the Reader will appreciate, or tolerate, this approach.

Propaganda and the propagation of information through many channels is the reality in which we live today. Incentives come to us from many places. It's worth taking a moment to acquire the proper terminology so that navigating this reality, which is full of pitfalls, will be more efficient. So let's cut to the chase.

NOTES

1 For: H.J. Shey, *Tyrtaeus and the art of propaganda*, Arethusa 1976, vol. 9, no. 1, pp. 5–28.
2 H.J. Shey, *Tyrtaeus and the art of propaganda*, Arethusa 1976, vol. 9, no. 1, pp. 5–28. gr. "αισχρής δε φυγής," which can be translated as "it is shameful to flee."
3 R. Walinski-Kiehl, *Pamphlets, propaganda and witch-hunting in Germany c. 156o-c. 1630*, Reformation 2002, vol. 6, no. 1, pp. 49–74.
4 R. Walinski-Kiehl, *Pamphlets, propaganda and witch-hunting in Germany c. 156o-c. 1630*, Reformation 2002, vol. 6, no. 1, pp. 49–74.
5 R. Walinski-Kiehl, *Pamphlets, propaganda and witch-hunting in Germany c. 156o-c. 1630*, Reformation 2002, vol. 6, no. 1, pp. 49–74.
6 R. Walinski-Kiehl, *Pamphlets, propaganda and witch-hunting in Germany c. 156o-c. 1630*, Reformation 2002, vol. 6, no. 1, p. 18.
7 R. Walinski-Kiehl, *Pamphlets, propaganda and witch-hunting in Germany c. 156o-c. 1630*, Reformation 2002, vol. 6, no. 1, p. 18.
8 P. Guilday, *The sacred congregation de propaganda fide (1622–1922)*, The Catholic Historical Review 1921, vol. 6, no. 4, pp. 478–494.
9 M.T. Prendergast, T.A. Prendergast, *The invention of propaganda: A critical commentary on and translation of Inscrutabili Divinae Providentiae Arcano*, in *The Oxford Handbook of Propaganda Studies*, ed. J. Auerbach, R. Castronovo, Oxford 2013, https://doi.org/10.1093/oxfordhb/9780199764419.013.016.
10 G.S. Jowett, V. O'Donnell, *Propaganda & Persuasion*, Sage, Los Angeles, London 2018.
11 R. Roldán-Figueroa, *Tomás Carrascón, anti-Roman Catholic propaganda, and the circulation of ideas in Jacobean England*, History of European Ideas 2013, vol. 39, no. 2, pp. 169–206.
12 R. Marlin, *Propaganda and the Ethics of Persuasion*, Broadview Press, Peterborough 2013.
13 C. Suciu, *Propaganda of the French Revolution*, 12.07.2019, https://about.proquest.com/en/blog/2019/propaganda-of-the-french-revolution.
14 R.C. Darnton, *Trends in radical propaganda on the eve of the French Revolution (1782–1788)*, PhD thesis, Oxford University 1964.

15 J. Wilke, *Propaganda*, in *The International Encyclopedia of Communication*, ed. W. Donsbach, Malden-Oxford-Carlton 2008.
16 J. Wilke, *Propaganda*, in *The International Encyclopedia of Communication*, ed. W. Donsbach, Malden-Oxford-Carlton 2008.
17 "Condemns all forms of propaganda, in whatsoever country conducted, which is either designed or likely to provoke or encourage and threat to the peace, breach of the peace, or act of aggression"; "To promote, by all means of publicity and propaganda available to them, friendly relations among nations based upon the Purposes and Principles of the Charter," United Nations General Assembly Resolution 110 (II), *Measures to be taken against propaganda and the inciters of a new war*, November 3, 1947, A/RES/2/110, http://www.un-documents.net/a2r110.htm.
18 See https://www.oed.com/dictionary/propaganda_n.
19 M.M. Miller, *The French periodical press during the reign of Louis XIV*, The French Review 1932, vol. 5, no. 4, pp. 301–308.
20 G.W. Allport, L.J. Postman, *Section of psychology: The basic psychology of rumor*, Transactions of the New York Academy of Sciences 1945, vol. 8, no. 2, pp. 61–81.
21 J. Wilke, *Propaganda ...*
22 J. Jarlbrink, F. Norén, *The rise and fall of 'propaganda' as a positive concept: A digital reading of Swedish parliamentary records, 1867–2019*, Scandinavian Journal of History 2023, vol. 48, no. 3, pp. 379–399.
23 Ref. https://cornucopiados.blogspot.com/2008/10/cantata-on-day-of-lenins-death-cita.html, [visited 12.02.24].
24 N. Tumarkin, *Political ritual and the cult of Lenin*, Human Rights Quarterly 1983, vol. 5, no. 2, p. 203.
25 R. Marcinkevičienė, *A dangerous language*, in *The Marketing of War in the Age of Neo-militarism*, ed. K. Gouliamos, C. Kassimeris, Routledge, New York 2013, pp. 35–53.
26 G. Orwell, *Politics and the English language*, in idem, *Shooting an elephant and other essays*, London 1950, after R. Marcinkevičienė, *A dangerous language....*
27 G. Orwell, *Politics and the English language*, in idem, *Shooting an elephant and other essays*, London 1950, after R. Marcinkevičienė, *A dangerous language...*
28 W.S. Lazarus-Barlow, *Cancer propaganda*, Acta Radiologica 1926, vol. 7, no. 1–6, pp. 142–146.
29 W.S. Lazarus-Barlow, *Cancer propaganda*, Acta Radiologica 1926, vol. 7, no. 1–6, pp. 142–146.
30 W.S. Lazarus-Barlow, *Cancer propaganda*, Acta Radiologica 1926, vol. 7, no. 1–6, pp. 142–146.
31 W.S. Lazarus-Barlow, *Cancer propaganda*, Acta Radiologica 1926, vol. 7, no. 1–6, pp. 142–146.
32 C.T. Salmon, T. Poorisat, *The rise and development of public health communication*, Health Communication 2020, vol. 35, no. 13, pp. 1666–1677.
33 S. Schwarzkopf, *What was advertising? The invention, rise, demise, and disappearance of advertising concepts in nineteenth-and twentieth-century Europe and America*, Business and Economic History Online 2009, vol. 7, pp. 27.
34 C. Higham, *Looking Forward: Mass Education through Publicity*, London 1920, p. 23, after S. Schwarzkopf, *What was advertising...*, p. 12.
35 E.L. Bernays, *Propaganda*, New York 1928.
36 S. Schwarzkopf, *What was advertising....*
37 R. Dodge, *The psychology of propaganda*, Religious Education 1920, vol. 15, no. 5, pp. 241–252.
38 R. Dodge, *The psychology of propaganda*, Religious Education 1920, vol. 15, no. 5, pp. 241–252.
39 R. Dodge, *The psychology of propaganda*, Religious Education 1920, vol. 15, no. 5, p. 3.
40 R. Dodge, *The psychology of propaganda*, Religious Education 1920, vol. 15, no. 5, p. 3.
41 R. Dodge, *The psychology of propaganda*, Religious Education 1920, vol. 15, no. 5, p. 3.
42 T. Jones, *Double-use of LGBT youth in propaganda*, Journal of LGBT Youth 2020, vol. 17, no. 4, pp. 408–431.
43 Permanent Select Committee on Intelligence, *Exposing Russia's effort to sow discord online: The internet research agency and advertisements*, https://democrats-intelligence.house.gov/social-media-content/.
44 C. Gandelman, *'Patri-arse': Revolution as analytic in the scatological caricatures of the Reformation and the French Revolution*, American Imago 1996, vol. 53, no. 1, p. 7.
45 C. Gandelman, *'Patri-arse': Revolution as analytic in the scatological caricatures of the Reformation and the French Revolution*, American Imago 1996, vol. 53, no. 1, p. 7.

46 C. Gandelman, *'Patri-arse': Revolution as analytic in the scatological caricatures of the Reformation and the French Revolution*, American Imago 1996, vol. 53, no. 1, p. 7.
47 V. van Dyke, *The responsibility of states for international propaganda*, American Journal of International Law 1940, vol. 34, no. 1, pp. 58–73.
48 G.F. Martens, *Recueil de traités [1817–1836]*, vol. 7, *[1800–1803]*, after V. van Dyke, *The responsibility…*, footnote 4.
49 V. van Dyke, *The responsibility….*
50 L.J. Gunn, F. Chapeau-Blondeau, M.D. McDonnell, B.R. Davis, A. Allison, D. Abbott, *Too good to be true: When overwhelming evidence fails to convince*, March 1, 2016, https://doi.org/10.1098/rspa.2015.0748.
51 E. Glatt, *The unanimous verdict according to the Talmud: Ancient law providing insight into modern legal theory*, Pace International Law Review Online 2013, vol. 3, no. 10, p. 316.
52 S. Livingston, W.L. Robinson, *Mapping fears: the use of commercial high-resolution satellite imagery in international affairs*, Astropolitics 2003, vol. 1, no. 2, pp. 3–25.
53 Amendment to 15 USC §5621: Prohibition on collection and release of detailed satellite imagery relating to Israel, Pub. L. 104-201, div. A, title X, §1064, Sept. 23, 1996, 110 Stat. 2653, https://www.congress.gov/104/plaws/publ201/PLAW-104publ201.pdf.
54 Amendment to 15 USC §5621: Prohibition on collection and release of detailed satellite imagery relating to Israel, Pub. L. 104-201, div. A, title X, §1064, Sept. 23, 1996, 110 Stat. 2653, https://www.congress.gov/104/plaws/publ201/PLAW-104publ201.pdf.

Chapter 2

Theoretical background

Information environments, and propaganda as modulation of information space

While discussing things like the Holy Office and its Congregation for Propaganda from the 17th century or other events from the rather distant past may be fascinating, it is not the main goal. After all, it doesn't really have much practical significance today. Now I start concretizing things. If you are already familiar with the subject, you can spend less time on this chapter and read on.

I have already used terms like "propaganda," "disinformation," or "information environment" without defining them and in some implied sense. To more effectively navigate this specialized subject area, these terms need to be precisely defined. This is necessary to understand or truly appreciate the subject matter. Theoretical issues are laid out in such a way as to be useful (especially for understanding in Chapters 6 and 7).

We will also not go into the historical specifics of the propaganda approaches in different countries at different times. This is certainly fascinating. It may carry some implications for today. This book, however, has other goals, more utilitarian. It is not a history book.

First of all, it is necessary to illuminate the very meaning of propaganda, as it has already been mentioned in Chapter 1. As I pointed out, the meaning of the word has been changing. New phrases have also emerged to describe more specific uses of the information craft (e.g., public affairs, PA). Accordingly, we will identify a specific range of meanings with propaganda, already without obscuring the term and without this historical ambiguity.

2.1 PROPAGANDA

There are many definitions (we were even tempted to mention one in the previous chapter), or analytical approaches. But rather than coming up with another one or reviewing them all over the years to justify their importance, we will simplify the matter by referring to the recognized ones. Several definitions are especially notable and worth knowing.

At the outset, it is worth noting that according to Goebbels, propaganda should be based on truth. If one still wants to create untruthful, false content (lie), then the only resilient way is to do this solely if it cannot be verified.[1] Morally, Goebbels is definitely a very questionable authority; in fact, he is not a moral authority at all. He is undoubtedly a war criminal and was responsible for what Germany did before and during World War II. In the German Third Reich, this man was in charge of propaganda. His name is one with especially bad connotations, a name that is recognizable, loud, and shocking. Of course, it is. We are not treating him as an authority here. Far from it. The moniker "Goebbelsian propaganda" is even a useful derogatory term. Even when it's actually used in some form of propaganda.

A similar view—of preferring the truth—is maintained by many experts, researchers, practitioners, and even contemporary military studies for use by armies. Already here I remind the Reader again that manipulations can also be created using true information.

DOI: 10.1201/9781003499497-2

2.1.1 "Academic" (political) definition

We'll start with a classic. According to Jaques Ellul (theologian, lawyer, and authority on the subject of propaganda): "Propaganda is the expression of opinions or actions carried out deliberately by individuals or groups with a view to influencing the opinion or action, of other individuals or groups for predetermined ends and through psychological manipulations."[2] It, therefore, involves acting in such a way as to achieve a certain influence on opinions or even actions. This message can be directed individually or in groups, which depends on the method and medium of choice. For example, a spot on TV or leaflets dropped on a massive scale from an airplane will be directing a general and identical message to audience groups of significant size. In contrast, micro-targeting or nanotargeting[3] is delivering content to small audiences, like to 10–100 people or perhaps even to each individual with tailored content, which in this age could, can, or will be achievable by means of information technology.

If we persisted, we could even argue that the abovementioned Ellul's definition of propaganda is also met by public relations (PR) activities or ordinary information campaigns or even advertising. These creations are aimed at reaching groups of recipients (people) with some kind of information message and using some kind of method to make them take action or change their views. But maybe not, after all, today, we have more and more accurate and precise words for such activities.

In practice, an actual propaganda "operation" can be much more complex than these previous few sentences suggest. I point out that Ellul's definition is concrete but quite technical—it does not valuate. It is coherent, concise, and describes the problem well. Still, the subject of propaganda can include various information campaigns. Ellul's work falls in the period after World War II and with the awareness of the propaganda of Hitler, Lenin, or Khrushchev.[4] His concepts are interesting, and those adapted from his book *Propaganda: The formation of men's attitudes*, already cited here, are sound. They are still relevant. Moreover, since that book was published during the Cold War, perhaps it fits well with the world in the third decade of the 21st century—a bit more than, for example, in the first two decades of this century. Even if some of the book's content has become severely outdated today, if only due to the development of technology. I do not intend to go into such deliberations excessively. I only point out that the book you read now fully appreciates these changes and anticipates (expects) more of them in the future. So, it is written with this in mind. Let's move on.

Let's take another quote from this work: "Propaganda is a set of methods employed by an organized group that wants to bring about the active or passive participation in its actions of a mass of individuals, psychologically unified through psychological manipulations and incorporated in an organization ...."[5] It is more convoluted, but here the key element is this "*set of methods*." The methods can vary. These can be tricks or techniques of expression or persuasion, referring to the wording and design of the message. But also the methods of reaching people themselves. These have changed tremendously since the 1970s. Technological changes matter, and such a rapid pace of change as we have had since the 2000s could not have been predicted in the 1970s.

Another compatible approach could be to consider propaganda as

> a process which deliberately attempts through persuasion-techniques to secure from the propagandee, before he can deliberate freely, the responses desired by the propagandist ... propaganda is a method of persuasion, not of compulsion: the victim is led to believe that the conclusion, the attitude, or the act that he adopts is really his own free choice.[6]

A clear definition of this complex issue is particularly important. So, let's look at the problem from another angle.

2.1.2 Military definition

Propaganda methods accompany military operations—for various reasons. They can build "one's own" advantage, solidifying the consensus and common goals of groups. They can also disintegrate and impede the "opponent's" actions.

The U.S. Department of Defense, in its handbook, formulates a definition according to which propaganda is: "any form of communication in support of national objectives designed to influence the opinions, emotions, attitudes, or behavior of any group in order to benefit the sponsor, either directly or indirectly."[7] With the term "sponsor" here implicitly referring to the progenitor (planner, maker) of the action: either a military or civilian person, or, say, "the organization behind the action." This modern definition is compatible with, essentially the same as the previous, "academic" definition from the 1970s. So, not much has changed here in terminology. This proves that we are on the right track. We won't deviate from it. Guided by a good selection of sources, we are moving on. While we're at it in the military manual, let's also learn about other terms[8]:

- **Black propaganda**—"propaganda presented as coming from a source other than the real one" (e.g., information claiming to be from an organization at which the propaganda is targeted; a definition quite close to today's concept of disinformation);
- **Gray propaganda**—"propaganda that does not identify any specific source" (its sources are of dubious quality, undetermined, unattributed);
- **White propaganda**—"propaganda disseminated and recognized by the sponsor or its accredited agency" (its source is established, its origin is known, it is an approved content).

Note that the above definitions are quite dated and historical. They refer to the concept of the source of information, and nowadays the more important criterion is often the type of content itself, its construction. I draw your attention to the fact that in various PR textbooks similar expressions appear, such as "black PR," "white PR," or "gray PR," which somewhat correspond to the above definitions. Only, of course, they don't use the word "propaganda," but "PR." Why this comment? Only for the sake of clarity, because it is not a matter of juxtaposing the two. In doing so, a digressive remark is necessary: in many areas, the use of "colored" terms for variants of different formulations is today rightly abandoned, and other terminology is adopted instead. However, I cite these old definitions for the sake of completeness, and also to allow the comprehension of the context of older works or references.

2.1.3 Nature of the propaganda content

Propaganda does not have to be particularly sophisticated. On the contrary, it is often quite simple (not to say simplistic) messages. It all depends on who the recipient is (and what mental or intellectual construction they have) and what the goal is. For example, in Nazi Germany, propaganda was omnipresent—it was conducted through all channels, influencing literature, the press, and advertising. Propaganda does not always have to be intelligent or "stealthy."[9] Sometimes, it is simply sufficient for whole groups of people to be constantly "immersed" in some crafted, created, manufactured version of reality. For this to work, of course, it is best to limit access to information "from the outside." For example, with censorship tools.

"Blunt" messages, even those that can be verified as untrue, are only one side of the coin. Because the contents can also be sophisticated, psychological, and subliminal.

Hostile propaganda, especially in a conflict situation, is worth identifying and combating. To be able to do so, every self-respecting State has or should have devoted structures. Although their activities may not always cover all the information channels available today.

Especially when these can be subject to rapid change, and bureaucratic-state structures may not be accustomed to rapid adaptation. Hence, the conclusion that adversaries' use of more and more new channels and techniques carries an obvious return on investment, because it may not be obvious that these channels or methods have been immediately adapted or used for such needs—potentially challenging the ability to identify or defend against it. But what are we talking about here, because it's starting to sound enigmatic? Let's make the example argument direct and to the point. At some point in the 2010s and 2020s, Instagram, TikTok, or even the communication tools of various computer or console games may have been considered relatively "novel" and not subject to monitoring. However, as these new channels gained popularity, it made sense to act upon it. After all, there are people and groups of people out there using those channels regularly—the audiences. Such new tools emerge on a fairly regular basis, sometimes in response to generational changes. Their adaptation may be useful, even crucial, both for offensive and defensive purposes.

Now, let's jump decades back. One of the more interesting, though not obvious, propaganda objects were postage stamps.[10] They could be used by States to emphasize the importance of countries (or existence at all). Argentina released stamps in 1936 with a map of Argentina covering the disputed territory of the Falkland Islands (controlled by Great Britain).[11] Such things are done intentionally and are not accidental. Policies using postage stamps with maps have been practiced by many countries[12]: Bolivia, Paraguay, Chile, Argentina, and others. It is worth recalling, for example, Ireland's disputes with Northern Ireland (British territory), Bohemia, and Moravia, where during the German occupation in 1939 postage stamps were issued with patriotic symbols of (then occupied) Czechoslovakia, which was overlooked by the German invaders.[13] And with that, I will conclude this specific paragraph about cartographic and philatelic propaganda. Another manifestation of the use of geography could arise when in 2023 Hungarian Prime Minister Orban showed himself wearing a scarf supporting the national soccer team—the scarf had outlined the contours of a map of Hungary within the pre-World War I borders, much larger than today, covering areas now belonging to other countries. That's also one way to do it.

Propaganda is created from information (from text, from multimedia) and delivered to the recipient through selected channels and methods, hence the direct conclusion that propaganda has *some source*, because someone creates material and delivers it to the recipient. In the following chapters, we will consider it more precisely, because these are important considerations for propaganda, information operations, and disinformation. This *someone*, therefore, controls and is responsible for the information payload. Counter-propaganda activities can be aimed at identifying such material (as propaganda) and its source, neutralizing it or publicizing it to reveal and debunk it. The source is not the same as the veracity or falsity of the messages.[14] In fact, propaganda does not have to use false content at all, and even often it should not. To combat propaganda easily verifiable as false it would be simple to disseminate information about these facts. This would allow to mark the entire influence campaign as untrue, undermining its effectiveness.

Situations may be more serious if the propaganda has the character of a more advanced operation, activity—when it is the assembly of various types of content in the specific, right way. Again, not necessarily false, merely presenting reality in a certain way. In a way that can influence the recipient due to the construction of such a method of influence, and perhaps due to the psychology of the recipient, the information environment (more on that later), or events that have actually occurred, are occurring, or perhaps are yet to occur (if one has knowledge of them or can predict them happening). A good example would be a pandemic of some infectious disease. If the message about the threat is adequately disseminated, it is informatively "available" to the minds of the public. Then, propaganda referring to the very fact of the pandemic, the very concepts associated with the pandemic situation (e.g., that one is working remotely), can be more easily accepted by some recipients (the mind can associate certain facts, awareness of the pandemic is more easily recalled, one even automatically looks for connections, as people love to rationalize things and seek connections, even when there are none). After all, something may sound true, something may be difficult to exclude; at the same time, this thing may be based on something unambiguously easy to identify—that there is an epidemic situation. And perhaps some action is actually being taken to deal with the epidemic, making it one point to mention or even "attack." We can imagine more of such "information levers."

Thus, determining the source of propaganda is not necessarily related to the veracity or falsity of the disseminated content. On the other hand, such content may be skewed in some direction (biased); it may be misleading. The military importance of information has been known for a very long time; it is not a product only of our time. What is changing, of course, is the information environment[15] and methods. Just as staff communiqués were once propaganda, later such value could be carried by the reports of some war correspondents or journalists (even if unwittingly—that's the information they got). The nature of war information reporting is changing further and can be, for example, conducted using tools such as social media, instant messaging, and video channels. Grassroots initiatives can have an impact precisely, thanks to social media, with a role also played by influencers of various kinds, that is, people who have an influence on certain environments or people; even if such people are not taken seriously, they can be listened to (and something will always remain in someone's mind).

This is all part of the information environment—new information channels, new media, new methods and means of exchanging information and data, their propagation and reception. That is, "technology" is changing.

2.1.4 Computational propaganda

It's worth introducing a rather novel, contemporary definition right now. Computational propaganda[16,17] is "the use of algorithms, automation, and human curation to purposefully distribute misleading information over social media networks."[18] It's the use of trolls and bots—something describing a method of propagation, of reaching an audience. A certain "assemblage of social media platforms, autonomous agents, and big data tasked with the manipulation of public opinion."[19] This definition, however, needs to be modified a bit, taking into account that computational methods can be used in propaganda on many levels, not just in propagation. There will be more on the use of these methods in the following chapters.

From here it is close to disinformation. However, I point out that due to the close relationship between these phenomena, the terms "propaganda," "disinformation," or "spreading misleading, false information" (misinformation) are sometimes used interchangeably,[20] which is not necessarily always accurate or justified.

2.2 MISLEADING, FALSE INFORMATION

Misinformation is false and untrue information subject to spreading, propagation,[21] but not intentionally. Thus, it can be the repetition of false information or messages (including rumors and hearsay) done involuntarily, without awareness of the purpose. This often well describes the so-called circles of enthusiasts of various kinds of conspiracy theories. It is about the process of unknowingly spreading false, untrue information. Helpful in the propagation of such ideas is the fact that sometimes it is actually difficult to establish the truth or veracity (or falsity) of certain theses and concepts, and sometimes it is even impossible.

Meanwhile, people may "demand certainty" and not be able to cope with the fact that modern science often talks about probability and statistical significance, because that's the way the world is.

For example, it is contemporarily believed that the existing reality was created as a result of the Big Bang, a physical (astrophysical, cosmological) process that, according to current knowledge, occurred about 13.8 billion years ago. In this sense, someone could argue that it is not known whether "something" (anything—matter, energy, etc.) could have existed or functioned at all "before" that moment. Any consideration toward what was or was not "before" the Big Bang is speculation at best, because it cannot be determined. On the other hand, it is certainly possible to establish scientifically and medically that vitamin C, while needed by the body and crucial in maintaining good health, is not a miracle cure for all ailments, such as cancer. It simply isn't and that's it. However, by unknowingly propagating such information, it can still be considered misleading to spread false information, perhaps unintentionally. After all, in pluralism one can have different views, and people very much like to hold views—their views, for example.

2.2.1 Why does it work? One explanation

Susceptibility to believing in false information is a matter of human psychology, and therefore it is psychological. In addition, it is difficult to effectively straighten out false information, which is related to how the human cognitive apparatus functions.[22] Even after a version has been corrected, an earlier dose of "poisoned" information can still influence people,[23] which is due to the so-called psychological continuing influence effect that contributes to the entrenchment of false information.[24]

2.2.2 So what to do?

There are two main approaches: spotting a fake and communicating on it, debunking, and doing this in advance, pre-bunking potential false information in advance.

A possible third approach could be not so much to straighten, correct, and debunk false information but to support reporting, media, and truthful information and promoting them[25]—the idea is to point out reliable sources of information. On the other hand, it is worth remembering that people may prefer to think that they (personally!) are not susceptible to disinformation or propaganda (among other reasons, that's why they usually are). Moreover, they may consider that it is these "other people" (and not themselves) who are susceptible to disinformation.[26]

So, the problem, then, are "those other people," because it doesn't work on "us" (or it works to a lesser extent, the so-called "third-person effect"[27,28]). And so 77% of respondents judged that "those other people" are more susceptible (than themselves).[29] There is a clear paradox here. Ultimately, it begs the question, had Goebbels, by any chance, been delighted, and perhaps even benefited from it? Maybe he did, only without the scientific theories that developed after his death. For example, the psychological third-person effect has been known since the 1980s.

2.3 DISINFORMATION

Disinformation is the deliberate spreading of false information. It is done knowingly, with the awareness that it is false. Perhaps even doing it methodically, efficiently, on a large scale. This is already an active measure that could fall under propaganda (information,

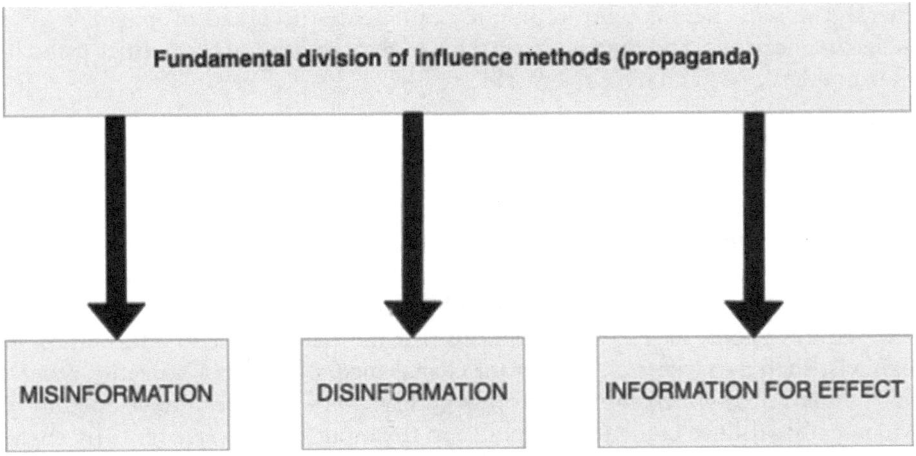

Figure 2.1 Methods of informational influence. Misleading (false) information, disinformation. But much can also be accomplished using truthful information.

Source: Own work.

disinformation, information warfare) operations. Of course, undertaken with some intent, with some purpose. In the case of disinformation, we have a clear goal and intention (intent). This is the main difference from merely propagating false information without being aware of its falsity (misinformation). Of course, someone can still be aware of the falsity of the information: then such a person uses disinformation as a method and exploits the unawareness or ignorance of the audience to propagate and amplify such messages. Uninformed people then become propagation nodes, and since they are unaware of this, at their level, we can consider it as unconscious spreading of false information (misinformation).

It is sometimes argued that disinformation is "any government-sponsored communication in which deliberately misleading information is passed to targeted individuals, groups, or governments with the purpose of influencing foreign elite or public opinion. This also defines propaganda."[30] And this may be the definition of disinformation. However, this definition only considers "government" (domestic, foreign) activities. This does not fit the times, where theoretically any citizen can potentially become an emitter (or intermediary) of information propagation, provided they have built the means and channels to do so. Similarly, information can be spread by commercial centers. Figures 2.1 and 2.2 display the primiary divisions of informational influence methods.

2.4 ACTORS, PRODUCERS OF PROPAGANDA, FALSE INFORMATION, DISINFORMATION

A broad issue is where such information transmissions come from. In today's information environment, this problem is complex, because they can be efficiently created by both state and non-state actors and institutions. Those actors can also be from third countries (foreign States). Propaganda and manufactured information messages affected many countries. There are examples of digital information activities on behalf of at least such States as Russia, China, Iran, France, or the United States. There's a whole cross-section.

In general, the issue here is who in practice can create or spread propaganda. There are many such classifications, and the manifestations of the activities of the entities listed here are discernible and have been all over the world[31]:

- **Trolls**—people interested in spreading provocative messages, perhaps intentionally false, so as to reach the audience and make a fuss, and introduce general chaos on a limited scale. They can use a wide variety of techniques: from referring to current events to social problems. They can be amateurs and enthusiasts of innocent discussions on the Internet, as well as professionals deliberately hired to do so, or someone who wants to make a living or has a certain sense of humor or simply a lot of free time;
- **Bots**—automations, scripts, and programs that mechanically send information through channels, such as Twitter/X, Instagram (social media in general), or any other service the "handling" of which can be automated. Bots may have been developed in ways to dynamically produce content in response to the input they receive (e.g., by engaging in "artificial" discussion with other, real, live peoples), and perhaps soon such capabilities will be deceptively human-like through AI/LLM (artificial intelligence, large language models, such as GPT) methods;
- **Substituted websites**—specially created sites containing false content or information relating to some event (e.g., pop culture, "geopolitical"), perhaps impersonating quality media, so crafted content that they may even constitute disinformation—these are simply sources of distorted messages, which can then be (also unknowingly) spread by others;
- **Social media channels**—like with websites, only that sometimes it can be easier to identify a personal or institutional source if such a person goes by name and gives a face to the content. These can also be all sorts of so-called analysts, experts, people interested in building audience channels, sometimes defense or geopolitical magicians/pundits, or self-proclaimed fortune tellers. Occasionally, they may be supported by other electronic or even traditional media. Their goal is not necessarily disinformation but money or fame, for which methods are adapted accordingly. Means based on the propagation of doubt, fear, or confusion, however, can closely resemble propaganda methods;
- **Enthusiasts of conspiracy theories**—as a center for the creation of such content, they need to attract an audience that will willingly pass such information on, propagate it, including unknowingly, in an unconscious way. On the other hand, the creators of these stories may believe in them themselves, but, they don't necessarily have to (then it's disinformation, on purpose). The important thing is that their dissemination pays off for them in some manner (as a hobby, financially, which the recipients of their content don't have to know);
- **Media**—may be interested in creating and promoting content according to ideological or other reasons, favorable to the chosen side of the political dispute, or because of financial considerations. Sometimes it may also happen that they spread stories not based on proper analysis or background research (if only due to misunderstandings of a covered topic);
- **Politicians**—they need to reach their audience, to win them over. To do this, they create content that may appeal or may shock, so that it resonates. They can promote distorted views of reality and take advantage of information asymmetry, that is, the fact that consumers of information propagate it without knowing what its true nature is, or that the information is untrue or worthless;
- **APT groups, APMs**—disinformation and information operations techniques can benefit from cyberattacks by APT (advanced persistent threat) groups, from stolen data, or from the implantation of false messages on hacked sites, exploiting their reputation or targeting psychological effects. APMs (advanced persistent manipulator), on the

other hand, are groups that create and spread propaganda and disinformation in an advanced, deliberate, and persistent manner (this will be discussed later);

- **Foreign governments**—and their security structures—can operate at any level (creation, propagation, etc.), using various channels or resources, including agents of influence, whether persuaded to act or hired. They can also use the previously mentioned techniques or groups. But also use special channels like diplomatic (which may also use social media profiles). We saw this very clearly in the case of the Russian Federation during the 2022–2023 war in Ukraine (which will be discussed as a case study);
- **Governments**—have a relatively large amount of power and can also exert informational influence internally. Internal by shaping information and messages internally and through various channels—in addition to those mentioned above, for example also through press conferences or other events.

2.5 CENSORSHIP

Censorship is the filtering or tampering of information. The trimming and editing of content (news, books, newspapers, posts on the Internet, social media, etc.), including the total or significant prohibition or blockade of information dissemination, at least that of unapproved origin, that is, "illegal" content (although in the second decade of the 21st century, political discussions in many countries began to introduce other euphemisms such as "harmful but legal"). Usually, it was the States that imposed censorship duties on information and the media that could distribute it, in accordance with the goals of the socio-political system.

Additionally, censorship can refer to ideology and some value system. It is a political issue (what is the purpose of such an action? In response to what? Is it related to state issues?), legal (what is the legal basis, what are the limitations and scope of censorship?), organizational (how do decision-making and executive structures work?), technical (how specifically is content trimmed? What and how can it be done in practice?). Issues of content moderation are also subject to the rules of use of websites, such as social networks. It could be, for example, removing content from posts and websites but also blocking calls.[32,33] The matter may also apply to cultural elements (content subject to censorship in the Age of Enlightenment. Or more contemporarily, in Soviet Russia, Communist China, including with regard to creative works such as literature or music). A historical example of cultural censorship is the non-performance of Wagner's music because of his National Socialist views.[34] And a completely contemporary interesting manifestation of attempts at censorship was the initiatives to ban Korean pop (K-pop) in China in the second decade of the 21st century because of (obviously) "national security" concerns.

The effects of censorship may be overestimated, and, more specifically, a belief may develop that it has a significant impact, but on "other people," not on "us."[35] However, this may be a reason to be more accepting of censorship methods. After all, with the assumption that these "other people" are particularly strongly influenced by media messages (e.g., disinformation), the temptation may arise to block certain information in order to protect these "other people." This is, again, a manifestation of the psychological third-person effect[36]—when one ascribes a particularly strong influence or effect to information messages, but on other people (personally, such people may believe that it does not affect them, of course, or affects them to a lesser degree).[37,38] All sorts of beliefs can arise about the pernicious effect of disinformation, propaganda, or even video games.[39] But "on other people" (to a greater extent).

As noted long time ago, it is also worth appreciating that censorship can seamlessly support propaganda,[40] because it does not have to be the mere blocking of certain information or information channels. It can be a disruption of the transmission of selected information, its circulation. When certain information does not appear, the full picture of the situation will not be formed—it will be distorted. Therefore, when using the tool of censorship, one should be wary of the potential impacts. At the same time, such caution was recommended by L.J. Clarke, who was responsible for official propaganda during the apartheid era in South Africa.[41] This can be considered a man who "knows his stuff," although let us point out that this is perhaps not the most fortunate reference.

In addition, special conditions and needs may arise in a war situation, requiring censorship measures. For example, during the Russian war in Ukraine in 2022, Ukraine blocked (comprehensively) Russian social media.[42] Western countries also blocked Russian media (including websites). This relatively simple action "solved" a large part of the problem of disinformation or propaganda, which until then allegedly "could not be dealt with," or rather, no one wanted to take action in the preceding years, which also contributed to the buildup of the phenomenon of "disinformation" as something popular, trending, which was allegedly so difficult to defend against. Censorship can prove to be a rather effective method. Even if restrictions can be technically circumvented, it does not mean that everyone will do so, or that it will even be done broadly. After all, in practice, it may be sufficient for censorship to simply have a certain high (90%, 95%, 99%) effectiveness—not necessarily a perfect one. In this sense, censorship can also help fight propaganda, not just support propaganda. It's a matter of point of view. It all depends on the goals, on the side from which a particular case is analyzed (by whom), and on the values, rights, and morals of those who decide about it, and the methods they possibly use—delicate stuff, prone to misuse or abuse.

2.5.1 Content moderation and its limitations

An important concept related to censorship is a variation of it—content moderation. This is the admission of "acceptable" content that complies with the rules of a particular platform (sometimes referred to as community rules) or ethical principles or legal regulations. For example, many platforms adopt in their moderation rules a prohibition on distributing illegal, copyright-infringing content. Others may "moderate" posts that encourage violence or contribute to the spread of hate speech.

Very often, moderation has to be automatic (at least to a great degree). Especially for large platforms, where there are actually so many new posts and content every hour that it is impossible for humans to analyze all of them. Content moderation is often a regulated area.[43] However, moderation itself faces many challenges. These stem from the fact that different States may have their own standards. The legal rules may vary, and consequently the expectations for content moderation may differ. This is because it is a matter of reconciling compliance with the law, but also—the right to freedom of expression. For example, different standards apply in the United States, in Europe, or in China. In Europe, for example, it is not strange to publish photos of ancient sculptures depicting nudity on a social media platform. However, there have been situations that for American platforms like Facebook, accustomed to standards in the United States, such vintage content was unacceptable. However, if taking down such a post would lead to it being blocked everywhere, it would be difficult to understand in Europe. So, this is a rather complex situation. Perhaps similarly, there was the issue of blocking by a generative artificial intelligence model from China's Alibaba of providing answers to an inquiry about Chinese leader Xi Jinping. Or doing exactly the same thing by the Midjourney model, built in San Francisco (subjecting itself to voluntary self-censorship). In the face of such challenges, it may be difficult to develop universally recognized moderation rules. This is also highlighted by the history of the International Telecommunications Union (ITU) and its failed attempts to develop telegraph codes.[44] It has not been possible to create a universal language for encoding information, and this is due to the existence of different types of languages, alphabets. Attempts were made for more than 50 years, starting in 1870.[45] At that time, some delegates made comments suggesting (in order to facilitate the work?) to omit some characters from other languages (because, according to them, they were unpronounceable, which only they themselves agreed with). The ITU standard project was abandoned in the 20th century, and today there is no longer any need for its existence. Technology changed. Still, this illustrates the problem of the construction of universally valid standards for information, as well as the fabrication of supposed reasons not to do something. Although currently there is luckily no problem with the notation of various letters or glyphs, thanks to character encoding and emojis.

2.6 PUBLIC RELATIONS, ADVERTISING, PUBLIC AFFAIRS

2.6.1 Public relations

The definition of PR is to shape the image or relationships between people and organizations and external audiences (perhaps customers). Of course, this can influence public opinion, exert influence, including even impacting political issues. This is not a book about PR, so more on this need not be added—except for the passages in the following chapters, where these methods are important and relevant. The object of such activities is to reach out with information, to influence opinions, and to shape them.

But the goals of political propaganda (or disinformation) are clear: they are political. Such is the nature of the influence to be exerted. Similarly, the objectives of military propaganda are military issues, such as the security of the State or the preparation of a campaign against a neighboring State. In this light, the purpose of advertising or commercial PR is economic. This should be quite easy to grasp. Even if arguments of a different nature are raised in the process, then it is done perhaps on occasion or due to its usefulness. Even if the actual methods of PR may be (technically) similar to those used in propaganda, and sometimes perhaps even the same—the goals, intentions, ethical considerations, even the source of the activity, the openness of the sponsors are different. In view of this, solely based on the similarity of the methods or techniques, these things cannot be fairly equated. These differences take place on various levels, qualitatively. A slightly different situation may be with political PR, when one promotes certain political solutions, approaches, or plans, or even a candidate in an election. Certain individuals—whether well-known, lesser-known, or not known at all—who should be brought to the public's attention (for some reason). However, everything then happens in accordance with the law and within the internal political order. Or at least it should.

In pluralistic societies, PR and advertising can be treated as issues of free speech issues.[46] And this is true even if the impact of selected PR campaigns can sometimes be seen or considered as something akin or identical to disinformation.[47] Indeed, sometimes such service providers may cross ethical boundaries by offering influence services more actively, such as in the field of political PR. In the following chapters, we will note that some of the methods used are exactly the same (technically). The field of action for PR and advertising, however, is much broader and includes interacting with virtually all areas of society: from sports through art to technology. We leave it a philosophical question whether, after crossing certain boundaries, PR and advertising still remain PR and advertising, or perhaps it transitions qualitatively to propaganda or disinformation.[48] Similarly with another question: at what point does journalism become PR or advertising? In these areas, however, we do not venture. Why? Well, if only because this book has to end somewhere.

2.6.2 Public affairs

Because various companies and organizations operate in a public setting, interactions within the socio-political system (and within the law) are necessary and are the subject of PA.[49] For example, when the head of a major technology company is asked to address the U.S. Congress or the European Parliament after a malfeasance scandal, this is the subject of public affairs and sometimes perhaps even crisis action. Public relations can also involve influencing the development of legislation (lobbying). Like advertising or PR, PA methods also have their place in the democratic order, and it should come as no surprise that various entities care about an effective and well-managed image and contacts with important parts of public life, although building competence and capacity in this area is by no means easy.[50] Usually, there is a special department within a company or organization working on this, with influence on communications policy. However, I would like to strongly emphasize that, of course, not every information campaign, such as political, can be considered in terms of propaganda as it is understood today; making politics can be based on methods of persuasion (of voters), just like that—how else? This is the essence of democratic systems and automatically equating such activities with propaganda is inadequate.[51] Although it can be done, even for political purposes. For example, when someone's actions are called propaganda (in the pejorative sense), even if those accusing someone of such "propaganda" use analogous methods—the "*propaganda of propaganda.*" This is a certain paradox and the beauty of the nature of political and journalistic discourse.

2.6.3 Public affairs in the military sense

Why do we refer so often to military sources already at this stage? Because such structures devote significant resources and thought to these issues—methodically, over years, decades, and even centuries.

At this point, it is worth referring once again to a good source of information—the U.S. Army terminology. There, PA in the military domain is considered

> public information, command information, and community engagement activities directed toward both the external and internal publics with interest in [Department of Defense]. Joint PA [Public Affairs] plans, coordinates, and synchronizes U.S. military public information activities and resources in order to support the commander's communications strategy and operational objectives through the distribution of truthful, timely, and factual information about joint military activities. PA contributes to the achievement of military objectives, by countering adversary misinformation and disinformation through the publication of accurate information.[52]

So, it is the publication of information that is considered reliable (from the point of view of the goals of the organization, here: the military, and more specifically the U.S. armed forces; although of course we should understand this more broadly) about military activities. Which can also counter hostile propaganda. A systematic approach to PA is necessary due to the fact that "hostile propaganda can actually be honest and direct. Propaganda is persuasive because it often uses elements to make information newsworthy [in the media]."[53] In essence, this is quintessential public communication. To a large extent, this definition can be translated to the goals and objectives of civilian, business Public Affairs—with appropriate modifications as to the objectives. With that said, this military handbook lists as one of its main objectives: "to tell the truth" (which is supposed to lead to trust-building), with consideration of narrative issues, that is, to build a story out of facts.[54] Historically, some U.S. politicians and military officials have maintained that it was the U.S. media that largely contributed to the U.S. defeat in Vietnam. Perhaps these experiences also lead to the construction of a professional approach to public affairs.

At this point, the Reader should feel reassured. The earlier reference to Goebbels is now clearly a kind of historical anecdote, given how we look at the man today (he was a criminal, as was his superior, and that whole regime). We recall him here because he emphasized the necessity of speaking the truth in propaganda. And this is the most appropriate approach. Of course, in his time there was no distinction (as there is today) between propaganda, Public Relations, and Public Affairs.

The U.S. Army, in an updated document on the concept of information, points out that truthful information can be effective in imposing narratives, views, and points of view. Informational impact can also be achieved by publishing content that is completely true, for example, when it is done in a certain, special way, at a certain time, for a certain purpose. After all, it may suffice, for example, to mention something (an event, an incident, a fact) in the context of other events—this can lead to a certain perception shift. This can also be a negative influence, even enabling "damaging credibility and capability of the targeted group."[55] In view of this, nowadays within the framework of propaganda, three basic elements can be distinguished for the purpose of producing some effects: misleading (false) information—*misinformation*, *disinformation* (deliberate), and *true information* (for effect).

2.7 APM AND FIMI—MANIPULATION AND FOREIGN INTERFERENCE

2.7.1 Advanced and Persistent Manipulator (APM)

The English-language term "advanced persistent manipulator"[56] is similar to the well-known cyber security term "advanced persistent threat," which describes a persistent and advanced cyber security threat from an advanced and determined threat group. In this sense, a literal meaning of APM would be in reference to the manipulation with information and the information environment.

As I write these words, the term APM is definitely not accepted as a standard, so one must approach the term with caution, as a certain novelty; however, let's treat it as a useful term. APM groups are specialized in propaganda, information operations, and information warfare. Their actions can target specific organizations, companies, state institutions, or even entire countries—their goals and objectives. They can manipulate public opinion, including by simply bringing up topics that (for some reason) the public just at a given moment "should" be concerned with (to avoid dealing with others, for example). Why does one sometimes—suddenly and completely unexpectedly—start talking about something or someone? For example, about someone previously unknown? Or an affair, concept, or initiative? These might not arise naturally; they can be the results of manipulations of various kinds.

APM groups may be funded by government structures and use a variety of methods, such as creating fake or substituted media accounts, including social media, fake personas, and directing information messages, the so-called "operational legend-building," building credible cover stories and backgrounds of the past, and lending credibility to stories, narratives, and people, for example when they appear seemingly out of nowhere. APMs can also gain access to some non-public resources, such as from groups responsible for cyber attacks and cyber operations, and use these resources to influence operations. Such collaborations of cyber-supported APMs can take over social media accounts, such as those belonging to an analyst, journalist, or politician. But activities don't have to be limited to social media or even just the Internet, as they can include the so-called "full information spectrum," activities online, offline, through various channels—also through selected media. An example of such an organization was the so-called Russian Troll Factory, the Internet Research Agency (IRA). Not only that, because APMs can also be fusions of information influence activities through social media and traditional media, state information, diplomatic means, etc. The systematic creation of "informational" content is of interest to many organizations: from intelligence through contracted PR firms to state governments.

2.7.2 Foreign information manipulation and interference (FIMI)

FIMI is a variant of the information activity and describes manipulation and information influence of "foreign" origin—foreign from the point of view of the State (or block) from whose point of view one looks at the process. The term largely overlaps with APM due to the fact that the terminology in this area is evolving and has not yet been widely adopted or standardized. FIMI can also describe disinformation activities or disinformation itself. The EU's diplomatic arm (external action service) describes FIMI activities as "*mostly non-illegal*"[57] (whatever that means: since clear reasons for "illegality" are not indicated). Legal issues will be discussed in later sections of this book. These are important things for strategy and stability, so if one says that something would be illegal, it is worth pointing out why, by virtue of what principles or laws. Otherwise, "illegality" becomes a rhetorical ploy, and loses meaning.

I will note that in 2022 alone (and the year-milestone is significant—that's when the Russian military attack on Ukraine occurred, which reverberated around the world), there were about 100 FIMI operations or incidents reported in the EU—and 750 by late 2023. And, interestingly, the EU report lists only two States as their sources—Russia and China.[58] The restriction to this area may sound natural and follows from the EU's internal and external policies and goals. The specifics of the steps and activities that make up the creation of operations will be discussed in later chapters.

2.8 PSYCHOLOGICAL OPERATIONS (PSYOP)

Propaganda or disinformation is also about playing on psychology or influencing the psyche of the audience. From there, it's close to the concept of military psychological operations. They can be succinctly defined as[59] causing or reinforcing the target's attitudes and behavior conducive to preconceived intentions. The intent of PSYOP is to influence perceptions.[60] NATO's definition provides for "[p]lanned activities using methods of communication and other means directed at approved audiences in order to influence perceptions, attitudes and behavior, affecting the achievement of political and military objectives."[61] Target group analysis is a very important part of such activities. Determining which groups are targeted for PSYOP messages will improve the efficiency of the process. So, it makes sense to identify the target groups that are the most suitable audiences, and select communication methods and means to reach them,[62] sometimes highlighting key communicators (e.g., influencers or other types of people who have an influence in a given environment) with which to best reach the desired audience groups.[63]

To reiterate, it is always most effective to use truth, truthful information.[64] A great fuss was created at one time by overfocusing on the so-called "fake news," that is, untrue information, which, as should be clear by now, is by definition not very effective (since it may be easy to demonstrate its falsity). NATO, too, recommends the use of true information: "[t]he use of false information is counter-productive to the long-term credibility and ultimate success of PSYOPS."[65]

In propaganda, influence and psychological effects can be of great importance. This can lead to influencing views toward some issues, and perhaps also to actions (taking them or not). In this sense, we are most interested in possible informational influence, but of course it is also worth bearing in mind non-informational influence, such as events in the physical world. In this sense, psychological operations are not something that can be reduced to propaganda.

Psychological operations are one of the things that can support information operations (IO, INFO OPS). There will be more about PSYOP later in this book, but the introduction of the term at this point is reasonable—it will enable to talk about certain events or materials.

2.9 INFORMATION OPERATIONS (IO)

This issue is central to this book. Information operation is a very important term. It is a series of coherent actions designed to lead to some effect or impact.

The military definition recognizes that it is the "integrated employment, during military operations, of information-related capability in concert with other lines of operation to influence, disrupt, corrupt, or usurp the decision making of adversaries and potential adversaries while protecting our own."[66]

It is, therefore, the use of information to achieve some goal.

This purpose may be to create confusion (information diversion), chaos, perhaps to introduce certain narratives, stories, or a certain way of seeing things. The importance of previously irrelevant things or concepts could be emphasized at some points to create information noise, force some topics into the public debate, and popularize them (e.g., to confuse, to stop other topics from being considered or discussed). The goal can also be to take some action that potentially influences someone's views, to lead to a certain activity. Such as going to a street demonstration, voting for an option in a referendum or election, or even taking subversive or violent actions. The goal can also be to discourage participation in elections (referendum). Detecting the fact that something constitutes an artificially created information operation may not be easy, for example, in the situation of ongoing elections in the State.[67] How to do so, what is the possible course—about this in Chapter 3.

While here we are talking about the military definition, we are referring to information operations also (formally) in peacetime. We can use the phrase "information warfare" to describe operations during war. Indeed, information operations have always been part of warfare. In this sense, the means of propagation (media) used in information operations can be equated, for example, with radio broadcasting, television broadcasting, websites, and social media[68] but also the good old staff communiqués during war, proclamations to the nation(s), diplomatic communications, and dropping leaflets from airplanes.

2.9.1 Information warfare

Information warfare is a term worth reserving for information activities during war (armed conflict), if only owing to the fact that the words have their specific meanings. After all, there is no point in talking about war during peace. Except when one wants to "amplify" one's statement, one wants to emphasize it (so this is a journalistic, or publicist issue). The latter, in principle, could be considered persuasion, the exertion of influence—in a sense, itself similar in nature to an information operation. Precision in terminology is worth paying attention to especially when we see that the era of high-intensity full-scale wars is not something in the distant past but rather a contemporary reality, which should be clear from 2022 onward.

Why is it better not to use the term "information warfare" for peacetime operations? Precisely because armed conflict (i.e., classic war) is not conducted in peacetime. Using terms with "war" connotations may enhance the information message, emphasize some points, but—again—it is purely "journalistic" or "publicist" in nature or form. If a State is at peace, and someone uses the term "war," what is the point? Sure, someone is "fighting" someone, although, of course, it is not an armed conflict between two countries. This is understandable, but especially in a world where full-scale and traditional wars are part of the reality we live in, it is inappropriate to use such vocabulary merely to "bolster" statements. A publicist and politician who uses terms like "war on drugs," and "war on traffic violations" puts the matter straight. And yet, after all, this is not about using artillery or bombing, for example, to fight them. To refer to peacetime struggles or competition between States, it is much better to use a different term: conflict. And in this sense, once conflict reaches the level of armed conflict—then it is a war.

Under wartime conditions, the objectives of such activities (information warfare, i.e., information operations during war) can depend on who the recipient is. Directing them inward, to one's own State and society, can boost morale, preparing them for a battle. Directing them outward, to enemies, for example, can encourage laying down of arms, discourage, deprave, corrupt, and demoralize. Directing them to allies and the societies of allied States would be aimed at leading to and maintaining support (in some form).

In summary, state structures, their contractors, military structures, parts of society, and even so-called militants, sometimes called terrorists by some,[69] may take part in the information warfare because of the means and methods used.

2.10 INFORMATION ENVIRONMENT

Another key definition is needed to build some model of conditions under which information impact occurs. For this purpose, the concept of information environment is very important and helpful. We won't reinvent the wheel, and in this kind of handbook, we will simply refer to a recognized definition—again, by the way—from the military community.

The information environment

> is the aggregate of individuals, organizations, and systems that collect, process, disseminate, or act on information. This environment consists of three interrelated dimensions which continuously interact with individuals, organizations, and systems. These dimensions are the physical, informational, and cognitive. The physical dimension consists of control and command systems, key decision makers and the supporting infrastructure that enables individuals and organizations to create actions (outcomes). The informational dimension determines where and how information is collected, processed, stored, disseminated and protected. The cognitive dimension encompasses the minds of those who send, receive and respond to or act on information.[70]

The information environment is, therefore, a complex socio-technical system and a certain model relating to reality. It aids in the detection and creation of information activities.

This definition can and should be adapted for civilian use, for our purposes. Following this line of reasoning, we can define such an "information environment" for ourselves or for the target under consideration. And then "our" information operations will "defend" our systems or interfere with the "adversary's" information environment. For example, if the goal of an information operation were to exert influence domestically, various actors are singled out, including, state actors (secret services, state structures, media, key individuals, selected companies), the media, the public, educational institutions, some non-governmental institutions, means like social media, perhaps also international organizations or the like from neighboring countries. One establishes how such actors operate and whether their activities can have some connection with the information operation being created, whether they can influence it, and whether they can be useful or harmful in the course of such operations. And so one modulates the message and the way of reaching the audience to take into account the elements of the information environment. One can describe it as playing the harp or the piano, pressing appropriate buttons and keys, and pulling the right levers.

Moreover, some information may be directed to specific actors within such an information environment. At the same time, the information environment can include different dimensions or domains, for example, physical, informational, and cognitive.[71] We are interested in the informational layer, at the interface between the physical and cognitive worlds, although the effects can come through the influence on the cognitive or physical layers. With that said, the information environment can also be dynamic (it usually is) as a result of its own or others' information activities. A hypothetical example is the public discrediting of a public figure, such as a politician. This person may have been respected, held a position of responsibility, been in power, and therefore was itself an important center within the information environment. As a result of some informational, active actions, such a person can be given even more importance or be degraded (lessening, diminishing of importance), or even removed from the information environment, deprived of influence. Information can be a powerful tool, even if it has no physical form. That's why delaying or failing to act in response to informational actions or following events can determine a losing battle—verbal, political, commercial, or perhaps even a military one.[72] These days, there may be little time to respond. It may even be a matter of hours or minutes to take action. Afterward, it may be too late to limit the damage.

The physical environment can also be influenced informationally, for example, by prompting the decision-making center to redeploy troops, and later, for example, describing the event accordingly (e.g., as preparations for war/aggression, although the action was taken for defensive purposes). But also actions in the physical environment can bring informational effect. For example, by aerial bombardment, one can exert pressure (i.e., have some effect) on enemy troops but also on society, on civilians. Studies are known about the psychological effects of the use of various types of warfare means: from bombardment and artillery, even to nuclear bombs. Which can, of course, lead to different kinds of decisions (and this is a cognitive layer). One should be aware that actions in different domains can affect others. These considerations are important in a purely civilian context.

For example, government alerts sent to the public—about weather threats, possible natural disasters, etc—can also affect individuals' actions. When one receives a message from the government's civilian early warning system (alert system), it can prompt people to make some kind of decision, such as not to go outside or to protect equipment from a windstorm. The same would be true, for example, in a radiation emergency due to radioactive contamination. It was precisely because of the lack of action in the 1986 Chernobyl power plant disaster that the local community was unaware of the risk and functioned as if nothing had happened. This undermined trust in the state authorities for years but also gave rise to a distrust of nuclear power. Spreading fear over nuclear energy worked for years afterward.

We noticed the limitations of the information environment during the pandemic in early 2020. Despite reports of spreading (SARS-CoV-2) virus infections in China, States did not take any measures in time and did not implement any restrictions on, for example, transportation from clearly exposed areas (from China) or in their own means of transportation. As a result, there was a rapid spread of the outbreaks in unprepared countries in Europe. It seemed sufficient, enough, to follow the news in January 2020. This was also done in the offices of the people in charge of States, but no action was taken. Of course, these are decision-making issues in complex state-bureaucratic environments, and we won't go into the details.

Figure 2.2 Amorphous information environment. Understanding its structure and operation makes it possible to make interventions.

Source: Adapted from Department of the Army, *Field Manual No. 100-6: Information Operations*, Washington 1996, https://irp.fas.org/doddir/army/fm100-6/.

2.10.1 Information advantage

2.10.1.1 What is information?

> [T]he purpose of information is to contribute to decision dominance, or a state in which commanders can act more quickly and effectively than their adversary. One achieves decision dominance by engaging in information advantage activities along five lines of effort: enabling decision-making, protecting friendly information, informing domestic and international audiences, influencing foreign audiences, and conducting information warfare.[73]

In this sense, information is data of some significance that is exchanged or delivered to recipients—domestic audience, allies, enemies, etc. Information is created to convey something, a message. To create or properly direct information, one needs some ability and competence. For example, when arranging messages, it is useful to take into account current events, situations, and cultural and environmental issues, to anchor it in something real. A message directed to a farmer in 19th century France looks different to a message directed to a city dweller in Western Europe in the 21st century; or to someone in an African province, to a representative of an ethnic minority in the United States, etc. It differs depending on the recipient. Thus, the cultural and historical context is important, as is even the context related to the worldview of the people and environments to which the message is directed.

2.10.2 Example of an operation to discredit a local dairy

The information environment is, therefore, a combination of people, institutions, various organizations, perhaps private companies.[74] The idea is to understand what potential for influence the various elements of such a "map" have—to understand what the interdependencies are. And by doing so, one may learn how information influence is distributed. And how one can act to exert influence. Let's analyze an example of a highly simplified information environment, establishing the goal of discrediting, for example, a local dairy. How do you define the information environment? It's the local media, social media, the dairy itself (let's assume it employs people responsible for communications or even PR), the local mayor, the village club, and the residents. If black PR is the goal, messages are created and spread on the internet, perhaps physical flyers are distributed, expecting that the events will be noticed as a "trend" or "grassroots effort," perhaps described over other means of information. We must also expect that the dairy will take countermeasures, such as engaging the media and local politicians to defend itself, that it will distribute leaflets itself. And also that it will eventually sue someone for violating its good image, for defamation.

The information environment can be "arranged" (roughly) for many countries and even interstate relations, although it would be much more complex, because it would include policymakers and politicians at the local level (with their possible connections or national or party affiliations) and at the central level (in both countries), traditional media with their ownership structure, social media, military structures, villagers, towns, etc. If, in addition, we imagine that we have a specific historical time (e.g., before the old wars), in addition, information can abound in the context of that historical reality, the beliefs of the time. Moreover, States actually actively shaped the public debate, for example, by means of censorship—certain information was removed, and the appearance of others may have been inspired. A complicated process!

2.11 INFORMATION SPACE

In democratic countries, pluralism performs a critical function. It is natural for there to be multiple media outlets, with different ownership structures. The point is that when there are different sources of information, in such conditions it is possible to create a civil society. Differing ways of describing or perceiving events or reality are then possible, and natural. The opposite of such an approach is a totalitarian system, where media messages are rigidly determined by the State, and the rest is subject to truncation or cuts, or complete suppression, be that by means of technical censorship or self-censorship. Under such circumstances, there may be a single image of the events, a single version of (approved) truth with regard to issues deemed important by the State.

The significant role of the media is manifold. They are able to modify or impose an agenda of opinion.[75] To influence what or who will be talked about, what topics will be considered, what will be given importance over others, and what topics will be left out, or suppressed. The weight assigned to events or information may have to do with whether a topic is addressed in the media.[76] Today, of course, it is not limited to traditional media, because if a topic is properly publicized, for example, on social media, it may also gain considerable uptake to become important and influential. Moreover, via such channels, the message can make its way into other electronic or traditional media, which will increase the reach and importance of some concept, topic, issue, or problem raised. The image or popularity of specific people—businessmen, politicians (current or aspiring), public figures, celebrities, etc.—can be shaped in a similar way. When they or their work receive frequent media attention and pickup, their importance in public perception may increase, or at least they may be perceived as significant. It is all about public perception then. For example, in Taiwan's 2019 local elections, a completely unknown man was apparently successfully promoted so that he won the election, and it was supposed to involve Chinese services active on social media.[77] It was, therefore, an artificial PR creation of a previously not especially known man. In the case of television, radio, or newspapers, after all, *someone* may decide that certain people, concepts, and products are shown often enough, over others. So, now let's consider the situation when some of those things don't happen by accident or naturally.

In a sense, this would be the shaping of the information space. For example, a significant popularity in the past (and perhaps even today) was enjoyed by those presenting the weather forecast. They are purveyors of important information, often positive (*it's going to be nice weather*!). They appear regularly. There is nothing wrong with it until someone wants to abuse such a position to exert political influence (this is not a joke).[78] In addition, if, due to global climate change, the issue of weather would become a political issue, and therefore subject to national and international political processes—it would not be surprising that it would be treated as a concrete political issue. It could also be then subject to instrumentalization—"for" and "against" attitudes. Why are we talking about this?

Now here's a surprise. Coincidentally, we've been touching on information space all along here. Information space, or infosphere, is a certain manifestation of the information environment. It includes the media, means such as radio, television, newspapers, social media, and, more generally, the entire space within which information appears or is propagated.

2.12 WEATHER FORECAST VERSUS RELIABILITY

From the moment information is created to the moment it reaches the recipient, many effects and dependencies may occur and be the case. In a highly polarized environment, information receipt can differ. In some environments, certain information may resonate strongly, spreading due to reactions of outrage (moral panic when rational judgment is suspended in a group of people) or catchy content. In other areas of the information environment, some content may spread much slower or not at all, if only because it is inconvenient or incompatible with the mental condition of the audience. Information, in order to achieve an effect, should be prepared in a form that is at least digestible for a particular audience. Going against established norms may not be the best approach to reach wide audiences.

The concept also includes people who can have an informational impact, that is, also the person announcing the weather. This just happens to be an ideal role, because the weather announcer says things that are very simple, content that everyone will understand. In addition, he or she tells the truth. The weather forecast quite often works sufficiently well, and when it does not, after all, it is not the fault of the presenter.[79] In a nutshell, a solid person, you can trust someone like that! Who knows, maybe someone would attempt to extend this trust to other areas of life as well, beyond voicing of the current forecast. After all, since he or she "knows" about the weather (he or she reads the forecasts prepared in advance by someone based on meteorological models of institutions involved in predicting the development of the weather situation), maybe he or she is also knowledgeable about other topics, such as energy security, economy, international security, or, say, geopolitics? I'll stop here, because I don't want the Reader to get the idea that weather prediction is an ideal way to build information or propaganda campaigns. However, we can see that such a seemingly innocuous element of the information space can have a wide reach and potential impact as well. And that was the point of this example.

2.12.1 The mechanics of public debate

All right, but how do the mechanics of public debate work? Certain content has access to debate in certain environments or populations, while other content does not. It's also a dynamic system: certain content is unacceptable at certain time or historical stages, and it may become relevant at other periods of time. The very phrase "information space" is popular in countries of the Eastern tradition, such as post-communist countries (Russia, Kazakhstan, etc.). This division between East and West may lead to confusion, because it is not necessarily clear to everyone what is being referred to: the "information space" or perhaps "information security" or "cyber security." Where in the West there is talk of securing IT systems against cyber attacks, in the East issues like electronic media, television, etc. may be attached to that topic. Thus, it can create a room for misunderstanding, where one side would consider something a "cyber attack," another would consider it an "information attack," and a third would consider it as nothing at all because they don't understand the issues.

2.13 OVERTON'S WINDOW

Overton's window is a concept derived from the social sciences (sociology), describing the space of debate and the flexibility, plasticity of that space.[80] In this book, we apply this model in a purely utilitarian and technical way. It is a model describing the introduction of a concept in such a way that it becomes socially *considered*, *acceptable*, and perhaps even reaches the *implementation* via legislative phase, at the political and legal level. It is natural that no one will seriously consider unknown or niche issues, without comprehending of their needs. People don't like change. Therefore, if there is a desire to make social changes, to influence legislation, it is necessary to get them into the information loop.

The mechanism of Overton's window describes the introduction of topics into the public debate. For example, one can use this terminology figuratively when considering the issue (purpose) of introducing into the information space matters concerning new medical therapies, which, after all, first need to be picked up and talked about, so that the concept or topic exists in the public debate, so that it will be familiar, then perhaps accepted by the public, society, and individual people.[81] Overton's window can also be useful in describing the conduct of information warfare.[82] After all, topics previously absent or even unacceptable in society can be introduced in such a way, including all sorts of socially bearing issues such as abortion, prohibition of slavery, obesity, antibiotic use, euthanasia, gender fluidity, brushing teeth twice a day, alcohol consumption, sexual orientations, and even culinary choices, voting by women or people under a certain age, adaptation of buildings and means of communication to the needs of people with disabilities, the role of a certain State in Europe, the use of physical violence against children and adolescents, legalization of marijuana (amphetamines, heroin, etc.), cleaning up after your dog while walking it, home possession of automatic rifles or rocket launchers, the suitability or inadequacy of a certain person as president, global warming or climate change,[83] and many others. It should be clear by now what we are considering here. It's debatable topics, including prior they even become known or debated at all.

At the same time, we do not have to attribute to any of the previously mentioned topics any particular valuations (for or against, good or bad), because we are talking about the method itself. Besides, it should be understandable that if one wants to handle a socio-political topic, it needs to somehow become in the interest of the public, society. Thus, it is introduced into the debate, this way altering the information space. After some time (months, years, decades), it may arrive at a point where the concept is not only understood as being a legitimate part of the discussed socio-political or technical issues, but it may become accepted as desirable. The key is the very introduction into the debate, into the public sphere of what is being talked about, of the very existence of the issue in the popular consciousness. The consideration of it, pulling it outside the social taboo (things that are not even mentioned) if it was there. Even if initially such a concept may be met with skepticism, hostility, or merely indifference, the space for debate may become extended, or expanded—be that naturally or artificially. Overton's window thus describes the impact on public perception. It is only a trifle that Overton's window also includes the point at which ideas are "not on the radar" of politics and the law, but can also appear on it, and in an extreme way, through overregulation. When it comes to the issue of propaganda and information operations, the very model of introducing concepts and topics is very relevant as it's also about the increase or decrease of information dynamics. For example, it is obvious and we accept it for granted that 2 + 2 = 4, and this cannot be changed informationally (without modification of educational programs in extreme ways). The window in this case is permanently and firmly "closed." Educational policy and programs stipulate exactly that 2 + 2 = 4. There is no point in even trying to change this fact, because an important part of propaganda or disinformation efforts is the need to limit to what is acceptable in a given society. But things may be different with other aspects, such as for example a concept like "eating certain types of food is associated with environmental impacts" may be more attractive in this context. Here, one might try to manipulate related topics within Overton's window, which may or may not lead to political or legal changes, or at least create information confusion.

As Figure 2.3 illustrates, initially a concept may be unimaginable, but by efficiently modulating the informational influence, it is possible to bring about a situation where it will not only become tolerable but will eventually become acceptable, and people will even demand for it, and therefore it will become sanctioned at the political-legal level. After all, it is not surprising that politicians care about votes, so they will adhere to what is popular in society, in social groups.[84] Some may care about enlarging the "windows" to gain new topics that

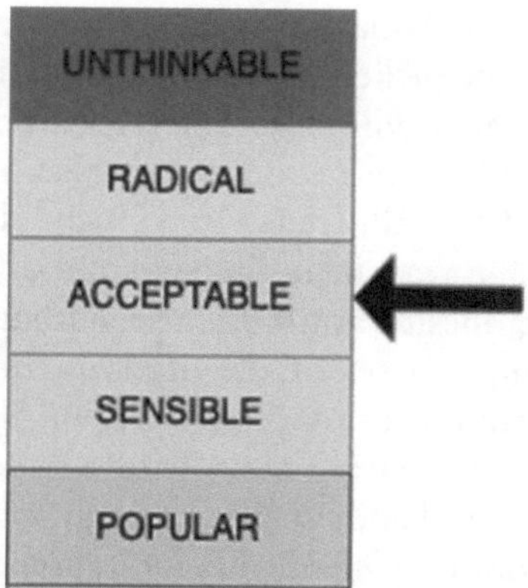

Figure 2.3 Overton's window concept.

Source: Adapted from J. Trevino, *Why the right-wing gets It – and why dems don't*, May 10, 2006, https://www.dailykos.com/stories/2006/05/09/208784/-Why-the-Right-Wing-Gets-It-and-Why-Dems-Don-t-UPDATED.

occupy social groups. Hence, creating seemingly relevant issues or popularizing certain concepts can be of great importance. Concepts are seemingly relevant, but sufficiently compelling, so that the topic is taken up at the socio-political level, at some stage in the media. An example is the legal prohibition of the death penalty, or rather the renunciation of[85] the use of this measure as a punishment for committed crimes. Because for the introduction of the measure it was necessary to build an understanding of the issue in society, although social groups may still find justification for such a method of punishment—if only a day after publicizing some horrific crime.

Manipulation of such an Overton's window can be done by propaganda, or information methods. This should be understandable; after all, what other methods could be used to change public perception or attitudes? In view of this, information or propaganda operations are able to "disrupt" and "disturb" the information environment, and "shift" various concepts on the Overton's window. How to do this? This is done by skillfully and meticulously adjusting techniques and tactics accordingly. By using appropriate methods and tools. We are slowly approaching this topic. Let's start with a certain technique that is quite modern.

2.14 MICRO-TARGETING

It will get more technical now. We were talking about reaching out to people, audiences, and social groups. But how to do it? It can be done in many ways. Spots on TV, billboards in the city, commercial ads, flyers—this will still be discussed. However, modern information technologies allow reaching audiences in a different, more precise way.

Micro-targeting[86] is the targeting of a message to certain small groups. Defining these groups can be complex and may include age, gender, location, residence, languages known (including foreign languages), that is, demographics. But also interests, whether someone is passionate about a particular topic or subject like business, technology news, or art. By overlaying a different configuration of such "personality profiles," one can build micro-groups. Men aged 35–45, living in Geneva (Switzerland), London (UK), or Poznan (Poland), and interested in the gardening industry, business news, and agriculture, while uninterested in art and eating cakes, may be few. If it's 1,000 or 2,000 people, we have defined a group to target. Targeting is "directing" the message based on some criteria (like those just mentioned). Thanks to new technologies, such as targeting ads on social media or on websites while browsing, it was possible to define such groups in multiple ways and reach them through different channels. Sometimes, targeting could include smaller groups, for example, of 100 or 20 people; it could even be individuals. This, however, was considered a serious privacy problem, so there are now typically limitations to the size of the targeted group, so that it is not too easy to target content to the really small groups. Such precautions may work most of the time. Privacy-improving advertising systems are being developed, and these are supposed to have built-in protection against overly precise micro-targeting. Technical methods in this industry are in motion, subject to development and evolution. This is a fast-evolving field. Those able to adapt and see opportunities fast will reap benefits.

2.14.1 The question of content

What can be directed? Text, images, video (multimedia)—all defined by those managing such an information-ad campaign. In the case of political messages, it may be an attempt to persuade viewers to support a particular point of view or a political party, and in the case of mass media, to appeal to held beliefs or views.[87] With micro-targeting, the same people could potentially receive similar or identical content through different channels, that is, be "immersed" in some specific message. And this already opens the room for building some stories and symbolic elements. Micro-targeting can be used intermittently (one or multiple times) or even continuously.

2.15 PSYCHOLOGY OF THE CROWD

Researchers in the social sciences have noted that people in groups, "in a crowd," such as at demonstrations, can behave in specific ways—different from being isolated individuals. When a person is a member of a group, certain standard bases of his or her judgment of the situation, his or her reasoning, are suspended.[88] In the words of Gustave Le Bon,

> [U]nder certain specific circumstances, and only under such circumstances, an aggregation of people presents new characteristics that are very different from those of the individuals who comprise it ... In certain situations, a half-dozen people may form a psychological crowd, which may not be the case with hundreds of randomly gathered men. On the other hand, an entire nation, although it may not be apparent in an agglomeration, may become a crowd under the action of certain influences.[89]

It is very interesting that the author of the basic work on crowd psychology made these observations at the end of the 19th century. Back then developed methods of social sciences, psychological research, were lacking, or at least were incomparable with later capabilities, not to mention those of today. Back then in the 19th century, it was difficult to verify hypotheses, certainly impossible to do on a large scale.

Why is this relevant to us? It is even critical! In social networks, on the Internet, "bubbles" of interests or interest groups may be formed. Perhaps, they can also sometimes be artificially "created" precisely through micro-targeting methods or through some other kind of mechanism for creating groups and segments of people aware that they are part of a group. What are these manifestations of special behavior? For example: "[T]he crowd is anonymous and consequently irresponsible, the *sense of responsibility that always controls individuals disappears completely*."[90] Sounds familiar? The apparent anonymity on the Internet is something often covered over the previous decades, and it, too, may contribute to a similar conviction of being anonymous. In this sense, a person could then act like an automaton, that is, react mechanically,[91] or irresponsibly. While upon first sight the following might not be so relevant to us, another observation is illuminating:

> [B]y the mere fact that [man] belongs to an organized crowd, ... he descends a few rungs in the ladder of civilization ... he *allows himself to be impressed by words and images* - which would be completely *ineffective against any of the isolated individuals* who make up the crowd - and to be *induced to do acts* contrary to his most obvious interests and his most familiar habits. An individual in a crowd is a grain of sand.[92]

In view of this, do people who are members of a similar kind of "Internet crowd" automatically regress in their development? This is not important to us and we do not make judgments (everyone can have their own view on this). What is important is precisely that they act in a particular way and that they may suddenly be more susceptible to "words and images." This is also the goal of propaganda or information operations.

Purchasing products out of stores in panic in the early days of the COVID-19 pandemic was a mass effect. It likely resulted from the exchange of messages on the Internet through various channels,[93] coverage in the media was instrumental in inducing such behaviors.

Similarly, it could be like that with the spread of conspiracy theories, as long as there are people who may amplify such messages (when these people are not there, such theories fade away).[94] As it happens, with the help of technology[95] and appropriate methods, today it is very easy to deliver textual, graphic, visual, and even audio content. And carry out influences of this kind on groups of the type of "crowds." Facebook, Twitter/X, Instagram, TikTok, and various kinds of forums can also be places where today "crowds gather."[96] Together with them, a corresponding dynamic of groups of people somehow connected, and acting in a unified or similar way or for a similar purpose is created. Such an atmosphere, in turn, drives the dynamics of spreading information among people, sometimes a lot of people, and sometimes at a very fast pace, and subject to sudden changes. The crowd, the groups, the possibility of communication between the people, and the reach of external influence with artificial content or micro-targeting—this is something completely new in terms of our civilization.

2.15.1 Effects of psychological bias

In psychology, we are familiar with the concepts of bias, which can lead to erroneous analytical conclusions. Particularly in this context, it is worth noting several human beliefs and convictions that directly affect perception, and sometimes several such burdens are associated with a specific bias in the perception of the world.[97] According to Oeberst and Imhoff, these include convictions that[98]:

1) human beliefs and experiences are an adequate and reasonable point of reference (or are they?);
2) man correctly assesses the world (or maybe not?);
3) "I'm good" (is that relative?);
4) The group I am in is a suitable and appropriate point of reference (and if not?);
5) other members of the group to which I belong are good (are they really?);
6) it is human qualities, not the context of action, that affect the final results of a person's actions.[99]

In a nutshell, it's about believing in one's own infallibility, and that one's environment has a kind of monopoly on being right. Since human actions are often based on beliefs and people may be being convinced of some truths, taking these six points into account, we come to a fractious conclusion. We are not objective, or even *right* by definition. But we tend to believe the opposite. It would be even worse for the culture of discussion if we decided that *we and only we* are right. People who are convinced that they are right are susceptible to manipulation, especially if someone, referring to this nature of theirs, would simply spout something that they think anyway, or concepts in line with such a person's beliefs. The question even arises whether it is still possible to speak of a social mechanism at all in such a situation, or whether it is already a purely technical one. Sometimes also with major implications for state security.

In a crowd, these beliefs may be exacerbated and reinforced. Moreover, a person in a crowd may act impulsively as a result of these effects. He or she may be more prone to propaganda and, as a result of it, even take some action that, using common sense and without external influence, he or she would not have taken but which he or she will regret.

2.15.2 When do we accept a point of view as true?

Another very specific reason why propaganda or disinformation can be effective in such environments is that when coming into contact with assessments that we already know—it is easier for us to accept them as true. In view of this, if people are bombarded with opinions on a certain subject, and this is done repeatedly, successively—there may be a situation where the propagated view may become more easily adopted. This is the so-called psychological *truth effect*.[100] This works for conspiracy theories as well as for some advertising. Interestingly, susceptibility to this effect occurs even when one has some knowledge of the subject.[101] This is why the "barrage" of falsehoods (misleading information, erroneous information, etc.) can have an effect—the information somehow enters the mind and perhaps influences decisions. This also means that once inaccurate or false content is disseminated, it will be very difficult to effectively correct it in the future.

Care must be taken when directing official information. Once announced, a version of events can take root, find a following, and if clarifying changes need to be made at some point, or in other cases official information needs to be changed in accordance with the state of the art, or new knowledge, it can lead to some audiences not believing the updated versions. This, in turn, is the so-called psychological *backfire effect*,[102] when an attempt to "correct" an earlier version may cause damage.[103] In view of this, sometimes it is better to be careful what one says, because changing the version can be ineffective and even cause harm.

2.15.3 Case study: missile hitting a hospital

Let's examine a specific event from 2023, when there was no one version. It is about the reports, published in the heat of the moment, regarding the explosion that occurred on October 17, 2023, at the Al-Ahli Arab Hospital in the Gaza Strip. Initially, the world's media duplicated Hamas' group news coverage that it was the result of an Israeli rocket launch. Such a message, in turn, caused widespread outrage. Only after some time and a proper reconstruction of the events was it realized that there was no certainty. Later, further analysis published by the security services of many States and experts indicated that the rocket was rather fired from the Palestinian area. There was an attempt to straighten out the messages spread earlier. But by then it was too late, as the earlier information had been effectively fixed in the minds of many recipients (and in the case of some, validated their worldviews or expectations/fears). This is how chasing sensationalism and propagating unverified information ends, unfortunately. In the time frame when the version about the Israeli missile was just beginning to spread, there was no evidence to support it, and yet many world media reported it.[104] Also later, false information about the event spread through many channels. People simply decided what they thought about it, and didn't need evidence to do so. The reports sparked mass protests in Arab countries, as well as in European countries, and impacted diplomacy and interstate contacts.

An important conclusion about the backfire effect: correcting some false or misleading information may make little sense, in fact. It may not pay off, because not only will it not help, but it may even cause harm. In general, once an information message finds fertile ground in social groups, it can be difficult to correct the situation later, to "straighten it out." Successfully convinced people do not like to change their minds,[105] especially when they recognize that they have come to some conclusions or views on their own (which may be the purpose of effective propaganda) and these are their "independent" conclusions.

2.16 TROLLS, TROLLING—MORE ON THE PHENOMENON

Who or what is a troll? It can be a person trying to disrupt a normal flow of discussion or debate, which may be due to his or her anti-social attitude,[106] but it can also be an expression of peculiar preferences or a sense of humor. Anyone can be a troll, and some may even enjoy it.

Trolls can also do paid work.[107] These are individuals hired to disrupt or paralyze the normal flow of information or debate, such as by asking unusual or even strange questions or by provocation.

A troll need not be a *strictly* evil person. He or she may be an intelligent person, and his or her high cognitive abilities may even be associated with tolerance for differing political views,[108] although this may not be apparent or expressed at the moment in the area of his or her goals or activities. Such a person, however, may be apt to "change his or her point of view" and manifest views quite different from the previous ones, in other words, be a tolerant or extreme cynic. Can people be blamed for their hobbies? The problem arises when a given troll gains a lot of publicity or the means to spread his or her "opinions." Then, he or she can introduce a chaotic element, destabilizing the environments in question and perhaps even the State itself, if such a person is placed sufficiently high. Imagine that a troll becomes the leader of a State, such as prime minister—an absurd vision, and even a very risky one. Effective trolling requires the ability to persuade others, eristic skills—so those necessary also in political discourse. One can *troll* on a variety of topics: from food issues to standards in a given society.

However, let's not confuse typical satire or pastiche with trolling. There's no sense to put a stamp of "disinformation" or "fake news" on humor. The troll, however, may do this with a stone-cold face expression, without necessarily giving clear indications of whether something is or isn't a joke, which can sometimes also pose a challenge to the so-called professional fact-checkers who explain jokes. Joke on them, one is only pretending?

Only recently has the term "troll" become relatively an infamous thing, thanks to the so-called Russian troll factory,[109] which routinely produces disinformation content directed at the West. That doesn't mean, however, that every troll is outright a "Russian agent." Some trolls make fun of public figures but at the same time subject the information space to useful stress tests. This can create confusion, but also, in the absence of a real crisis, it may show people to be wary of incoming information. Thus, it's a form of education. Therefore, trolling can be a manifestation of an unhealthy mental condition, but it can also be quite a comforting phenomenon.

2.16.1 Hypothetical situation when trolls take over the country

Of course, such an attitude cannot be universal, because the framework of a civilized society could not function when everyone is a troll. As usual, moderation is a virtue. It is important because an excess can be a threat, including to state security. Trolls placed in strategic places (media, public offices, political positions, etc.) could pose a serious threat to the security of the State, and certainly to its informational integrity.

What is the easiest way to counteract that? "*Don't feed the trolls*,"[110] that is, don't overly (or not at all) engage in discussion, interaction, don't give them satisfaction, don't publicize them, don't share their content. However, it may become impossible not to do this—not to interact—if such individuals were acceptable, legitimate public figures, in high places. Therefore, such a situation would be very dangerous. A limited number of trolls in those high offices would probably be tolerable but exceeding a certain limit—it could be a bit scary. A few psychopaths or sociopaths can be dealt with, but exceeding a critical mass could even lead to the collapse of the State.

2.16.2 Don't feed the trolls

Anyone can be a troll, anyone can take such actions[111]; no psychosocial predisposition or deep factual knowledge is necessary (although it may help). Fortunately, most trolls are rather lousy—that is—easy to detect and ignore. Then, all one have to do is apply the golden rule: don't feed the troll. And the problem is solved. Worse when the troll is actively malicious (being rewarded for it or not, because some people may enjoy such "activity")[112,113] and wastes someone's time and cognitive and mental cycles, which perhaps is supposed to be his or her goal. Provocateurs who "wind up" arguments can introduce an element of confusion by either imposing or silencing certain things in public debate.

2.17 SOCIAL GROUPS

People may be members of social groups. Whether consciously or not, as it is not necessarily their choice—it may be a classification. Often, it is simply a classification based on objective criteria, such as demographics. For example, one can be a member of a Nation, a citizen of a State (a group distinguished by citizenship), one can be of a certain age or gender. And this determines to which social group someone is "assigned." Groups may also form due to various kinds of preferences or views. For example, someone may support a particular political option, may be interested in art, or may be a vegetarian (groups distinguished by views and preferences). Group formations are a fascinating research problem. Realistically, groups are of great practical importance, for example, for politicians, their campaign experts, advertisers, and PR people. That's because it makes sense to target an information message to a specific audience, so that the message is effective—those audiences that may be expected to pick up specific lines of communication, but not others. Just as there is no point in "talking to a brick wall," it is better to target the message to some existing people in such a way that members of such identified groups will accept the message. The formation of groups is a fascinating problem,[114] and what groups someone becomes a member of may depend on his or her mental or physical condition, also on his or her appearance. Those are the basics of social psychology. We need not delve deeper into that.

Belonging to a group can also mean being able to limit oneself to communication within groups, and potentially isolating oneself from outside information, creating "information bubbles,"[115] closed circles of information circulation, and echo chambers. This is not necessarily a consequence of technology and social networking, as people may prefer interacting with like-minded people in general, including in offline lives.

2.17.1 Radical effects—thresholds for action

Now, let's turn to considerations at a higher risk level. Groups may become targets of information operations. At the same time, let's recall that the purpose of propaganda or information influence is to produce some effect, to induce targets to take some action, or particular behavior. Such behavior can also be influenced by the environment, for example, people may be more likely to take some action when they see others engaging in the same or similar things.[116]

2.17.2 Crossing the thresholds of radical action

When this threshold is reached, certain boundaries may be crossed, like—street violence may erupt—such as throwing a stone at a store window. It can even lead to the formation of radical groups whose goal may be social or political upheaval, including by terrorist means. This is why radical individuals, including artificially radicalized ones (provocateurs), are important within these groups. If a person is faced with the choice of whether or not to join an armed revolution, he or she will take into account the actions of those around him or her. By leading through information to disorder and creating conflict situations, one can be "assisted" in "making" such "decisions." The point is that the perceived individual cost (risk) of revolutionary actions may decrease as more and more people decide to take part in these actions.[117] If "everyone" starts throwing stones, bottles, Molotov cocktails—the perception of risk may become altered as part of radicalization or escalation. This may encourage more and more people to engage in such behavior. And then such a group can become a cell of action that shatters the social order.

Think about it: if 95% of the people within your social group join revolutionary actions, what would you do? What percentage of people should take up these actions to get you to do so as well?

How many radicalized people around you is enough for you to throw a stone at a store window? If we have a group of 100 people, is 20 enough? Or maybe 80? And where is the beginning of action here? Because if the thresholds are low, it may suffice to notice only the radical behavior of five people. So after all, it would only take five deliberate provocateurs, artificially making a fuss,[118] and then everything happens, as if it were automatic or natural. The threshold theory concept considers just such elements: what are *the conditions for individuals to be radicalized*, to take extremist, fundamentalist, anti-social, anti-state actions, etc. This model can be used to explain the dynamics of social action from the French Revolution through the October Revolution to the events of our time.

These considerations correspond with the previously analyzed issues of crowd psychology. For a propagandist, this is important knowledge, because if the goal is to influence, to create effects, it is useful to have some general estimate of how susceptible the social groups are. One can analyze limited riots. Even if it starts with kicking a trashcan, it may go toward the disintegration and the breakdown of the social order, if only on a limited scale. And this beautiful theory of applied sociology (you don't have to be a sociologist to appreciate it) becomes very relevant with the mechanics of information activities.

2.18 HOW MANY PEOPLE DOES IT TAKE TO BRING ABOUT A COUP AND REVOLUTION IN A STATE? SUBVERSION OF THE STATE BY INFORMATION METHODS

Let's start with another question: what percentage of the population is enough to bring about a coup?

The causes of subversive and revolutionary activity are quite complex, depending on the quality of life when the conditions of existence become, in the conception of groups of people, difficult or unbearable (which does not have to be confirmed objectively).[119] Note that as late as 1917, Lenin doubted whether "we old people will live to see the decisive battles of the coming revolution." And yet how fortunate he was, as he succeeded. The conditions for this arose soon after he and his accompanying group were transported by the Prussian army in a sealed train car. Conditions for spreading revolutionary sentiment in Czarist Russia and bringing about the collapse of the previous order. This, therefore, did not happen from the grassroots, on its own.

Today, of course, there are many methods other than the "*charismatic leader of a political movement*," as more and more researchers wonder whether, by chance, the very possibility of social media and its popularity does not pose a risk to the cohesion of society.[120] Simplifying and reducing the problem to the minimum number of people necessary, it is considered that in order to bring about a coup d'etat with a reasonably good chance of success, it is enough to involve about 3–5% of the population,[121] although some argue that more may be needed—25%.[122] But let's say that those 3–5% may at times be sufficient. At a scale of the population, it is relatively a modest figure if it was hypothetically sufficient to sustain the momentum and possibly suppress attempts at resistance. Also due to the fact that such numbers may result in a reasonably good chance that members of the forces of order may recognize that people in their circle are already involved in revolutionary activities. This, then, could blunt the desire to suppress unrest. Among those in power (the elite circles, the authorities), it may cause all sorts of doubts, perhaps leading to a change of sides.

This is how we moved from merely considering the concept of a social group or bubble to purely revolutionary actions on as scale of an entire State or Nation—induced initially by information. At the same time, let's admit that it is essentially unknown what these thresholds of radicalization look like for a given social group, a given Nation, and a situation. But similar mechanics can be applied to the propagation of various ideas: from the need to fight climate change, through the issue of the right to abortion, the support for some concepts or political options, to other political processes and issues.

The dynamics of rumor propagation or disinformation can also be explained in a similar way. If it is done by a negligible part of a social group or society—there are obvious limitations. At some point, a critical mass, a *certain threshold*, may be crossed. From that moment such a "rumor" can be propagated more strongly, gaining credibility. Social media make it possible to create perceptions: many different kinds of bots, trolls, and influencers can propagate some concepts. Making them credible, if only by the number of participating people. This is why the phenomenon of bots and influencer abuse can be dangerous.

2.19 FIGHT AGAINST DISINFORMATION AND PROPAGANDA

What to do about information operations? The methods and the possibilities vary and will be discussed later. Here, I will mention two exemplary, general concepts.

2.19.1 Reactive action

If one identifies a campaign of disinformation, one can try to *debunk* abuses, reality bending, or "twisted" stories by exposing them,[123] disseminating and publicizing correct versions, perhaps widely. This is a reactive action. For example, if we had a campaign of disinformation (rumors, conspiracy theories) about a human infectious disease (e.g., COVID-19) spreading via telecommunications networks (e.g., 5G cellular networks), as at times happened during the pandemic of 2020–2022, "correcting" this obvious and absurd falsehood would include a solid explanation of why this is impossible and why there cannot be any connection between the two.

2.19.2 Proactive action

An example of proactive, preemptive action is to *pre-bunk*,[124–125] that is, preparing social groups and the public for possibly incoming information campaigns and materials, and exposing these. This method can be effective in building psychological resistance to disinformation, according to many studies.[126] Pre-bunking may benefit from provision of novel information and factual explanations to the user; when successful, it may contribute to decrease of fraud.[127] In other words perhaps—treat the audience seriously and offer useful advice, not simply stamp content.

Pre-emptive action can be compared to informational inoculation, building immunity. An example would be anticipating that there will be disinformation campaigns targeting war refugees in connection with the war in Ukraine. Debunking or pre-bunking may also be considered social engineering.

2.19.3 Social engineering

Debunking and pre-bunking are examples of information interventions. They can be controversial, because depending on who is making them, there may (but not necessarily) arise a problem of social engineering by States or companies. Propaganda itself also meets the conditions of social engineering. So, when it is carried out by external actors, such as hostile States, it should come as no surprise that the targets of aggression (specific targets in a State or an entire State) want to defend themselves. But, there still may be societal costs. The risks of these methods will be discussed further on.

Now it's time for more technical stuff.

NOTES

1 L.W. Doob, *Goebbels' principles of propaganda*, Public Opinion Quarterly 1950, vol. 14, no. 3, pp. 419–442.
2 J. Ellul, *Propaganda: The Formation of Men's Attitudes*, Vintage Books, New York 1973, p. 6.
3 O. Barbu, *Advertising, microtargeting and social media*, Procedia – Social and Behavioral Sciences 2014, vol. 163, pp. 44–49.
4 J. Ellul, *Propaganda ....*
5 J. Ellul, *Propaganda ...*, p. 61.
6 E.H. Henderson, *Toward a definition of propaganda*, The Journal of Social Psychology 1943, vol. 18, no. 1, p. 9.
7 Department of Defense, *Dictionary of Military and Associated Terms*, Skyhorse Publishing, Washington 2007, p. 295.
8 Department of Defense, *Dictionary of Military and Associated Terms*, Skyhorse Publishing, Washington 2007, pp. 76, 236, 589.
9 W.C. Garrison, *Information Operations and Counter-Propaganda: Making a Weapon of Public Affairs*, US Army War College, Carlisle Barracks 1999, https://apps.dtic.mil/sti/pdfs/ADA363892.pdf.
10 B. Davis, *Maps on postage stamps as propaganda*, "The Cartographic Journal" 1985 vol. 22, no. 2, pp. 125–130.
11 B. Davis, *Maps on postage stamps as propaganda*, "The Cartographic Journal" 1985 vol. 22, no. 2, pp. 125–130.
12 B. Davis, *Maps on postage stamps as propaganda*, "The Cartographic Journal" 1985 vol. 22, no. 2, pp. 125–130.
13 B. Davis, *Maps on postage stamps as propaganda*, "The Cartographic Journal" 1985 vol. 22, no. 2, pp. 125–130.
14 NATO, *Allied Joint Doctrine for Psychological Operations*, AJP-3.10.1(A), October 22, 2007, https://info.publicintelligence.net/NATO-PSYOPS.pdf.
15 N. O'Shaughnessy, *Weapons of mass seduction: Propaganda, media and the Iraq war*, Journal of Political Marketing 2004, vol. 3, no. 4, pp. 79–104.
16 S.C. Woolley, P.N. Howard, *Automation, algorithms, and politics: Political communication, computational propaganda, and autonomous agents. Introduction*, International Journal of Communication 2016, vol. 10, p. 9.
17 S.C. Woolley, P.N. Howard, *Computational Propaganda Worldwide: Executive Summary*, Oxford 2017, p. 6.
18 S.C. Woolley, P.N. Howard, *Computational Propaganda Worldwide: Executive Summary*, Oxford 2017, p. 6.
19 S.C. Woolley, P.N. Howard, *Automation...*, p. 5.
20 A.M. Guess, B.A. Lyons, *Misinformation, disinformation, and online propaganda*, in *Social Media and Democracy: The State of the Field, Prospects for Reform*, ed. J.A. Tucker, N. Persily, New York 2020.
21 A.M. Guess, B.A. Lyons, *Misinformation, disinformation, and online propaganda*, in *Social Media and Democracy: The State of the Field, Prospects for Reform*, ed. J.A. Tucker, N. Persily, New York 2020.

22 U.K. Ecker, S. Lewandowsky, J. Cook, P. Schmid, L.K. Fazio, N. Brashier, P. Kendeou, E.K. Vraga, M.A. Amazeen, *The psychological drivers of misinformation belief and its resistance to correction*, Nature Reviews Psychology 2022, vol. 1, no. 1, pp. 13–29.
23 U.K. Ecker, S. Lewandowsky, J. Cook, P. Schmid, L.K. Fazio, N. Brashier, P. Kendeou, E.K. Vraga, M.A. Amazeen, *The psychological drivers of misinformation belief and its resistance to correction*, Nature Reviews Psychology 2022, vol. 1, no. 1, pp. 13–29.
24 H.M. Johnson, C.M. Seifert, *Sources of the continued influence effect: When misinformation in memory affects later inferences*, Journal of Experimental Psychology: Learning, Memory, and Cognition 1994, vol. 20, no. 6, p. 1420.
25 A. Acerbi, S. Altay, H. Mercier, *Research note: Fighting misinformation or fighting for information?*, January 12, 2022, https://misinforeview.hks.harvard.edu/article/research-note-fighting-misinformation-or-fighting-for-information/.
26 S. Altay, A. Acerbi, *People believe misinformation is a threat because they assume others are gullible*, New Media & Society, February 17, 2023, https://doi.org/10.1177/14614448231153379.
27 O. Ştefăniţă, N. Corbu, R. Buturoiu, *Fake news and the third-person effect: They are more influenced than me and you*, Journal of Media Research 2018, vol. 11, no. 3.
28 W.P. Davison, *The third-person effect in communication*, Public Opinion Quarterly 1983, vol. 47, no. 1, pp. 1–15.
29 S. Altay, A. Acerbi, *People believe....*
30 W.C. Garrison, *Information...*, pp. 6–7.
31 J.A. Tucker, A. Guess, P. Barberá, C. Vaccari, A. Siegel, S. Sanovich, D. Stukal, B. Nyhan, *Social media, political polarization, and political disinformation: A review of the scientific literature*, Political Polarization, and Political Disinformation: A Review of the Scientific Literature, March 19, 2018, http://dx.doi.org/10.2139/ssrn.3144139.
32 C.S. Leberknight, M. Chiang, H.V. Poor, F. Wong, *A taxonomy of Internet censorship and anti-censorship*, December 31, 2010, pp. 52–64, https://www.princeton.edu/~chiangm/anticensorship.pdf.
33 R.S. Raman, A. Stoll, J. Dalek, R. Ramesh, W. Scott, R. Ensafi, *Measuring the deployment of network censorship filters at global scale*, February 2020, https://www.ndss-symposium.org/wp-content/uploads/2020/02/23099-paper.pdf.
34 P. Hall, *The Oxford Handbook of Music Censorship*, Oxford University Press, Oxford 2017.
35 H. Rojas, D.V. Shah, R.J. Faber, *For the good of others: Censorship and the third-person effect*, International Journal of Public Opinion Research 1996, vol. 8, no. 2, pp. 163–186.
36 R.M. Perloff, *The third-person effect*, in *Media effects: Advances in theory and research*, ed. by J. Bryant, D. Zillmann, Mahwah 2002, pp. 499–506.
37 J. Yang, Y. Tian, *'Others are more vulnerable to fake news than I am': Third-person effect of COVID-19 fake news on social media users*, Computers in Human Behavior 2021, vol. 125.
38 N. Corbu, D.A. Oprea, E. Negrea-Busuioc, L. Radu, *'They can't fool me, but they can fool the others!': Third person effect and fake news detection*, European Journal of Communication 2020, vol. 35, no. 2, pp. 165–180.
39 M. Schmierbach, M.P. Boyle, Q. Xu, D.M. McLeod, *Exploring third-person differences between gamers and nongamers*, Journal of Communication 2011, vol. 61, no. 2, pp. 307–327.
40 L.J. Clarke, *How censorship becomes propaganda*, Index on Censorship 1987, vol. 16, no. 5, pp. 5–6.
41 L.J. Clarke, *How censorship becomes propaganda*, Index on Censorship 1987, vol. 16, no. 5, pp. 5–6.
42 Y. Golovchenko, *Fighting propaganda with censorship: A study of the Ukrainian ban on Russian social media*, The Journal of Politics 2022, vol. 84, no. 2, pp. 639–654.
43 K. Langvardt, *Regulating online content moderation*, Georgetown Law Journal 2017, vol. 106, p. 1353.
44 H. Tworek, *History explains why global content moderation cannot work*, December 10, 2021, https://www.brookings.edu/techstream/history-explains-why-global-content-moderation-cannot-work/.
45 H. Tworek, *History explains why global content moderation cannot work*, December 10, 2021, https://www.brookings.edu/techstream/history-explains-why-global-content-moderation-cannot-work/.

46 C.A. Pratt, *First Amendment protection for public relations expression: The applicability and limitations of the commercial and corporate speech models*, Journal of Public Relations Research 1990, vol. 2, pp. 205–217.
47 L. Edwards, *Organized lying and professional legitimacy: Public relations accountability in the disinformation debate*, European Journal of Communication 2021, vol. 36, no. 2, pp. 168–182.
48 L. Edwards, *Organized lying and professional legitimacy: Public relations accountability in the disinformation debate*, European Journal of Communication 2021, vol. 36, no. 2, pp. 168–182.
49 P. Harris, C.S. Fleisher, *Handbook of Public Affairs*, New York 2005.
50 C.S. Fleisher, *The development of competencies in international public affairs*, Journal of Public Affairs 2003, vol. 3, no. 1, pp. 76–82.
51 A. Godber, G. Origgi, *Telling propaganda from legitimate political persuasion*, Episteme 2023, vol. 20, no. 3.
52 Department of the Army, Department of the Navy, *Joint Operations*, August 11, 2011, p. 69, https://www.moore.army.mil/mssp/security%20topics/Potential%20Adversaries/content/pdf/JP%203-0.pdf.
53 Department of the Army, Department of the Navy, Department of the Air Force, *Public Affairs*, November 17, 2015, p. 69, https://www.jcs.mil/Portals/36/Documents/Doctrine/pubs/jp3_61.pdf.
54 Department of the Army, Department of the Navy, Department of the Air Force, *Public Affairs*, November 17, 2015, p. 69, https://www.jcs.mil/Portals/36/Documents/Doctrine/pubs/jp3_61.pdf.
55 Department of the Army, *ADP 3-13: Information*, November 2023, pp. 1–11, https://armypubs.army.mil/epubs/DR_pubs/DR_a/ARN39736-ADP_3-13-000-WEB-1.pdf.
56 M.N. Miller, *Digital threats to democracy: A double-edged sentence*, May 2020, https://securityandtechnology.org/wp-content/uploads/2020/07/cnas_report-hti-double-edged_sentencev.pdf.
57 *Tackling disinformation, foreign information manipulation & interference*, October 27, 2021, https://www.eeas.europa.eu/eeas/tackling-disinformation-foreign-information-manipulation-interference_en.
58 *1st EEAS Report on foreign information manipulation and interference threats*, February 2023, https://www.eeas.europa.eu/sites/default/files/documents/2023/EEAS-DataTeam-ThreatReport-2023.pdf.
59 Department of the Army, *Psychological Operations*, January 7, 2010, p. 9, https://irp.fas.org/doddir/dod/jp3-13-2.pdf.
60 Department of the Army, *Psychological Operations*, January 7, 2010, p. 9, https://irp.fas.org/doddir/dod/jp3-13-2.pdf, p. 24.
61 NATO, *NATO Military Policy on Psychological Operations*, MC 0402/2, June 22, 2012, p. 4, https://info.publicintelligence.net/NATO-PSYOPS-Policy.pdf.
62 Department of the Army, *Psychological Operations Tactics, Techniques, and Procedures*, FM 3-05.301 (FM 33-1-1) MCRP 3-40.6A, December 2003, https://irp.fas.org/doddir/army/fm3-05-301.pdf.
63 Department of the Army, *Psychological Operations Tactics, Techniques, and Procedures*, FM 3-05.301 (FM 33-1-1) MCRP 3-40.6A, December 2003, https://irp.fas.org/doddir/army/fm3-05-301.pdf.
64 Department of the Army, *Psychological Operations Tactics, Techniques, and Procedures*, FM 3-05.301 (FM 33-1-1) MCRP 3-40.6A, December 2003, https://irp.fas.org/doddir/army/fm3-05-301.pdf.
65 NATO, *Allied Joint Doctrine for Psychological Operations*, AJP-3.10.1(A), October 2007, p. 21, https://info.publicintelligence.net/NATO-PSYOPS.pdf.
66 Department of the Army, Department of the Navy, Department of the Air Force, United States Coast Guard, *Information Operations*, November 27, 2012, p. 19, https://irp.fas.org/doddir/dod/jp3_13.pdf.
67 T. Caulfield, J.M. Spring, M.A. Sasse, *Why Jenny can't figure out which of these messages is a covert information operation*, in *Proceedings of the New Security Paradigms Workshop*, September 2019, pp. 118–128.
68 J. Weedon, W. Nuland, A. Stamos, *Information operations and Facebook*, April 27, 2017, https://fbnewsroomus.files.wordpress.com/2017/04/facebook-and-information-operations-v1.pdf.

69 H.J. Ingram, *The strategic logic of Islamic State information operations*, Australian Journal of International Affairs 2015, vol. 69, no. 6, pp. 729–752.

70 Department of the Army, Department of the Navy, Department of the Air Force, United States Coast Guard, *Information Operations...*, p. 19.

71 R. Cordray III, M.J. Romanych, *Mapping the information environment*, IO Sphere, Summer 2005, pp. 7–10, https://www.hqmc.marines.mil/Portals/147/Docs/MCIOC/IORecruiting/MappingtheInformationEnvironmentIOSphereSummer2005.pdf.

72 D.M. Murphy, J.F. White, *Propaganda: Can a word decide a war?*, The US Army War College Quarterly: Parameters 2007, vol. 37, no. 3, p. 23.

73 Department of the Army, *ADP 3-13: Information advantage*, after S.P. White, *The organizational determinants of military doctrine: A history of Army information operations*, Texas National Security Review, Winter 2022–2023, p. 23, https://tnsr.org/2023/01/the-organizational-determinants-of-military-doctrine-a-history-of-army-information-operations/.

74 C.A. Theohary, *Defense primer: Information operations*, CRS Report, December 2020, https://crsreports.congress.gov/product/details?prodcode=IF10771.

75 M.E. McCombs, D.L. Shaw, *The agenda-setting function of mass media*, Public Opinion Quarterly 1972, vol. 36, no. 2, pp. 176–187.

76 M.E. McCombs, D.L. Shaw, *The agenda-setting function of mass media*, Public Opinion Quarterly 1972, vol. 36, no. 2, pp. 176–187.

77 P. Huang, *Chinese cyber-operatives boosted Taiwan's insurgent candidate*, Foreign Policy 2019, vol. 26.

78 J. Rosen, *Coming next: the weather as a political issue*, Et Cetera1989, vol. 46, no. 1, p. 30.

79 J. Rosen, *Coming next: the weather as a political issue*, Et Cetera1989, vol. 46, no. 1, p. 30.

80 N.J. Russel, *An introduction to the Overton window of political possibilities*, January 4, 2006, https://www.mackinac.org/7504.

81 D.J. Morgan, *The Overton window and a less dogmatic approach to antibiotics*, Clinical Infectious Diseases 2020, vol. 70, no. 11, pp. 2439–2441.

82 G. Bobric, *The Overton window: A tool for information warfare*, Academic Paper, International Conference on Cyber Warfare and Security, February 2021, https://www.proquest.com/openview/d14239dd5c1f67e37109feb2573f50e1/1.pdf?pq-origsite=gscholar&cbl=396500.

83 L. Calv, *Moving the Overton window*, The Lancet Planetary Health 2021, vol. 5, https://www.thelancet.com/pdfs/journals/lanplh/PIIS2542-5196(21)00293-X.pdf.

84 H. Berghel, *The QAnon phenomenon: The storm has always been among us*, Computer 2022, vol. 55, no. 5, pp. 93–100.

85 Second Optional Protocol to the International Covenant on Civil and Political Rights on the Abolition of the Death Penalty, adopted in New York on December 15, 1989, OJ. 2014, item 891.

86 O. Barbu, *Advertising, microtargeting and social media*, Procedia - Social and Behavioral Sciences 2014, vol. 163, pp. 44–49.

87 L. Cleveland, *Symbols and politics: Mass communication and the public drama*, Politics 1969, vol. 4, no. 2, pp. 186–196.

88 G. Le Bon, *The crowd: A study of the popular mind*, Beyond Books Hub., London 1897.

89 G. Le Bon, *The crowd: A study of the popular mind*, Beyond Books Hub., London 1897, p. 20.

90 G. Le Bon, *The crowd: A study of the popular mind*, Beyond Books Hub., London 1897, p. 24.

91 G. Le Bon, *The crowd: A study of the popular mind*, Beyond Books Hub., London 1897, p. 24.

92 G. Le Bon, *The crowd: A study of the popular mind*, Beyond Books Hub., London 1897, p. 26.

93 E. Brindal, N. Kakoschke, A. Reeson, D. Evans, *Madness of the crowd: Understanding mass behaviors through a multidisciplinary lens*, Frontiers in Psychology 2022, vol. 13, https://www.frontiersin.org/articles/10.3389/fpsyg.2022.924511/full.

94 E. Brindal, N. Kakoschke, A. Reeson, D. Evans, *Madness of the crowd: Understanding mass behaviors through a multidisciplinary lens*, Frontiers in Psychology 2022, vol. 13, https://www.frontiersin.org/articles/10.3389/fpsyg.2022.924511/full.

95 C. Hayden, *From connection to contagion*, Journal of the Royal Anthropological Institute 2021, vol. 27, pp. 95–107.

96 C. Hayden, *From connection to contagion*, Journal of the Royal Anthropological Institute 2021, vol. 27, pp. 95–107.

97 A. Oeberst, R. Imhoff, *Toward parsimony in bias research: A proposed common framework of belief-consistent information processing for a set of biases*, Perspectives on Psychological Science 2023, vol. 18, no. 1.
98 The questions in parentheses are from me and I submit them for the Reader's consideration.
99 A. Oeberst, R. Imhoff, *Toward parsimony*....
100 S. Mattavelli, J. Béna, O. Corneille, C. Unkelbach, *People underestimate the influence of repetition on truth judgments (and more so for themselves than for others)*, Cognition 2023, vol. 242.
101 L.K. Fazio, N.M. Brashier, B.K. Payne, E.J. Marsh, *Knowledge does not protect against illusory truth*, Journal of Experimental Psychology: General 2015, vol. 144, no. 5, p. 993.
102 B. Swire-Thompson, N. Miklaucic, J.P. Wihbey, D. Lazer, J. DeGutis, *The backfire effect after correcting misinformation is strongly associated with reliability*, Journal of Experimental Psychology: General 2022, vol. 151, no. 7.
103 U.K. Ecker, *Why rebuttals may not work: The psychology of misinformation*, Media Asia 2017, vol. 44, no. 2, pp. 79–87.
104 Y. Mounk, *How the media got the hospital explosion wrong*, The Atlantic, October 23, 2023, https://www.theatlantic.com/ideas/archive/2023/10/gaza-hospital-explosion-misinformation-reporting/675719/.
105 U.K. Ecker, S. Lewandowsky et al., *The psychological drivers*..., pp. 13–29.
106 J. Cheng, M. Bernstein, C. Danescu-Niculescu-Mizil, J. Leskovec, *Anyone can become a troll: Causes of trolling behavior in online discussions*, in *Proceedings of the 2017 ACM Conference on Computer Supported Cooperative Work and Social Computing*, February 2017, pp. 1217–1230.
107 F. Ezzeddine, L. Luceri, O. Ayoub, I. Sbeity, G. Nogora, E. Ferrara, S. Giordano, *Characterizing and detecting state-sponsored troll activity on social media*, November 8, 2022, https://europepmc.org/article/ppr/ppr568700.
108 S.H.R. Rasmussen, S. Ludeke, *Cognitive ability is a powerful predictor of political tolerance*, Journal of Personality 2022, vol. 90, no. 3, pp. 311–323.
109 S. McCombie, A.J. Uhlmann, S. Morrison, *The US 2016 presidential election & Russia's troll farms*, Intelligence and National Security 2020, vol. 35, no. 1, pp. 95–114.
110 R. MacKinnon, E. Zuckerman, *Don't feed the trolls*, Index on Censorship 2012, vol. 41, no. 4, pp. 14–24.
111 J. Cheng, M. Bernstein et al., *Anyone can*..., pp. 1217–1230.
112 E. March, G. Steele, *High esteem and hurting others online: trait sadism moderates the relationship between self-esteem and internet trolling*, Cyberpsychology, Behavior, and Social Networking 2020, vol. 23, no. 7, pp. 441–446.
113 E. March, *New research shows trolls don't just enjoy hurting others, they also feel good about themselves*, September 16, 2020, https://theconversation.com/new-research-shows-trolls-dont-just-enjoy-hurting-others-they-also-feel-good-about-themselves-145931.
114 J. Halberstadt, J.C. Jackson, D. Bilkey, J. Jong, H. Whitehouse, C. McNaughton, S. Zollmann, *Incipient social groups: An analysis via in-vivo behavioral tracking*, PloS one 2016, vol. 11, no. 3.
115 D. Spohr, *Fake news and ideological polarization: Filter bubbles and selective exposure on social media*, Business Information Review 2017, vol. 34, no. 3, pp. 150–160.
116 M. Granovetter, *Threshold models of collective behavior*, American Journal of Sociology 1978, vol. 83, no. 6, pp. 1420–1443.
117 M. Granovetter, *Threshold models of collective behavior*, American Journal of Sociology 1978, vol. 83, no. 6, pp. 1420–1443.
118 M. Granovetter, *Threshold models of collective behavior*, American Journal of Sociology 1978, vol. 83, no. 6, pp. 1420–1443.
119 J.C. Davies, *Toward a theory of revolution*, American Sociological Review, 1962, vol. 27, no. 1, pp. 5–19.
120 S. González-Bailón, Y. Lelkes, *Do social media undermine social cohesion? A critical review*, Social Issues and Policy Review 2023, vol. 17, no. 1, pp. 155–180.
121 D. Robson, *The '3.5% rule': How a small minority can change the world*, May 14, 2019, https://www.bbc.com/future/article/20190513-it-only-takes-35-of-people-to-change-the-world.
122 D. Centola, J. Becker, D. Brackbill, A. Baronchelli, *Experimental evidence for tipping points in social convention*, Science 2018, vol. 360, no. 6393, pp. 1116–1119.

123 L.Q. Tay, M.J. Hurlstone, T. Kurz, U.K. Ecker, *A comparison of prebunking and debunking interventions for implied versus explicit misinformation*, British Journal of Psychology 2022, vol. 113, no. 3, pp. 591–607.
124 S. Lewandowsky, S. Van Der Linden, *Countering misinformation and fake news through inoculation and prebunking*, European Review of Social Psychology 2021, vol. 32, no. 2, pp. 348–384.
125 J. Compton, *Inoculation theory*, in *The SAGE Handbook of Persuasion: Developments in Theory and Practice*, edited by J.P. Dillard, L. Shen, New York 2013, pp. 220–237.
126 J. Roozenbeek, S. Van Der Linden, B. Goldberg, S. Rathje, S. Lewandowsky, *Psychological inoculation improves resilience against misinformation on social media*, Science Advances 2022, vol. 8, no. 34.
127 J. Carey, B. Fogarty, M. Gehrke, B. Nyhan, J. Reifler, Prebunking and Credible Source Corrections Increase Election Credibility: Evidence from the US and Brazil.

Chapter 3

Technological methods of digital propaganda and information operations

Like propaganda, disinformation has existed for a long time. That much is obvious. Let's not succumb to the mannerism of ritually prefacing analyses and articles with truisms like: "*disinformation is nothing new*." Because that's what they are, truisms. With such disclaimers, one may try to signal that they are knowledgeable about the subject, cautious to call things "new," and are aware of past methods. That one does not succumb to current trends, fads, as the consideration of the problem of disinformation has experienced a kind of renaissance since 2016.

It's true, disinformation *as a concept* is nothing new. In fact, propaganda and disinformation (even when not named as such) have been around for centuries, even if formally just for a few hundred years. They have been used on a mass scale for just over 100 years. Still, there are elements of novelty all the time. In other words, while some claim that *disinformation is nothing new*—I argue that in fact, new technologies qualitatively justify to claim that things and methods *are new*.

What is changing here?

The environment is changing. The methods are changing. The knowledge is changing. For example, human knowledge. We develop knowledge of certain psychological rules and effects, they are studied and analyzed meticulously, using scientific methods, systematically. This enables the building of effective influence operations, properly tailored, properly constructed, implemented, and targeted. Let's reiterate once again (it's important to reinforce this) that the most effective can be the use of truth, truthful information.[1] And modern technology methods help in operationalizing the use of true information for influence, even if malign.

The technology, techniques, and methods are of great importance. Not only the theory of propaganda, information activities, and influence but also the practice of propaganda methods. And that's what this chapter deals with in terms of technical issues and the basics. Sometimes, the description in this chapter may seem complex, even low-level (detailed), also somewhat technical—it is anchored in information technology. This is helpful, sometimes indispensable. But if the Reader finds that this content is not suitable for him or her (e.g., in places where source code is discussed), or already has the topic mastered—they can simply try to skip these parts, moving on.

For today's communication methods, anyone can be its element. A "node," a "relay," or even a producer, an emitter in a system of disinformation or propaganda. It is easier than ever before to achieve the necessary basics: use a method to create content, post it in the right places, find an audience, and reach them. This is now possible on a grand scale, previously unavailable. This is also why reducing the problem to a simple statement that disinformation is nothing new misses the point completely. Because the changes in the information environment today are both quantitative and qualitative. This is something absolutely new

DOI: 10.1201/9781003499497-3

that was never available before. Of course, just because everyone has a possibility to use it in theory, it does not mean that everyone has it in practice—it depends on many factors. We will analyze them.

Techniques used in a systematic and deliberate manner by determined actors can lead to previously unattainable effects.

3.1 DUAL-USE AND DUAL-PURPOSE METHODS

Undoubtedly, some of the influence techniques are seemingly ordinary advertising or public relations (PR) techniques—techniques, and therefore solutions, approaches, and methods. It is difficult to consider clear separation. But there's much more to that. Of course, there are activities reserved for "foreign," and domestic, as one prefers (but this chapter is about technical issues) pure propaganda and disinformation methods (neither advertising nor PR). But in many cases, these are only elements, specific details. For it turns out that these methods can simply have multiple uses. So, instead of ridiculing or taking a swipe at something as supposedly not particularly sophisticated and not very specialized, it is better to follow other criteria. The criterion of effectiveness. After all, it's not that something must necessarily be sophisticated, specialized, unique, advanced, one-of-a-kind. The most important criterion is effectiveness. The effect achieved. And this threshold can be achieved by applying theoretical foundations and practical information capabilities—technical approach, good design.

Such methods can be used for awareness-raising (information campaigns, e.g., health-related), advertising, PR, so civil, friendly, not demonic at all, or Goebbelsian, so to speak. But the same methods can also be used by groups (including those external) interested in carrying out diversionary activities, and information operations. These can be civilian groups but also military ones, although such structures can have the largest field of action during actual military operations, like during wars. The quintessential feature of some information methods is that they can be used in both civilian and military areas.[2]

An example is the memetic technique, or perhaps even conflict, competition, maybe even warfare.[3,4] Creating memes—attention-grabbing, succinct descriptions or comments of a situation, events, or reality, perhaps humorous—can have satirical purposes. But it can also be a method within politics, or even warfare—both defensive (preparing grounds of one's side for battle, boosting morale, siding allies) and offensive (discouraging the opposing side). In this chapter, specific applications are of lesser importance. What counts are technique, technology, and methods. It is just worth noting that methods can be used by different people or people from different structures or sides, for different purposes. What matters, therefore, is *who* is doing *something* and *why*—for *what* purpose. Many techniques and methods can be applied in both military and civilian areas. Those based on information processing and propagation can be particularly difficult to separate and can be used in hostile operations below the threshold of armed confrontation.

Obviously, I am not comparing memes with tanks or missiles. Those serve different purposes. But if we consider memes as a method of warfare, couldn't this pose a challenge to arms control or disarmament processes? In practice—no. This is because legitimate informational influence has its place in social and civilian life. Still, in view of this, it makes no sense to say that hostile information activities are some sort of a purely military issue reserved for the "bad guys" (or the opponent side) who want to do harm. These measures may be of this nature, but in most cases it will then be a civilian issue, a so-called journalistic, political issue. However, we will consider differently an article in the press or a TV program, and differently the technical possibilities of the application of information methods, such as the construction of a spam system (for the propagation of fishy advertising content), or a bot farm intended to propagate certain ideas, more or less aggressive, but also warnings or threats in a war situation, or dropping leaflets. Likewise with the ways of conducting such activities: one can use algorithmic message targeting, algorithmic content generation (e.g., using AI (artificial intelligence) methods, LLMs (large language models), bots and automatons, or humans too. This is an issue that needs to be considered on many levels. Not only in the context of sociology and psychology but also (perhaps even more so) on a technical, mathematical, and IT level. Understanding and appreciating the nature of such methods requires the application of expertise from many fields—social as well as technical. Naturally, today technical methods are crucial because they are the actual methods of identifying and acquiring "targets," as well as reaching them, but the role of constructing information messages cannot be underestimated, because this is a very important part of the information payload. This, however, is no longer a situation of the kind as 100 years ago or so, when the issue of technology was quite limited, maybe to the construction and maintenance of radio broadcasting infrastructure, its direction and power, and the provision of radio receivers to people to absorb this information—to listen to music or speeches of state leaders.

3.2 SOME SAY DISINFORMATION IS NOTHING NEW

Let's recap this analytical pitfall again to clear the way for the rest of this book. In essence, disinformation itself (as a concept) is nothing new. But the real novelty is the modern possibilities offered by technology. Today, the information sphere is an integral part of many (almost all) people's lives. We use cyberspace to communicate, to exchange information, to obtain it, and to keep up with the latest developments—news, reports, announcements, also memes ("funny cat pictures"). We use social media. Many people are active on them and have their profiles there. We can interact with other people. It is not a passive absorption of information (as it was with newspapers, with theater, with radio, with television, decades or centuries ago). In the past, one could malign and angrily wave fists at the TV in response to the program content. Today, anyone can express disapproval or even speak out directly to the online account or profile of a particular public figure or politician, below their posts, including using terms commonly considered offensive. Such is the beauty of technology. That's pretty new. To say that disinformation is nothing new is akin to saying that traveling using locomotive motion is nothing new. I mean, sure, but electric cars are pretty different to traveling with steam engine-powered vessels, if only due to speed and comfort.

3.2.1 Look, here is the novelty

What is *completely* new is such because of the information environment; methods of informational interaction and news consumption have changed. The change was the strengthening of the active role of the user, the human being, and the citizen. A hundred years ago, the broad masses of people were limited to passively receiving information (and actively disseminating—but usually on a tiny scale), such as from the radio or newspapers, often with a long delay, meanwhile today everything has accelerated. The circulation of information is continuous. So, it can immediately have an impact on social groups. The dynamics are completely different than in the past. This is not only about speed of exchange but also qualitative differences and evolution of human expression due to fast pace of information consumption. In this sense, disinformation or propaganda is a novelty, because it has changed its face considerably.

So, in other words, the new issue here—both quantitatively and qualitatively—are the methods. Importantly, these methods will become increasingly numerous, advanced, and versatile.

And they are so at different levels. At the level of content generation, there are issues of generative AI, at the level of identification and outreach, there are new channels of information (platforms, social networks) or the evolution of existing ones, at the level of comprehension of human nature, we know more and more about psychology and the functioning of human brain and mind. So, we are talking about methods, and these are the result of developments in science and technology. The importance of organizational issues can also be mentioned. In cases of grassroots groups, however, this is of little importance, because their potential activity or reach is limited, and fragmented.

In the case of supporting the actions of one's own State—as various groups are doing during Russia's war in Ukraine—it may be similar, that is, loosely structured formats, perhaps with some leadership or coordination. In military cases, the structures may be more apparent, as there is a hierarchy in the military. This form, like bureaucracies and formal approach, however, can somewhat slow down development and adaptation to change. This is well described by the so-called Martec's law,[5] stating that "technological change is exponential, while organizational change is logarithmic."[6] In simple terms: technological changes happen very quickly, but organizational changes (absorbing these technological changes) happen much more slowly compared to the technological ones. This explains the limited absorption of new developments by large companies, organizations, and state institutions. In a parliamentary democracy, at least in places, this is enforced by the elections calendar. From time to time, voters have a chance to "reset the current settings," and when they recognize the need, they have this opportunity, at least in theory. They may also be *aided* in such a choice—with information activities.

In general, however, Martec's law illustrates a major challenge for organization and management. This challenge is increasing as technology develops rapidly. And this is something we are facing in the current era, in the 21st century. Organizational absorption capacity is limited. And as time goes on and there is no action taken to adapt, the gap between technology development and the organizational level grows very quickly. This also constrains regulations and laws.

3.2.2 Okay, but so what?

Excellent question. Simply put, it can be difficult for companies and States to detect or counteract the propaganda and disinformation methods being used when they are simply much behind and the adversary has assimilated the new solutions and is using them effectively.

Then, the situation is more or less like bringing a knife to a gunfight. Now, let's get to the specifics.

3.3 BOTS AND TROLLS

I have already mentioned that it is important to identify the social groups that are to be the recipients of information, of some message. But how to reach them? If we have a platform, such as a social media platform like Meta/Facebook, X/Twitter, Meta/Instagram, or any other that has users creating and consuming content, one method is to create a coordinated group of automatons, agents, or even groups of people acting in a coordinated manner.

3.3.1 Bots

If we are talking about automated traffic, the proper term for such automatons is a "bot" (from the word "robot").[7] This can be an algorithmically controlled platform that, after registering a profile within a communication platform (such as a social network), will propagate some content and post messages. Still, a bot is an algorithm, a program that performs certain actions. It is not a human. It is an automaton controlled by software, an agent that can spread messages, publish information or posts at certain times, and interact with other humans (or bots). It can create an "artificial crowd," that is, artificial traffic, giving the impression that someone's (human) posts are popular, that the person has many followers, by which other people may have confidence in such a profile. Since someone has a big observer/follower count, their posts are viewed many times, so they have more reach, and perhaps appear to be a more serious person (which, of course, does not have to be true).

A bot can be programmed to interact with people for specific purposes, for example, to harass or simply engage someone's attention and use/waste their time. Or respond to posts relating to selected issues, such as current events, a particular person, product, or political party. Humans can be behind the production of the content (or content templates), but it can also be generated fully automatically, for example, by AI methods through large language models (LLMs) such as generative pre-trained transformer (GPT) or others.

Such bots should not be confused with "chat bots" (conversation bots), which can be used by institutions or companies to talk to people (users, customers) and provide information. These serve primarily to reduce costs, as it is not necessary to engage human support (technical or customer service) to solve simple problems. They are often limited and can't solve real problems. Then, it's just a waste of the user's (customer's) time, as such useless solutions provide little apparent help, and in fact may even cause harm. Both malicious bots and chatbots may, therefore, burn mental cycles of humans. However, in the case of legitimate chatbots, this is not done on purpose, and the reason is rather incompetence or a fad. This example shows that bots per se do not necessarily serve purely harmful disinformation or propaganda, underlining the issue of intent. In fact, a bot that posts the current weather or this type of information on a chat channel is not harmful, it is helpful. So we can't equate the term "bot" exclusively with bad actions. That would be a mistake. Bots can be programmed, and it is only up to the intentions of the creator and the implementation to define how they will work.

When it comes to fraud, it is important to detect and combat the malicious use of bots. This is not easy for an individual without access to the technical details of the digital platform. One can be guided by limitations in the content generated, meaningless responses, etc. There's a lot of guesswork here, and conclusions may be unjustified. As LLMs and generative text content creation become more popular, such detection will become even more complicated and time-consuming.

The use of bots consumes mental, thought cycles—including those of analysts. Such bots for "consuming mental cycles" may, therefore, become dangerous. If only to divert attention or create an information overload to hide other activities.

Thus, perhaps there will eventually be situations where it will be difficult to immediately detect whether we are dealing with a real person. Then, a simplified method might be to simply limit ourselves to people known from the real world, some form of verification of a person's profile or experience of past interactions with that profile. This, however, would be a drastic solution. However, who really feels like "talking" to an automaton is a time well spent?

3.3.1.1 Recipe for creating a bot farm, botnet

It is up to the platforms to detect and combat bots. They often do so effectively. The creation of a farm, botnet (from bot network) itself may seem simple on the surface:

1) **Selecting the target group**—the audience. This requires finding answers to the questions, where are they? Why and how to engage them? What can we target? How many bots are needed? One can imagine targeting specific environments (information bubbles)

to either reinforce beliefs within them or disintegrate them. But it is not necessary to take active measures. If it's just bots for situational analysis (without interacting with other users), then of course the matter is greatly simplified. Recipients can be classified as groups,[8] based on traits such as demographics (age, gender), interests, preferences, and opinions (either for or against a certain view) but also by keywords in their earlier online activities. The content itself is irrelevant; it's all about whether the identified people are interested in certain topics.

2) **Choosing a platform for bots** depends on where the target audience is. These can be platforms like Twitter/X or Instagram. Based on the selection of the target group further down the platform, one can narrow the focus to certain keywords, concepts, and account names. Or maybe the target is making voice calls (phone calls, instant messaging)? Then, content generation software libraries must take this into account and support automatic speech generation or voice cloning, for example, using neural networks,[9] which is possible.[10] Then, too, input data in the form of account names or phone numbers and audio samples are needed, which may violate data protection laws. But if someone is interested in unethical or even illegal activities, this may be acceptable to them. As a matter of defense, one must be aware of this. Illegality of actions does not mean their impossibility.
3) **Choosing a format for the bots.** Programming them through the use of software, and various types of control libraries. This is an important point, because platforms are (rightly) fighting botnets, and attackers may want to evade detection. One has to decide whether to use the API (application programming interface), if it is provided by the platform as the standard way of posting content, or whether this should be based on mechanization (instrumentation, programming) of the web browser, for example, using libraries such as Puppeteer,[11] for the Chrome web browser, automating web browsing,[12] with extensions to further hinder the detection of the platform's use (stealth).[13] Since platforms may not tolerate the use of their standard API for something they would consider abusive (i.e., their terms of service prohibit this), unofficial methods remain: standard access software and the use of a web browser or an application. Of course, then such an approach must take into account if the fact of using such a library is not easily detected, as this too may not be tolerated by the platforms, but with some effort, it can be concealed. It is not necessarily so difficult. I write this from experience. For research purposes, I have "automated" such interfaces many times, both for analyzing the web, which means browsing many websites (even thousands of sites per second, thanks to the execution environment in cloud services), and within social networks or even advertising networks. And these actions have never been detected or blocked as abusive. This is how I correctly obtained data for the scientific research and analyses I was developing. The research, of course, was ethical (privacy measurements). With these experiences, it is not difficult for me to imagine constructing a purely offensive system. At the same time, the standards and methods in this field (automation of network use, websites) are changing quite rapidly.
4) **Choice of masking and concealment methods**. Masking should primarily hide the fact that the profile is not real but is "automated." That is, detection of the use of the software libraries should be evaded. Then, it's about the practice of uses to avoid leaving detectable behavioral traces. Running too many bots from the same device and network address is not a good idea. Sending 10 posts per second over a period of 24 hours, from several accounts, from a single IP address and from the same web browser, may look suspicious. That's also why it's a good idea to use various types of services, like proxies, to mask the network (IP) address. Perhaps also to mask the actual country of origin of the network traffic. In this way, one may create network traffic pointing to

different countries. There are many technical solutions: from networks like Tor (acutely easy to detect) to setting up own proxy/VPN (Virtual Private Network) servers, for example, in some cloud or academic environment, or other approaches.[14] Such systems are even offered by companies like Apple (Private Relay). One may also use hacked servers (which is illegal) or workstations of ordinary users (paying them to enable such activities) and install proxy servers on them. Of course, they don't have to be aware of the actual purpose of such solutions, or at least they can adopt such a line of defense in a possible court proceeding or counterintelligence investigation. It will also be unethical and illegal. I do not recommend making one's own homes available for such applications to make money for oneself in this way. In fact, I advise against such a way of passive income. Masking is also a matter of content.

5) **The selection of a content generator methods and content generation.** First, it is important who the message is directed to. This must be determined beforehand. Second, how should it be generated? It can be done manually, but it is not a good idea to have 1,000 bots sending the exact same message. It then becomes obvious that something is not right. This is suspicious, unreliable, and even embarrassing for the developers. Another way is to construct templates, decompose the message into its component parts and take into account several such parts, randomizing these elements, which, however, may still be easy to detect in the long run. One can also engage people to generate content. However, these methods may gradually lose their relevance. Methods based on natural language processing, that is, methods using AI,[15] may be an effective solution. They may work much better because they are scalable and do not require significant human intervention. For example, this is how generative AI (such as GPT and other variants) can construct entries for bots:

Eating meat is harmful to health and the environment. Red meat is high in fat and saturated fatty acids, which can lead to heart disease and atherosclerosis. In addition, meat production is very environmentally unfriendly and contributes to greenhouse gas emissions. It is worth considering a change to a vegetarian or vegan diet.

Eating meat is good for your health, as it is a source of protein, iron, zinc and magnesium, as well as B, A, E and C vitamins.

The meat industry is a manifestation of ruthless capitalist exploitation. The fight against social inequality starts from the plate—choose vegetarianism.

Eating meat is an important part of a healthy diet, rich in protein and nutrients. In addition, the meat industry generates profits for the economy and provides jobs. As a leader, I have always encouraged increased meat production to provide the public with a quality source of food.

Eating insects is a useful and economical alternative to meat. Insects are rich in protein and have a low environmental impact, which is in line with our values. Introducing insect farming on an industrial scale can benefit the economy and provide food for the poorer segments of society.

Eating insects is a manifestation of bourgeois degeneration. The insect farming industry is another way to exploit nature and exploit the proletariat. Moreover, the consumption of insects can contribute to the development of diseases and endanger people's health. In our revolutionary society, we should oppose such practices and work for the development of vegan food.

Party X is the only force that can bring about the victory of the proletarian revolution and achieve socialism. Party Y, on the other hand, is a bunch of vermin and thieves who seek only to enrich themselves at the expense of the people. As Marxist-Leninist revolutionaries, we should fight against reactionary forces like Party Y and strive to establish a just socialist government.

All of these entries were generated automatically (LLM/GPT). Indeed, for some entries, I instructed the generator to use a specific style, such as Marxist-Leninist. And it did so. One can configure such things freely, according to one's own preferences, or rather goals. Moreover, using such automatic methods, one may do it "on an industrial scale." One may dynamically generate responses in the course of a conversation. Then, such a botnet of thousands of profiles could make quite a stir, especially if launched at the right time and in the right way. I do not recommend testing this at home. However, such a solution could be effective especially on platforms where short entries are preferred.[16] Moreover, the problem of detecting synthetic content created in this way could be a challenge.[17] This one in general refers to lexical analysis of whole blocks of text or individual sentences, in search of various kinds of suspicious patterns (i.e., forms that a human would rather not use); the possibilities and limitations of such methods will be continually established and clarified. It will be a race: offense versus defense. With access to an LLM, content can be efficiently generated in a variety of ways that are relatively difficult to detect. Of course, the use of content from generators under certain circumstances may be detectable.[18,19] According to some studies, however, at some stage, such detection may be impossible, and this is even proven with mathematical precision.[20] Botnet developers may take this into account, although they will probably not go into the details of the mathematical evidence and simply take it for granted. The most important criterion anyway would be whether the system works, whether it produces results, such as monetary income.

6) **Selecting methods of engagement.** One can respond to everyone or to selected posts relating to a particular topic (e.g., based on the keywords used). Engage in discussions with some people. Produce "fake discussions" under other people's posts. It all depends on your goals. However, the defense is obvious: don't get involved. At the same time, this may be easier said than done.

3.3.2 So now we have a functioning botnet—final remarks

The preceding considerations are part of the typical way of modeling the activity of mechanized systems for information operations[21]: *target identification, selection of information methods, selection of content, and delivery of content.* Of course, the chapter is for illustrative and educational purposes only. I am not encouraging anybody to do anything. There's also no special need, or sense, to include source code listings in this book, as technical solutions will change. This is the main reason. It is doubtful that merely considering such systems is unethical. On the contrary, it is necessary to talk about them, because the problems of abuse are real, they will stay with us and evolve. How else to develop defenses?

For those interested in the topic, it should not be difficult to develop this solution on their own. However, without access to technical competencies, one can't do it, especially if one has to modify existing solutions, assemble them into a whole system, and sometimes modify the source code. In any case, consideration of the points indicated in the previous section is necessary for the development of any anti-bot system. It takes little time to create a single, basic bot. It is a matter of tens of minutes, hours at most. Expansion is more time-consuming. It is also a matter of developing a control platform for such a botnet, to synchronize activities. This would require more work. So, developing a full botnet on a large scale can take some time, more than if one only needs to control 1-10 bots. Maintenance of such a platform is a challenge—which means reacting to necessary changes in the target platform in the case of programming issues, but this is a detail. It is worth spending enough time considering the basic issues, that is, a good design of such a solution.

When it comes to spreading content of differing nature (multimodal—text, audio, video, images), it is worth bearing in mind other "dynamic" details, for example, the specifics of spreading and propagation of textual records are different from those of image-type formats. Detection of images and video records is different and can be more difficult.[22]

It is worth elaborating on the issue covered in point 4 above, that is, the choice of masking methods. Bot farms or proxy servers are known to have been installed by ordinary citizens in Ukraine during the war and made available to external actors; similar cases have also occurred in other countries. Bot networks are combated by online or social media platforms when their use can be established, for example, by detecting abuse and coordination of activities (which can be trivial without masking). In general, the challenge in creating a botnet is not so much the software of the system itself but operating it in such a way that it evades detection (for which many techniques and methods have been developed[23–24]), if used on a wider scale. This is not black magic. This knowledge is largely acquired through practice—by trial and error. So, it requires resources: time, money, tolerance for risk. I don't want it to sound like I'm encouraging such activities or even claiming that it's not a problem. Successfully putting together such a system is a challenge and must cost money. However, this is not rocket science or space technology of the type of the Mars landing, or the Manhattan Project.

It should be noted, however, that States are waging a battle against the practice of botnet farms spamming, brokering (for cyber attacks), or facilitating the masking of source addresses for propaganda and disinformation purposes. Due to the defensive war, takedowns of such botnet farms used by Russia in Ukraine are particularly noteworthy. In 2023, there were also the first serious attempts at legal bans. The first ideas arose in the United Kingdom, where a ban on the "manufacture, import, sale, rental and possession of SIM farms" was being considered, which was defined as devices that can use more than four SIM cards.[25] SIM cards enable the use of telecommunications networks. Using more than one SIM may make sense when one wants to use different operators, for example, when traveling. But four is quite a lot, and so it would seem a reasonable limitation, with some exceptions, for which it might be worth introducing legal authorization. The assumption is that having the technical capability to use more than four SIM cards could be a premise suggesting abuse. Will such a ban on production and sales have an effect? Perhaps, although even in the case of a ban, creating the equivalent of a bot farm using USB connectors and controlling small-sized Raspberry-type computers is possible. Then, the construction of a bot farm is not technically difficult, it can be done in a short time by anyone with basic hardware and software proficiency. So why bother with prohibiting that with the law? Possession is also to be banned, so the legal basis for prosecuting and criminalizing such practices when they are detected arises here. And in this sense, such a ban can be justified as having a practical effect.

An alternative may be to buy such a service from vendors that create such botnet platforms on a larger scale. There may be some risks associated with this. First, someone will know that we are the ones doing something. Second, they may know what that "something" is—who (what) the actions are taken against. Third, in the event that information about such "cooperation" is leaked or blocked in some way, it can be highly embarrassing. Fourth, it costs money, although developing your own solution can also mean expenses. Fifth, is it a good idea to engage in activities that are, let's face it, unethical? Even if our actions are ethical, by buying into and supporting the activities of such a "bot platform," we may be contributing, if indirectly, to abuse.

3.3.3 Trolls

Although trolls have already been mentioned, here we will approach the topic in a purely technical way. Strongly simplifying, a troll can simply be "a bot that is human". It doesn't sound like much: a human taking semi-automatic actions but applying human ingenuity? However, it could also be even a fairly popular person or profile who engages in such activities for some reason. For his or her own satisfaction (healthy or not), going much beyond the capability of simple bots—if only due to human ingenuity factor. Or perhaps also in the service of someone or something, such as for political purposes[26] or in the interest of a foreign country. Also to support some idea, some party, to show a preference for some product, even if only a certain diet. Or simply, trolling for a fee. Someone may also be bored. They may have problems accepting reality. They may have political goals. Reasons may vary. Coordinated groups of trolls can waste someone's time, or get on someone's nerves. The solution has already been discussed: do not feed the trolls. That is, ignore or block them. Sometimes blocking is even recommended, because tolerating a situation in which a troll notoriously links to "real" posts (and their responses are in the threads) may serve to lend him or her credibility or be seen as an expression of at least tolerance for the content expressed. But what if such activity is coordinated and does not originate from a single profile? It can be much more engaging, annoying, and time-consuming.

Trolls also can synchronize (coordinate) their activities and can effectively contribute to the disruption of the "order" in the information space[27]; they can also compromise their targets—people (e.g., public figures), or help them compromise themselves. It can be particularly effective especially when such methods are facilitated by the intellectual composition of such a target, and the selected activities effectively take advantage of those certain preconditions and lead to this happening in the open. These can, of course, be grassroots activities, that is, groups of enthusiasts, coordinating messages or goals. But it could also involve something completely different and of a different nature, with no specific goals to achieve, not any "Russian military intelligence," even if their actions actually or only seemingly support such opinions. This in view also risks compromising analyses of this kind: if person X says Y and Russia or China says Y, then person X "is certainly" an agent of Russia or China. Although, in the absence of evidence, one can say: someone's statements support or repeat the Russia/China/whatever line. Then such an "analyst" might sound "more serious." Another approach may be "analyses" of which reliability is limited to journalism of the type: take three or four cases, describe them as related facts, put them all together, and draw general conclusions. This may indeed draw attention to certain phenomena, and even be a legitimate journalistic method! But it does not necessarily prove conspiracies, operations, or coordination in the strict, analytical, expert, or scientific sense.

Trolls can organize themselves. They can also use persuasion or eristic methods to steer discussions, discredit targets (here: individuals), create general confusion, and waste the time of such a target.

3.3.3.1 Arena of action—social media

Of course, if we're talking about influencing people, action happens where the people are.

So, the arena of activity may involve social media platforms like Twitter/X, Instagram, Facebook, TikTok, YouTube, and others. Simply speaking: anything being in use by sufficient numbers of people, or the right people. At one time, it could also be comments under news/media articles in the old days when someone still read them. As with bots—the arena of activity are sites that have users. After all, there is no point in writing to empty spaces. Unless it's someone's whim, but then it's relatively harmless (useless). Unless such a message is (paradoxically!) reinforced by enthusiasts tracking down misinformation, fact-checkers, and the likes. Oddly, sometimes that's the case. A niche message, devoid of wider relevance and one that should be completely ignored, gets scooped up and loudly "debunked." And thus it is spread and amplified. Activities made on the cheap get noticed and gain audience—for free (or for taxpayer's money of the State of the targeted Nation).

As a curiosity, I cite the 2022–2024 controversy over TikTok. Due to its Chinese provenance and existing laws in China, it was alleged that this platform has close ties (subordination) to the Chinese Communist Party.[28] Such considerations are also important, because if one directs information messages through a platform, and that platform becomes discredited (or not), this may (or may not) affect the reception of the communication. But in themselves, of course, such platforms remain a tool to reach their users. Which to some may be more important than provenance. And these tools will, therefore, be in use because of the people being there.

3.3.4 Amplification

Amplification is the spreading of a message. Methods to make some content recognized and disseminated. People are induced to share it and spread it. This can be done with bots, for example, when 1,000 accounts "pass on" some post, perhaps real persons will recognize that there is something in it, and will be inclined to pass it on as well. And then with such synthetic and manufactured, artificial support, some content gets amplified.[29] Instead of being read by a few or a few dozen people, it can reach hundreds, thousands, or maybe even millions of recipients. When the content from the post is written about (or of interest to) traditional or electronic media, the effect is even greater.

Such signals of apparent credibility can be disrupted,[30] for example, by inserting descriptions, labels, and context messages, like "this is subject to debate," "harmful content," and other such contextual information becoming standard on social media. If spreading opinions or links to websites include a warning such as "this is a known hoax," "this is subject to dispute," or "this comes from the government media of country XYZ," it can reduce the potential for propagation of such content.[31] In the early days of social network development, there was no support for such descriptive additions. Therefore, it was possible to spread fakes or misleading posts effectively and without restrictions, on a large scale. Now, however, standards are evolving. Certain requirements are also imposed through regulation. In a word, the bar has gone up to the benefit of users.

3.3.5 Algorithmic amplification and gaming of recommender systems

Content amplification can be done algorithmically, by recommender systems. If these are based on content analysis and interaction with it, it may be possible to "game" them in such a way that they will amplify selected, foul content. It was found that such gaming of recommender systems effectively promoted extremist content.[32–33] Recommendation systems are subject to modification, so methods of playing with them will also evolve.

Recommender systems are subject to laws and regulations, especially in Europe. The so-called Wild West is coming to an end. Of course, there will always be opportunities to game the systems, the safeguards—but the simple methods have been gated.

3.3.6 Influencers, public figures, politicians

Just for the sake of completeness of the argument, I recall that disinformation or propaganda content can also be spread by people with natural capabilities to do so. People who have already gained a substantial audience for themselves. If they have an audience and ways to reach them, they become communicators or producers of content.

People such as politicians can spread misinformation or false information and this is a fact, it happens all over the world,[34,35] probably for various reasons, it does not necessarily have to be a deliberate harmful act, sometimes it may simply be in self-interest or party interest. This phenomenon applies to all kinds of political options (the specific political alignment is less important here), and their followers or supporters may willingly spread the content further, including uncritically, without realizing its true nature, and at other times knowing it exactly. Such influencers may also use all sorts of techniques, tricks, methods, and gimmicks to get their message across.

3.4 DEEPFAKE, GENERATIVE CONTENT

Deepfake is a huge topic. These are methods of generating content that is untrue, misleading, and false, yet looks realistic, to the point of being deceptively real. More formally, deepfakes are generative AI creations: from text to voice, image, or video content. This can be, for example, a video in which a so-called famous person[36] (politician, whoever) utters messages that they never said. Yet, the video depicts the "person" as saying just that. So it's a technology for fabricating events. Deepfake may introduce significant rule-breaking to the game of propaganda, including in political, artistic, and other expressions.[37] Such content released at the right time can lead to significant misunderstanding or damage. Therefore, it is necessary to create conditions to detect and remove such creations.

Detection of deepfake content is an important research topic.[38–39] Such methods may highlight certain signatures that indicate the artificial, or generative, nature of a video recording. These are situations when, for example, the generated hands (image) look obviously fishy and untrue, when eye blinking[40] does not occur or is artificial, when there are various exaggerations, missing shadows, and other such "artifacts." Detection involves the detection of inaccuracies or imperfections of generative content. This is an analysis of appearance (physical, physiological issues) or behavior (behavioral issues). There are many such details that can still be analyzed. However, it is worth noting that generative technology is moving forward. It may become increasingly difficult to detect with such signs as image imperfections, because the generation will be of better quality and such "little details" easy to catch may be missing. Generative AI models solved the issue of generating human depictions whose hands had more fingers than five, or whose hands or fingers were twisted in unnatural ways (see Figure 3.1). It was funny when it lasted, but now it may be over. But if the generated scene is near-perfect, what then? The origin of the image, that is, the reliability of the source, will become important. Such content, after all, never spreads automatically. The fact that someone creates a fake video depicting an athlete, an artist, a well-known person, a popular politician—who does something, says something—it still means nothing. Because the point is to deliver such content to the people. Broadly.

If the proliferation process is effectively disrupted, the relative impact of fakes will be greatly reduced, diminished, perhaps even to zero, none. In fact, it is not at all crucial that such content can be created and generated. This is only a stage. That's not the point. The most important thing is to find and reach the audience. That's why obligations are imposed on digital platforms to combat the propagation of such content. They also have this in their rules for using their services. Such fake creations have already been created multiple times. This is in no way a novelty—including with many politicians, and as part of the war in Ukraine, with Zelensky[41] or Putin. But they were successfully detected and removed, bringing the harmful impact to zero or minimizing it.

Thus, combating the propagation of harmful and untrue content should not be merely about the possibility of generating it—that cannot be blocked, the genie is permanently out

Figure 3.1 The image of hands generated by AI methods left much to be desired in the early 2000s—it did not look real.

Source: Author's generation.

of the bottle. The emphasis should be on detection and elimination of such content. And removing content by digital platforms is quite simple, at least technically. It is sufficient to know the signature of such a file and permanent removal from the platform takes place almost instantly. Naturally, the challenge remains in detecting such content for removal. This will not always be possible prior to the start of this content gaining popularity. But once the content is spread, someone may eventually notice it, analyze it, determine that something is wrong, and report it. The file will then be analyzed further, and removed, if only as a result of widespread reporting by many users, which may be even more accurate than automatic detection,[42] though mixed approaches may be worthwhile. Yes, it will still probably be spread in less popular, niche, or obscure places, on niche platforms, in circles of people susceptible to *non-standard worldview theories*, but the reach (and that's what counts!) will be small, minimal in such a case (unless some individual decides to physically act upon the content, that is).

Thus, there is no question of the "end of truth," as some analysts or columnists despaired of in the early 2020s. If someone allows himself or herself to be misled, it may also have something to do with the fact that he himself or she herself may have expected and anticipated such content from someone else in particular, for example, that a specific politician is a really bad person, perhaps a thief or a drunkard. Wouldn't you be inclined to believe that the politician you do not necessarily like is inherently a bad person? So, it would be more indicative of the condition of the people who give credence to the falsehood; this could still involve damage. Of course, there can certainly be subtle exceptions. But let's put the extremes aside. Personally, I'm not worried that someone will "accidentally" start a war on the basis of a deepfake that has been circulated. For a simple reason: wars are not started in such an impulsive and ill-considered ways. And information confusion can be triggered in completely different ways (here, I recommend re-reading the earlier parts about the missile falling).

One need only to point to the precedent of the deepfake of Ukrainian President Zelensky (2022). When it was determined that such content was produced and would be spread, pre-bunking methods were used, preparing the public (and the international community) that such an action may occur. Later, the hoax was straightened out, and its content was quickly removed and blocked by the platforms. As a result, the impact of this operation was virtually nil—but conference presenters had some content to speak about. In addition, the production quality of this fake was relatively low. However, this was a precedent. Another example is the deepfake of Russian President Putin (2023), of much better quality. The propagation element was better—this was done via hacked television (control of broadcasting was taken over), where this content was simply aired.

Anyway, "generative" productions can find their place as part of the "technical platform" for the production and distribution of falsehoods, disinformation, and propaganda. However, it is necessary to think of it as whole systems (even factories): from the idea to production to delivery to the recipient. This will become clear later in the chapter, where the elements that make up information operations will be discussed, from beginning to end (not including the possible consequences if this were to be the actual end).

On the other hand, there is no doubt that the production of multimodal (audio, video, text) generative content, at least initially or in stages, may cause problems for digital societies and platforms. Also, text detection (as already mentioned) will be necessary for bot detection.[43] These are techniques and technologies that may come at a cost to societies.[44] It is clear that large technology platforms are developing solutions to detect the use of such methods, and some results are also being made public, such as those developed with research collaborations between Meta/Facebook and academic teams.[45] In simple terms: such methods aim to identify the "technical fingerprints," revealing that an image is a processed, artificial one. By analyzing the traces, one can determine the degree of likelihood that the tested image is or is not a fake. If one has such an automaton, it can be used against any file uploaded by the user and against all files uploaded so far.

So, generative methods can produce "synthetic" content. This content can also be detected to some extent. But the key challenge is to propagate them, to deliver them to the audience, to make them credible. Are then, deepfakes a security risk? Certainly, both to persons and to States. It can be used in so-called hybrid operations, in disinformation, or in propaganda. These methods can also be used in war. Or in elections.

To appreciate this risk, let's imagine a scenario of a conversation held over a video conferencing system (Skype, Teams, Meet, Zoom, whatever, etc.). Let's assume that someone has hacked one point of such a conversation (e.g., taking over someone's login credentials, or perhaps even controlling someone's computer) and joins in, but with the help of deepfake-software methods presents a face generated by an AI model. Not only the face, also the voice, and the text to be read is based on other texts of the person it impersonates to mimic the style. And now such an automaton "communicates" with the target. Would that be easy to detect for you?

3.4.1 Scenario of using deepfake as part of the war

These issues are important[46]; imagine a (false) order of surrender or calling to perform some other action during hostilities. Let's imagine that communication systems are hacked and an attempt is made to "implant" a false command/order (such scenarios were considered by the U.S. military as early as around 1999). We would like it to be impossible, because in warfare, certain decisions should not made hastily—there is a defined path of communication and authentication, authenticating the source. But who knows what could happen during the chaos of war. Undoubtedly, the fake video with Ukrainian President Zelenski demonstrated an attempt to give recommendations or orders—in the fake, the image called on the military to lay down their arms and surrender.[47] Thus, this is not just a purely theoretical matter. In the case in question, it failed for several reasons: the low quality of the production, the early detection and publicity, and a clear institutional (hierarchical) path for issuing instructions (orders). In this case, it was also spectacular perhaps, however, mainly to audiences in the West, where it fell on fertile ground of expectation of the inevitable uses of deepfakes. In practice, it was simply unbelievable. But what if the actions were more subtle, credible, perhaps aimed at smaller decisive targets, such as specific military units, at specific times? The risk in the case of information chaos and lack of verifiability could be a potential decision dispute. Funny thing, but recall the movie "Crimson Tide" (1995), which depicted a U.S. submarine cut off from staff communications, where decisions to launch nuclear weapons were in the hands of isolated submarine commanders, operating in a situation of receiving ambiguous orders (i.e., uncertainty). This is, of course, a (hopefully) fictional and untrue scenario. Today, however, it should give us food for thought as to how the crew would behave in such a situation, receiving a falsified order. Not necessarily a deepfake of the audio-video recording kind.

So, the basic problem: the material created is directed to selected groups of people or selected military units. This is a challenge for the command authorization path, so it is largely an illusory problem, except perhaps in some emergency situations.

3.4.2 Micro-targeting scenario of political and social groups by sending generative content (deepfake)

Another risk is micro-targeting, that is, precisely targeting content and delivering it to specific audiences. If one correctly identifies social groups that potentially may be particularly susceptible to some content (e.g., acutely politically engaged to the point where they might be suspected not to doubt manufactured content), one can target synthetic, generative, untrue (deepfake) content precisely to them.[48] Some content consumers pay attention not so much to the (in)credibility of the content, but rather to whether (and how) it fits into their worldview.[49] To quote from the research citing one surveyed person: "If my worldview matches with a video, I will definitely share it even if it's fake. Whatever they are saying, whatever views they hold doesn't matter. If I like it, I will share it."[50] Some people may, therefore, at times be convinced of their own views so that extreme content could work particularly well on or against them. They are susceptible to it, even if momentarily, and it is something that can potentially be exploited (if one wishes). Such a combination of methods and techniques can, therefore, result in some influence. But the important element here is the mental-intellectual condition of the social groups being targeted, so not the mere potential to create a hoax or the mere delivery of it for the sake of it. It has to be all at once.

3.4.3 Advantages of using generative and deepfake technologies

The problem, therefore, will be detection, but it is also worth mentioning cases in which deepfake (and more broadly generative) technology can be used to the benefit of people. Consider the automatic generation of advertisements or even political spots. In India, for example, there are many communities that speak different languages, and already in 2019, one politician used generative technology to create ad content that take this fact into account. In these spots, the person spoke in different languages—including ones he didn't know. This allowed people from many communities, perhaps disadvantaged ones, to participate in political and social life. Another idea is to clone an actor's voice and use it to deliver messages in any languages. Cloning the voice of a smartphone owner to create voice messages is already possible.

Still another problem is the possibility of creating spots with people who are, well, on longer alive. Imagine a politician who is no longer alive but is still popular, and some political force wants to take advantage of this. So, it generates spots with this person in which they say something that they never said (when alive). It may even be possible to hide the fact that a politician or state leader is dead, at least for a while. Imagine what would have happened if such a technology had been available in the past, such as in the USSR. As Stalin died, his followers, whose careers depended on him, might have been tempted to "prolong" the dictator's existence by creating generative content, as if the dictator was still in power. So, it's a paradox, because thanks to generative technology, such a politician or leader doesn't even have to be alive anymore.[51] This, of course, is not a problem of technology per se. Nor is it a joke. Back in 2020, I foresaw such a risk. It was realized at least during Indonesia's 2024 election campaign when a politician used the image of Suharto, the late dictator/president to create an election video where "Suharto," who died in 2008, exhorted people to vote for this political party.[52]

Another possibility is political PR and the creation of spots automatically, on the fly. The political candidate would not have to do anything, because the content would create itself—and it would be heavily profiled for a specific audience, delivered with micro-targeting, for example.

As of end of 2023, Google has introduced new rules under which "synthetic," generative AI (deepfake) material cannot be used in political advertising. This can't be done unless such creations are clearly labeled—as generated, synthetic content about situations that didn't happen. As long as they present stories that didn't happen, which can mislead people. This applies to multimedia: videos, audio recordings, photos.[53] Such "disclosure must be clear and conspicuous, and must be placed in a location where it is likely to be noticed by users."[54] And these are good principles, fitting into the public debate at the international level, and into emerging standards and laws. These are reasonable rules, giving grounds for removal of such content in the case of non-compliance.

3.5 SIGNATURE OF FALSE AND DISINFORMATION CONTENT

If there already exists a phenomenon of propaganda production of false, disinformation content, spreading it, can it somehow be detected? It's complicated, because a lot of content is not necessarily simple to verify. The best deliberate propaganda should be based on truthfulness; otherwise, it may be easy to establish falsity and question the entire message and the sources spreading it. Then, the signature would be obvious, taking into account two possibilities: true or false. In practice, however, this can be more complicated. But what can be done? As I explained with regard to deepfake, there are some approaches and methods for detecting such content.

Sometimes content intended to mislead may contain special characteristics. They may differ from such more credible, better-quality content.[55] Differential characteristics may correspond to disinformation content, conspiracy theories, content designed to make one pick it up and take an interest in it (clickbait), false or hateful content, "junk science," and rumors.[56] By categorizing content in this way, it is possible to try to detect it automatically by analyzing patterns and using methods of natural language processing and computational linguistics. Among other things, this would be an attempt to detect the creation style of such content.

For example, a short entry: "We will all going to die soon. We know the cause and the date. Click here for details" is an obvious clickbait—it encourages people to click in order to open an article, read it, thereby bringing revenue to the website (because of the ads displayed). It appeals to ultimate issues and to emotions. It is also arguably fake. So, perhaps an analysis of the construction of such sentences and specific words could enable a technical method of detecting them. Detect the template of their creation. By recognizing linguistic patterns, giving them weight and meaning, we could potentially determine the nature of some information. For example, bogus information can be (on average, more often) more negative in tone than fact-based information. True information is also more lexically diverse. Junk news are more likely to address the emotions of the audience. They are also easier to digest.[57] If such information is easy to read, this can contribute to its propagation. After all, junk content that is easy to consume (e.g., presents a simplistic or even straightforward model of reality)[58] may gain many recipients, if only because the bar of comprehension will hang low—to increase accessibility for the audience.

However, this suggests a method of defense: present the real content in a clear and understandable way, without complicating it unnecessarily. Not everyone can do this, because not everyone is (nor they need to be!) a good communicator. Early detection of a fake can be valuable, because if it were to gain popularity—preemptive action can be taken (pre-bunking, see also Chapter 2).

3.6 CONTENT CREATION METHODS AND TECHNIQUES

An important feature of new technologies and social media is the relative reduction in the cost of creating information campaigns, their content load, and reaching their audiences,[59] which can support populist or extremist circles.[60] But how to do it? In the simplest terms, the idea is to develop a system that, if functioning effectively enough, would work like a stream. From acquiring information about current trends and events (research, observations, emerging trends), analyzing related events, selecting strategies, and delegating this task to an expert group (or to an automaton, which would reduce costs), which would develop a detailed strategy and actual content. And further—to transfer this content to the broadcast systems. Technically, this could be trolls, bots, perhaps also people—if there are available enthusiasts of the topic, specific influencers.

A well-created information payload, content,[61] is a very important thing. Content creation itself can be done manually, semi-automatically,[62] and fully automatically, thanks to natural language processing techniques, and generative techniques of LLM/AI. Such content can be created in various ways: as text, images, audio recordings, videos, etc.[63] However, they should be based on something concrete:

- on knowledge (school education, cultural, information in relation to movies watched, series, books read, current events, etc.),
- on the specifics of the people who are to be the targets (recipients, victims) of propaganda.

The point is that communications must relate to something. People (for the most part) have a short memory of events, so the propaganda content itself also has to evolve quickly. This is an important part of decoding information/propaganda messages: figuring out what they refer to. For example, they may refer to historical disputes: with the Soviet Union, with Russia, with Germany, with France.[64] And only by taking into account the intellectual composition of the "audience" can the actual impact of the communication be decoded. Without the right intellectual background, it will not be possible to "correctly" decode the "desired" information message. However, designing a message constructed incorrectly may still not trigger these processes in the minds of the audience as expected. Hence, the conclusion is that when generating propaganda content it is worthwhile to involve intelligent people capable of processing information of different nature, from different channels, within multiple contexts. This is an important observation: not everything can be fully automated. Especially if someone cares about efficiency and results. Of course, technology can be a big help here; in fact, most activities must be supported technically and automatically. For example, generative AI methods are capable of creating convincing propaganda messages.[65] But that's not all, after all, in addition, they are able to create content in multiple languages (internally translate automatically into other languages) and use different styles of speech. This offers tremendous cost efficiency and increased scalability of information operations. This is worth keeping in mind, as one of today's opportunities is to use platforms to build and spread propaganda as a service.[66] Perhaps this is the future, where you pay for the service and get the result. What remains to be analyzed is the actual quality of such messages when they are delegated to a "sub-provider."

With the use of new technologies such as AI methods or LLMs, it will be more difficult to identify that a given piece of content constitutes propaganda, because these methods can create credible messages at low cost—in large quantities.[67] The issue to be determined is the actual cost and limitations of using LLMs for propaganda, because after all, if these were to be controlled by large corporations or companies, these could (they do) build in restrictions, some kind of censorship, limitations to counter abuse. However, there are many indications that the local launch of specialized language models—without the involvement of external companies—will be possible in the future. Particularly if we are dealing with state, military, intelligence, or diversionary actors with significant budgets—it is clear that one way or another they will gain access to unrestricted solutions. If only because they will create such for their own purposes. In the first half of 2023, some still argued that large generative models would find their way into the hands of rather large companies (and the military, intelligence, etc.), but the situation quickly evolved. Work was underway to improve the models' performance. Already in the second half of 2023 it was possible, and not that difficult, to run an entire complex LLM on a smartphone, in a web browser. So, widespread access to this technology will not be out of the question. The safest assumption is that these methods will eventually become widespread, widely adopted, and used, and will not be subject to restrictive limitations, which will be untenable. This, then, is the scenario when such models would be widely available, rather than only through selected companies or suppliers. In short, this scenario would legitimize the hypothesis of gradual adoption of these models as a standard tool. In many industries, including those related to PR, information operations, or propaganda, this could lead to serious consequences in the creation and propagation of content.

3.6.1 More on artificial intelligence, large language models

Since this is a chapter on technical issues, it should be mentioned that many things can be automated. This speeds up work, reduces costs, and even increases the reach of payloads. Automated content creation has been possible for a long time, but advanced automation of textual or multimedia content generation has greatly accelerated with generative AI methods. There are many methods of AI (machine learning), but in this book we will focus on a select one—LLM.

How it works follows. As with most AI methods, one needs a lot of data, for example, from books, websites, graphic content, etc. Good quality input data for "training" is essential for high-performance LLMs.[68] This data is extracted, processed, and used for training the models. After such "training," the model can be applied. In the case of LLMs, they perform the function of expanding of the input data. The expansion occurs in the most probable way.

We have the initial words; the model inserts the next most probable words afterward (with some randomness), taking into account the previous ones; the analysis is more complex, the so-called self-attention functions are used to interpret the meaning of individual words. For example, the expansion answer to the phrase "twinkle twinkle little" will be "star," as it is a natural continuation of this popular nursery rhyme. Sometimes, however, very different, even nonsensical content may be generated. Such responses depend on a number of factors (e.g., if the scale of randomness, called temperature, is increased in the LLM model used, the generated response may be a much less sensible text of the kind: "Twinkle, twinkle, zubidoo bliggle, Zooping through the sky with a sniggle, Flibbering flibberets, oh so friggle"). In general, however, LLMs may elaborate on the input data, and they do so quite well, analyzing that data and extracting key context from it.[69]

Large language models can generate slogans, essays, articles, as well as social media posts. Everything works quickly, in an automated manner. From the very beginning, serious risks of abuse have been identified. One of them is the use of these techniques to generate spam and misinformation.[70] This is a legitimate concern, because LLMs are able to create very realistic content, and in addition, do it very quickly, which increases the efficiency of applying these solutions to information operations. Now social media bots could be much more compelling. And while it is claimed that such abuses can be countered, after all, sooner or later players in this industry may gain access to their own specialized models, without any restrictions, or use providers of such propaganda production services. These undoubtedly can be created,[71] and even be cost-effective. Having said that, who knows, perhaps eventually anyone will be able to create such influence, information operations, even from an armchair at home—without the need for entire teams of people, hardware, and software. There is no doubt that the performance and capability of such LLM systems will rise, rapidly and significantly.[72] Specialized LLMs have been emerging. In medical knowledge, in cybersecurity, and even in cyber-crime. There will be more specialized versions.[73]

Ultimately avoiding these kinds of uses is impossible. We have to live with it. This is because for such use, all that is needed is that: (1) such a model exists; (2) works well; (3) there is access to it; (4) it is possible to reach the audience effectively with the generated content.[74] All of these points are achievable, especially the first three. It is reasonable to consider that the only place to defend against is the fourth point. So, platforms must look for such abuses, prosecute them, analyze them, and fight them. Of course, it is necessary that there are also susceptible audiences, and these can be properly educated to acquire immunity. However, it is doubtful that this can be an effective and scalable solution. Still, it remains a case of building resilience. The problem of disinformation is appreciated broadly. The World Economic Forum's Global Risks Report (2024) indicated very serious concerns about the issue of misinformation and the spread of misleading, false information. Even though putting issues of disinformation at the top of the risk ranking might have been somewhat exaggerated, considering the generally unstable situation in the third decade of the twenty-first century, it cannot be said that the problem does not exist. It does. Such a report is clearly a sign of the times. The same year, 2024, during one of the peak interest of concerns around manufacturing harmful content using AI technologies multiple key technology companies announced devoted TechAccords with voluntary rules at the Munich Security Conference—a form of voluntary pledge to fight the issue of deepfakes used in the context of elections activity. Called "Deceptive AI Election Content," it foresees scrutinizing "convincing AI-generated audio, video, and images that deceptively fake or alter the appearance, voice, or actions of political candidates, election officials, and other key stakeholders in a democratic election, or that provide false information to voters."[75] The announcement includes a pledge to develop detection mechanisms allowing to take down such detected content and communicate the detected events to the public.

3.6.2 LLMs problems, LLM bot detection

A particular aspect of LLMs is that they may not be very effective in describing ambiguous things, at least the early ones. Those, however, are essential for the real world and human matters.[76] Yet, LLMs need not be perfect to be very good, and in some tasks much better than many people. It is worth noting that the content produced by such models may be of much better quality than propaganda content made by humans, because it depends on the competence and talents of the people involved, and cheap trolls do not guarantee high quality. Such use can be difficult to detect. Although in 2024, engaging social media bots would be detectable by asking such an automaton bot a single question based on tasks that are easy for humans but difficult for LLM bots, such as symbolic manipulation, noise filtering, randomness, and some elements of graphical reasoning.[77]

For example, GPT3 gave the wrong answer in the task: "State the number of occurrences of *t* in eeooeotetto"—there are three, meanwhile, the LLM was able to state that there are five.[78] More such "tricky" questions and tasks can be imagined. In the first half of the third decade of 2020s, it is difficult to say whether, or how long, the human advantage will last. It is also possible to use the capabilities of LLMs against them. For example, ask to list the capitals of all the states in the United States, and if the answer is given (quickly), there is a slight chance that we are dealing with a human being. Alternatively, ask for a few dozen digits from the expansion of the number pi (π; 3,14159265358979323846264338327950288 4197).[79] I am not saying that no human is capable of giving such an answer. However, such people are few. If, dear Reader, you don't believe it, then ask, let's say, five random people you encounter on the street to name the first 30 digits from the expansion of the number π and see what happens. Good luck.

3.7 RISK OF EXPOSURE TO FALSE MESSAGES AND HARMFUL INFORMATION CONTENT

To appreciate when propaganda or disinformation can be effective, one must understand that it is not sufficient to be exposed to false content, to propaganda, disinformation, etc. This may not be enough to influence a person to take action. It is not that simple.

Exposure alone is not enough. This simple fact has been known for long and has been scientifically confirmed numerous times. Most recently also, in the case of disinformation activities on the occasion of the COVID-19 pandemic. And this is an important case from modern times, because undoubtedly the pandemic was accompanied by disinformation campaigns of considerable scale on the one side, and public information campaigns on the other. Legitimate campaigns, and illegitimate ones—conducted by internal actors (skeptics; political parties who wanted to increase support; publicists and influencers of various kinds, public figures), and external actors (similar categories of people, but from "foreign" countries, to include information and intelligence services of neighboring States, for example, Russia,[80] although it may be inadequate,[81] or simplistic, to ritually reduce everything in disinformation "always" on Russia; in the case of COVID-19, as with many other topics, there are simply all sorts of "internal actors," the conditions are complex, even if some issues are similar or the same "as Russia.")

The reach or impact of such information is often limited, even negligibly small—even when individuals are repeatedly exposed to it. But the crucial point is that the links between exposure to disinformation and future opinions and views are not at all directly causal.[82] So it's not as if someone just read a post or an article to immediately, automatically become a brain-washed zombie under the influence of propaganda. Shaping people's views, influencing them—this is a difficult art.

In the said case of COVID-19—to make things funnier!—the combined effects of pro- and anti-vaccine campaigns contributed to an increase in vaccination.[83] Perhaps a good summary of such a result is the slogan: "Advertising is the engine of trade," or the maxim: "it doesn't matter what they say about you as long as they spell your name right." The conclusion is that changing and influencing people's specific behavior is not easy.

By the way, typical totalitarian propaganda template works just like this: people are immersed in propaganda messages, or messages that reinforce them. These permeate all spheres of life: from advertising, the press, the media, education, and even storefronts. Living in such an environment, one can be influenced—no other information content has access. But in pluralism people have access to information and stimuli from many sources or sides, and sometimes information from one source "overrides" those coming from another—the choice is of the citizen (at least in the ideal, model situation; such choices may sometimes be illusory). Ultimately, it is not the case that groups of bots and trolls, influencers on social media on one or even several information channels will lead to the immersion of "whole lives" of people in a propaganda message. What's different is when this is coherently matched by communications from "everywhere"—the media (radio, TV, press), education (schools, universities), and other sources such as hospitals, advertising leaflets in stores, etc. When the message is repeated in many places. For the purposes of effective propaganda, it is important that one and the same message (or similar ones) be repeated many times (preferably all the time), preferably through different channels. For example, we are currently going through a renaissance of gender mainstreaming and equality policies for women. Hence, it can be interesting to politically reach audiences precisely on the basis of gender; one does not have to be for or against any particular view to reach audiences using these concepts. It should be noted that there are techniques by which one can deliberately target a message to specific audiences and do that continuously or at least for quite a long time.[84] For example, by gender, since it so happens that many politicians want to portray themselves as those who will support women, women's rights. These are certainly laudable goals! But it's worth noting that in targeting this kind of information, they use standard outreach techniques, sometimes with a message that the recipient is eager to hear. And if he or she hears it often enough and widely enough, he or she may even adopt these attitudes and views as his or her own. Because that's just the way it works, regardless of the issues raised.

This is related to a broader issue: targeting messages based on identity (*identity-based* messaging or targeting) or even targeting content based on specific problems or issues (*issue-based*),[85] such as gender equality and their roles in society, views on the economy, the ozone hole, CO2 emissions levels, global warming, genetically modified organisms. Sometimes, certain issues are indeed important, and thus frequently and widely raised. To reach people, one has to jump on such a "bandwagon" and consciously plug into a trend, a current of thought, swim in that current, and perhaps even shape its flow direction or speed. If one puts together such campaigns in such a way that the messages are consistent and frequent, some effect may be attained. While it may be difficult to measure it, for example, because it may take some time (months, years, decades). Here, however, the important point is that certain groups may be more or less susceptible to different kinds of messages and communications.

What's important here? We have confirmed that identity-based targeting of communications can enhance their effectiveness. Targeting messages to different groups (segments) of society is a fact.[86] And it is done in such a way that it is effective. For example, "women's topics" raised by women politicians or activists actually reach other women more strongly.[87]

3.7.1 Remember the continuous influence effect

Continuous influence effect cannot be underestimated. Once read, experienced, or acquired information, it can have a somewhat lasting influence on the perception of events in the future.[88,89] In view of this, some informational input can disturb people's view of future information, events, and reality—influence perception, expectations, and evaluations of future events. This was the case, for example, with the alleged fake birth certificate of U.S. President Obama, supposed to indicate that he was not born in the United States. People familiar with the subject were quicker to absorb any new "reports," recalling the previous data, and more easily considered them as "confirmation."

Therefore, it is better not to rush to announce public information: once disseminated, it may be difficult to "straighten things out" later; doubts may arise (justified or not). It is worth recalling here once again the case of the fall of a rocket on a hospital in the Gaza Strip and what the consequences were of publicizing the first, unverified version, which, however, was accepted by whole crowds of people around the world.

Thus, we have drawn another important conclusion. Overestimating the mere fact of reaching an audience with false information (or propaganda) can lead to a misconception about the effectiveness of an information campaign. Exposure alone is not and cannot be a measure of the effectiveness of an information operation, and certainly not the degree of "importance" (severity) of such activities. It follows that exposure alone does not necessarily imply a measure of impact. Sometimes, however, the goal is not to influence opinions or decisions, but, for example, to familiarize the public with a concept or person (to promote it, one must first make people aware that it exists). This contrasts with propaganda or disinformation influence goals—and here exposure can be enough.

3.8 REACHING OUT TO THE PUBLIC

It is not enough to produce content. It is still necessary to be able to reach an audience with them. A few decades ago, messages could be transmitted by word of mouth, by rumor, by verbal exchange of information, and through newspapers. During wars, leaflets were distributed from airplanes or helicopters. Messages can be propagated through radio, television, the Internet, and various types of media. Nowadays, it is possible to reach audiences through social media platforms—for example, Twitter, Facebook, Instagram, TikTok—as long as such a platform has (ideally, the relevant) users. And this is a key problem, because if one generates even an excellent educational, announcement, or propaganda content, one still has to reach the audience. As it happens, digital platforms, for example, have introduced restrictions in this regard—content moderation. For example, it is forbidden to spread content that has been stolen (e.g., hacked), as well as to engage in activities of an informational or propaganda operation nature, as the Russian, Chinese, American, or French armies, for example, have found out. Such activities were systematically detected by Facebook and not only prevented but also publicized. Certain strictures can also be imposed by legal regulations (see Chapter 5).

Now, how to reach the audience in other ways?

3.9 TECHNICAL ISSUES—STANDARDS, NOTIFICATIONS

Notifications are often used in new technologies. Everyone is familiar with them, they are short messages displayed from time to time on devices, such as smartphone screens. The displayed message may be accompanied by sound. Apps are able to send them and the best example is an alert about an important message (in a news app), about a change in the weather, about the fact that something has occurred in a smartphone game, or about an SMS received. Notifications are very useful. But how do they work? Technically, they use the software layer in the smartphone's operating system[90] or web browser.[91] The delivery and display are carried out by the corresponding infrastructure.[92]

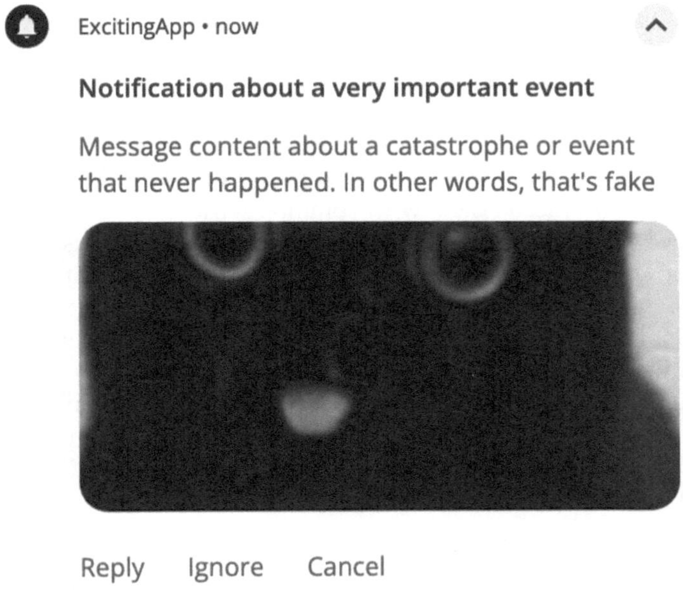

Figure 3.2 Example of a notification.

Source: Own (Cat blep picture easily found on the internet).

Such a sample message delivered for display on a smartphone or web browser is shown in Figure 3.2. But how would it get there? After all, it is only permissible to send such content after knowingly, intentionally, installing an app or giving permission for it to be displayed on some website. That is, in essence, users are in control of what messages will be displayed to them. Since they give permission to display notifications, it's in response to their desires.

Let's take a moment to think about situations in which such capabilities could be abused—used against the user. Such capability is exactly what is in the hands of the people who control the infrastructure responsible for displaying messages and notifications. It's just that they don't abuse it in this way. There is a rather slim chance that someone serious would want to send spam, "junk news," slurs, or propaganda and disinformation through their infrastructure. They would not desire to risk shooting themselves in the foot by doing so—people would uninstall such rogue applications or block the display of notifications. Accidental sending of communications might happen, but if so, it would be rather harmless. Abuse could still take place here. How?

Such infrastructure can become the target of a cyberattack. This is a risk point. Taking control over it can be valuable. If someone or something has the ability to send messages, through a platform that has credibility, to hundreds, thousands, or perhaps even millions of recipients—that's the potential for a large-scale blunder or even a small-scale information disruption. The risk arises when someone (e.g., a disgruntled employee or unauthorized person) gains access and control of such infrastructure. Then false and harmful content can be sent. When I explained the existence of this risk in 2019,[93] these were hypothetical considerations. A few years after that, actual cases emerged. In 2023 in Pakistan, users of a popular app for ordering transportation and package delivery[94] one day started receiving offensive content. It happened due to hacking of the notification infrastructure—the attackers have taken control over it. Once someone gained such access, they could send whatever they liked, and send it to nearly 100,000 people. In this case, the actual effect could have been to mildly upset the recipients and cause damage to the company's reputation, that is, the information security of that company came under question, including brand reputation.

The history of abuse of these functions indicates that this is not a common problem, but it does happen.[95,96] However, imagine a popular respected newspaper (such as the *Financial Times*), an online medium. There is a good chance that notifications from this source are read by many and are taken seriously. That's a credible information source. It may, therefore, be a tempting target for cyber attacks, and once control of such infrastructure is gained, fraud or abuse can occur. It is worth keeping care when giving websites permission to display notifications. Now, how to defend oneself? With common sense. Be cautious. When the content displayed by notifications deviates strongly from the norm, it can be suspicious. The message "warning about poisoned water source in your tap" may sound sensitive, but it is unlikely that a world-scale newspaper application would direct so geographically precise information just to you. But it is imaginable that at least some people would act upon receiving such information—if only by overwhelming the emergency line or the water company phone line. Another thing is that it is often difficult to predict how unexpected reality can be. You could of course disable these features globally in the smartphone or the browser settings. But it's probably not worth it, as these features are useful.

Another option for targeting content is advertising.

3.10 CONTENT DISTRIBUTION CHANNEL—AD TARGETING

Advertisements on the internet is a graceful way to target content to users. That's what it's for, actually. Technically, it's the display of text or multimedia on publisher resources—websites, mobile apps, smart TVs, etc. Usually, there are places within these solutions where advertising content appears. Such content, however, can range from product advertising, to political, or other more or less successful messages. However, it is undoubtedly a way of reaching the user. Campaigns can be programmed either legally, by purchasing the appropriate subscriptions and creating content, or illegally—by hacking the providers' infrastructures. Such ad infrastructures may also target content to the audience, quite precisely.

3.11 SELF-SABOTAGE OF TECHNOLOGY TO TRANSMIT INFORMATION

Political content can also be included in the software users install. This is exactly what happened during the Russian invasion of Ukraine in 2022. At that time, politically motivated (or perhaps ethically, activist) developers of widely used open-source software libraries (such as NPM packages for NodeJS) decided to include some custom, non-standard features in their software.[97] Such packages usually facilitate the use of additional features. This is a standard thing for programming.

In some cases of such activism (such as the node-ipc NodeJS package), the effects would be destructive: overwriting data on disk. Instead of data or text — a heart emoji: ♡ would be placed, effectively overwriting (destroying) the data previously held there. That is, it would be a data removal. Later, it was changed to just display a message to the programmer. The effects were to be limited to computers located in Russia and Ukraine.[98] Naturally, this caused a huge controversy. As a rule, users and developers should have confidence in open-source software, especially one that is widely used, and the one in question was being downloaded (worldwide) millions of times a week.

It was also a precedent due to the fact of the first such a full-scale war, in a situation where computerization and software are widespread and IT infrastructure is actually in reality quite fragile—a change of one package may lead to paralysis or losses on a grand scale, and such packages are commonly included in large quantities. Further down the line, the developer responsible for the software created a special package called Peacenotwar. This one was limited to the displaying of an anti-war or peace message, in various languages. Here is that message:

> War is not the answer, no matter how bad it is. War brings tragedy and destruction, robbing generations of precious moments and hope for the future. The goal should always be peace. The soldier puts on their boots for their country, obeying the orders of their government. Find the strength to forgive, come together, and stand up to real injustice and evil. We are all connected through humanity and only separated because of geographic lines. We may feel insignificant as individuals but when enough people act with the same intention, we create big movements. Do what you think is right, follow your own morals. May God bless you and your family. Stay safe.[99]

Another developer added this message to his software's license:

> By using the code provided in this repository you agree with the following:l.
>
> - Russia had illegally annexed Crimea in 2014 and brought the war in Donbas followed by full-scale invasion of Ukraine in 2022.
> - Russia has brought sorrow and devastation to millions of Ukrainians, killed hundreds of innocent people, damaged thousands of buildings, and forced several million people to flee.[100]

This was the use of software for the purpose of expressing protest (protestware), a political stance.

Developers, programmers, and people who maintain some kind of systems, software, or programming libraries also have some kind of power or control: they can exert informational influence. I just demonstrated the manifestation of this.

Of course, this was an act of self-sabotage—sabotage of one's own creation, there was no hacking, breaking through security, and "injecting" modified versions. The whole thing happened at the level of the "supply chain" (the library delivered to users when they updated or installed software). For some developers and users, however, this was very unwelcome, unexpected, and even shocking and unethical. However, as it turned out, these are also methods of taking action. Except for the more "active" kind of activities like deletion of data—mostly informational, by implementing appropriate technical functions in the source code of popular software libraries on which popular software is based.

We live in the information age. One of its manifestations is the important role of IT workers. Consider what would happen if significant numbers of them, in various institutions and companies, decided to carry out some kind of protest or lead to paralysis. What percentage of systems important to society would stop working? Who has the power here? Partial answer: certainly not these IT specialists, because it is difficult to imagine that large numbers of unconnected people would want to take such a risk and do so in a coordinated manner. Or at least, we would all like to believe so.

3.12 GROUPING SOCIAL MEDIA COMMUNICATIONS

Social media posts can be amplified—artificially but also naturally, gaining sudden popularity, becoming the so-called virals, rapidly spread content.[101,102] When a viral is a hoax—false information, like a textual post, or a photo—for example, relating to medical, public health,[103] or political content—it can even have the potential to be dangerous. Such content can also be unintuitive, being counterintuitive to the so-called mainstream news, and the established norms, so it can attract the attention of people interested in such counterculture climates—and gain popularity.

Sometimes, the avalanche starts with one such news item, such as a tweet/xeet message that started a campaign for conspiracy theory believers to visit and film local hospitals to show that they were allegedly empty,[104] thus arguing that the effects of the COVID-19 pandemic were a hoax. Of course, it is dangerous to public health when an outsider enters the premises of an infectious disease hospital, in an unauthorized manner, perhaps without proper safety measures. Such messages were reinforced on social media by popular accounts, including those of politicians (giving them credence, for political purposes). Messages of this kind appeared in many countries, as if some form of connection, even if not coordination, perhaps inspiration, had occurred. Most such accounts in the English-speaking sphere were not bots, but profiles run by people,[105] but it was likely the posts from high-follower count figures, like politicians and popular activists that reinforced it.

Such content may spread through various interest groups centered around specific content and based on certain special concepts. These can be different kinds of diets, political views, thoughts on the state of the world, and horoscopes. Groups can bring together geopolitical enthusiasts, supporters, or opponents of certain ideas, concepts, ideologies, etc. In other words, the amplification can have an identity background.[106] Analyzing this as a phenomenon, it is essentially unnecessary to go into the details of the issues toward which such groups may be enthusiastic or skeptical or even hostile. The mechanism works the same way and has done so for decades,[107] and perhaps for centuries.

People trust certain sources of information, and these are the ones they prefer—a kind of habit. There may be many such people—they may form groups; they may create identities. And all sorts of recommendation algorithms[108] can detect what content users interact with. For example, users click "like," which is a signal for the recommendation system to assign them to some segments and show them similar posts or ads. There are legitimate allegations that recommendation system engines are deliberately created in such a way as to make some users (e.g., children[109]) dependent. Recommendation systems are not bad in themselves—their job is to recommend selected content to users. There is no need to browse through thousands or millions of posts or suggestions—the recommendation engine will point out those few or dozens of appropriate ones.[110] Recommendation systems learn who the user is: what and with whom he or she interacts, what he or she likes and dislikes, what actions he or she takes. And based on this, it presents content, guided by algorithms. How the algorithms work depends on their configuration and on the platform. YouTube, for example, pays attention to the amount of time we spend watching some videos with certain content, suggesting more videos we'd like to spend a certain amount of time watching (optimization for viewing intent). TikTok's rating functions, on the other hand, work to avoid presenting content that is too similar and to avoid boring the viewer, optimizing the performance due to the length of time the user spends on the app.[111] Such knowledge is derived from how the user uses the platform. And it can be used to increase the chances that a given user will spend more time on that platform, consuming more content, absorbing more information, and information messages. Continuously suggested content may be addictive, seemingly it may look like there's always something new, and that content never ends.

The disinformation content itself and its spread can be understandably visualized under the assumption that it propagates like a viral pathogen.[112] A helpful tool in mapping such phenomena is visualizing information flows, or mapping what profiles and content they share.[113] Hence the notion of an "information bubble," in which the user is supposedly locked in, meaning that he or she receives information that is consistent with his or her worldview and preferences—without those of others he or she dislikes or disagrees with. However, these so-called "bubbles" are not necessarily just a matter in the domain of social media and the Internet. In the real (offline) world, too, people may prefer to consume content (read, watch) that they like, that they (in some ways) agree with, and even surround themselves with people who are similar to themselves, holding similar views or opinions (though of course they also interact with others). Who knows, it may even be more effective on the Internet to go beyond such an echo chamber, after all, other kinds of content, information, and websites are readily available there. It's just a matter of choice. In other words, the view of the ubiquity of Internet information bubbles and their alleged ill effect should be revised.[114,115]

The Web and the Internet can foster radicalization but also open up more sources of information.[116] So, why did the view of the ubiquitous and allegedly, supposedly destructive effects of Internet information bubbles[117] gain popularity? Perhaps because it was easy to understand, accept, and explain certain phenomena this way, to rationalize it to oneself, and this was helped by the information that people increasingly get from social media. The dots were connected in a simplistic ("it surely must be this!") way, recognizing that algorithms could be the culprit. Some of these technologies may be part of the problem, but perhaps they should not necessarily be immediately recognized as the core, main, or sole cause of a complex phenomenon. At least initially, the source of interest in the problem was strictly American-centric phenomena. These were the events surrounding the 2016 U.S. elections, their outcome and reactions to that outcome (when Trump won, to some degree perhaps it may have caused a form of a cognitive dissonance, at least in the cases of some people). Perhaps this is also why this view of information bubbles was spread, and even political decisions were made with it in mind; also outside the United States, like in Europe. What a bummer. Let's not discount the social effects of such phenomena without a sound analysis. Furthermore, taking things out of proportions and attributing too much impact to disinformation activities may also be misguided—and then even help the actors responsible for such campaigns, when the one side publicly exaggerates the alleged impact of an otherwise low-impact activity.[118]

3.13 TECHNIQUES USED IN PROPAGANDA OPERATIONS

The fundamental issues in the case of influence operations, information operations, disinformation, or propaganda are: who, how, and what.[119] This refers to the so-called ABC model (*Actors, Behavior, Content*), specifying that the phenomenon (and operations) can be efficiently analyzed by making distinctions based on who performs the actions, who is responsible for them (actor), how they do it (behavior), and with what information load, content.

Influence campaigns can be analyzed according to a number of criteria[120]: the ideology and purpose of the campaign, the context in which the propaganda occurs, the identification of the actor (propagandist), the structure of the propaganda organization, the target group, the technique of using different media/channels, special techniques for maximizing effects, the reaction of the audience, and the effects and their evaluation.[121] For example, the context of the moment, current events, or circumstances may be relevant. Does the propaganda campaign use them in some way? Does it allude to them? To epidemics, war, elections, global climate change, and other topics? To things that are happening or being talked about? How does it do it, how does it allude or refer to it, what connections does it see with the current atmosphere? Effective propaganda and information messages refer to concrete things and try to build their message on something real[122] and current. For example, it makes no sense to refer to some events from 2004, 2014, 1994, or 1894. To put it bluntly and practically, hardly anyone would care anymore. By referring to something that was and is not, time is wasted.

Therefore, it is more efficient to focus on the here and now. Has something recent happened or is about to happen? So, it would be an analytical matter to establish links between messages and possible events, national or international situations. That's also why it's impossible to do effective propaganda without some scope of knowledge, and it's not just a need to involve people from the field of sociology or international relations, because these specific events or "clichés" should be identified properly and appropriately given the goals and objectives. Or, alternatively, just people who may be aware of what's going on in domestic or international matters. Simply speaking, someone intelligent may suffice. No particular education background is necessarily required.

3.14 PERSUASION AND MANIPULATION TECHNIQUES

It is worth noting a well-known truth: a lie repeated by many and multiple times can be accepted as true information. This is the so-called psychological *effect of illusory truth*[123,124]: repeated claims are more likely to be accepted as true than claims that are not repeated (or are novel).[125] Of course, exposure to false content cannot be equated with the power of persuasion. There is no guarantee that someone, having seen something even multiple times, will be permanently convinced by such content, taking it as a certainty. People live in different environments, and what happens around them affects them, which will not be changed by displayed information, a message in the media, such as social media. If, after turning off the computer, putting the smartphone in a pocket, and leaving the house, the world looks to that person differently from what the propagandist wanted to portray, argue, or suggest, people may not be convinced—because they just got other information. Therefore, it may be more difficult to explain the dangers and real risks of global warming to people when it's freezing outside the window (this may not be the most appropriate time, and it's more effective to do it in the summer when it's hot, unless a particularly warm winter occurs). Warming and climate change are global, descriptions of the phenomenon take into account the extent of change around the world, but people may still be limited to seeing what is local. A perverse idea to convince such doubters could be to set fire to local forests, for example, to help argue about the warming climate, but this scenario seems (hopefully) improbable, even absurd. Right?

Various takes can be countered by verifying information and publicizing the bogus ones (debunking them). However, one must be careful and not over-publicize the debunking, lest one accidentally reinforces such a message and helps it propagate (i.e., help it reach a larger audience). If something is niche, why "fight" it on a wider scale? However, if doing so, then it is better to do it thoughtfully, basing the message on credible facts. Warning the audience without using manipulation techniques. Cover bogus content or distorted messages, and explain them reliably in a simple language, so that the message is clear and understandable to a wide audience, so that they do not feel manipulated. And definitely do all this without unnecessary repetition of the "original" false content.[126] Otherwise, there may be a risk of accidental amplification. And unfortunately, it has happened that the services or news services of various countries have unknowingly amplified such messages. If you need to refer to it, rephrase it.

Once we have this necessary introduction and the elements of "safeguards" behind, we can move on to discuss specific techniques,[127–128] tricks, tactics, and methods that can be used in creating false or misinformation content. In demonstrating the use of these techniques, I will refer to the issue of sugar consumption. This is a good example. Undoubtedly, the excessive consumption of sugar is harmful. With propaganda techniques, it can be remedied, even if only in the short term.

3.14.1 Presenting irrelevant data

Presenting irrelevant data can be used to justify some theses, phrases, or lines of argument. This technique refers to authority in the form of data, reports, and perhaps even scientific results. It is a method to justify an information message in some "objective" way. It matters less in what way, because it may turn out that the sources to which someone refers are wrong, erroneous, or unrelated, off-topic. But who is going to dig into that, especially in the heat of an online argument on social media? Such data must, of course, be somehow—if only seemingly—related to the content one wants to present.

For example, in order to make a propaganda case for the health benefits of sugar as a food, one can selectively choose studies showing some positive effects associated with sugar consumption: that sugar provides a quick dose of energy, that it can, after all, be part of a well-balanced diet (without going into details). Of course, one must ignore studies showing negative consequences, if only for excessive sugar consumption. It is, therefore, a presentation of some data one-sidedly.

3.14.2 Obfuscation, intentional vagueness, confusion

Introducing doubts about the perception of an issue, complicating the conversation on a topic, suggesting the existence of ambiguities, perhaps a hidden agenda, or some unknown processes can lead to a change in the topic of conversation. For example, from the main topic one can switch to side topics.

When it comes to sugar, the case is clear. One can at least introduce niche, scientific terminology (biological, chemical, medical, etc.) into communication. It may be familiar to a small audience. Others may accept the information uncritically in the belief that since specialized terminology is used, someone knows what they are talking about, and may even be trustworthy (gives the impression that they know it). Different kinds of arguments can also be shuffled together. So, the idea is to obscure the essence of the message.

For example, it can be mentioned that sucrose (a disaccharide consisting of glucose and fructose) undergoes complex metabolic transformations in the body. Once ingested, sugar contributes to the activation of various enzymatic pathways involved in glycolysis, gluconeogenesis, and lipogenesis. These complex metabolic interactions can disrupt the body's delicate homeostatic balance, disrupting insulin signaling, promoting lipogenesis, and potentially leading to subtle physiological changes. The influx of glucose resulting from sugar consumption stimulates pancreatic beta cells to release insulin, a key hormone involved in glucose regulation. Scientific findings indicate that excessive sugar intake can affect the composition of the gut microbiota, potentially altering the gut-brain axis and affecting neuroendocrine signaling. These physiological changes could affect appetite regulation, satiety signaling, and even mood and cognitive function, etc.

After this block of jargon, one inserts the thesis that this argument would support. This block of text actually adds little (although scientifically it may be correct). The insertion of this element also has the effect of exhausting the mental capacity (fatigue) of the audience, which can facilitate the weakening of defensive capabilities.

3.14.3 Black and white vision (fallacy)

This is a deliberate analytical and sometimes logical error. The idea is to argue that the situation is (apparently) clear, that we have only two alternatives: for or against, true or false, etc. There is nothing in the middle. Often the real processes are more complex. Reduced to an alternative, the problem is simplified (and the more complex context, background, is lost). This is a clever manipulative technique when one needs to take sides. Express a clear view. There is no room for anything in between. This allows exaggeration of some elements of the problem.

In the case of sugar, the issue is clear. Those who consume sugar and sweetened products lead lives of joy, fulfillment, and pleasure. Those who avoid or consume sugar in moderation deprive themselves and their families of joy. There is no in-between. What do you choose? What is noteworthy here is how the details of the negative consequences of sugar consumption are omitted.

3.14.4 Whataboutism (relativism)

In response to some kind of topic, the method of whataboutism is to question things, to relativize them. It's an approach that presents concepts in a way that would indicate that arguments of this kind are meaningless. Discounting them.

For example, someone could state that according to studies, people who consume excessive amounts of sugar gain weight. And this is true. But a propagandist could counter this by claiming that someone is only quoting selected studies (accusing someone else of bias). And besides, after all, other products consumed in excess can also have harmful effects (e.g., radioactive cobalt, Co-60), and therefore there is no reason to focus on the harmfulness of sugar when "everything" can do harm. This technique can also be used to try to accuse someone, or show hypocrisy.[129]

3.14.5 Use of loaded language

It is a certain verbal extremism when we are using "big" words, perhaps extreme, bombastic, also offensive (swearing). Language that draws more attention to emotions than to substantive issues. There is no room for evidence, discussion, or reliability.

With sugar, the issue is clear. A propagandist can refer to sugar as a "sweet delight" or "source of happiness," using language that appeals to positive emotions and associations. This approach aims to create favorable perceptions and feelings of pleasure. By using "charged" language, the propagandist seeks to influence people's attitudes and beliefs using emotions. This technique can influence public opinion by creating fear, desire, or other strong emotions.

This is a technique often used in political messaging, all over the world. It is used because (apparently?) it is effective.

3.14.6 Stereotyping, labeling

It is to portray the audience by a certain name, so those are attacks also aimed directly at the adversary or a group of recipients, defining some attitudes pejoratively. This may be aimed at discrediting or belittling. The technique is meant to challenge credibility or take it away.

In the case of sugar, for example, it's referring to those promoting moderate (low, zero) sugar consumption as "food police," "food extremists," implying that their views are extreme, unjustified, and unreasonable. Any recommendations by scientists can be dismissed with claims that they are paid, and corrupt. One can recall the situation decades ago, when scientific authorities were used to advertise cigarettes (of which harmfulness is unquestioned today). Moreover, labeling creates a negative perception of people and views, if only by portraying them as overly harsh, and irrational. People in favor of limiting sugar intake can be portrayed as bored, devoid of joy in life, of advanced age, of a certain gender or skin color, or simply people whose time has passed. They can be said to be boring, monotonous people, leading lives devoid of taste and pleasure. On the other hand, on the opposite side, one will put sugar eaters: carefree, happy, joyful, and living life to the fullest.

3.14.7 Misrepresentation of someone's position (Straw Man)

The idea is to use the voice, opinion, or arguments of another person (perhaps an "authority") but to process (twist) it in such a way that in reality it will be a representation of content completely different. However, still attributed to someone else, which can be very clever. This is a fallacy of extension or straw-man.[130] Because it can be aimed directly at someone: misrepresenting someone's opinion (in their own words) to refute such a representation. Someone says one thing, we process this voice into something similar and refute this new argument, presenting it as a refutation of the source thesis. Simple and effective. It also shows why the use of analogies is riddled with problems: when one starts talking about analogies instead of concretes.

Imagine a well-known nutritionist arguing for the need to limit sugar consumption. As propagandists, we could creatively and selectively misrepresent such a position, such as quoting the same nutritionist when he or she admits that some doses of sugar can have positive effects. One would have to completely ignore other points made in criticism of sugar consumption. In such a way, this nutritionist would be portrayed as an advocate of sugar consumption. And since he or she is a well-known authority, one could extend this conclusion to a general character. One could also selectively describe the definition of things done by such a person and point out flaws in them—but within the definition and framing of the issue that we have created, not actually in what this person has said. However, putting words in someone's mouth this way can be considered offensive and can even be refuted quite easily when it becomes clear when this fact is realized.

3.14.8 Appeal to "authority"

Few people are recognized experts on everything. It is more effective to cite some recognized expert sources, including scientific content and publications. Someone with a professor's title may always sound credible, no matter the content being spoken. After all, every professor is a professor. So, it may be advisable to call on some authority to justify or challenge controversial views. In Communist times, such authorities might have been Marx or Lenin. Today, it is sometimes the same, although of course the names have changed. Bringing the discussion down to what an "authority" thinks or says on a given topic (real or apparent) can end it.

In the case of sugar, for example, arguments can be invoked from consumer organizations, ice cream manufacturers, well-known professors, experts, and celebrities. Leading experts in nutrition and dietetics, including Professor X, who has many years of experience and is a well-known, respected, and trusted authority, have concluded that sugar can be part of a healthy diet if consumed in moderation. Citing such a respected authority, the propagandist tries to convince that his or her position on sugar consumption is in line with the experts' opinion. And if the experts have opined, who are we to question their enlightened views? This can also be done instead of presenting factual arguments, supported by scientific literature. Or cite such, but providing a link to closed journals, that is, those paywalled, requiring a subscription when it is expected that there is little chance that anyone in the audience has a subscription or that they are able to factually analyze such a paper. Usually, few people have the time or qualifications to do so anyway (understandably), so an argument from authority generally gets the job done.

3.14.9 Exaggeration or minimization

Exaggeration or minimization (belittling) is a method of going to extremes and focusing on extreme issues, exaggerating (or downplaying) them. Exaggeration and minimization ensure the clarity of the message. One can only support or oppose something. The result of adding 1 + 2 is either 1 or 4—you have to advocate something, there is nothing in the middle (3). Exaggeration and belittling are extremes that can distort reality, the truth, that can mislead. Using these techniques, the propagandist seeks to influence, without presenting a balanced and evidence-based view. It is an uncritical outlook.

Since sugar is harmless in moderate amounts, concerns are greatly exaggerated. And that's it. This is trivializing the negative effects and consequences. They have no place here.

3.14.10 Flag-waving (identification with the group)

"Flag-waving" is an approach based on solidarity of groups. These can be interest groups, opinion groups, national groups, but also other groups with different characteristics. Basically, any group defined by some term, word, or perhaps even an acronym can be subsumed under this.

For example, since we're all one global family, and agriculture is a cornerstone worldwide, there's nothing wrong with traditional sugar beets and the sugar industry. No one from a foreign country will spit in our faces and push sweeteners or stevia on us, because we remember history well. The technique leverages emotional attachment to a unifying idea, even though that idea may be entirely unrelated to the topic at hand (here: the harmful effects of sugar).

In this international context, consuming sugar is not just about enjoying sweetness; it's a celebration of our global heritage and cultural identity. Traditional desserts from various cultures have for centuries brought families and communities together, strengthening our bonds and fostering a sense of unity. From beloved pastries like French croissants, Italian cannoli, Polish poppyseed cakes, Japanese mochi, and Indian gulab jamun, to Mexican churros, sugar plays a crucial role in our rich culinary traditions. Indulging in these sweet delights pays homage to our ancestors and preserves the essence of what it means to be part of the global community. Embracing sugar consumption becomes an act of global unity, reflecting our love for humanity. We can savor the pride associated with consuming sugar that is inclusive of the LGBTQ+ community! Just like the vibrant colors of the rainbow flag, symbolizing unity and integration, enjoying sugar celebrates diversity and love within the LGBTQ+ community. Let's immerse ourselves in the delightful world of sugar that invites everyone, regardless of sexual orientation or gender identity. Each bite of inclusive treats brings a sense of joy and acceptance, reminding us that love is sweet and knows no boundaries.

3.14.11 Slogans

Slogans are short statements meant to overly simplify a problem. They are a non-entry into a discussion, even if they pretend to be one. They are messages of a few sentences or even one sentence. When cleverly arranged, they can draw attention and even persuade people. These are well-known techniques used in political influence, including in totalitarian states, such as communist ones.[131]

Examples of slogans include "Vote for the Communist Party" or "Against Fascism!".[132] "Let's choose the future" is also a good slogan. And in the case of sugar, "Savor the sweet side of life."

3.14.12 Thought-terminating cliché

It's a very short message, requiring no creativity. The idea is to cut off discussion and discourage going into detail. Without knowledge of the subject (on the part of the propagandist but also on the part of the recipient), it is more effective to communicate in generalities.

In the case of sugar, doubts can be disposed of like this: "Sugar is just a natural part of life, so why worry? Enjoy the sweetness and forget about the rest." Enjoy it and have lots of health.

3.14.13 Doubt

The idea here is to create a situation and atmosphere of uncertainty—doubt—to introduce elements that challenge some views, perhaps to raise fears.

For years, we have been bombarded with alarming claims about the dangers of sugar. But isn't this just sowing fear? Many experts question the validity of these claims, suggesting that the alleged dangers of sugar may be exaggerated. Are we being misled by sensationalist headlines and selective studies? It's time to cast doubt on the anti-sugar crusade and examine a balanced perspective. Moderate sugar consumption, when part of a well-balanced diet and active lifestyle, can bring pleasure without compromising health.

3.14.14 Appeal to fear or prejudice

Danger ahead. This is an extreme playing on emotions, intended to arouse fear or prejudice. It's a technique that can all too easily lead to bad consequences, if only to aggression. Fear can be evolutionarily built-in (e.g., of wild animals, snakes), but it can also be acquired (e.g., of "others," some social group). It can arise in response to current news or reports (after reading that a crime has occurred in several parks in the country, we avoid going to the park). In particular, some people may like to be afraid (of social groups, financial crashes, cold or heat) or have a predisposition to it because of their history, but in the latter case you would need to have information about a specific person, so you wouldn't be able to use it on a wider scale. It seems to me, dear Reader, that it won't be difficult for you to identify a few things that people in your group or society more broadly fear. Building messages on these concepts would be an application of this method, which I would prefer not to write more about, because the content follows from the name itself.

I leave the preparation of a statement praising sugar using this method as an exercise for the Reader.

3.14.15 Bandwagon (and jumping on one)

It is worthwhile to ride in the same cart with others, you can jump on the moving cart or wagon (bandwagon) and fit into the existing trend. If a lot of people adhere to a certain view or idea, then surely they are true and right, there's something about them. Since *everyone* is doing or thinking something, maybe there is something in it and it should be accepted. This is herd thinking. In this technique, doubts are overlooked, taking for good measure that "others do it too" (and there are plenty of them). If people want to feel that they are actually part of such a whole (they are riding on the same boat of ideas), then social media is perfect for this: there are many people, repeating the same or similar opinions. The meeting place for such people is a demonstration or public protest.[133]

With sugar, the issue is clear: millions of people around the world consume sweets in large quantities. So, surely this is commendable, positive, and worthy of recommendation. Let us do the same! Right?

3.14.16 Repetition

Continuous repetition of the same thing, even in different words, wears out the mental cycles of the audience, especially when they don't notice what's happening, and engage in such a process, to their doom. Repetition is also an amplification of the message, because if something is repeated many times, even when it is defined in words only somewhat similar in meaning, it can build the impression of the weight of the arguments for something. This is a flawed logic.

It's now about sugar again. The sweet way to happiness! Enjoy the sweetness of life with sugar. Let sugar be your companion from morning to evening. Start your day with a cup of sweet coffee, enjoy a sweet break for an afternoon boost of sweet energy and end your day with a delicious dessert. Sugar, sugar, sugar—let this be the soundtrack of your day. Sucrose! Glucose! Fructose! Glycoside! Saccharin! Sugar is the key to unlocking a world of happiness. (On a side note, have a nice diabetes).

3.14.17 Reductio ad Hitlerum—guilt by association with something or someone evil

Bringing everything down to Hitler is also a propaganda opportunity. It is known that Hitler is considered pure evil, one of the worst people in history. So why not reduce something—people, views, opinions, you name it—to Hitler? Justify that something is in line with Hitler, his views, conduct, preferences. Since it's Hitler, it couldn't be worse. By the way, such a construction of the argument is not very reasonable. We all breathe, and there is no doubt that Hitler also breathed, but making an analogy to indicate some connection with Hitler is, after all, unjustified—it is pure absurdity (and it disarms this kind of "analogy"). No conclusion can be drawn from this.

In the case of sugar, one can refer to the "thought police," that is, anti-sugar views, and compare them to Hitler's actions.

It's an argument along the lines of: person X is bad/good, person X is for/against something; therefore, that something is bad/good.

In the case of sugar, it's also simple the other way. If Hitler liked sweets, then sweets and sugar are by definition bad.

3.14.18 Oversimplification

This is a very dangerous technique that may be effective. Somehow, it turned out that the world and real life are quite complicated. Many real problems, issues, and processes are very complex in nature. Few people can have the full picture of information or even the predisposition to analyze the whole big picture, and draw conclusions. What can be done here? Just simplify it all. However, many dangers lurk in simplification. Artificially and deceitfully simplifying, by presenting a certain distorted—precisely by over-simplification—picture, one can explain natural phenomena such as earthquakes or global climate change, as well as political processes, wars, etc. with simple conspiracy theories. For example, freemasons and Illuminati are behind wars, vaccines are harmful because the cousin of a father-in-law's daughter went to the hospital after being vaccinated (e.g., got hit by a car, thinking about the vaccination), and global climate change is not there, because it is now winter and in February, it is relatively (subjectively) cold outside the window, maybe even there is a slight frost, and on the other hand—in the summer it is hot and under some circumstances a fire broke out or there is a flood—so someone might want to try to oversimplify and present this (without a broader analysis of the situation) as evidence of climate change, too. This is also related to the previous technique—misrepresentation of data. All that is needed is to cut out—biased, selective—a certain piece of information from a complex report, news story, or scientific publication and use only it to justify a point of view or challenge another.

With regard to sugar, this is an ideal method—to present a simplistic and overly optimistic view. We can state that "sugar is simply a source of energy, and in addition, it makes you feel better." And that is true! The idea here is to focus on this single dimension, ignoring others, and thus demonstrate the benefits of sugar, arguing that it is unequivocal, beyond doubt. This ignores details such as long-term effects (weight gain, diseases, etc.).

If you are a propagandist, you certainly appreciate this technique.

3.14.19 Summary

These techniques can be used in practice. Both in propaganda or disinformation operations but also in other situations where there is a need to influence, to use methods of persuasion. I used one example—the consumption of sugar—to illustrate the applicability. In practice, of course, various methods can be used for different purposes, to present different information messages. The use of a single example may seem absurd and perhaps raises the suspicion that these techniques are not very effective. I do not believe that anyone can believe, based on the sentences quoted above, that consuming sugar in excess is healthy and harmless. The example only serves to demonstrate how to use these techniques. It is not meant to convince anyone of anything. Furthermore, the *sugar consumption examples* were generated with the help of LLM (GPT), which demonstrates that the tool can formulate statements with appropriate context and style. This shows that it can be built into a technical system for generating and propagating informational, propaganda content.

Another example is worth considering.

In the European Union, countries have been introducing a method of labeling products according to a unified nutritional scale—Nutri-Score.[134] It is to be mandatory in the EU. According to this measure, some unhealthy products, such as those containing harmful sugar (carbohydrates) can be labeled as good—category A, B. Others, on the other hand, such as salmon or olive oil, are labeled unhealthy—category D. The technique of referring to authority here has been taken to unprecedented heights. Everything is legal—this method was introduced by European law. What adds fuel to the fire of the matter is that this system is recommended by the European Commission and the World Health Organization. Of course, its use can make sense when comparing products in the same category (two salmon varieties, two different oils, and not oil vs. pudding vs. salmon)—that is its intention. That is, comparing salmon and pizza is not foreseen as appropriate by the designers of this system, while comparing a different assortment of pizzas (same food category) is. But who knows about it? There is no common knowledge and transparency here, so, for example, when comparing highly processed frozen pizza and olive oil, one can come to the absurd conclusion that it is the pizza that is healthier. There is no screaming information about this little detail on the front of the package. No disclaimer. In contrast, while sugar in excess is harmful, it can be consumed—but in moderation.

3.15 FOREIGN INTERFERENCE AND INFORMATION MANIPULATION

Foreign Information Manipulation Interference (FIMI)[135] is a formal term for disinformation or propaganda activities when the subject are external actors (e.g., States) and the object is the situation within a State (another). We are talking about intentional, not accidental actions. This chapter handles technical elements, and conflict or even war situations have their place in the following chapters. So why are we already considering this? Because it is possible to refer to formal analytical or classification categories in such an analysis.

Such a methodology is DISARM (DISinformation Analysis and Risk Management).[136] This classification can be considered as technically as possible, relevant to defense. However, one must look at the subject critically. While the methodology itself is interesting, it has some peculiarities, perhaps weaknesses. I will not overlook them. The DISARM framework is a methodology to classify different elements of an information operation in different phases. DISARM also highlights opportunities for defense. The methodology distinguishes[137] tactics and operation techniques.

3.15.1 Plan strategy

For example, in the initial plan strategy (tactic TA01) of the attacking party, there are various techniques, for example, such as dismiss, distort, distract, dismay, and divide, which could be used as part of an information campaign (when compared with the propaganda techniques discussed earlier, many of them may be used as part of this tactic). For example, "divide" involves positioning information activities in such a way as to build divisions within the social group under attack.

It is also pointed out that as part of this initial tactic, it is necessary to identify the targets, that is, who the audience is, which will help select information techniques. Already at this stage, one can notice an apparent, potential inadequacy of this DISARM methodology. Well, in order to defend against such action planning, one of the suggested defense techniques is to require to charge a fee for the use of the platform/social media (C00006). This doesn't look like a sensible advice, because the facts are that large groups of people gather on platforms that are not paid for. So, making such a requirement would be a shot in the foot from the point of view of a digital platform. As a side note, for those platforms that did offer payment options—did that improve things?

Still, in addition, charging for a service is something that could only be decided by the platform. Thus, this cannot be considered a useful, general, actionable recommendation, with more similar ones suggested as part of the DISARM framework. For example, another recommendation—the creation of a regulation (law) (C00012)—seems more sensible. But is it really? How would potential targets of disinformation, such as a city hall or a company, defend themselves by introducing new laws? Do they even have the initiative to do so? Such initiatives can be taken by States, meanwhile, in the European Union they could even be barred from introducing such laws (because this is already regulated by European law, for example). This recommendation, therefore, is also not very practical. It is not bad in itself, but it is reserved exclusively to the competence of state bodies (which is noted in the methodology). One should be aware that the DISARM framework mixes these different orders—companies, researchers, states matters, etc.

Another "exotic" recommendation is to outlaw news stations that broadcast on a 24-hour cycle (C00020). Perhaps this has some justification, since the minute-by-minute news aisle encourages quick reactions, outrage, controversy, and the reception of events when there is not yet full knowledge of them. But let's be serious: who would dare to impose such informational restrictions on the media? On freedom of speech? This also indicates that the DISARM authors are recommending censorship methods.

3.15.2 Plan objectives

Another tactic is planning objectives (TA02). This is an assessment that can determine how to act. An example technique might be the creation of grand narratives (T0003), stories designed to justify something or invalidate something else. The DISARM authors give an example of such a grand narrative: Russia as an (alleged) victim of outside attack. The rest of the communication should subsequently be built around this theme. This is the kind of element that would be expanded.

Here, the creators of this framework change the approach somewhat, as they indicate as one method of defense (C00029) the creation of fake websites designed to "counter-narrative" such a hostile message. That is, the creators consider taking "proactive" actions by applying information techniques.

3.15.3 Developing people

In this development, it's about the technique (T0007) of creating (building stories) fake social media accounts (but authenticated), for example, influencers and fake experts (technique T0009). These are information centers that will send content to the audience (targets), which also means, for example, pages of fake media that distribute crooked information. This, of course, can also be contracting the right company that already has both accounts and people.

Defense against it? Actually, one form of defense could be regulation (this will be discussed in Chapter 5) but also active prosecution and suppression (which digital platforms do). Another method could be to make it more difficult to set up accounts: requiring verification of phone number, credit card, etc.

3.15.4 Developing the network

Since we already have "developed" people, or rather their profiles with some background of previous activity, or profiles of "experts" and influencers, they can create networks composed also of ordinary people who have been persuaded to do something, for example, they believe in some conspiracy theory, are against something, in opposition to recognized standards and information, because that is their preference.

How to counter this? By targeting the center of such a network (i.e., key profiles/persons), perhaps targeting people individually with the message, but also engaging other well-known people, such as influencers (C00009), to help defuse such fake campaigns and train them to spot abuses or misuses.

Another interesting tactic could be to take control of someone's social media accounts and use them for disinformation, and propaganda (T0011). Such accounts already exist (they have an audience, followers, a certain reputation), so it's a tempting target. Such actions have already targeted experts and journalists, and well-known websites.

One of the defense tactics would be to move away from social media, to abandon it (C00056). This is yet another instance where this framework proposes unrealistic actions. This highlights that the framework must be approached with caution.

3.15.5 Micro-targeting

Within the framework of this tactic (TA05), one can list many techniques for reaching audiences with precision. From my perspective, the best tool for this has always been advertising networks. Here, the creation of websites to generate finances, funding campaigns, and acquiring fake ad clicks are also mentioned.

Singling this out as a separate tactic is not the most appropriate when done in such a broad way, in addition to confusing the operational goals with the end goals (so to speak) of generating money.

3.15.6 Developing content

We are talking about audience-directed content. It can be developed in many ways—either with the help of humans or with the help of automatons. This has already been explained earlier. Here, we can note the mentioned technique of creating memes—graphics with an accompanying description, sometimes funny, sometimes shocking, controversial, iconoclastic—to express some ideas quickly and efficiently. We have seen the use of memes on many occasions, including during the war in Ukraine (by both sides, more on which in Chapter 7).

3.15.7 Channel selection

The operation is all about reaching the audience. The choice of the best channel is dictated solely by this. There is no point in using channels without an audience (users). A channel can be radio, TV, newspapers, and from a modern perspective—digital platforms like YouTube, Instagram, LinkedIn, and Twitter/X. The people are there, it's all about reaching them.

The simplest defense method imaginable is content moderation (C00107), it is even suggested to buy more ads than the adversary (C00105)—that is, cause information overload and proactive measures.

3.15.8 Pumping

It's all about engaging people and the media—getting into an argument, debating when messages are exchanged, and demanding "insurmountable" proof for some thesis (T0040). For example, demanding that it be proven "beyond a reasonable doubt" that vaccines do not cause complications. Or (T0042) referring to the "seed kernel of truth," that is, juggling factual and bogus information in such a way as to reverse the audience's prior perception of things. Here, false experts, indicated in the previous point, can also be helpful, although the possibility of questioning the authority of such an "expert" will immediately arise.

One of the suggested methods of defense (C00112) is particularly bizarre: it is a demand for assurances that someone proves that they are not a propagandist or part of an information operation. In this sense, this methodology for classifying and fighting propaganda itself recommends exactly the same methods (fighting fire with fire).

3.15.9 Exposure

The methodology also lists active actions targeting specific individuals—influencers, experts, and public figures—in such a way as to discredit these innocent people. This includes harassment of users.

A defense could be content moderation (C00122), for example.

3.15.10 Physical activities

These activities involve getting out of the information or virtual zone by organizing demonstrations, protests, riots, etc.

3.15.11 Persistence

Persistence is related to creating content in such a way that it can't be easily removed from platforms or from the network. It is, therefore, redundancy—storing information in multiple places.

3.15.12 Measuring efficiency

This is very useful in information operations. Since some action is being taken, it is useful to determine what effect it is having. Same may be useful for defense, by the way.

3.15.13 Summary

Preparing an information operation requires considering many technical and social issues. You can use technology (automated targeting and display ads, social media accounts, bots) and people (building interest networks and "enthusiasts") to do this. The DISARM framework mentions such elements and in places does it very well.

Unfortunately, some of the items (suggested defense tactics) are, to put it mildly, unrealistic, making it unhelpful to even post them as part of such a methodology. For example, one recommends censorship (C00122). This is about content moderation, but the word "censorship" (C00016) was used. I have already mentioned other examples of problematic elements. Nevertheless, the methodology is used (selected aspects of it) and various official reports refer to it. It is worth exercising caution here and selecting some solutions, certainly not all.

3.15.14 Returning to FIMI

The FIMI methodology describes the characteristics of an operation, and within that provides evaluation criteria: severity (very low, low, medium, high), duration (short, medium, long), impact, and motivation. Determining such characteristics can be tricky, for many reasons.

For example, in determining the degree of importance (the effect of an event), it is taken into account how many viewers saw the message. However, it is not clear how appropriate this criterion is as a measure of effect, because whether a one-time message is seen by 100 people or 1000 people, maybe even a million—it actually makes little difference if it has no real effect, or impact. After all, it is not the case that after exposure, someone is "instantly" "infected" and becomes a propaganda-programmed, unmotivated robot. This is especially not the case in pluralistic societies, where people do not live in a totalitarian world dominated by propaganda. However, no "local" cultural, social, or political conditions have been taken into account (difficult to do on a global scale). In other cases, seeing a message only one time may bring an effect, if the source is universally seen as credible.

These criteria of seriousness (validity) function a bit better in the "medium" case, understood as a non-information effect (e.g., people taking to the streets in peaceful demonstrations), and in the "high" case (attacks on people, destruction of property, riots). In this sense, in the "low" or "very low" case, there are no effects at all.

Various other approaches can also be used to detect propaganda, such as SCAME[138] (Source-Content-Audience-Media-Effect analysis). This is an analysis of sources (who is behind it, what is used in propaganda), content (what is it: multimedia, quality, tailored to the audience), audience (who is the target group), media (why were particular information channels used), effects (what are the effects of these activities).

3.16 SUMMARY

This chapter was about technical aspects, and ultimately it is worth noting the close relationship between cyberoperations (achieving cyber, intelligence, or military effects, which may require breaking security, hacking information systems, etc.) and information operations. On the subject of cyber security, I recommend another book I authored, *Philosophy of Cybersecurity* (2023), which contains many helpful explanations that go well with the content in this (and other) chapters.

The two dimensions (cyber, info) are quite closely related and can even sometimes support each other. For example, cyber operations can give access to platforms through which various types of information can be spread or the source of the messages can be masked.[139]

Techniques are constantly evolving. In the past, much attention was paid to radio. This is understandable, as it was an important medium for disseminating information. Channels and technologies are constantly evolving. In particular, computing and information processing techniques have introduced major changes and are leading to more of them. Therefore, one must constantly explore new possibilities and pay attention to channels, techniques, technologies, and potential solutions. It is necessary to study what is used in the broad practical range of applications, not only for evident propaganda, for example, state or military propaganda.

NOTES

1 Department of the Army, *Psychological Operations Tactics, Techniques, and Procedures*, Field Manual No. 3-05.301 (FM 33-1-1) MCRP 3-40.6, December 31, 2003, https://irp.fas.org/doddir/army/fm3-05-301.pdf.

2 J.A. Alic, *The dual use of technology: Concepts and policies*, Technology in Society 1994, vol. 16, no. 2, pp. 155–172.

3 B.J. Hancock, *Memetic warfare: The future of war*, Military Intelligence 2010, vol. 41.

4 A. Kingdon, *The meme is the method: Examining the power of the image within extremist propaganda*, in *Researching Cybercrimes: Methodologies, Ethics, and Critical Approaches*, ed. by A. Lavorgna, T.J. Holt, Palgrave Macmillan, Cham, London 2021, pp. 301–322.

5 S. Brinker, *Martec's law: Technology changes exponentially, organizations change logarithmically*, Chief Marketing Technologist, June 13, 2013, https://chiefmartec.com/2013/06/martecs-law-technology-changes-exponentially-organizations-change-logarithmically/.

6 D. Wiljer, Z. Hakim, *Developing an artificial intelligence-enabled health care practice: Rewiring health care professions for better care*, Journal of Medical Imaging and Radiation Sciences 2019, vol. 50, no. 4, pp. 8–14.

7 E. Ferrara, O. Varol, C. Davis, F. Menczer, A. Flammini, *The rise of social bots*, Communications of the ACM 2016, vol. 59, no. 7, pp. 96–104.

8 F.N. Ribeiro, K. Saha, M. Babaei, L. Henrique, J. Messias, F. Benevenuto, O. Goga, K.P. Gummadi, E.M. Redmiles, *On microtargeting socially divisive ads: A case study of Russia-linked ad campaigns on Facebook*, in *Proceedings of the Conference on Fairness, Accountability, and Transparency*, Association for Computing Machinery, New York 2019, pp. 140–149.

9 A. Lieto, D. Moro, F. Devoti, C. Parera, V. Lipari, P. Bestagini, S. Tubaro, *'Hello? Who am I talking to?': A shallow CNN approach for human vs. bot speech classification*, in *ICASSP 2019–2019 IEEE International Conference on Acoustics, Speech and Signal Processing (ICASSP), 12–17 May 2019*, Brighton, UK 2019, pp. 2577–2581.

10 E. Wenger, M. Bronckers, C. Cianfarani, J. Cryan, A. Sha, H. Zheng, B.Y. Zhao, *'Hello, It's Me': Deep learning-based speech synthesis attacks in the real world*, in *Proceedings of the 2021 ACM SIGSAC Conference on Computer and Communications Security*, November 2021, pp. 235–251.

11 See https://pptr.dev/; https://github.com/puppeteer/puppeteer.

12 S. Wiefling, N. Gruschka, L. Lo Iacono, *Even turing should sometimes not be able to tell: Mimicking humanoid usage behavior for exploratory studies of online services*, in *Secure IT Systems: 24th Nordic Conference, NordSec 2019, Aalborg, Denmark, November 18–20, 2019, Proceedings 24*, Springer 2019, pp. 188–203.

13 Puppeteer-extra-plugin-stealth, https://www.npmjs.com/package/puppeteer-extra-plugin-stealth.

14 Y. Govil, L. Wang, J. Rexford, *MIMIQ: Masking IPs with migration in QUIC*, in *10th USENIX Workshop on Free and Open Communications on the Internet (FOCI)*, 2020, https://www.usenix.org/system/files/foci20-paper-govil.pdf.

15 K. Shu, A. Bhattacharjee, F. Alatawi, T.H. Nazer, K. Ding, M. Karami, H. Liu, *Combating disinformation in a social media age*, WIREs: Data Mining and Knowledge Discovery 2020, vol. 10, no. 6, e1385.

16 G. Spitale, N. Biller-Andorno, F. Germani, *AI model GPT-3 (dis)informs us better than humans*, Science Advances 2023, vol. 9, no. 26, eadh1850.

17 R. Tang, Y.N. Chuang, X. Hu, *The Science Of Detecting LLM-generated Texts*, February 4, 2023, https://arxiv.org/pdf/2303.07205.pdf.

18 H.S. Heidenreich, J.R. Williams, *The earth is flat and the sun is not a star: The susceptibility of GPT-2 to universal adversarial triggers*, in *Proceedings of the 2021 AAAI/ACM Conference on AI, Ethics, and Society*, July 2021, pp. 566–573.

19 A. Garcia-Silva, C. Berrio, J.M. Gómez-Pérez, *An empirical study on pre-trained embeddings and language models for bot detection*, in *Proceedings of the 4th Workshop on Representation Learning for NLP (RepL4NLP-2019)*, August 2019, pp. 148–155.

20 V.S. Sadasivan, A. Kumar, S. Balasubramanian, W. Wang, S. Feizi, *Can AI-generated Text be Reliably Detected?*, March 17, 2023, https://arxiv.org/pdf/2303.11156.pdf.

21 S.J. Terp, P. Breuer, *DISARM: a framework for analysis of disinformation campaigns*, in *2022 IEEE Conference on Cognitive and Computational Aspects of Situation Management (CogSIMA)*, June 2022, pp. 1–8.

22 J.A. Tucker, A. Guess, P. Barberá, C. Vaccari, A. Siegel, S. Sanovich, D. Stukal, B. Nyhan, *Social Media, Political Polarization, and Political Disinformation: A Review of the Scientific Literature*, March 19, 2018, http://dx.doi.org/10.2139/ssrn.3144139.

23 S. Gaonkar, N.F. Dessai, J. Costa, A. Borkar, S. Aswale, P. Shetgaonkar, *A survey on botnet detection techniques*, in *2020 International Conference on Emerging Trends in Information Technology and Engineering (ic-ETITE)*, February 2020, pp. 1–6.

24 S. Cresci, *A decade of social bot detection*, Communications of the ACM 2020, vol. 63, no. 10, pp. 72–83.

25 UK Home Office, *Preventing the use of SIM farms for fraud: Consultation (accessible)*, May 3, 2023, https://www.gov.uk/government/consultations/preventing-the-use-of-sim-farms-for-fraud/preventing-the-use-of-sim-farms-for-fraud-consultation-accessible.

26 J.C. Ong, J.V. Cabañes, *When disinformation studies meets production studies: Social identities and moral justifications in the political trolling industry*, International Journal of Communication 2019, vol. 13, pp. 5771–5790.

27 A. Giachanou, X. Zhang, A. Barrón-Cedeño, O. Koltsova, P. Rosso, *Online information disorder: Fake news, bots and trolls*, International Journal of Data Science and Analytics 2022, vol. 13, no. 4, pp. 265–269.

28 R. Lee, P. Luttrell, M. Johnson, J. Garnaut, *TikTok, ByteDance, and their Ties to the Chinese Communist Party*, March 14, 2023, https://www.aph.gov.au/DocumentStore.ashx?id=a7e2a076-1112-4414-ba0f-f129e0cd39fe&subId=735418.

29 W. Yaqub, O. Kakhidze, M.L. Brockman, N. Memon, S. Patil, *Effects of credibility indicators on social media news sharing intent*, in *Proceedings of the 2020 Chi Conference on Human Factors in Computing Systems*, April 2020, pp. 1–14.

30 G. Pennycook, A. Bear, E.T. Collins, D.G. Rand, *The implied truth effect: Attaching warnings to a subset of fake news headlines increases perceived accuracy of headlines without warnings*, Management Science 2020, vol. 66, no. 11, pp. 4944–4957.

31 G. Pennycook, Z. Epstein, M. Mosleh, A.A. Arechar, D. Eckles, D.G. Rand, *Shifting attention to accuracy can reduce misinformation online*, Nature 2021, vol. 592, no. 7855, pp. 590–595.

32 M. Yesilada, S. Lewandowsky, *A Systematic Review: The YouTube Recommender System and Pathways to Problematic Content*, June 2, 2021, https://osf.io/preprints/psyarxiv/6pv5c/.

33 J.B. Schmitt, D. Rieger, O. Rutkowski, J. Ernst, *Counter-messages as prevention or promotion of extremism! The potential role of YouTube: Recommendation algorithms*, Journal of Communication 2018, vol. 68, no. 4, pp. 780–808.

34 J. Lasser, S.T. Aroyehun, A. Simchon, F. Carrella, D. Garcia, S. Lewandowsky, *Social media sharing of low-quality news sources by political elites*, PNAS Nexus 2022, vol. 1, no. 4, pgad158.

35 M. Mosleh, D.G. Rand, *Measuring exposure to misinformation from political elites on Twitter*, Nature Communications 2022, vol. 13, no. 1, p. 7144.

36 Y. Li, X. Yang, P. Sun, H. Qi, S. Lyu, *Celeb-DF: A large-scale challenging dataset for deepfake forensics*, in *Proceedings of the IEEE/CVF Conference on Computer Vision and Pattern Recognition*, 2020, pp. 3207–3216, https://openaccess.thecvf.com/content_CVPR_2020/papers/Li_Celeb-DF_A_Large-Scale_Challenging_Dataset_for_DeepFake_Forensics_CVPR_2020_paper.pdf.
37 C.S. Pinhanez, G.H. Flores, M.A. Vasconcelos, M. Qiao, N. Linck, R. de Paula, Y.J. Ong, *Towards a New Science of Disinformation*, 2022, https://arxiv.org/pdf/2204.01489.pdf.
38 P. Yu, Z. Xia, J. Fei, Y. Lu, *A survey on deepfake video detection*, IET Biometrics 2021, vol. 10, no. 6, pp. 607–624.
39 B. Dolhansky, J. Bitton, B. Pflaum, J. Lu, R. Howes, M. Wang, C.C. Ferrer, *The Deepfake Detection Challenge (DfDC). Preview dataset*, June 12, 2020, https://arxiv.org/pdf/2006.07397.pdf.
40 P. Gupta, K. Chugh, A. Dhall, R. Subramanian, *The eyes know it: Fakeet-an eye-tracking database to understand deepfake perception*, in *Proceedings of the 2020 International Conference on Multimodal Interaction*, October 2020, pp. 519–527.
41 M. Boháček, H. Farid, *Protecting President Zelenskyy Against Deep Fakes*, June 24, 2022, https://arxiv.org/pdf/2206.12043.pdf.
42 M. Groh, Z. Epstein, C. Firestone, R. Picard, *Deepfake detection by human crowds, machines, and machine-informed crowds*, Proceedings of the National Academy of Sciences 2022, vol. 119, no. 1.
43 M. Gambini, T. Fagni, F. Falchi, M. Tesconi, *On pushing DeepFake Tweet Detection capabilities to the limits*, in *14th ACM Web Science Conference 2022*, June 2022, pp. 154–163.
44 D. Gamage, K. Sasahara, J. Chen, *The emergence of deepfakes and its societal implications: A systematic review*, in *Conference for Truth and Trust Online 2021*, October 2021, pp. 28–39, https://truthandtrustonline.com/tto-2021/accepted-talks-and-papers-2021/.
45 V. Asnani, X. Yin, T. Hassner, X. Liu, *Reverse Engineering of Generative Models: Inferring Model Hyperparameters from Generated Images*, June 15, 2021, https://ai.facebook.com/blog/reverse-engineering-generative-model-from-a-single-deepfake-image/.
46 M. Muna, *Technological Arming: Is Deepfake the Next Digital Weapon*, UC Berkley, May 11, 2020.
47 D.L. Byman, C. Gao, C. Meserole, V.S. Subrahmanian, *Deepfakes and International Conflict*, January 2023, https://www.brookings.edu/articles/deepfakes-and-international-conflict/.
48 T. Dobber, N. Metoui, D. Trilling, N. Helberger, C. de Vreese, *Do (microtargeted) deepfakes have real effects on political attitudes?* The International Journal of Press/Politics 2021, vol. 26, no. 1, pp. 69–91.
49 F. Shahid, S. Kamath, A. Sidotam, V. Jiang, A. Batino, A. Vashistha, '*It matches my worldview*': *Examining perceptions and attitudes around fake videos*, in *Proceedings of the 2022 CHI Conference on Human Factors in Computing Systems*, April 2022, pp. 1–15.
50 F. Shahid, S. Kamath, A. Sidotam, V. Jiang, A. Batino, A. Vashistha, '*It matches my worldview*': *Examining perceptions and attitudes around fake videos*, in *Proceedings of the 2022 CHI Conference on Human Factors in Computing Systems*, April 2022, p. 8.
51 F. Shahid, S. Kamath, A. Sidotam, V. Jiang, A. Batino, A. Vashistha, '*It matches my worldview*': *Examining perceptions and attitudes around fake videos*, in *Proceedings of the 2022 CHI Conference on Human Factors in Computing Systems*, April 2022, p. 8.
52 *Late Indonesian President Suharto Appears as a Deepfake.* (January 12, 2024). The Sydney Morning Herald. https://www.smh.com.au/world/late-indonesian-president-suharto-appears-as-a-deepfake-20240112-p5ewv8.html.
53 *Updates to Political Content Policy (September 2023)*, Google, Advertising Policies Help, September 2023, https://support.google.com/adspolicy/answer/13755910?hl=en&ref_topic=29265.
54 *Updates to Political Content Policy (September 2023)*, Google, Advertising Policies Help, September 2023, https://support.google.com/adspolicy/answer/13755910?hl=en&ref_topic=29265.
55 B. Horne, S. Adali, *This just in: Fake news packs a lot in title, uses simpler, repetitive content in text body, more similar to satire than real news*, in *Proceedings of the International AAAI Conference on Web and Social Media*, May 2017, pp. 759–766, https://ojs.aaai.org/index.php/ICWSM/article/view/14976/14826.
56 C. Carrasco-Farré, *The fingerprints of misinformation: How deceptive content differs from reliable sources in terms of cognitive effort and appeal to emotions*, Humanities and Social Sciences Communications 2022, vol. 9, no. 1, pp. 1–18.

57 C. Carrasco-Farré, *The fingerprints of misinformation: How deceptive content differs from reliable sources in terms of cognitive effort and appeal to emotions*, Humanities and Social Sciences Communications 2022, vol. 9, no. 1, pp. 1–18.
58 C. Carrasco-Farré, *The fingerprints of misinformation: How deceptive content differs from reliable sources in terms of cognitive effort and appeal to emotions*, but compare with studies with the opposite result (based on a smaller scale of data) – M. Tavakoli, H. Alani, G. Burel, *On the readability of misinformation in comparison to the truth*, in *Proceedings of the Test2Story'23 Workshop, Dublin*, April 2, 2023, https://ceur-ws.org/Vol-3370/paper6.pdf.
59 J. Bartlett, *Populism, social media and democratic strain*, in *European Populism and Winning the Immigration Debate*, ed. C. Sandelind, Falun 2014, pp. 99–114.
60 S. Engesser, N. Ernst, F. Esser, F. Büchel, *Populism and social media: How politicians spread a fragmented ideology*, Information, Communication & Society 2017, vol. 20, no. 8, pp. 1109–1126.
61 C. François, *Actors, Behaviors, Content: A disinformation ABC*, September 20, 2019, https://www.ivir.nl/publicaties/download/ABC_Framework_2019_Sept_2019.pdf.
62 P.N. Howard, B. Kollanyi, *Bots, #StrongerIn, and #Brexit: Computational propaganda during the UK-EU referendum*, June 20, 2016, https://arxiv.org/ftp/arxiv/papers/1606/1606.06356.pdf.
63 V. Ng, S. Li, *Multimodal Propaganda Processing*, February 17, 2023, https://arxiv.org/pdf/2302.08709.pdf.
64 V. Ng, S. Li, *Multimodal Propaganda Processing*, February 17, 2023, https://arxiv.org/pdf/2302.08709.pdf.
65 J.A. Goldstein, J. Chao, S. Grossman, A. Stamos, M. Tomz, *Can AI write persuasive propaganda?* April 8, 2023, https://osf.io/preprints/socarxiv/fp87b/.
66 E. Bagdasaryan, V. Shmatikov, *Spinning Language Models: Risks of propaganda-as-a-service and countermeasures*, in *2022 IEEE Symposium on Security and Privacy (SP)*, May 2022, pp. 769–786.
67 J.A. Goldstein, G. Sastry, M. Musser, R. DiResta, M. Gentzel, K. Sedova, *Generative Language Models and Automated Influence Operations: Emerging Threats and Potential Mitigations*, January 10, 2023, https://arxiv.org/pdf/2301.04246.pdf.
68 S. Gunasekar, Y. Zhang, J. Aneja, C.C.T. Mendes, A. Del Giorno, S. Gopi, M. Javaheripi, P.Kauffmann, G. de Rosa, O. Saarikivi, A. Salim, S. Shah, H.S. Behl, X. Wang, S. Bubeck, R. Eldan, A.T. Kalai, Y.T. Lee, Y. Li, *Textbooks are All You Need*, June 20, 2023, https://arxiv.org/pdf/2306.11644.pdf.
69 M. Shanahan, *Talking about Large Language Models*, December 7, 2022, https://arxiv.org/pdf/2212.03551.pdf.
70 J.A. Goldstein, G. Sastry et al., *Generative Language Models....*
71 E. Bagdasaryan, V. Shmatikov, *Spinning Language Models,...*
72 C.Y. Hsieh, C.L. Li, C.K. Yeh, H. Nakhost, Y. Fujii, A. Ratner, R. Krishna, C.Y. Lee, T. Pfister, *Distilling Step-by-Step! Outperforming larger language models with less training data and smaller model sizes*, May 3, 2023, https://arxiv.org/pdf/2305.02301.pdf.
73 *WormGPT – The Generative AI Tool Cybercriminals are Using to Launch BEC Attacks*, July 13, 2023, https://slashnext.com/blog/wormgpt-the-generative-ai-tool-cybercriminals-are-using-to-launch-business-email-compromise-attacks/.
74 *WormGPT – The Generative AI Tool Cybercriminals are Using to Launch BEC Attacks*, July 13, 2023, https://slashnext.com/blog/wormgpt-the-generative-ai-tool-cybercriminals-are-using-to-launch-business-email-compromise-attacks/.
75 A Tech Accord to Combat Deceptive Use of AI in 2024 Elections. 2014. Retrieved 17 February 2024, https://www.aielectionsaccord.com/uploads/2024/02/A-Tech-Accord-to-Combat-Deceptive-Use-of-AI-in-2024-Elections.FINAL_.pdf.
76 A. Liu, Z. Wu, J. Michael, A. Suhr, P. West, A. Koller, S. Swayamdipta, N.A. Smith, Y. Choi, *We're Afraid Language Models aren't Modeling Ambiguity*, April 27, 2023, https://arxiv.org/pdf/2304.14399.pdf.
77 H. Wang, X. Luo, W. Wang, X. Yan, *Bot or Human? Detecting ChatGPT Imposters with a Single Question*, May 16, 2023, https://arxiv.org/pdf/2305.06424.pdf.
78 H. Wang, X. Luo, W. Wang, X. Yan, *Bot or Human? Detecting ChatGPT Imposters with a Single Question*, May 16, 2023, https://arxiv.org/pdf/2305.06424.pdf.

79 H. Wang, X. Luo, W. Wang, X. Yan, *Bot or Human? Detecting ChatGPT Imposters with a Single Question*, May 16, 2023, https://arxiv.org/pdf/2305.06424.pdf.
80 M.R. Gordon, D. Volz, *Russian Disinformation Campaign Aims to Undermine Confidence in Pfizer, Other COVID-19 Vaccines, US Officials Say*, March 7, 2010, https://www.wsj.com/articles/russian-disinformation-campaign-aims-to-undermine-confidence-in-pfizer-other-covid-19-vaccines-u-s-officials-say-11615129200.
81 S. Gunitsky, *Democracies can't blame Putin for their disinformation problem*, Foreign Policy, April 21, 2020, https://foreignpolicy.com/2020/04/21/democracies-disinformation-russia-china-homegrown/.
82 C. de Saint Laurent, G. Murphy, K. Hegarty, C.M. Greene, *Measuring the effects of misinformation exposure and beliefs on behavioral intentions: A COVID-19 vaccination study*, Cognitive Research: Principles and Implications 2022, vol. 7, no. 1, p. 87.
83 C. de Saint Laurent, G. Murphy, K. Hegarty, C.M. Greene, *Measuring the effects of misinformation exposure and beliefs on behavioral intentions: A COVID-19 vaccination study*, Cognitive Research: Principles and Implications 2022, vol. 7, no. 1, p. 87.
84 M.R. Holman, M.C. Schneider, K. Pondel, *Gender targeting in political advertisements*, Political Research Quarterly 2015, vol. 68, no. 4, pp. 816–829.
85 I. Nenadic, K. Bleyer-Simon, *Issue-based advertising*, RSC Research Report 2021, https://cadmus.eui.eu/handle/1814/74326.
86 C. Erfort, *Gendered targeting: Do parties tailor their campaign ads to women?* March 20, 2023, https://osf.io/5vs9b.
87 M.R. Holman, M.C. Schneider, K. Pondel, *Gender targeting …*
88 H.M. Johnson, C.M. Seifert, *Sources of the continued influence effect: When misinformation in memory affects later inferences*, Journal of Experimental Psychology: Learning, Memory, and Cognition 1994, vol. 20, no. 6, p. 1420.
89 S. Lewandowsky, U.K. Ecker, C.M. Seifert, N. Schwarz, J. Cook, *Misinformation and its correction: Continued influence and successful debiasing*, Psychological Science in the Public Interest 2012, vol. 13, no. 3, pp. 106–131.
90 *Notifications Overview*, https://developer.android.com/develop/ui/views/notifications.
91 *Notifications API Standard*, https://notifications.spec.whatwg.org/; *Push API*, https://w3c.github.io/push-api/.
92 M. Thomson, E. Damaggio, B. Raymor, *Generic Event Delivery using HTTP push RFC 8030*, https://datatracker.ietf.org/doc/rfc8030.
93 *Opinion: Websites Ask for Permissions and Attack Forgiveness*, https://www.wired.com/story/opinion-websites-ask-for-permissions-and-attack-forgiveness/.
94 D. Das, *Pakistani Cab App Bykea Hacked. Indians the Usual Suspects*, June 13, 2023, https://theprint.in/go-to-pakistan/pakistani-taxi-app-bykea-hacked-indians-the-usual-suspects/1625386/.
95 *Browser Notification Spam Tricks Clicks for Ad Revenue*, August 2, 2021, https://www.trendmicro.com/en_no/research/21/g/browser-notification-spam-tricks-clicks-for-ad-revenue.html.
96 *How push notifications are abused to deliver fraudulent links*, July 22, 2022, https://blogs.vmware.com/security/2022/07/how-push-notifications-are-abused-to-deliver-fraudulent-links.html.
97 R.G. Kula, C. Treude, *In war and peace: the impact of world politics on software ecosystems*, in *Proceedings of the 30th ACM Joint European Software Engineering Conference and Symposium on the Foundations of Software Engineering*, November 2022, pp. 1600–1604.
98 See https://nvd.nist.gov/vuln/detail/cve-2022-23812.
99 NPM, *Peacenotwar*, https://www.npmjs.com/package/peacenotwar.
100 *Terraform Module*, https://registry.terraform.io/modules/terraform-aws-modules/eks/aws/18.10.0.
101 M. Guerini, C. Strapparava, G. Ozbal, *Exploring text virality in social networks*, in *Proceedings of the International AAAI Conference on Web and Social Media*, March 25, 2011, https://arxiv.org/pdf/1203.5502.pdf.
102 L. Weng, F. Menczer, Y.Y. Ahn, *Virality prediction and community structure in social networks*, Scientific Reports 2013, vol. 3, no. 1, pp. 1–6.
103 S.B. Naeem, R. Bhatti, A. Khan, *An exploration of how fake news is taking over social media and putting public health at risk*, Health Information & Libraries Journal 2021, vol. 38, no. 2, pp. 143–149.

104 A. Gruzd, P. Mai, *Going viral: How a single tweet spawned a COVID-19 conspiracy theory on Twitter*, Big Data & Society 2020, vol. 7, no. 2. https://doi.org/10.1177/2053951720938405.
105 A. Gruzd, P. Mai, *Going viral: How a single tweet spawned a COVID-19 conspiracy theory on Twitter*, Big Data & Society 2020, vol. 7, no. 2. https://doi.org/10.1177/2053951720938405.
106 S.J. Taylor, L. Muchnik, M. Kumar, S. Aral, *Identity effects in social media*, Nature Human Behaviour 2023, vol. 7, no. 1, pp. 27–37.
107 S. Chaiken, *Heuristic versus systematic information processing and the use of source versus message cues in persuasion*, Journal of Personality and Social Psychology 1980, vol. 39, no. 5, p. 752.
108 A. Narayanan, *Understanding Social Media Recommendation Algorithms*, March 9, 2023, https://knightcolumbia.org/content/understanding-social-media-recommendation-algorithms.
109 *Prepared Remarks of Commissioner Alvaro M. Bedoya, Federal Trade Commission*, February 7, 2023, https://www.ftc.gov/system/files/ftc_gov/pdf/national-academies-speech-bedoya.pdf.
110 L. Thorburn, P. Bengani, J. Stray, *How Platform Recommenders Work*, January 20, 2022, https://medium.com/understanding-recommenders/how-platform-recommenders-work-15e260d9a15a.
111 B. Smith, *How TikTok Reads Your Mind*, December 5, 2021, https://www.nytimes.com/2021/12/05/business/media/tiktok-algorithm.html.
112 S. Van Der Linden, *Misinformation: Susceptibility, spread, and interventions to immunize the public*, Nature Medicine 2022, vol. 28, no. 3, pp. 460–467.
113 A. Narayanan, *Introducing Visualizing Virality*, May 8, 2023, https://knightcolumbia.org/blog/introducing-visualizing-virality;https://virality.brown.columbia.edu/.
114 P.M. Dahlgren, *A critical review of filter bubbles and a comparison with selective exposure*, Nordicom Review 2021, vol. 42, no. 1, pp. 15–33.
115 S. Flaxman, S. Goel, J.M. Rao, *Filter bubbles, echo chambers, and online news consumption*, Public Opinion Quarterly 2016, vol. 80, pp. 298–320.
116 S. Flaxman, S. Goel, J.M. Rao, *Filter bubbles, echo chambers, and online news consumption*, Public Opinion Quarterly 2016, vol. 80, pp. 298–320.
117 M.M. El-Bermawy, *Your Filter Bubble is Destroying Democracy*, November 18, 2016, https://www.wired.com/2016/11/filter-bubble-destroying-democracy/.
118 Wilde, G. From Panic to Policy: The Limits of Foreign Propaganda and the Foundations of an Effective Response.
119 C. François, *Actors* ....
120 J. Bartlett, *Populism* ....
121 J. Bartlett, *Populism* ....
122 J. Bartlett, *Populism* ....
123 V. Vellani, S. Zheng, D. Ercelik, T. Sharot, *The illusory truth effect leads to the spread of misinformation*, Cognition 2023, vol. 236, Article no. 105421.
124 H.R. Arkes, C. Hackett, L. Boehm, *The generality of the relation between familiarity and judged validity*, Journal of Behavioral Decision Making 1989, vol. 2, no. 2, pp. 81–94.
125 S. Van Der Linden, *Misinformation* ....
126 S. Lewandowsky, U.K. Ecker, et al., *Misinformation and its correction* ....
127 R.C. Chang, C.M. Lai, K.L. Chang, C.H. Lin, *Dataset of Propaganda Techniques of the State-sponsored Information Operation of the People's Republic of China*, June 14, 2021, https://arxiv.org/pdf/2106.07544.pdf.
128 C. Miller, *Propaganda Analysis*, New York 1937.
129 D. Dimitrov, B.B. Ali, S. Shaar, F. Alam, F. Silvestri, H. Firooz, P. Nakov, G. Da San Martino, *Detecting Propaganda Techniques in Memes*, August 7, 2021, https://arxiv.org/pdf/2109.08013.pdf.
130 C. Miller, *Propaganda Analysis*, New York 1937.
131 H.D. Lasswell, D. Blumenstock, *The technique of slogans in communist propaganda*, Psychiatry 1938, vol. 1, no. 4, pp. 505–520.
132 H.D. Lasswell, D. Blumenstock, *The technique of slogans in communist propaganda*, Psychiatry 1938, vol. 1, no. 4, pp. 505–520.
133 R. Marlin, *Propaganda and the Ethics of Persuasion*, Broadview Press, Peterborough 2013.

134 Regulation (EU) No. 1169/2011 of the European Parliament and of the Council of October 25, 2011 on the provision of food information to consumers, amending Regulations (EC) No. 1924/2006 and (EC) No. 1925/2006 of the European Parliament and of the Council, and repealing Commission Directive 87/250/EEC, Council Directive 90/496/EEC, Commission Directive 1999/10/EC, Directive 2000/13/EC of the European Parliament and of the Council, Commission Directives 2002/67/EC and 2008/5/EC, and Commission Regulation (EC) No. 608/2004, Official Journal of the EU L 304 of 22.11.2011, p. 18, as amended.
135 *Foreign Information Manipulation Interference (FIMI) and Cybersecurity – Threat Landscape (ENISA)*, https://www.enisa.europa.eu/publications/foreign-information-manipulation-interference-fimi-and-cybersecurity-threat-landscape.
136 S.J. Terp, P. Breuer, *DISARM: a framework for Analysis of Disinformation Campaigns*, in *2022 IEEE Conference on Cognitive and Computational Aspects of Situation Management (CogSIMA)*, June 2022, pp. 1–8.
137 *DISARM Disinformation TTP (Tactics, Techniques and Procedures) Framework*, https://github.com/DISARMFoundation/DISARMframeworks.
138 Department of the Army, *Psychological Operations Tactics*, ...
139 UK Ministry of Defence, *Cyber Primer*, October 2022, https://assets.publishing.service.gov.uk/government/uploads/system/uploads/attachment_data/file/1115061/Cyber_Primer_Edition_3.pdf.

Chapter 4

Commercial propaganda and PR

It is necessary to start this chapter by emphasizing that whatever is written here, there is a very clear difference between information about commercial products and services (marketing, economic, business issues) and information (more or less reliable) coming from States, and concerning security, defense, conflict, or war. There is a huge difference between political or military (war) propaganda and commercial "propaganda"—advertising, PR. These are qualitative differences. You cannot put an equal sign between these two distinct areas. In general, it would be unfair. There is a clear difference in goals, as well as means, sometimes even involving concealment of the source of activities. However, it must be acknowledged that certain PR activities can be covert or non-obvious.

With these necessary explanations behind us, we can move on to the point. For the sake of consistency in the book, we will still refer to various types of activities as propaganda, which is, after all, justified, given the classical definitions (see Chapter 1 for the discussion of the use of the term "propaganda" in relation to health information, etc.). These things are not the same, but nevertheless methods used as part of PR (public relations), PA (public affairs), and even HR (human resources) can be considered forms of propaganda.[1] By the way, in Spanish, the word "propaganda" simply means advertising. What does this imply? Not much—just a detail of the language. It is, however, telling, isn't it?

We won't condemn advertising itself here. According to research, it may be helpful and useful thing for consumers—if it is not necessarily useful for someone, it does not mean that it is useless for everyone. For example, if someone is interested in a certain range of products, he or she may be interested in emerging news. He or she may actively seek them out, but sometimes he or she doesn't have to. Still, sometimes the advertised content can be harmful, to recall the products appearing decades ago with admixtures of radioactive elements, cigarettes, or products laden with sugar, which, as we know today, may be quite harmful.

With advertising, however, ethical criteria and industry standards are important, which should be guarded by regulations and possibly industry codes. While self-regulation may not always work, hard regulations may impose restrictions or prohibit certain types of advertising, such as harmful foods, ads directed at children, and political advertising. Exposure to advertisements for beverages or other food products has been reported to have a pronounced effect on children's cognitive functions.[2] In general, consumers recognize these products, remember them, and are able to recall them in memory, including in certain situations, spontaneously (feeling of craving), and perhaps while shopping.

Still, it is crucial to ensure that certain boundaries are not crossed. In this context, the chapter will present situations where various boundaries have nevertheless been crossed.

DOI: 10.1201/9781003499497-4

4.1 PERSUASION AND AUDIENCE OUTREACH

An important requirement for successful commercial activity is persuasion. Persuading an audience to an idea, a concept, a service, or a product is the goal of advertising or promotion. When a new kind of laundry detergent, a brand of cookies, or a beverage appears on the market—how is the consumer supposed to know of their existence? How is he or she supposed to make a decision about wanting to try it, to purchase it? This is done by reaching out to the consumer, and it is perfectly legal and widely accepted. Since persuasion techniques have been exhaustively discussed in Chapter 3, I will not repeat that content here. But these techniques can be applied to advertising or PR communications (let's be careful and think about it for a moment!).

What is advertising? Mechanically, technically—these are campaigns that create informational messages. They involve paying to reach an audience. The effectiveness of advertising campaigns is also verified (measuring how many people the message reached, and whether it affected sales). Advertising targets may also include the so-called *brand awareness*, that is, activities to build awareness of brands, and products—the familiarity with names, logos, vendors. Surely most readers of this book are able to name some manufacturers of smartphones, clothes, and beverages. This is the result of reaching consumers with messages. We know these brands because we have heard about them or seen them in various places. Probably a much smaller fraction of readers are able to name the brands of modern manufacturers of lawn mowers or agricultural plows, because these are things of interest to a rather narrow audience and their ads may not reach everyone, as it would make limited sense—it would constitute a waste of resources for an advertising campaign.

These are important differences from the so-called state or military propaganda, especially in totalitarian States, where propaganda may be widespread or ubiquitous. In democratic countries, however, and in the advertising industry, specific audiences are reached, rather than all and without exception.

4.1.1 Real-time auctions

Online ads are targeted so that they are displayed in a specific place: on a website, in a smartphone application, etc. They can be contextual, non-profiled ads (linked with the viewed content) that do not include additional information about the consumer. The more accurate ones, profiled or targeted to audiences with specific interests (rock music, cars, books), may offer better precision. Such methods work by sharing and using user data,[3] a practice that has raised privacy concerns (when I write these words, proposed improvements are underway). For example, in 2014, I studied information flows in such a basic ad targeting infrastructure, real-time bidding (real-time auctions). Without access to ad infrastructures internals, I established that the cost of a display ad (combined with user data exchange) can be relatively low: $0.0005. However, the crucial point is that such a price is subject to significant fluctuations, such as the price being affected by geographic location and user characteristics, among other things—profiling. In essence, however, these are small sums, and no wonder. If one were to pay much more per display, it would be unprofitable to reach out people with ads on a mass scale—simple economics in action. This system of targeting ads will be discussed further in subsequent chapters, as micro-targeting and algorithmic advertising techniques can be important elements in information operations. With that said, the real-time bidding platforms of the 2020s are changing, and it now looks like they will largely migrate to a more open, user-friendly form. Let's hope so!

Commercial activities can also amount to pure abuses. Much has been said about how modern advertising infrastructures work. When a user accesses a website, the infrastructure—consisting of scripts running on the site (in a mobile app)—signals the visit to an advertising platform, and eventually an ad is displayed. Finally, payment is directed to the website where the ad was displayed. In view of this, such a system funds websites. But what if they host unreliable, sensational content, or even spread false, distorted information? Such situations have happened—a high-profile case was the funding of websites publishing bogus information about the COVID-19 pandemic.[4] The targeting of funds to such entities is, or was, based precisely on the idea of supporting display advertising. The chosen strategy of publishing sensationalist content, conspiracy theories, and "neglected topics" may attract enthusiasts. But is financial support for such activities truly socially positive? No, it isn't. The abuse here is or was, formally, on the part of the content publisher, that is, someone who developed such a website and embedded advertising scripts on it. In response to this phenomenon, existing regulations (hard and soft) require providers of such advertising systems to defund and demonetize content such as harmful misinformation.

4.2 WHAT CAME FIRST—ADVERTISING OR PROPAGANDA?

I am not judging which came first—the egg or the chicken. Were advertising techniques applied to propaganda first, or propaganda techniques applied to advertising? It doesn't matter to us. Now, it is what it is and that's it, case closed; this is not a book about history but about security in the information age. About what is important today and what will be important in the future.

4.2.1 Propaganda methods in World War I—the birth of modern public relations

Undoubtedly, the heyday of advertising and PR came after World War I.[5] Involved in the development were experts who had previously supported the military in the war effort. They were the ones who later set the standards for the emerging field of PR. These are the facts, and there is no point in arguing with them.

As early as the 1930s, it was noted that advertising messages and content use propaganda techniques. These are methods involving, for example, appealing to the *desire to* be popular, attractive, to follow the crowd, to the *fear of* being neglected, unattractive, fear of social disapproval, and fear of old age or disease.[6] These themes can be seen even in advertising for toothpaste or food.[7] This may be a kind of inconvenient fact for today's enthusiasts of spreading techniques to detect disinformation, since traces of the application of these techniques can be found in many spheres of life, if one approaches the topic of detection from such a naive side. In view of this, it is better to clarify these differences, so that people do not have cognitive dissonance after an "enlightened expert" reveals the secrets of disinformation detection, and people, taking it for granted, suddenly recognize that, after all, "here it is used in advertising," or "this or that influencer, person, politician, applies it." Why do they do so? They follow the approach because it is effective, but that does not make them propagandists of war (or something like that). However, in order to do so properly—to distinguish properly, to view the difference—propaganda education needs to be introduced in school curriculum, honestly explaining the issue and demonstrating when the use of persuasion methods is acceptable (and to what extent!), and when it can or should be considered harmful and perhaps even illegal. There is a clear difference between advertising dishwashing liquid, writing out theses on the Internet that are identical to the line of hostile States (especially before or during wars) and doing so in cooperation with foreign intelligence services, in addition, deliberately, and fully knowingly.

But getting back to the point of this chapter, it is a fact that appeals to fear can be detected in advertising, with which one can at least undermine the motivation and morale of social groups that become the target of such actions.[8] One can be afraid of many things, such as disease, death, war, terrorist attacks, fascism, dictatorship, migrants, and getting hit by a bus. It depends on the specific social group, as well as the situation and circumstances. When the topic of terrorism is raised frequently, it is easier to scare people with it, as it then exists in the public consciousness; it is much more difficult to scare people with niche and unknown topics—an important premise for effectiveness.

This creates fertile ground for spreading informational content that emphasizes a state of insecurity arising from or related to something. How can fear then be exploited in advertising? For example, by promoting information about some disease and advertising means or solutions that can reduce or eliminate the risk of such a disease. However, when appealing to fear, it is necessary to ensure that the message is credible. This can be fostered by the circumstances, and the credibility of the source. For example, when talking about a disease, the advertising may involve medical doctors or actors dressed as medical doctors (although when exaggerated, this can be unethical or even illegal).

4.2.2 Calibrating the right level of fear

The challenge can be to effectively calibrate (choose) a certain level of fear. Exaggeration can have the opposite effect—lowering credibility. However, to some extent, and point, a linear relationship may exist, that is, the more fear, the greater the effect.[9] To be clear: this whole time, we are still talking about advertising issues. When this technique works, it can positively influence the willingness to purchase a specific product. A specific one, after all: it's hard to imagine that, based on fear, it would be possible to (easily) advertise ice cream with chocolate frosting and a sprinkling of nuts. But such advertising is effective for items such as a battery-powered lamp (which can be used in the event of a power outage), a condom (to protect against AIDS), pepper spray (for defense in the face of rising crime in an area), anti-tank artillery (when there is a war going on in the world), or chocolate (a good source of energy when you go on a hike in the mountains and the weather is poor), or 500 rolls of toilet paper (when there is talk of a pandemic or war on TV).

Fear can be detrimental to some sectors. For example, fear of a pandemic has had a negative impact on the tourism sector[10] but still a positive impact on the production of masks, disinfection gels, etc. These products in 2020–2022 were recommended (even required) by state services, sanitation, and health experts. Two years of widespread advertising of such products and solutions did the job.

Of course, it is not just about fear. In general, consumer decisions are influenced by emotions.[11] Some of them, such as hatred, can severely damage brands and products. On the other hand, if a feeling of guilt is aroused in the consumer (e.g., because of humanity's impact on climate change), he or she may turn to certain services or products (choose paper straws instead of plastic ones, or products of companies emphasizing, more or less truthfully, neutrality toward climate change and not harming the environment). It is always necessary to be cautious when stirring up certain emotions.

4.2.3 Negative messages use evolutionary adaptation

The focus on negative messages leads to increased consumption of information[12]: watching TV and browsing the Internet. This explains those various kinds of flashy or sensationalist news headlines of the type:

WE'RE ALL GOING TO DIE

THREE ASTEROIDS ARE APPROACHING. DO WE HAVE A PROBLEM?

DANGEROUS VIRUS STRAIN CERBERUS

EXPERT: 10% OF THE POPULATION WILL DIE

IT HAS BEGUN...

NOW IT WILL BEGIN

JOE DID NOT KNOW THAT THE MICROPHONE WAS ON AND RECORDING....

And so on.

Seeing this kind of headline—that is, the headline template itself, which is supposed to scare people, as a rule—people may be willing to click on it, watch the video recording, and read the article. And this may pay off, because, after all, such content (e.g., low-quality) can be financed by display ads. Why does it work? The interest in negative content is rooted in human nature: evolutionary activation of threat detection and defense.[13] According to research, the inclusion of negative keywords in the content of news or information clearly contributes to increased click-through rates.[14] Ruthlessly preying (deliberate exploitation) on this evolutionary condition may, therefore, have purely financial motivations. Since people "like to be afraid"—they are evolutionarily conditioned to do so and for some people it may be a perverse form of infotainment—they are getting what they want. Although these days, of course, there is no saber-toothed cat lurking in the wilderness—the fear-inducing signals must be different. In addition, headlines containing "positive" (rather than "negative") words are negatively correlated with their popularity. The more positive a news item sounds, the less people will be interested and click on it. So, it seems that people just love to be afraid. This trait can be exploited by many "experts," charlatans, fortune tellers, geopolitics experts, etc. Inciting fear works—it is scientifically proven!

4.3 THE SEED OF INFORMATION SOWN CAN HAVE LONG-TERM EFFECTS AND IS DIFFICULT TO REMEDY

Why is spreading bogus, misleading, or distorted information a problem? A clue can be found in the results of scientific analyses indicating that false information is very difficult to address, fix, and correct. For example, it is difficult to "invalidate" or refute a scientific falsehood once it's spread. Often, efforts do not have a significant effect, and the dynamics of such actions can be observed in many cases. A nice example is the spread of false information during the coronavirus pandemic.[15]

Here are examples of such illogical nonsense, which have nevertheless been subject to some (let's point out: niche) propagation: embedded electronic circuits in a vaccine, somehow interacting with telecommunications networks in the 5G standard[16] or the induction of autism by vaccines. Another example is bogus or misleading reports of forest fires.[17] Forests sometimes burn; every now and then there are larger fires. This has always been and will always be the case to some degree (sometimes it is even beneficial for the forest in the long term). This is a natural process, not necessarily always due to beliefs about, for example, the effects of climate change. But are the causes always natural? Or unnatural? People may feel the *need to seek explanations for* phenomena and those "responsible." They like to rationalize reality. Successful propagandists or promoters of conspiracy theories should know this. And I assure you that those successful ones do.

So, what to do with information or comments concerning natural catastrophes? The correct action in such a case is not to make one's own assumptions but to refer to the communication by the relevant state services or reputable and respected scientific centers, because they have the tools and procedures to determine the causes. Such means are not available to people sitting at home in front of a computer or in front of the TV.

It is especially difficult to correct bogus information that makes someone feel good. The best response is to give honest, comprehensive explanations. The idea is to offer the audience a new model for thinking about the world, about a particular subject, as they may rely on one built on falsity or wrong assumptions. They can function in such an alternative world for themselves, rely on such untruths, and make decisions, such as credit decisions, based on them. For example, someone might see disinformation on YouTube about how banks and financial institutions are about to collapse. And the first thing they do is to make decisions that are detrimental to them or give such advice to others.

4.3.1 Challenges of straightening falsehoods

It is more difficult to straighten out false information in a situation of social polarization—when groups of people can base their views on ideology and political views, and several camps with opposing views or beliefs emerge. Thus, one has to take into account the nature of false information, true information, the socio-political environment, recent events, etc. In view of this, from the point of view of legitimate (e.g., state ones) information services, one cannot simply issue a communiqué or provide some information. Limiting to showing the "other side" of things, dissenting information, may even entrench someone in their (false) beliefs.[18] And, after all, this is not the point of straightening something out, to confirm a false view of reality. It has to be done in a certain way, in response to current conditions. That's why communications and PR people have to be careful in such a situation, understanding its complexity.

We are said to trust science, so hear this. Interestingly, science communicators themselves can introduce ambiguity or outright falsehoods, such as when they overlook the limitations of the research they describe or try to stretch the results. Introducing mistakes already at the level of initial communication about scientific results[19] can result in false views about a scientific field, results, or even disillusionment and skepticism about science itself! Straightening falsehoods, if done, must happen quickly[20]; the longer one waits, the more strongly such false information can take hold, and then it can be more difficult to rectify the situation.

Let's return to commercial issues. From the above discussion, we may conclude that when one conducts mass education, spreading messages, even advertising, it may be difficult to reverse the direction of opinion later on. These earlier opinions are rooted somewhere, they sit somewhere, and they influence minds. This is partly due to the psychological *effect of availability bias*,[21] which is that when one has material and information on a topic in the memory, the very fact of familiarity with a particular topic has an effect on future inferences, or actions taken, for example, when interacting with such topics. This is also why it is worth being very careful when disseminating educational or informational campaigns—these actions can have long-term effects.

It is better to be sure that the disseminated knowledge is of good quality. This is because it may be tricky to "reverse" previously built awareness.

4.4 FALSE BUSINESS-COMMERCIAL INFORMATION

4.4.1 Cigarette smoking, gender equality, heroin, coke, pot

Years ago, people could see TV commercials extolling the virtues of smoking cigarettes. The commercials might even have involved a "medical doctor" or someone who looked like one (a technique of appeal to authority). Years later, we know that smoking does harm. However, few today may remember that the first spectacular cigarette advertising benefited from the emerging emancipation movement. It was like that: several women were engaged (hired) to walk in the Easter Parade in New York City, smoking cigarettes,[22] which of course appealed to the theme of *women's freedom*, gender equality, the emerging emancipation movement, and feminism. The resonance of this campaign was substantial, and the advertising was visible.

Similarly, today we have advertising campaigns relating to various social and environmental topics, such as climate change, where companies can promote their sensitivity to such topics. Is this ethical, or more specifically, was it ethical to hijack the topic of gender equality to advertise cigarettes? I leave that to the Reader's judgment. However, it worked the other way too: in 1968, propaganda methods designed to discourage cigarette smoking were tested on children. The results were not satisfactory, although in selected cases there were successes.[23] It was suspected quite early that scaring people with the consequences of smoking cigarettes was not effective.[24]

So, do people like to be afraid but are not afraid of the health consequences that are not immediate or those that will not come soon? If only it was that simple. None of these studies took into account the fact that at the time cigarette advertising was legal and quite common. Since this was the case, *there was pluralism* here, there were *several points of view*, information coming from many sources of different kinds: those scientific and medical, and those commercial, convincing people of "feeling good" or being fashionable. *People could, therefore, juxtapose* them—and make decisions. Such a situation definitely did not exist when suffragettes advertised cigarettes, referring to equality issues, because then the scientific understanding of cigarettes' harm to health was less recognized. So, then the information could be quite one-sided, and the juxtaposition of a product advertisement with a vibrant, emerging social movement was a perfect thing from a PR point of view.

Today, on the other hand, things are different: cigarettes are no longer in vogue, and people prefer to spend their time in other ways, such as watching TV series, playing computer or console games, consuming candy, e-cigarettes (sometimes), or amphetamines[25] (of course, there have been many educational campaigns against drugs[26]). With that said, I personally do not recommend either cigarettes or drug consumption to the Readers, and I am not going to argue this using any of the techniques in the previous section. I will only say that it is simply unwise, in view of what is known about their effects on health.

4.4.2 Abuse, opinion manipulation, celebrities, and influencers

But what if false information is spread by the head of a large company, or a well-known and popular person (celebrity) hired for such "advertising"? This can, again, be an application of the propaganda technique of appeal to authority. Of course, here there is no case of an objective authority but of a well-known person—being an "authority" here is determined by wealth, fame, recognition—speaking on a topic. By nature, people, as well as the media, will pay attention to such voices, and perhaps even spread them, since this is partly how the world and the information-business ecosystem works. However, sometimes even large companies can have problems with fakes. Just to name Tesla, straightening out the reports that their "fully autonomous car" had an accident, which in that case was not entirely true (an accident did occur but the cars were not fully autonomous).[27] False information can very negatively affect companies, product reputation, and brands. But abuse and fraud in the other direction are also possible.

4.4.3 False product reviews and ratings

A variety of business ventures and companies happen to organize actions of writing false reviews about their own products—in online stores, consumer rating sites, blogs, etc. They can do it themselves "out of the blue" but also hire people to do it: ordinary Internet users but also celebrities. In the United States, there was even a fine ($615,000) imposed on companies involved in spreading false comments in order to exert political influence on the regulator (Federal Communications Commission).[28] This political influence was attempted by impersonating ordinary citizens (even dead ones) without their consent—by writing millions of comments on the Internet.[29] In this case, however, these were not such ordinary comments, because the companies were audacious enough to use this method to send opinions directly to the regulator, as part of a public consultation campaign. This was done at a cost of $4.2 million and through a company contracted to do it. So, the process was deliberate and systematic. Apparently, they overdid it with the quantity, because someone began to suspect something.

Likewise, unfair practices can occur precisely when rating services or products—positive ones for one's own, and negative ones for competitors, for example. Moreover, such practices can be hidden, concealed, or disguised. They can be conducted unofficially, without informing the audience, they can be made by well-known people and celebrities. Such marketing is frowned upon by regulators in Europe.

Fake reviews (e.g., on Google Maps, Amazon) can be bought; there were entire industries devoted to the activity.[30] Companies and regulators are aware of this practice and want to combat it. Lawmakers and regulators recognize the problem. The U.S. Federal Trade Commission has proposed that every time a consumer sees a false review, the company behind it should pay a fine of $50,000.[31] That is, if such messages are seen by 100 people, the fine would be $500,000. This would be a strong deterrent. Penalties were to cover a wide range of actions. For example, it was envisioned to prohibit

> §465.5 [Insider Consumer Reviews and Consumer Testimonials] It is an unfair or deceptive act or practice and a violation of this Rule for: (a) an officer or manager of a business to write or create a consumer review or consumer testimonial about the business or one of its products or services that fails to have a clear and conspicuous disclosure of the officer's relationship to the business,[32]
>
> as well as "false consumer reviews, or celebrity recommendations," which includes "the writing, creation or sale by a company of consumer reviews, consumer opinions or celebrity opinions"(§465.2).[33] Indeed, this is an "unfair and deceptive" practice.[34]

Similar recommendations have emerged elsewhere. In the United Kingdom, they were issued by the Competition and Markets Authority.[35] In France, a relevant law has been enacted, also providing for bans on advertising of certain regulated services (e.g., a ban on plastic/aesthetic surgery advertising); the activity itself must be clearly labeled; failure to comply may be punishable with two years' imprisonment and a €300,000 fine.[36] Consumer protection also extends to influencer referrals, as statements recommending or discouraging something may of course (potentially) also contain unverifiable or untrue content—thus constituting false content and perhaps even misinformation. This may conceptually seem similar, but in principle, however, it is quite a different matter to introduce certain messages, narratives, even to propagate content of a political or military nature.

To some extent, authoring fake reviews can also be detected by automated techniques.[37]

4.4.4 Influencer manipulation and manipulation of employees or subcontractors

Employee behavior can be manipulated, as Uber has been demonstrating, for example, by influencing where and when drivers work.[38] But more broadly—platforms themselves can make subtle modifications to content display algorithms to determine certain emotional states of users, such as whether they are depressed. Facebook, for example, conducted such research on more than 689,000 users (and that's a lot!). What kind of manipulations are these? For example, removing certain types of content (such as those with negative overtones) from the timeline (displayed posts or messages) to determine changes in emotional states. Such influence is possible on a mass scale.[39] Although the study itself was about whether people's emotions can influence others. They can, it was confirmed. However, *in the process of such studies*, the vast capabilities of *the platforms themselves* and the consequences of manipulating the content displayed were demonstrated. The initial research was conducted back in 2012, and Cornell University was apparently outraged by the negative response after it was published. An additional announcement was made that the ethics of the research were guaranteed. However, by 2023, the communiqué was no longer online—it had disappeared somewhere. But the critical reception—measured by the large number of publications and articles—remained. Perhaps the design of internal university systems was changed or the website was modified—we don't know. But as a result, doubt may arise: since the information from this university disappeared, can it be assumed that it was withdrawn? Sometimes, all it takes is doubt.

Ultimately, another conclusion is more important. Digital platforms are able to manipulate the emotions of their users. They have the means to do so. This is scientifically confirmed, on a pretty large scale, and now cannot be disputed. These abilities are a very big power. How it can be used—this will be discussed in the following chapters. Such social engineering activities have been carried out in practice.

4.5 DARK PATTERNS—DIGITAL SUBLIMINAL MANIPULATION

A problem related to the manipulation of consumer action is the so-called anti-patterns of design, or "*dark patterns*." Such patterns are the design of programs, applications, and information systems—to manipulate user behavior.[40]

This can be done by placing elements of the user interface (application design, program) in different places, changing the colors of some elements so as to reduce the chance that the user will notice them or use such functions, for example, the function to express disagreement with the processing of someone's personal data. The creation of such patterns can be based precisely on the analysis of people's behavior, psychological, sociological, and anthropological research, and the use of this knowledge against users in a conscious manner (when done deliberately, that is). This can be deliberate obstruction, making it difficult to take certain actions, especially those that the user is entitled to or can expect (e.g., requesting the removal of an email address from a mailing list through which spam, or unwanted information, is sent).

Many techniques can be used,[41] such as coercion, confusion (e.g., asking questions that the user may not understand), distraction (attracting the user's attention or distracting him or her from his or her current activities), exploitation of mistakes (while using the service), and others. Such practices may be a violation of antitrust and consumer protection rules.[42] The European Commission gives examples: "publishing only positive reviews and removing negative ones; linking a consumer's recommendation to content other than the content the consumer intended to recommend."[43] The Digital Services Act provides a concise definition:

> practices that materially distort or impair, either on purpose or in effect, the ability of recipients of the service to make autonomous and informed choices or decisions. Those practices can be used to persuade the recipients of the service to engage in unwanted behaviors or into undesired decisions which have negative consequences for them.[44]

These are actions intended to influence the user, analogous to persuasion. They may even be considered aggressive business practices through the exertion of unlawful pressure.[45] They may be subject to restrictions and actions against such manipulation. As I write these words, there has been no known situation where someone has gone to jail for such practices.

4.6 EXAMPLES OF MANIPULATION OF COMMERCIAL ACTIVITIES, IMPACT ON STOCK MARKET, COMPANY LISTINGS

The information sphere, such as in social media, can have an impact on the value of companies, on stock market shares.[46] For example, in 2022, due to the confusion on Twitter caused by the introduction of a paid version of a "verified account," which in practice anyone could obtain, many fake accounts appeared. People registered such "verified accounts," inserted logos and descriptions of well-known companies in the profile descriptions, and wrote bogus messages, perhaps as a joke.[47] In one such example, someone pretending to be the listed pharmaceutical company Eli Lilly announced that the company would be making its important product, insulin, available free of charge. The stock went down 4.5%.[48] Another example of real information impact on stock market value is the situation with Freeport, which distributes liquefied natural gas (LNG), as a result of the publication of information (a tweet) about physical damage to the pipeline. This affected the value of the gas market on the exchange.[49] The (fake) information was allegedly published by someone posing as a stockbroker, followed by the publication of another false message—allegedly signed by the company operating the oil pipeline. Similar phenomena were occurring on Chinese social media[50] and may have related to issues such as the supposedly upcoming changes in rules (laws) in various economic and industrial sectors. At least one such consulting firm (Esteel) was fined by the regulator for publishing false content—employees of that company put out information that a city that is the headquarters of a steel manufacturer was about to introduce some restrictions. In response, stock market for iron prices went down (by 7.6%).[51] Such "leaks" or "rumors" are a growing problem. In another industry, we have a similar phenomenon, the so-called Kremlinology, when, faced with a lack of information, Western analysts at times pounce on every possible scrap of information, such as various posts, on various accounts on the Telegram platform, including the bogus ones, sometimes—to a far from perfect effect.

But these are also issues of interpenetration between commercial and military activities. During the war in Ukraine, it became clear that communications companies can have a major impact on battlefield operations. If only by the mere fact of making communication capabilities available or not (which is crucial in war).[52] They can be turned on; they can be turned off. Such control means a lot of power and influence.

4.7 SUMMARY

The basic ability to spot eristic tricks, influence, and persuasion moves in commercial and advertising messages is useful. In a well-run education system, such skills should be taught in school. An important social safeguard is at stake. As a matter of fact, propaganda methods, when used, do not have to be considered in moral terms, for example, relating to some value system (although they may fit into it or seemingly relate to it). This is because the premise is to benefit, to be effective.

In view of this, when it comes to commercial issues, we are specifically talking about informational influence intended to bring financial benefits. Such motivations can be seen in many cases in the promotion of services or products, but also in the situation of influencing regulations intended to cover some sectors (food, technology, AI). Of course, this does not mean that an exemplary influencer in social or electronic media is immediately a propagandist, although, after all, even if they may be one, and some may parlay that. However, it is worth keeping in mind the right proportions, while still noticing the crucial subtleties and differences. It would be unreasonable, and certainly tiresome, to look for some hidden influence everywhere.

The topic of this chapter is also a good argument for regulating services and markets, such as advertising. If only so that, in response to a well-recognized topic (scientifically researched), we can avoid running advertising of certain products or substances, like substances deemed harmful to certain audiences (e.g., children).

This is also why this chapter does not put an equal sign between "propaganda" in the modern sense and "advertising" and related activities. This can be done for journalistic purposes, but in the current sense of the words, it would be expertly or scientifically imprecise. Despite the fact that commercial and state/war activities can use exactly the same techniques and even exactly the same technical solutions—the differences are clear. These are differences in purpose, and they will be highlighted in the following chapters.

NOTES

1 J. Ellul, *Propaganda: The Formation of Men's Attitudes*, Knopf Doubleday Publishing Group, New York 1973.
2 N. Lei, Z. Liu, L. Xiang, L. Ye, J. Zhang, The extent and nature of television food and non-alcoholic beverage advertising to children during Chinese New Year in Beijing, China, *BMC Public Health* 2022, vol. 22, no. 1, pp. 1–16.
3 C. Castelluccia, L. Olejnik, T. Minh-Dung, *Selling off privacy at auction*, in *Network and Distributed System Security Symposium (NDSS)*, November 2014.
4 E. Taylor, L.M. Neudert, S. Hoffmann, P.N. Howard, *Follow the money: How the online advertising ecosystem funds COVID-19 junk news and disinformation*, in *COVID-19 Series COMPROP Working Paper 2020*, August 3, 2020, https://demtech.oii.ox.ac.uk/research/posts/follow-the-money-how-the-online-advertising-ecosystem-funds-covid-19-junk-news-and-disinformation/.
5 B. Maartens, The Great War, military recruitment and the public relations work of the Parliamentary Recruiting Committee, 1914–1915, *Public Relations Inquiry* 2016, vol. 5, no. 2, pp. 169–185.
6 A. Jewett, Detecting and analyzing propaganda, *English Journal* 1940, vol. 29, no. 2, pp. 105–115.
7 A. Jewett, Detecting and analyzing propaganda, *English Journal* 1940, vol. 29, no. 2, p. 5.
8 P.R. Baines, Evaluating the effect of the fear appeal in advertising: Implications for information operation campaigns, *Journal of Information Warfare* 2009, vol. 8, no. 1, pp. 20–31.
9 M.S. LaTour, H.J. Rotfeld, There are threats and (maybe) fear-caused arousal: Theory and confusions of appeals to fear and fear arousal itself, *Journal of Advertising* 1997, vol. 26, no. 3, pp. 45–59.
10 D. Zheng, Q. Luo, B.W. Ritchie, Afraid to travel after COVID-19? Self-protection, coping and resilience against pandemic "travel fear," *Tourism Management* 2021, vol. 83.
11 S. Khatoon, V. Rehman, Negative emotions in consumer brand relationship: A review and future research agenda, *International Journal of Consumer Studies* 2021, vol. 45, no. 4, pp. 719–749.
12 C.E. Robertson, N. Pröllochs, K. Schwarzenegger, P. Pärnamets, J.J. Van Bavel, S. Feuerriegel, Negativity drives online news consumption, *Nature Human Behaviour* 2023, vol. 7, no. 5, pp. 812–822.
13 C.E. Robertson, N. Pröllochs, K. Schwarzenegger, P. Pärnamets, J.J. Van Bavel, S. Feuerriegel, Negativity drives online news consumption, *Nature Human Behaviour* 2023, vol. 7, no. 5, pp. 812–822.
14 C.E. Robertson, N. Pröllochs, K. Schwarzenegger, P. Pärnamets, J.J. Van Bavel, S. Feuerriegel, Negativity drives online news consumption, *Nature Human Behaviour* 2023, vol. 7, no. 5, pp. 812–822.

15 M.P.S. Chan, D. Albarracín, A meta-analysis of correction effects in science-relevant misinformation, *Nature Human Behaviour* 2023, https://www.asc.upenn.edu/sites/default/files/2023-06/A%20meta-analysis%20of%20correction%20effects%20in%20science-relevant%20misinformation.pdf.
16 I. Himelboim, P. Borah, D.K.L. Lee, J. Lee, Y. Su, A. Vishnevskaya, X. Xiao, What do 5G networks, Bill Gates, Agenda 21, and QAnon have in common? Sources, distribution, and characteristics, *New Media and Society* 2023, Article no. 14614448221142800.
17 G.M. Jones, E.K. Vraga, P.F. Hessburg, M.D. Hurteau, C.D. Allen, R.E. Keane, T.A. Spies, M.P. North, B.M. Collins, M.A. Finney, J.M. Lydersen, A.L. Westerling, Counteracting wildfire misinformation, *Frontiers in Ecology and the Environment* 2022, vol. 20, no. 7, pp. 392–393.
18 M.P.S. Chan, C.R. Jones, K. Hall Jamieson, D. Albarracín, Debunking: A meta-analysis of the psychological efficacy of messages countering misinformation, *Psychological Science* 2017, vol. 28, no. 11, pp. 1531–1546.
19 J.D. West, C.T. Bergstrom, Misinformation in and about science, *Proceedings of the National Academy of Sciences* 2021, vol. 118, no. 15, Article no. e1912444117.
20 N.M. Brashier, G. Pennycook, A.J. Berinsky, D.G. Rand, Timing matters when correcting fake news, *Proceedings of the National Academy of Sciences* 2021, vol. 118, no. 5.
21 A. Tversky, D. Kahneman, Availability: A heuristic for judging frequency and probability, *Cognitive Psychology* 1973, vol. 5, no. 2, pp. 207–232.
22 M. Topić, An analysis of the smoking debate ahead of Bernays' 'Torches of Freedom' campaign through the lens of the New York Times coverage (1870–1929), *Journal of Historical Research in Marketing* 2021, vol. 13, no. 3–4, pp. 214–230.
23 W.W. Holland, A. Elliott, Cigarette smoking, respiratory symptoms, and anti-smoking propaganda. An experiment, *Lancet* 1968, vol. 291, no. 7532, pp. 41–43.
24 M.S. Spelman, P. Ley, Knowledge of lung cancer and smoking habits, *British Journal of Social and Clinical Psychology* 1966, vol. 5, no. 3, pp. 207–210.
25 M. Collison, In search of the high life: Drugs, crime, masculinities and consumption, *The British Journal of Criminology* 1996, vol. 36, no. 3, pp. 428–444.
26 B.M. Stone, The war on drugs has unduly biased substance use research, *Psychological Reports* 2022.
27 M. Nayak, J. Schneider, *Driver who Claimed Tesla's Autopilot Caused a Crash that Left her with Facial Injuries Loses What's Believed to be the First such Case to go to Trial*, April 22, 2023, https://fortune.com/2023/04/21/tesla-autopilot-crash-lawsuit-los-angeles/.
28 *Attorney General James secures $615,000 from companies that supplied fake comments to influence FCC's repeal of Net Neutrality Rules*, May 10, 2023, https://ag.ny.gov/press-release/2023/attorney-general-james-secures-615000-companies-supplied-fake-comments-influence.
29 See https://ag.ny.gov/sites/default/files/oag-fakecommentsreport.pdf.
30 S. He, B. Hollenbeck, D. Proserpio, The market for fake reviews, *Marketing Science* 2022, vol. 41, no. 5, pp. 896–921.
31 Federal Trade Commission,16 CFR Part 465: Trade Regulation Rule on the Use of Consumer Reviews and Testimonials, July 31, 2023, https://www.federalregister.gov/documents/2023/07/31/2023-15581/trade-regulation-rule-on-the-use-of-consumer-reviews-and-testimonials.
32 Federal Trade Commission,16 CFR Part 465: Trade Regulation Rule on the Use of Consumer Reviews and Testimonials, July 31, 2023, https://www.federalregister.gov/documents/2023/07/31/2023-15581/trade-regulation-rule-on-the-use-of-consumer-reviews-and-testimonials.
33 "§ 465.2 [Fake or False Consumer Reviews, Consumer Testimonials, or Celebrity Testimonials]. (a) It is an unfair or deceptive act or practice and a violation of this Rule for a business to write, create, or sell a consumer review, consumer testimonial, or celebrity testimonial: (1) by a reviewer or testimonial list who does not exist; ... (b) It is an unfair or deceptive act or practice and a violation of this Rule for a business to purchase a consumer review, or to disseminate or cause the dissemination of a consumer testimonial or celebrity testimonial, about the business or one of its products or services, which the business knew or should have known." Federal Trade Commission,16 CFR Part 465: Trade Regulation Rule on the Use of Consumer Reviews and Testimonials, July 31, 2023, https://www.federalregister.gov/documents/2023/07/31/2023-15581/trade-regulation-rule-on-the-use-of-consumer-reviews-and-testimonials.

34 Federal Trade Commission, 16 CFR Part 465: Trade Regulation Rule on the Use of Consumer Reviews and Testimonials, § 465.2, July 31, 2023, https://www.federalregister.gov/documents/2023/07/31/2023-15581/trade-regulation-rule-on-the-use-of-consumer-reviews-and-testimonials.
35 *Influencer marketing: What you need to know – competition and markets authority*, April 30, 2019, https://competitionandmarkets.blog.gov.uk/2019/04/30/influencer-marketing-what-you-need-to-know/.
36 La loi n° 2023-451 du 9 juin 2023 visant à encadrer l'influence commerciale et à lutter contre les dérives des influenceurs sur les réseaux sociaux, https://www.legifrance.gouv.fr/jorf/id/JORFTEXT000047663185.
37 R. Mohawesh, S. Xu, S.N. Tran, R. Ollington, M. Springer, Y. Jararweh, S. Maqsood, Fake reviews detection: A survey, *IEEE Access* 2021, vol. 9, pp. 65771–65802.
38 N. Scheiber, *How Uber Uses Psychological Tricks to Push its Drivers Buttons*, April 2, 2017, https://www.nytimes.com/interactive/2017/04/02/technology/uber-drivers-psychological-tricks.html.
39 A.D. Kramer, J.E. Guillory, J.T. Hancock, Experimental evidence of massive-scale emotional contagion through social networks, *Proceedings of the National Academy of Sciences* 2014, vol. 111, no. 24, p. 8788.
40 C.M. Gray, Y. Kou, B. Battles, J. Hoggatt, A.L. Toombs, *The dark (patterns) side of UX design*, in *Proceedings of the 2018 CHI Conference on Human Factors in Computing Systems*, April 2018, pp. 1–14.
41 M. Leiser, Illuminating manipulative design: From 'dark patterns' to information asymmetry and the repression of free choice under the Unfair Commercial Practices Directive, *Loyola Consumer Law Review* 2022, vol. 34, p. 484.
42 G. Day, A. Stemler, Are dark patterns anticompetitive?, *Alabama Law Review* 2020, vol. 72, no. 1.
43 Commission Notice – Guidelines on the interpretation and application of Directive 2005/29/EC of the European Parliament and of the Council concerning unfair business-to-consumer commercial practices in the internal market (2021/C 526/01), OJ C 526, 29.12.2021, p. 1.
44 Regulation (EU) 2022/2065 of the European Parliament and of the Council of 19 October 2022 on a Single Market For Digital Services and amending Directive 2000/31/EC (Digital Services Act) (Text with EEA relevance). PE/30/2022/REV/1 OJ L 277, 27.10.2022, p. 1–102.
45 Articles 8 and 9 of Directive 2005/29/EC of the European Parliament and of the Council of May 11, 2005 concerning unfair business-to-consumer commercial practices in the internal market and amending Council Directive 84/450/EEC, Directives 97/7/EC, 98/27/EC and 2002/65/EC of the European Parliament and of the Council and Regulation (EC) No. 2006/2004 of the European Parliament and of the Council ("Unfair Commercial Practices Directive"), Official Journal of the EU L 149 of 11.06.2005, p. 22, as amended.
46 E. Blankespoor, G.S. Miller, H.D. White, The role of dissemination in market liquidity: Evidence from firms' use of Twitter™, *The Accounting Review* 2014, vol. 89, no. 1, pp. 79–112.
47 R. Mac, B. Mullin, K. Conger, M. Isaac, *A verifiable mess: Twitter users create havoc by impersonating brands*, November 11, 2022, https://www.nytimes.com/2022/11/11/technology/twitter-blue-fake-accounts.html.
48 Eli Lilly Dves on Twitter Chaos, Taking Novo, Sanofi with it, *Investor Business Daily*, November 11, 2022, https://www.investors.com/news/technology/lly-stock-dives-taking-novo-sanofi-with-it-after-fake-twitter-account-promises-free-insulin/.
49 *An Unconfirmed Tweet about Freeport LNG is Upending Gas Markets*, November 11, 2022, https://www.bloomberg.com/news/articles/2022-11-11/an-unconfirmed-tweet-about-freeport-lng-is-upending-gas-markets.
50 T. Hale, C. Leng, *Chinese Regulator Takes Aim at Market-moving 'Little Essays' on Social Media*, July 7, 2023, https://www.ft.com/content/2d4d1ec2-b7a9-4454-ab2a-46bc159faf5c.
51 T. Hale, C. Leng, *Chinese Regulator Takes Aim at Market-moving 'Little Essays' on Social Media*, July 7, 2023, https://www.ft.com/content/2d4d1ec2-b7a9-4454-ab2a-46bc159faf5c.
52 P. Sholdra, *Elon Musk Command of the Ukrainian Military*, October 20, 2022, https://www.theruck.news/p/elon-musks-command-of-the-ukrainian.

Chapter 5

Norms, rules, international law—legality of propaganda and disinformation

Is disinformation legal; is it lawful? To answer that point, it is necessary to address another question: in accordance with what, whose law? So, it's a question of jurisdiction—aspects of the legal principles, the reach of a State's justice system. It is not my purpose to dissect the legal principles of all, or even a select few countries. That would be tedious and not really useful for our purposes.

This chapter also serves as a general clarification of when we are dealing with combat or information warfare. Without the basics, it can be difficult to determine this objectively, and not just publicistically or informally, that is, throwing the word "war" in every sentence, completely without substance. Without clearly establishing what we stand on, it is also not possible to determine at least when the use of, for example, deepfake creations could constitute war crimes. Because, after all, it could be. But the key question is: under what circumstances?

Certain principles need to be specified, although I will simplify things to make matters digestible and coherent. The reference of choice will be international law, European law, and in certain cases the laws of different States. European law are laws and rules established by the institutions of the European Union (EU) or treaties to which European States accede. These laws may be directly applicable in EU Member States, and are sometimes subject to transposition, when their basis is introduced into laws of a Member State, perhaps expanded to account for some local special considerations. European law consists of, among other things, treaties, regulations, directives, and, of course, judgments of the Court of Justice of the European Union. Also important are issues of the so-called soft law, such as those issued by regulatory or supervisory agencies. Such soft law was, for example, the EU Code of Conduct on Disinformation.[1] In addition to European Union law, the European Convention on Human Rights[2] and the judgments of the European Court of Human Rights are worth noting.

Other elements of international law are treaties and sometimes rules set by the United Nations or its agencies. Such rules indicate how a State should behave (and sometimes obliges it to do so) at least in relations between States. Sources of law are treaties, customary law, norms, etc. International bilateral (between two States) and multilateral agreements can also be relevant. And that's enough for us, after all, we won't go into the details of the order established by the treaties of the Peace of Westphalia (1648) and the latter ones here.

If the Reader finds that the issues raised in this chapter do not necessarily fascinate him or her or do not seem particularly useful, he or she can quickly review it (perhaps devoting more time to some elements) and move on.

DOI: 10.1201/9781003499497-5

5.1 DEEPFAKE AND WAR CRIMES

5.1.1 Deepfake and regulation

Many rights can be violated when distributing deepfake content. It all depends on the circumstances, that is, at least on what the multimedia content represents. It could be a simple joke, but it could be something more serious.

There may be violations of national rights, such as defamation and a violation of the right to one's image protection. But this is also a matter of European law. The directive on combating violence against women and domestic violence[3] in Article 7(b) makes it mandatory to punish

> the production of images, videos or other content which give the impression that another person is engaged in sexual activities, without that person's consent, or the manipulation of such images, videos or other content, and then making them available to multiple end-users by means of information and communication technologies.

That is, producing a deepfake with such content relating to an existing person. The ban also applies to threats to create such material.

5.1.1.1 Artificial Intelligence Act and Digital Services Act versus deepfake

The Artificial Intelligence Act (AI Act)[4] text stipulates a requirement of disclosing the use of deepfake technology to produce content by labeling it: "Deployers of an AI system that generates or manipulates image, audio or video content constituting a deep fake, shall disclose that the content has been artificially generated or manipulated,"[5] while "deep fake" content is defined as "AI generated or manipulated image, audio or video content that resembles existing persons, objects, places or other entities or events and would falsely appear to a person to be authentic or truthful."[6]

In addition, the Digital Services Act[7] in Article 35(1)(k) stipulates an obligation to ensure

> an item of information, whether it constitutes a generated or manipulated image, audio or video that appreciably resembles existing persons, objects, places or other entities or events and falsely appears to a person to be authentic or truthful is distinguishable through prominent markings when presented on their online interfaces, and, in addition, providing an easy to use functionality which enables recipients of the service to indicate such information.

Such productions must, therefore, be properly marked. The laws legalize the uses of deepfake (generative content) in the EU, including commercially. However, they impose requirements when in use: labeling obligations, limiting abuse and spread. This is an obligation imposed on large digital platforms of the likes of Google, Facebook/Meta, TikTok, Instagram, etc. There are heavy fines for violating these obligations.

5.1.1.2 Deepfake in China

Restrictions on the use of deepfake have also been introduced in China.[8] Here, it is worth remembering that the rules for regulating technologies such as AI in China explicitly have to promote *socialist values*. More specifically, content created by generative AI (such as LLM, but also just deepfake) "should embody core socialist values and must not contain any content that subverts state power."[9] These apply to both deepfake multimedia and the text being created. In Europe, of course, European values are the ones preferred, which also can and do translate into laws and technologies.[10]

Now that we know that deepfakes are on the radar of lawmakers and regulators, and that the technology is even included in existing laws, let's take it to another level. One can imagine many abuses and problems associated with deepfakes. One can also imagine the use of a deepfake on the battlefield.

5.1.2 Deepfake, war propaganda, war

Deepfakes can be used to misrepresent certain people and create the impression of non-existent situations or statements—as if they happened. They have already been used in wartime conditions, more specifically in Ukraine in 2022–2023. Just note the poorly produced deepfake with President Zelensky, who supposedly recommended laying down arms and surrendering, or the series with President Putin.

"Disarming" the deepfake with Zelensky was not difficult, and the mere fact of its creation had no major negative consequences, as it was not possible to spread the message to the right audience. In view of this, the public focused on the fact of creation, which, of course, in itself did not lead to any effects or consequences. Similar situation happened in 2023, when a fake with Russian President Putin was created and propagated via hacked television. Control of the means of disseminating the information was taken over, and through it a "message" was broadcast that "Ukrainian troops armed to the teeth by NATO, with the approval and support of Washington, had invaded the regions of Kursk, Belgorod, and Bryansk" and that martial law had been imposed and three regions bordering Ukraine had been evacuated. Of course, this was false information. No apparent effects of the broadcast of this material are known.

5.2 TYPES OF PROPAGANDA

Propaganda always accompanies conflicts and wars. It can be targeted at the recipients:

- **Internal**—with the goal of strengthening society or army morale, shaping the understanding of reality in the way desired by the State;
- **External**—toward the enemy—undermining enemy morale, disinformation, inspiration, inducing practical influence aimed at the military and state services, as well as at the public;
- **Third countries**—presenting own version, seeking support, weakening support for the enemy, influencing societies in such countries, etc.

Depending on whether third countries are neutral or side with either side—they too may carry out actions in favor of the supported side (or its cause), weakening the side they do not favor.

The war in Ukraine has demonstrated a full spectrum of propaganda reflecting the above criteria, carried out according to this pattern. That is how it is with war situations. However, one should be aware of this. If only so that one does not accidentally believe one's own propaganda and remain able to evaluate the various messages in their correct proportions and contexts, which may be necessary when making strategic, or even personal decisions.

However, these are general and rather political issues. How is it with the issue of war? How does it relate to aspects of law?

First, we must note that the conduct of propaganda activities, including information operations or disinformation, is in accordance with the laws of war (restrictions and rules, will be discussed further). In this case, we are talking about International Humanitarian Law, also known as the Laws of Armed Conflict. This is a set of principles derived from the observation of past warfare, developed or observed customs, codified, for example, in the Geneva Conventions. Their purpose is to improve the situation of the warring parties—actually, the soldiers and civilians. The main rationale is precisely to spare civilians and not subject them to hostilities. Similarly with civilian objects like power plants, water supply infrastructure (etc.) necessary for the survival of the population.

This law stipulates how to conduct warfare in a civilized, humane way, so to speak.

5.2.1 Propaganda in war is legal—except in the case of perfidy

Propaganda is, therefore, legal in warfare. Moreover, the Geneva Conventions explicitly legalize the use of disinformation. The English word "misinformation" is used in this context, today meaning spreading false information in an unintentional, perhaps unconscious manner. This, however, is also a reason why the terminology must be approached with caution. For it turns out that in the past the word "disinformation" was not used in the sense of today's English term but meaning "misinformation" (which can be translated as "false information"). Okay, but what is it about? It's about Article 37(2) of Additional Protocol I to the Geneva Conventions[11]:

> Ruses of war are not prohibited. Such ruses are acts which are intended to mislead an adversary or to induce him to act recklessly but which infringe no rule of international law applicable in armed conflict and which are not perfidious because they do not invite the confidence of an adversary with respect to protection under that law. The following are examples of such ruses: the use of camouflage, decoys, mock operations and misinformation.

This provision states that ruses of war are possible, and a ruse is deliberate misinformation (i.e., disinformation, in today's terminology). Misinformation (disinformation), and therefore propaganda, is listed as such a ruse. So everything is clear. Propaganda is allowed on the battlefield. But there are some exceptions and rules.

In this context, an important exception is an action of "perfidy." The cited provision prohibits this. How does Article 37(1) define perfidy?

> Article 37 — Prohibition of perfidy
>
> 1. It is prohibited to kill, injure or capture an adversary by resort to perfidy. Acts inviting the confidence of an adversary to lead him to believe that he is entitled to, or is obliged to accord, protection under the rules of international law applicable in armed conflict, with intent to betray that confidence, shall constitute perfidy. The following acts are examples of perfidy:
>   a) the feigning of an intent to negotiate under a flag of truce or of a surrender;
>   b) the feigning of an incapacitation by wounds or sickness;
>   c) the feigning of civilian, non-combatant status; and
>   d) the feigning of protected status by the use of signs, emblems or uniforms of the United Nations or of neutral or other States not Parties to the conflict.

Thus, a perfidious act is a violation of the presumption of trust, that is, inducing a party to behave in such a way that it will bring death to them, despite their belief of safety. Now this is critical: the result of such propaganda must be an effect with a violation of legitimate trust, resulting in harm. Let's repeat it: in the case of perfidy, there must be an effect of injury or death to the individuals who were misled by such a method. This is, therefore, a very narrow understanding of things. But such actions would constitute war crimes in a direct and unquestionable manner. One may imagine the lethal targeting of injured, surrendering soldiers, or ones at a hospital, previously creating a perception of safety in their minds.

If disinformation and propaganda methods lead to such a situation, such use of these methods may be illegal and may constitute a war crime. False information that can bring danger to civilians, such as terrorizing them (including with information), is also prohibited.

Specifically, the following examples of propaganda are understood as appropriate:

> Transmitting misleading messages by radio or in the press; knowingly permitting the enemy to in tercept false documents, plans of operations, dispatches or information items which actually bear no relation to reality; using the enemy [radio - L.O.] wavelengths, passwords, wireless codes to transmit false instructions; pretending to communicate with reinforcements which do not exist; [..] using signals for the sole purpose of deceiving an adversary; resorting to psychological warfare methods by inciting the enemy soldiers to rebel, to mutiny or desert, possibly taking weapons and transportation; inciting the enemy population to revolt against its government etc.[12,13]

That is to say, propaganda as such is permitted, except in the case of perfidy.

So, while propaganda, misinformation, and disinformation during an armed conflict are permitted, there are clear limitations. These stem from the principles of humanitarianism. For example, influence campaigns, psychological operations, and information operations cannot encourage violations of the principles of international humanitarian law, such as calling for genocide.[14] Prohibitions on incitement and encouragement—these are already specific restrictions. However, I want to again underline (to avoid any doubts) that the prohibition applies to situations in which the encouragement actually led to or conceivably could have contributed to actions that violate legal prohibitions. Merely directing false messages and disinformation, the content of psychological operations is not sufficient to check the box.

What does this have to do with deepfakes? The simplest example: one waring party creates a multimedia recording with a "president" or an important "general" in which they recommend surrender, laying down arms, and putting their adversaries in control—and as a result of these actions, the side kills soldiers. Then, it could imaginably constitute an example of forbidden methods (perfidy). Trust has been violated. More such examples could be given.

Here, however, let's return to the previously mentioned deepfakes of the presidents of Ukraine and Russia. Are these war crimes? No. They definitely are not examples of war crimes. This is due to the fact that the mere publication of these materials had no effect. The mere creation, or even propagation, is not the problem. The problem is the delivery to the audience and getting that audience to take action that would be fatal for them. Manipulation of information content is as old as the world, and there is no shortage of examples. The very emergence of deepfake capabilities is just another method, contemporary to us. In addition, the rules even legalize deepfake methods in war (bar the exceptions mentioned, when it would be forbidden).[15] From this comes the conclusion that the use of deepfake methods in war is permissible (bar the exceptions). In contrast, clearly the misuse of deepfakes outside of war—other laws operate here—breaches laws in many cases.

There are other rules as well.

5.3 WAR-MONGERING PROPAGANDA IS PROHIBITED

Warmongering is prohibited. This is the lesson that humanity has learned from the experience of World War II, and it has become the basis for codification.

Also in view of the past experience of nations, Article 20 of the International Covenant on Civil and Political Rights[16] states: "Any propaganda for war shall be prohibited by law." Here it is worth noting that "propaganda for war."[17] This implies that it refers to war-mongering propaganda. Similar provisions are found in the laws of many countries.[18,19]

Such restrictions, moreover, are consistent with the right to freedom of expression (speech).[20] Prior to World War II, a number of proposals under consideration aimed at having each State introduce such restrictions in the law against incitement to war or hatred in a way that threatens peace.[21] This was to be part of the so-called "moral disarmament,"[22] which was to include the removal from school textbooks of any content that might incite hatred.[23] The idea of "moral disarmament" was part of a trend of work aimed at preventing another major war. However, these proposals have not been implemented. The "Global Declaration on Information Integrity Online,"[24] launched in 2023 by the Netherlands and Canada and supported by 27 countries, is part of this trend. The proclamation provides for countering misleading information and disinformation and the means of rapidly spreading and sharing it, including generative content created by methods using artificial intelligence (AI). This document is in the form of a proclamation, but there is a process of its implementation in the UN arena. It is not out of the question that this initiative, in combination with others, will lead to the issuance of some binding rules. Let's just hope they are more realistic than the demands made before the start of World War II.

5.4 REGULATION OF PROPAGANDA

In addition to warmongering, States identified propaganda as a problem fairly early, in the 19th century. Napoleon, for example, advocated limiting the role of non-state actors in exerting propaganda influence on other States and tried to get Great Britain to do so as well—unsuccessfully.[25] Anyway, to this day, something like this has not been comprehensively introduced in principle (some States still hope for such rules), which has been eagerly used by all sorts of dissidents since the 1920s, in various States. This shows, however, that first—the issue is not new, and second—that solving it was not to everyone's liking. For some, it was even very much not to their liking, as there are examples of States that made pacts to spread propaganda against other States. In the 20th century, the situation changes, because the exchange of letters, leaflets, or speech can be regarded as something of a small scale, something fading into history. What was different was when mass media such as radio appeared. From that point on, States took an interest in it as a problem.[26] In general, since the 20th century—even before World War II—one can see a "booming" of this interest. Until today, even.

5.5 POLISH-GERMAN PROPAGANDA CONFLICT AND REGULATIONS MITIGATING IT

Before World War II, Poland and Germany tried to establish, from today's perspective, a breakthrough and a pioneering agreement limiting propaganda activities. During the efforts to incorporate Silesia into Poland, the propaganda activity (Poland, Germany) was very clear and evident. The problem continued to grow until an interstate agreement was concluded

(Reichs-Rund Funk-Gesellschaft—Polskie Radio, March 1931), a precursor to[27] agreements relating to large-scale propaganda activity,[28] providing, among other things, that the parties "take all reasonable steps to prevent broadcasts over their respective stations prejudicial to the spirit of cooperation and understanding in the fields of politics, religion, and economy."[29] Although in the agreement, each party "reserves the right to some positive propaganda of its state activities in various fields" and undertakes "to ensure that its broadcasts in no way offend the national feelings of listeners in the other country."[30]

For this, the agreement on the exchange of programs[31] provided for the broadcast of "artistic propaganda" (here in the sense of simply broadcasting programs). A contemporary example of cooperation can be found in the ongoing process between the Russian Federation and the People's Republic of China.[32] It provides for the exchange of media content between the services in order to inform the public, in a similar and identical manner, about specific issues, including socio-political ones, with the aim of "promoting objective, comprehensive and accurate coverage of major world events." Among the listed signatory entities are media institutions but also companies, such as Huawei.

5.6 PROPAGANDA AND RADIO BROADCASTING

Various agreements and motivations resulted in the International Convention concerning the use of broadcasting in the cause of peace,[33] providing in Article 1 that States are to

> prohibit and, if occasion arises, to stop without delay the broadcasting within their respective territories of any transmission which to the detriment of good international understanding is of such a character as to incite the population of any territory to acts incompatible with the internal order or the security.[34]

In other words, it prohibits propaganda against other States, particularly incitement to war (Article 2). The Convention obliges signatory States to stop such acts executed from their territory, by anyone. The convention was created in the 1930s and entered into force in 1938. Its signatory included the Union of Soviet Socialist Republics (today: Russian Federation). The outbreak of World War II the following year suffices as a commentary on the effectiveness of this convention. Although, in all fairness, let's admit that the ban applied only to the signatories of this convention. Signatory States, however, denounced it (Czechoslovakia in 1991, the Netherlands in 1982, and France in 1984). No wonder. Signing it does not provide protection; instead, it imposes restrictions on States guided by the rule of law.

So, before World War II, rules were created to limit radio propaganda targeting other countries. But a geographical curiosity—Europe is relatively small, which mattered when high-powered radio transmitters began to be established. By the end of the 1930s, the transmitting stations were already quite sizable. In addition, there were many national minorities in the countries of Europe. In the French city of Strasbourg, it was understandable to broadcast in German, and so a reception of such signals was possible also in Germany, which, after all, was the real purpose. Broadcasting to the German-speaking residents of Strasbourg was not the actual aim. The same was true elsewhere on the continent.

5.6.1 Satellite broadcasting versus information interference

The 1982 UN General Assembly resolution dedicated to satellite broadcasting[35] may sound like a niche thing, obscure, outdated, or at most dedicated to specific areas of information transmission, yet it gives an idea of priorities at the time of early space activities: non-intervention in the internal affairs of States (by other States, via their satellites). One can see the connection here with the concerns raised today about outside interference in the information space (via TV, radio, social media) in both the West and the East. Concerns justified, or not necessarily so, as this is always subject to interpretation, and as one can easily imagine—each side has its own opinion, and in this sense it is difficult to be objective. However, allegations of interference are made all over the world, whatever we think about it, whichever side we support against another. Of course, the so-called moral issues and ethical considerations can vary widely. Again, as Stephen King put it when talking about opinions—everyone has their own. The Satellite Broadcasting Resolution indicates that any "disagreements" should be resolved by "peaceful means" (Article 7). However, it also imposes "international responsibility" in the area of information transmission (Article 8). Does this matter? Well, it may, because it creates a formal premise for the prosecution of abuses of the type of "Radio Hate" in Rwanda, systemically carrying out the broadcast of hateful content and calls for murder, for genocide (content that does not comply with international law, which prohibits genocide or calling for it). The satellites are in space, but the responsibility falls on the States controlling them or agreeing to launch them.[36] Incidentally, in 2019 North Korea claimed to have launched a satellite, Kwangmyongsong-2, transmitting "revolutionary songs"[37] in honor of General Kim Ir Sen. That is one way to do it.

5.7 STATES' OBLIGATION TO USE PROPAGANDA

Let's recall an actual "recommendation" resulting from an UN resolution.[38] In 1947, the UN General Assembly adopted the resolution "Measures to be taken against propaganda and the inciters of a new war." This creation has been drafted following the previously concluded World War II. It may also be an extension of pre-1939 measures heading in the same direction, and initiated by the concerns of many countries. The resolution condemns "all forms of propaganda, in whatsoever country conducted, which is either designed or likely to provoke or encourage any threat to the peace, breach of the peace, or act of aggression." But as it is, let's pay attention to the phrase "whatsoever country conducted."

Doubts can be dispelled very quickly, because the resolution goes on to recommend: "to promote, by all means of publicity and propaganda available to them, friendly relations among nations." The resolution provides for state propaganda means and orders that they are used in a certain way. This is very interesting and well summarized in other words:

1) States have the means of propaganda,
2) Propaganda should be directed to spread messages.

Here, of course, it is about very laudable things: the promotion of peace and friendly relations between States. Propaganda so understood is a tool. This view has been formalized—as already indicated by the analysis in Chapter 1. Here, I add that the resolution discussed here also refers to space, that is, including satellite infrastructure that can be a transmitter of content. It is also worth noting that some have argued that certain forms of propaganda should be tolerated as a tool if used in lieu of military action if they allow an agreement to be reached,[39] but it may still be difficult to balance and avoid escalation. In and of itself, there are no functioning and universally recognized regulations of propaganda. However, certain things can be successfully achieved, and in Europe it is happening. In contrast, here I will note that while it is not easy to consider propaganda as a use of force or armed attack, the Geneva Conventions nevertheless prohibit the sowing of terror by propaganda methods. Article 13(2) of the Second Additional Protocol to the Geneva Conventions provides that "the civilian population as such, as well as individual civilians, shall not be the object of attack. Acts or threats of violence the primary purpose of which is to spread terror among the civilian population are prohibited." In view of this, during hostilities, it is illegal to use propaganda that sows terror. What could such terror be? One can imagine spreading information that could cause panic or riots, fear of environmental, nuclear, biological, and chemical disaster, etc. Such actions can be considered a violation of the rules under certain war circumstances. In this case, it is an act of violence. Merely inducing some action is not enough, and it is clear that it cannot be as absurd as, for example, inducing enemy soldiers to consume methanol[40] by spreading false information about its health-promoting properties (to be clear: this is a poison, please do not consume it). The problem is that military action can very often have a terror effect, such as when a bomb, rocket, or tactical nuclear weapon goes off. However, the rule indicated is about situations where sowing terror is the main purpose of the action[41]—so it is not about side effects, indirect effects, etc.

5.7.1 "Hate radio" in Rwanda and "Der Stürmer" in Germany

Radio broadcasts spreading hateful content, such as statements like: " By 5th May the elimination of the Tutsis should be finished,"[42] during the Rwandan conflict,[43] can be an illustration of terror and incitement to crime. This example should be a warning to everyone what the construction of media propaganda messages, dehumanizing some groups of people, society, can lead to. Genocide, ethnic cleansing has its origin, its beginning somewhere. Similarly, in Nazi Germany, the propaganda role of inciting ethnic cleansing was fulfilled by the media, such as the newspaper "Der Stürmer."[44]

These things do not come out of nowhere. The question is, how can they be remedied? Legally, the paths are limited. Genocide is treated as a war crime. But according to Article 3(c) of the Convention on the Prevention and Punishment of the Crime of Genocide,[45] "direct and public incitement to commit genocide" is also punishable. Such actions can be carried out through various means, including mass media (radio, television, social media). Of course, the practical element remains: someone (some State, tribunal, etc.) must be able to investigate and bring about a verdict. In the case of Germany, that was successful at Nuremberg, and similarly in the case of the genocide on the territory of the former Yugoslavia.[46] The people responsible for hateful propaganda on the radio (Radio Télévision Libre des Mille Collines) in Rwanda were convicted by the Tribunal.[47]

In this case, a cause-and-effect relationship was also found: people criticized in such media (here: in the Rwandan newspaper *Kangura*) lost their employment and even their lives.[48] However, such formal tribunals and criminal trials are rare.

5.8 CENSORSHIP

Speaking of propaganda, it is necessary to pay attention to censorship, that is, deliberate restrictions of the flow of information and communication in order to hinder or block access to content, or information. Nowadays, the easiest way to imagine this is to pick up a newspaper or read an article on the Internet and imagine that certain sentences are removed or blackened in such a way that they cannot be read. Similarly with the content of communication between people—certain messages could be blocked or truncated, or it would be impossible to use telephony, SMS, or instant messaging (WhatsApp, Signal, etc.) at all. Such a blockade is technically possible. And what is the situation with legal rules?

Let's start with the fact that the means of broadcasting and transmission are a technical issue. Censorship is also a technical issue. In view of this, if something can be printed, published, broadcast, distributed, transmitted, etc., it can also be blocked. In different situations, this can occur at the level of individual companies, States, and transnationally. For example, Article 39 of the UN Charter[49] provides for the UN Security Council to take action. Military contingents can be sent ("stabilizing"), armed activity of other countries can be authorized (to "stabilize" the situation in another country), or no action can be taken (as during the war in Ukraine, because it so happened that a country on the Security Council can effectively block any action). Let's put reality aside, because it's clear that taking action depends on who the action would be taken against—something that was established after World War II and is difficult to change today. However, let's return to the possibility of blocking communications.

5.8.1 UN Security Council and the right of information blockade against a State

The Security Council, according to Article 41 of the UN Charter, has an interesting option: blocking communications within a country or with a country directly. This is listed as a soft action, weaker than military action by air (bombing), naval, or land forces. Thus, there can be a "complete or partial interruption ... *of the means of communication*." What are "*means* of communication"? They are not defined precisely, but several are listed: "postal, telegraphic, radio, *and other*." As one can easily imagine, these technologies—*means*—are subject to change. They looked very different in 1945 than they do today. Back then, it might have been all about the telegraph, radio, and postal service. Today, those "*others*" are rather more important.

What could those "*others*" be? It could be telecommunications—internet, television. Tomorrow—who knows—anything else that enables communication. It is known that the provisions in this article are about the exchange of information (mentioned: postal, telegraph, radio), so the interpretation of what these modern "others" are is obvious and not up to debate. It is about any means of information exchange, that is, for example, also excluding some State from the Internet, which is technically possible.

5.8.2 The State itself can introduce information blockades and censorship at home

States can also do it themselves domestically according to their own rules and needs. The International Communication Union (ITU) is the UN's telecommunications agency. The ITU Constitution[50] provides in Article 34(1) that

> [m]ember States reserve the right to stop, in accordance with their national law, the transmission of any private telegram which may appear dangerous to the security of the State or contrary to its laws, to public order or to decency, provided that they immediately notify the office of origin of the stoppage of any such telegram or any part thereof, except when such notification may appear dangerous to the security of the State[51]

and in para. 2 of that article, that "[m]ember States also reserve the right to cut off, in accordance with their national law, any other private telecommunications which may appear dangerous to the security of the State or contrary to its laws, to public order or to decency."[52]

From this article, we can draw several conclusions. The blocking and seizure of telecommunications content is legal, so there may be technical capabilities to do so—if the States so desire. This is at the discretion of specific countries. And these implement such rules in various ways.

5.9 RIGHTS AGAINST CENSORSHIP

What is the situation from the other side? We have the right to freedom of speech, to expression, and to exchange views and information.

In the Universal Declaration of Human Rights,[53] we find Article 19 which reads: "Every individual has the right to freedom of opinion and expression; this right includes the unfettered freedom to hold opinions and to seek, receive and impart information and ideas, by all means and without distinction as to frontiers." Thus, the ability to receive and impart information by "all means" and, in addition, "without regard to frontiers" is provided for. The International Covenant on Civil and Political Rights reads:

> Everyone shall have the right to freedom of expression; this right shall include freedom to seek, receive and impart information and ideas of all kinds, regardless of frontiers, either orally, in writing or in print, in the form of art, or through any other media of his choice (Article 19(2)).

This probably needs no comment.

In the European Convention on Human Rights, we have guarantees of "freedom to hold opinions and to receive and impart information and ideas without interference by public authority and regardless of frontiers" (Article 10(1)). The European Court of Human Rights said that the exchange of information on the Internet is an element of basic expression and the means by which people exercise their right to communicate: "The Internet has now become one of the principal means by which individuals exercise their right to freedom of expression and information."[54] Thus, these principles directly apply to the Internet as well, as the European Court of Human Rights has explicitly confirmed.[55]

The 2023 Declaration on Freedom of Communication on the Internet[56] stipulates that States should not impose restrictions on online content that deviate from such applied to other means of information exchange. It also said that "[t]he authorities should not, through general blocking or filtering measures, deny access by the public to information and other communication on the Internet, regardless of frontiers." However, an exception was added: "This does not prevent the installation of filters for the protection of minors, in particular in places accessible to them, such as schools or libraries."[57] Permission is also provided that "measures may be taken to enforce the removal of clearly identifiable Internet content or, alternatively, the blockage of access to it, if the competent national authorities have taken a provisional or final decision on its illegality." That is, legal, judicial review must be preserved for blocking decisions.

According to Principle 3(a) and (b) of the Organization for Security and Cooperation in Europe's (OSCE) Declaration on Freedom of Expression and the Internet,[58]

> a. Mandatory blocking of entire websites, IP addresses, ports, network protocols or types of uses (such as social networking) is an extreme measure—analogous to banning a newspaper or broadcaster—which can only be justified in accordance with international standards, for example where necessary to protect children against sexual abuse. b. Content filtering systems which are imposed by a government or commercial service provider and which are not end-user controlled are a form of prior censorship and are not justifiable as a restriction on freedom of expression.[59]

Article 11(1) of the EU Charter of Fundamental Rights[60] also provides for "the right … to receive and impart information and ideas without interference by public authority and regardless of frontiers."

5.9.1 Why did I mention all this?

I did so *to make it clear* that the right to receive, transmit, and broadcast information is guaranteed to people. This right has been developed for a long time and is well established. It is worth keeping this in mind. Freedom of speech has strong legal guarantees; political expression is specially protected. Curiously, this is also why political advertising cannot be banned outright and completely—the freedom of such expression is simply protected.[61] The basic principle in Europe is that there is very little room for restrictions on political expression (e.g., speech).[62] Simply put—it is illegal to tamper with legitimate political expression. This stands, as it would appear, in contrast to the 2023 ideas of the European Parliament for a ban on targeted political advertising, as well as, for example, a restrictive ban on disinformation and even propaganda, if we are talking about the expression of political opinion (which, as I have already explained, is subject to special protection). This fascinating topic merits further research, and I invite others to delve into it. This book, however, has its priorities and focus elsewhere.

Such rights impose limits on regulating debate, which one must be aware of. For a similar reason, there may be problems with banning or regulating expression on such political issues as epidemics (coronavirus, bird flu, swine flu, or any in the future), global warming, etc. These are political issues only because they are part of the public debate and even taken up by political parties; this may suffice to consider the topic political.

The only thing that can be said here is: *dura lex sed lex*. It's the law: respect it and abide by it. This is a challenge of sorts, as for several years now States around the world have been looking in detail at the problems of disinformation,[63] considering how to curb certain forms of expression. At one stage even referring to them as "fake news," not quite correctly. The real challenge is not so much the truthfulness or falsity as such, but how something is used, presented, and framed.

5.10 EU LAW AND DISINFORMATION

In the European Union, influenced by the trends and fashions considering disinformation, a number of new regulations have included relevant provisions relating to such activities. According to the Digital Services Act, digital platforms shall somehow deal with the problems of "illegal content, online disinformation and other social risks" (recital 2). We've already talked about advertising, so let's quote it directly:

> When recipients of the service are presented with advertisements based on targeting techniques optimised to match their interests and potentially appeal to their vulnerabilities, this can have particularly serious negative effects. In certain cases, manipulative techniques can negatively impact entire groups and amplify societal harms, for example by contributing to disinformation campaigns or by discriminating against certain groups.
> (recital 69)

Such threats exist and are real. They must be dealt with. It's a good thing that laws have been created to anticipate the existence of these problems, because they were overlooked in 2016 (the U.S. presidential election), as well as earlier during several elections in European countries.

The law stipulates the obligation to analyze risks and take appropriate countermeasures. However, in 2023, European Commissioner for Internal Market and Services Thierry Breton had twice issued warnings to digital platforms, announcing that they would be banned from operating in the European Union if they did not combat fake content (remove it immediately)—which sounds threatening, because as I explained in the case of the crisis with the missile fall on the Gaza hospital, even big media, quality media, like the *New York Times*, have had some bad experiences here when the story they initially disseminated had to be rewritten completely. But to ban such media right away sounds drastic. It is true that the reach of an international newspaper is far greater than the distorted or inaccurate views spread by social media. To be clear: nobody threatened the *New York Times* to be blocked in Europe. This juxtaposition should serve as a cautionary tale to be heeded should it occur to the trigger-happy officials or States to exercise their powers too hastily.

5.11 SUMMARY

Binding and functionally universally applicable international regulations of propaganda, disinformation, and information influence do not exist. Still, there is no shortage of laws and rules themselves, both at the international level (some of which I haven't even mentioned, as they are niche today), European level, and national level. These are issues relating to combating specific abuses such as propaganda or disinformation. Those are also measures that are more active, such as blocking content or information exchange (censorship). No universally accepted international treaty to regulate the "information space" seems possible, or simple to agree on, despite Russia's (repeated!) attempts.[64] Russia's 2023 proposal argues that the use of information in the "military and political as well as other spheres in order to undermine or infringe upon the sovereignty, violate the territorial integrity, social and economic stability of sovereign States, interfere in their internal affairs." It also includes remarks about the "disseminati[on of] information through information and communications technologies that is detrimental to the socio-political and socio-economic foundations, spiritual, moral and cultural environment of States and is threatening the lives and safety of citizens." In other words, there is a clear desire here to ban cyber attacks (methods and tools for carrying them out), as well as "hostile" information activities, that is, propaganda, disinformation, and PR, and potentially also media broadcasts.

In the United States, freedom of expression has a solid foundation. Freedom of political expression is subject to special protection also in Europe in particular. This places restrictions on enthusiasts modulating what is allowed in a debate and what is not. Perhaps this is for the better, because otherwise there would be a risk of a different kind: the formation of political systems and governments with a monopoly on the truth. And a total monopoly at that, not only of its creation but also of its distribution, and thus inclined to suppress the dissemination of other points of view. We know such approaches from history. Too often they did not end well.

In the past, a king, a dictator, or a ruler established what is allowed and what is not—what information the public receives and what it does not. This facilitated social control, as well as making politics, diplomacy, and wars. In the 20th century, there have been some changes here, also dictated by the experience of totalitarian systems. Nevertheless, the information space is a field where many actions can be taken, including hostile and even offensive ones, it is a field of competition between States. This is what the last chapters are devoted to.

NOTES

1 See https://digital-strategy.ec.europa.eu/en/library/2018-code-practice-disinformation.
2 Convention for the Protection of Human Rights and Fundamental Freedoms, drawn up in Rome on November 4, 1950, subsequently amended by Protocols Nos. 3, 5 and 8 and supplemented by Protocol No. 2, OJ. 1993, no. 61, item 284.

3 Proposal – Directive of the European Parliament and of the Council on combating violence against women and domestic violence, March 8, 2002, COM/2022/105 final, https://eur-lex.europa.eu/legal-content/PL/ALL/?uri=CELEX:52022PC0105.

4 Proposal – Regulation of the European Parliament and of the Council laying down harmonized rules for artificial intelligence (Artificial Intelligence Act) and amending certain Union legislative acts, April 21, 2021, COM/2021/206 final; PROVISIONAL AGREEMENT RESULTING FROM INTERINSTITUTIONAL NEGOTIATIONS [2.2.2024], Article 52(3). https://www.europarl.europa.eu/meetdocs/2014_2019/plmrep/COMMITTEES/CJ40/AG/2024/02-13/1296003EN.pdf.

5 Proposal – Regulation of the European Parliament and of the Council laying down harmonized rules for artificial intelligence (Artificial Intelligence Act) and amending certain Union legislative acts, April 21, 2021, COM/2021/206 final; PROVISIONAL AGREEMENT RESULTING FROM INTERINSTITUTIONAL NEGOTIATIONS [2.2.2024], Article 52(3). https://www.europarl.europa.eu/meetdocs/2014_2019/plmrep/COMMITTEES/CJ40/AG/2024/02-13/1296003EN.pdf.

6 Proposal – Regulation of the European Parliament and of the Council laying down harmonized rules for artificial intelligence (Artificial Intelligence Act) and amending certain Union legislative acts, April 21, 2021, COM/2021/206 final; PROVISIONAL AGREEMENT RESULTING FROM INTERINSTITUTIONAL NEGOTIATIONS [2.2.2024], Article 52(3). https://www.europarl.europa.eu/meetdocs/2014_2019/plmrep/COMMITTEES/CJ40/AG/2024/02-13/1296003EN.pdf.

7 Regulation (EU) 2022/2065 of the European Parliament and of the Council of October 19, 2022 on the single market for digital services and amending Directive 2000/31/EC (Digital Services Act), Official Journal of the EU L 277 of 27.10.2022, p. 1, as amended.

8 E. Hine, L. Floridi, New deepfake regulations in China are a tool for social stability, but at what cost?, *Nature Machine Intelligence* 2022, no. 4, pp. 608–610.

9 国家互联网信息办公室关于《生成式人工智能服务管理办法(征求意见稿)》公开征求意见的通知-, 中共中央网络安全和信息化委员会办公室 http://www.cac.gov.cn/2023-04/11/c_1682854275475410.htm.

10 A. Andersdotter, L. Olejnik, Policy strategies for value-based technology standards, *Internet Policy Review* 2021, vol. 10, no. 3, pp. 1–26.

11 Additional Protocols to the Geneva Conventions of August 12, 1949, concerning the Protection of Victims of International Armed Conflicts (Protocol I) and concerning the Protection of Victims of Non-International Armed Conflicts (Protocol II), drawn up in Geneva on June 8, 1977, OJ. 1992, no. 41, item 175, as amended.

12 *Commentary on the additional protocols: of 8 June 1977 to the Geneva Conventions of 12 August 1949*, ed. C. Pilloud, Y. Sandoz, C. Swinarski, B. Zimmermann, Leiden 1987, p. 443, § 1521.

13 *Protocol Additional to the Geneva Conventions of 12 August 1949, and Relating to the Protection of Victims of International Armed Conflicts (Protocol I), 8 June 1977. Commentary of 1987*, https://ihl-databases.icrc.org/en/ihl-treaties/api-1977/article-37/commentary/1987.

14 T. Rodenhäuser, The legal boundaries of (digital) information or psychological operations under international humanitarian law, *International Law Studies* 2023, vol. 100, p. 16.

15 D.N. Allen, Deepfake fight: AI-powered disinformation and perfidy under the Geneva Conventions, *Notre Dame Journal on Emerging Technologies* 2022, vol. 3, no. 2.

16 International Covenant on Civil and Political Rights opened for signature in New York on December 19, 1966, OJ. 1977, no. 38, item 167.

17 International Covenant on Civil and Political Rights opened for signature in New York on December 19, 1966, OJ. 1977, no. 38, item 167.

18 H.J. Heintze, H.H. Frederick, International legal prohibitions against media content advocating war, racism and genocide: Indisputable principles, varying enforcement, *Department of Justice Journal of Federal Law and Practice* 1990, vol. 11, pp. 91.

19 W.W. Van Alstyne, The first amendment and the suppression of Warmongering propoganda in the United States: Comments and footnotes, *Law and Contemporary Problems* 1966, vol. 31, pp. 530.

20 United Nations High Commissioner for Human Rights, General Comment No. 11: Prohibition of propaganda for war and inciting national, racial or religious hatred (Art. 20), July 29, 1983, https://www.ohchr.org/sites/default/files/Documents/Issues/Opinion/CCPRGeneralCommentNo11.pdf.

21 M. Wolos, The activities of polish diplomacy in 1931, *The Polish Quarterly of International Affairs* 2009, vol. 18, no. 1, pp. 61–95.

22 League of Nations, *Moral Disarment.* Memorandum from the Polish Goverment, September 23, 1931, https://libraryresources.unog.ch/ld.php?content_id=31462481.
23 M. Wallach, *The Activities.*
24 Ministerie van Buitenlandse Zaken, *Global Declaration on Information Integrity Online*, September 20, 2023, https://www.government.nl/documents/diplomatic-statements/2023/09/20/global-declaration-on-information-integrity-online.
25 V. Van Dyke, The responsibility of states for international propaganda, *American Journal of International Law* 1940, vol. 34, no. 1, pp. 58–73.
26 E.A. Downey, A historical survey of the international regulation of propaganda, *Michigan Yearbook of International Legal Studies* 1984, no. 5, p. 341.
27 H.S. LeRoy, Treaty regulation of international radio and short wave broadcasting, *American Journal of International Law* 1938, vol. 32, no. 4, pp. 719–737.
28 E.A. Downey, *A historical survey.*
29 H.S. LeRoy, *Treaty Regulation*, p. 11.
30 Transcript of the agreement in the historic 1934 issue of the Journal Des Telecommunications, No. 11, https://www.itu.int/bibar/ITUJournal/DocLibrary/ITU011-1934-11-fr.pdf.
31 C. Birdsall, J. Walewska-Choptiany, Reconstructing media culture: Transnational perspectives on radio in Silesia, 1924–1948, *Historical Journal of Film, Radio and Television* 2019, vol. 39, no. 3, pp. 439–478.
32 China-Russia Media Cooperation Agreement, July 29, 2021, https://www.documentcloud.org/documents/23558638-china-russia-media-cooperation-agreement-july-2021.
33 International Convention concerning the use of broadcasting in the cause of peace, Geneva, September 23, 1936.
34 International Convention concerning the use of broadcasting in the cause of peace, Geneva, September 23, 1936.
35 UN General Assembly, Principles Governing the Use by States of Artificial Earth Satellites for International Direct Television Broadcasting, A/RES/37/92, December 10, 1983, https://digitallibrary.un.org/record/41084.
36 L. Olejnik, *The Outer Space Treaty and Promoting Responsible Use of Space*, June 7, 2009, https://www.justsecurity.org/86823/the-outer-space-treaty-and-promoting-responsible-use-of-space/.
37 *N. Korea says Satellite Transmitting Revolutionary Songs*, April 5, 2009, https://www.reuters.com/article/idUSSEO85480/.
38 UN General Assembly, Measures to be taken against propaganda and the inciters of a new war, A/RES/2/110, November 3, 1947, http://www.un-documents.net/a2r110.htm.
39 R.A. Falk, On regulating international propaganda: A plea for moderate aims, *Law and Contemporary Problems* 1966, vol. 31, no. 3, pp. 622–634.
40 H. Lahmann, Protecting the global information space in times of armed conflict, *International Review of the Red Cross* 2020, vol. 102, no. 915, pp. 1227–1248.
41 S. Breau, Low-yield tactical nuclear weapons and the rule of distinction, *Flinders Law Journal* 2013, vol. 15, p. 219.
42 F. Misser, I. Jaumain, Rwanda: Death by radio, *Index on Censorship* 1994, vol. 23, no. 4–5, pp. 72–74.
43 W.A. Schabas, Hate speech in Rwanda: The road to genocide, *McGill Law Journal* 2000, vol. 46, no. 141.
44 C.S. Maravilla, Hate speech as a war crime: Public and direct incitement to genocide in international law, *Tulane Journal of International and Comparative Law* 2008, vol. 17, no. 113.
45 Convention on the Prevention and Punishment of the Crime of Genocide, adopted by the General Assembly of the United Nations on December 9, 1948 (ratified in accordance with the law of July 18, 1950), OJ. 1952, no. 2, item 9 as amended.
46 Ministry of Justice, *International Criminal Tribunal for the Former Yugoslavia*, https://www.gov.pl/web/sprawiedliwosc/miedzynarodowy-trybunal-karny-dla-bylej-jugoslawii.
47 C.A. MacKinnon, Prosecutor v. Nahimana, Barayagwiza, & Ngeze. Case No. ICTR 99-52-T, *American Journal of International Law* 2004, vol. 98, no. 2, pp. 325–330.

48 C.A. MacKinnon, Prosecutor v. Nahimana, Barayagwiza, & Ngeze. Case No. ICTR 99-52-T, *American Journal of International Law* 2004, vol. 98, no. 2, pp. 325–330.
49 Charter of the United Nations, Statute of the International Court of Justice and Agreement Establishing the United Nations Preparatory Commission, OJ. 1947, no. 23, item 90.
50 Constitution and Convention of the International Telecommunication Union, drawn up in Geneva on December 22, 1992, OJ. 1998, no. 35, item 196; Amendment Document to the Constitution and Convention of the International Telecommunication Union, drawn up in Geneva on December 22, 1992 and revised by the Plenipotentiary Conference in Kyoto on October 14, 1994, drawn up in Minneapolis on November 6, 1998, OJ. 2003, no. 10, item 111.
51 Constitution and Convention of the International Telecommunication Union, drawn up in Geneva on December 22, 1992, OJ. 1998, no. 35, item 196; Amendment Document to the Constitution and Convention of the International Telecommunication Union, drawn up in Geneva on December 22, 1992 and revised by the Plenipotentiary Conference in Kyoto on October 14, 1994, drawn up in Minneapolis on November 6, 1998, OJ. 2003, no. 10, item 111.
52 Constitution and Convention of the International Telecommunication Union, drawn up in Geneva on December 22, 1992, OJ. 1998, no. 35, item 196; Amendment Document to the Constitution and Convention of the International Telecommunication Union, drawn up in Geneva on December 22, 1992 and revised by the Plenipotentiary Conference in Kyoto on October 14, 1994, drawn up in Minneapolis on November 6, 1998, OJ. 2003, no. 10, item 111.
53 Universal Declaration of Human Rights, UN General Assembly Resolution 217 A (III), adopted December 10, 1948 in Paris, https://libr.sejm.gov.pl/tek01/txt/onz/1948.html.
54 ECHR judgment of December 18, 2012 in *Ahmet Yildirim v. Turkey*, Application No. 3111/10.
55 ECHR judgment of June 23, 2020 in *Engels v. Russia*, application no. 61919/16.
56 Council of Europe, Declaration on freedom of communication on the Internet, May 28, 2023, https://rm.coe.int/16805dfbd5.
57 Council of Europe, Declaration on freedom of communication on the Internet, May 28, 2023, https://rm.coe.int/16805dfbd5.
58 UN, OSCE, OAS and ACHPR, Joint declaration on freedom of expression and the Internet, https://www.osce.org/fom/78309.
59 UN, OSCE, OAS and ACHPR, Joint declaration on freedom of expression and the Internet, https://www.osce.org/fom/78309.
60 Consolidated version: Official Journal of the EU C 202, 7.06.2016, p. 369.
61 ECHR judgment of April 22, 2013 in *Animal Defenders International v. the United Kingdom*, Application No. 48876/08, paras. 13–15.
62 ECHR judgment of November 25, 1996 in *Wingrove v. the United Kingdom*, Application No. 58080/11, para. 58.
63 B. Baade, Fake news and international law, *European Journal of International Law* 2018, vol. 29, no. 4, pp. 1357–1376.
64 *Updated concept of the convention of the United Nations on ensuring international information security*, 2023, https://docs-library.unoda.org/Open-Ended_Working_Group_on_Information_and_Communication_Technologies_-_(2021)/ENG_Concept_of_UN_Convention__on_International_Information_Security_Proposal_of_the_Russian__Federation.pdf.

Chapter 6

Political and state propaganda

In this chapter, we continue the exploration of two important topics: the uses of propaganda methods in politics and state affairs. The next chapter is devoted to military issues, information warfare, and war propaganda.

6.1 BASIC DISTINCTION AGAIN: PR VERSUS PROPAGANDA, INFORMATION PLURALISM

Distinctions can be made between "ordinary" political PR (e.g., in an election campaign), awareness-raising or educational campaigns, and information operations. These are important activities in a democratic State with pluralism. These may also be relevant activities for every state system or regime. As explained, such activities may be considered forms of propaganda—the techniques or methods may be the same, or very similar. However, this does not immediately mean that we are talking about outright totalitarian propaganda, such as we had to deal with, for example, in Germany during the time of Hitler and his NSDAP political party[1] or in Soviet Russia. In totalitarian environment, propaganda was total and covered the full spectrum: from state information, to radio, literary, commercial, even medical content. It saturated the information environment. Breaking through this wall of information then was very difficult or even impossible. In such a situation, propaganda may gain great powers. This is when there is no input or feedback from other sources, from other points of view. In contrast, when we have pluralism, it can be challenging for propaganda to achieve a "totalitarian" level of power. This is impossible, even if large segments of society draw information from only one source, because other segments of society may seek information from other sources, and information saturation on a full scale in the majority of society will not occur. And this is why democratic systems can function more fairly than totalitarian ones. Although the openness of societies may mean a certain weakness and vulnerability to pitting one social group against another.[2] Various activities can be conducted. The picture, therefore, is nuanced, the scales of intensity are broad; there is more to that than simple extremes, totalitarian-or-not. Propaganda was never limited to a particular type of government. Simply speaking, forms, and their honesty qualities, differ.

However, due to the diversity of access to information in a pluralistic society, we do not equate PR, educational campaigns, or even ordinary propaganda with "totalitarian propaganda." These are different orders, and need not be mixed.

Various terms will be used in this chapter: "propaganda," "political advertising," "educational campaign," "PR," "announcement," "proclamation," etc. There will be a talk of both internal informational influences—focused on the population in the country. But also about external influence—information activities aimed at external audiences, such as those in other States and their affairs. Reading this chapter will also help to appreciate the problems and

DOI: 10.1201/9781003499497-6

undesirable effects that may occur when a side believes its own propaganda. For example, in the propaganda of success, which portrays reality in a certain way, while in the "real reality," the situation is somewhat different and more complex. Believing in one's imaginary reality is a fundamental mistake, an analytical error, and a self-induced flaw.

6.2 MULTI-CHANNEL INFORMATION EFFORTS

Information activities can be conducted through multiple channels. To repeat: these may include traditional media, state information services, and state diplomacy. And today, of course, also social media which such centers of information may use. The unfortunate phrase "fake news" appearing in the second decade of the 21st century needs to be confronted again. The use of this term has led to the problem of disinformation being too closely identified not only with aspects of simple true/false dichotomy but also with media and journalistic issues.[3] This is an excessive reduction of the subject matter—by which one can even harm oneself, when one believes in this illusion and accepts it as reality. Such a reduction, however, may have served various politicians or influencers.

6.2.1 Disinformation and propaganda is not primarily an issue of news reporting or of journalism

Information operations, propaganda, and disinformation are a realm far beyond the reductive single-dimensional perception of this as "something related to journalism or press." That would be a pure oversimplification. Terminology is very important, because words can dictate the understanding of issues. Fortunately, the unfortunate use of the term "fake news"[4] has been noticed and started to be phased out as a short-term fashion. Although it took some time and effort for this knowledge and perception to gain ground and spread. Until then, the phrase has unfortunately managed to become quite established. So, why is that an issue? In the extreme case, equating propaganda or even disinformation with "fake news" can in itself carry the full weight of false, misleading information, and even disinformation—if done on purpose. And why uses of this term were unfortunate? Primarily because it is difficult to define "fake news," "false information" (here narrowed down to news, i.e., media information), or to reduce a complex phenomenon to a single binary division fake-true. It may be difficult to clearly define the veracity or falsity of press or media information (or even scientific reporting, or publications) in relation to a journalistic article (which is supposed to describe a topic). After all, in most cases, information is based on something, which involves a dose of trust, or relevance of quality. But incredulous takes can also be corroborated with qualities, and even be shaped to be believable (especially when unverifiable). So, to make matters worse, fake/true is an ambiguous meaning, prone to manipulation.

After all, one can't use the term "fake news" in the sense of something you disagree with, and that's how it also used to be—as a slur, an insult, a belittling term. This is then instrumentalizing the topic using means of persuasion—perhaps it is even propaganda. So, to stress: what matters here is propaganda. That is a concept worthy of attention, not "fake news."[5] To reduce a multidimensional issue to a single realm would make it impossible to analyze the true nature of the issue of influence.

Another situation arises with disinformation. Disinformation can be treated as a tool of propaganda[6] and does not have to use false information at all. Demonstrating untruths cuts across the usefulness—especially when there is a risk that falsehoods will be detected. If one does use messages based on falsehoods—one should only do it if one cannot be caught in a lie, what, to reiterate, was assimilated by Goebbels' propaganda machine.[7]

These are valid arguments, but one does not have to limit oneself to them. Further on in this chapter, I will explain why mere lies, too, can have an effect on certain audiences. So, it is important to note that both approaches are possible—but used in different ways, for different purposes. At the very least, it is worth being aware of the two approaches, including if you are a consumer of information.

Moreover, sometimes it may even be difficult to believe the truth, for example when it is inconvenient, unintuitive, unexpected, unwelcome, or defies common sense of previously held beliefs. And then such a propagandist would even have to bend the reality (falsify it) in order to make matters easier to grasp, to believe the real information. Oh, the paradox! In other words, when directing information it must be made in ways so it is acceptable, including for the true information (unless the goal is causing disbelief—belief in the opposite—in the audience). This shows that public communication requires a certain amount of flexibility, but overstepping the bounds can be unethical.

6.2.2 Ability to impose an agenda—topics that are discussed

It is also useful to be aware of the agenda-setting process of traditional and electronic media. What is described and how it is described has an impact on what is talked about or not talked about, covered, or picked up. The media may not have as much influence on what we think about a topic compared to what we already believe about it,[8] and how it is talked about.[9] However, their activities can result in practical implications. Often, what's barred from entry to the public debate is obscured, or effectively does not exist. Instead, place is awarded to other concepts (sometimes, it may also be too soon to cover certain views, as simple as this). Especially in the past, the role of the media was significant.

Times are changing. A partial diffusion occurs, as traditional media are losing some of their past flair or importance—to electronic or social media, other such new channels, and it is these ones that win capabilities to influence agendas. How? Let's give a direct, if blunt, example! For example, a person can be portrayed as a crook and a thief or as a hero—depending on how the information is conveyed and demonstrated, how it is related to each other, and what context is formed. Events can gain little or a lot of importance through this. Or be treated as not significant at all.

6.2.2.1 Shaping the messages about global warming

The same is true of scientific studies, even those of questionable quality. Because the average viewer may not notice the difference between scientific papers or publications—papers are papers, after all, and who cares who authors them? If one paper confirms the fact of global warming and the other does not (or reports results to the contrary), one can do a lot with this fact, handling it informationally, molding, and modeling the message. One medium may then describe the progressive process. Another may act as if the problem did not exist, or even suggest that "someone" cares about making people believe that some climate processes are occurring (or not). The latter case describes a manipulation that convinces people that a manipulation is taking place. It is the presentation of the situation in a layered way, the so-called stacked, or multi-level conspiracy.

6.2.2.2 Shaping the message about the ozone hole and Y2K

Abuse can also be related to the use of the timeline. Time, as we know, only moves forward. It is difficult to change the past. But perceptions of the past are something else—these can be changed in the future. For example, in 2023, one can write an article about how concerns about the ozone hole in the 1980s and 1990s were exaggerated, and justify it on the grounds that a catastrophe was predicted. And yet "*today we can see that nothing happened*"—No.

The catastrophe did not happen precisely because there was some preventive action taken globally (such as reducing the use of freons/CFCs, or chlorofluorocarbons) that saved us. But we have no comparison with a situation in which nothing was done. Because there is only a single timeline! We cannot have two worlds put side by side and test alternatives of taking or not taking actions. To say that the problem was contrived is, therefore, incorrect. A biased article may simply fail to mention it, especially if one likes to go against "recognized standards", imposed by the "world government," etc.

A similar mechanism was at function in the case of other issues. An example is the so-called "millennium bug" (Y2K), when computer systems were supposed to fail when their clock went from 1999 to 2000, or actually (this was the problem) to 1900. In computer systems, where the year was counted with only two digits, this was what the effect could be: going from 99 to 00, so effectively from 1999 to 1900 instead of 2000—going in reverse, not forward. A lot of systems could have been affected by this since our lives, regulations, laws, payrolls, etc.—they work in function of the passing time. And time should flow forward, not backward. Once the problem was realized, and communicated to experts and to the public, time (including of experts and policymakers) and resources were devoted to solving it. We don't know with 100% certainty what the full situation would have been if no action had been taken against the ozone hole, Y2K (or COVID-19). We don't know because there is only one timeline; we can't go back and test a different approach. This is the fundamental nature of our world and we need to live with it.

This fact can be used by fraudsters or charlatans to convince naive and gullible people of strange theses. Similar aerobatics can be done on any subject from the past, where some decision had to be made and it had some consequences (the consequences of not making a decision, for obvious reasons, were not experienced).

6.3 FADING STATE CONTROL OF THE INFORMATION ENVIRONMENT?

The information environment is something in which societies (as a whole, as individuals) are immersed. In which they live and function. Different information can circulate at different speeds. Today, news or hot information can spread very rapidly. This is because of technology and the preference for rapid consumption of information.

After all, it is enough for the parties propagating the information to send a message via the notification infrastructure. Then, the information is nearly instantly displayed in web browsers or on other devices (like smartphones). This happens very quickly and on a large scale. Tens, hundreds of thousands of recipients can be informed of an event even immediately. Such information can include interpretations of events right away. All this shapes the public debate, but also the information environment, that is, the system we discussed in Chapter 3.

In the 21st century, the information environment is a very dynamic space, but also an amorphous one. In the 19th century, people could obtain information from other people, and they learned about it from newspapers; in the 20th century, radio, then the Internet appeared. All of this may have been subject to state control, and therefore also to censorship. Today, this form of information control does not function as it used to (at least on a daily basis and in democratic States), people can get information from many different sources. If only they want to, because many can, of course, limit themselves to only a certain type of content, that is, content that they like, that entertains them, because of which they do not experience an uncomfortable feeling of cognitive dissonance. This also suggests a subtle form of manipulation: overload of cognitive abilities of recipients or giving them information so that they are tempted to focus on some topics, and ignore others. An informational and digital temptation.

6.3.1 Amorphism of the information environment and its formation in a democratic society and the rule of law

The amorphism of the information environment manifests itself precisely in the fact that information can be drawn from a plethora of channels of various nature. Many elements of the information environment can shape it in one way or another and influence it. Shaping such an environment is quite difficult—no one has a monopoly on the information message. These are not the days when one big newspaper is read by almost everyone and has a huge influence on what people know, what they don't know, and what they think. These are no longer the days when the proverbial university professor didn't have an opinion on a topic until the newspapers subscribed to by his or her university's Department of This and That arrived—and after reading a new issue, he or she then suddenly knew what they were supposed to think on a given topic.

Today, such a message can be broadcast at any time. It can be short, concise, and quickly set the tone for events that are underway—it can influence them. Such a message sent immediately and irresponsibly can also contribute to practical actions: protests, riots, even revolutions. Or to refer to events that are yet to come, because, after all, some people may know about them beforehand, and thus it is possible to effectively preemptively set the tone, anticipating the construction of a certain narrative. Although this particular term is sometimes used awkwardly, it is often misused. It nonetheless has its justified uses. So what is a narrative?

6.3.2 Narratives

The Oxford Dictionary of English definition states that narrative is "an account of a series of events, facts, etc., given in order and with the establishing of connections between them; a narration, a story, an account."[10] The definition is telling, and good, but perhaps it is not the most ideal or appropriate in the context we are concerned with here. For our purposes, a much better definition is this military-realm one[11]: "a spoken or written account of events and information arranged in a logical sequence to 'influence the behavior of a target audience.'"[12] Thus, it is some kind of information line—a short, concise description of a story, or a situation. It can also illuminate or distort things. Factually, or not, justify or explain the phenomena taking place. Fit the happening events into some track of thought logically—for example, by someone established. It is necessary for the story to be self-consistent and generally fitting and logical. For example, with an appropriately constructed narrative, one may absolve someone of guilt by shifting it to other people, groups, or environments—or put the guilt on someone. One may also impose a certain way of understanding events, including historical events, even very distant in time.

6.3.3 The beginning of modernity—the radio

Radio was the first technical means of mass broadcasting and reaching audiences over long distances. The origins of strident radio propaganda were in the 1920s—shortly after the so-called plebiscites were held, in which, after World War I, the population of many places in Europe voted on the issue to which State the lands should belong. Germany, for example, directed its propaganda to the German-speaking population of Silesia. Poland did not give up the field, launching transmitters many times more powerful than the German ones (until the Nazis came to power in Germany and, with a full understanding of the importance of propaganda, increased the power of the transmitters).[13] The strategic value of radio stations such as (then, German territory) Breslau (Wroclaw today) and Gleiwitz (Gliwice today) was clear at the time. Today, we may underestimate this by analyzing the German provocation "under a false flag," the Gleiwitz incident, when a feigned "attack on Germany" was carried out by German individuals disguised as Polish soldiers. World War II began and was "justified" with this.

Radio propaganda was very useful in large countries. For example, it allowed to reach the Chinese countryside (where in the 1950s illiteracy levels were high), which was important in consolidating the socialist system. The practical problem of not having a large number of radios was solved, if only by building a system for receiving radio signals and broadcasting through loudspeakers. In 1962 there were already 6.7 million of them in the country.[14] An additional "advantage" of such a system of broadcasting was the inability to turn off such a loudspeaker, as well as the opportunity to observe who turned up to listen to the broadcast (and who did not). And everyone had to listen—such obligations were introduced. If someone did not turn up to listen, could such a person be considered an honest communist citizen?

6.3.4 For consideration—Hitler won the election despite being barred from using radio

In Germany during World War II, listening to foreign radio was a crime, passing on information so received was punishable by death.[15]

It is worth noting, however, that election candidate Adolf Hitler (and his political party, the NSDAP) "never had access to the radio in Germany before he came to power. The denial of radio facilities to him (exploited by the Nazis as a form of persecution) was one of the factors that helped him win in the end."[16] This is counterintuitive: it may have helped because the Nazis portrayed themselves as victims of persecution. But still, the rivals were able to use these then very new means of reaching their audiences, and that apparently was not enough.

In 1941, radio was considered the best existing means of disseminating propaganda. Goebbels introduced a basic principle of Nazi radio: radio must be entertaining (interesting),[17] so that the recipients simply wanted to listen to it. If, on the other hand, propaganda is directed to external countries—one must understand the internal situation, culture, and mentality of the people there.[18] This observation still holds true today with regard to the use of any means of communication. For example, in 2005, a woman not wearing a bra perhaps might have caused a sensation somewhere, but directing a similar message in France would be futile.

6.3.5 "Hate radio," Balkans, information blockades

In the 1990s, as I mentioned, radio played a crucial and tragic role in the Rwandan genocide.[19] So, due to stabilization and humanitarian issues, there were calls to build a capacity to jam radio broadcasting—as I explained in the previous chapter, this is possible and legal. Here, I refer to the powers of UN peacekeeping missions.[20]

Jamming radio involves broadcasting a signal on the same radio frequencies. As for media jamming, this was successfully done by NATO in 1997 during the Balkan crisis—by jamming or physically taking control of broadcasting systems.[21] Prior to that, stations in Belgrade at the time referred to U.S. President Bill Clinton as "Bill Hitler," "Adolf Clinton," "Führer"—calling him a war criminal,[22] so on. The headquarters of Serbian media outlet Radio Televisija Srbije was also bombed in 1999 due to its involvement in propaganda, and satellite broadcasting was later cut off; EUTELSAT satellites were controlled by Western countries.[23]

6.3.6 Contemporary stuff—social media and Internet from satellite

Could an analogous solution today be to shut down telecommunications networks, the Internet? In the case of social media, there is some centralization here—someone controls them. This someone would either have to shut them down (e.g., being forced by state services), or the transmission of network packets would have to be blocked from identified servers. This could be problematic but it is not impossible.

During the war in Ukraine, disabling information systems seemed to be one of Russia's goals. However, it failed to do so. Information—photos, videos, posts, descriptions—flowed in a wide stream around the world, having a great impact on Western societies. This was possible, thanks to a good Internet connection, as well as the Starlink satellite Internet system. The information flowing in a wide current meant that Russia was on the losing end of the information war from the beginning. Then again, there may not even have been an opportunity to impose an agenda here on Western States or their societies, but the incoming information only strengthened the will to help. And limited the ability of Western States to engage in appeasement.

6.4 AUDIENCE SEGMENTS, INFORMATION BUBBLES

6.4.1 Customer groups, segments

Since we have said that people are consumers of information, let's add that people may be classified into certain groups or segments. This can be done using advertising terminology, such as "people interested in new technology content," "people who drink carbonated beverages," and "people who use an electric kettle to brew coffee." One can also use demographic criteria: classify groups by age, gender, place of residence, education level, etc. In addition, one can include views on some specific topics, such as gender equality, abortion, LGBT, climate change, meat consumption, and vacationing in the mountains or by the sea. One can conduct polls and study the sentiments of such groups.

People divided into such groups can form peculiar communities bound in some way, such as demographically or by interests. These people don't necessarily know each other—something, however, connects them. And this makes it possible to reach out to these groups. Such groups may have a preference for certain topics, for example, vegetarians will be friendlier to information pointing out the benefits of their diet (for reasons of health, environmental protection, etc.), while such information may not necessarily appeal to people who do not attach such importance to diet and, for example, enjoy consuming the traditional German Schweinhaxe mit knödel und sauerkraut (pork hock with sauerkraut and knodel dumpling), sipping beer.

Different groups may prefer particular lines of messages. In view of this, the next step is to draw information from sources that mostly provide them with messages in line with their views (e.g., ideological line). In the case of social media, this can happen due to the use of recommendation algorithms. That is, when one clicks on some content a number of times, when one marks some content as preferred ("likes" it, adds it to "favorites," etc.), when one adds a comment under some post—algorithms receive and interpret such a signal. They then cue up content that is consistent with those interactions and choices, and perhaps dim others. This might lead to information isolation, when non-preferred content is not surfaced. Such a person will then be stuck in his or her own information bubble and will not recognize some content. Perhaps this will make him or her feel very comfortable. His or her feelings or views will not be hurt. However, he or she will not learn about many other important things.

Certain events, phenomena—war or cataclysm, or perhaps the peace and well-being of society, because it is not just brutal violence and disasters everywhere—may surprise him or her.

For example, regarding the war in Ukraine, many may have had a feeling of strong cognitive dissonance. Well, because how was that possible—such a war happening in the 21st century? It's so outdated, unfashionable, and pointless; after all, there was supposed to be harmony and peace in our times, and wars were supposedly a thing of the past. And then suddenly a large-scale war breaks out; suddenly there are pictures of corpses of dead civilians lying in the streets—victims of war. (By the way, this then raises the question of whether or not such content should be blocked. According to the rules of many digital platforms, purging them would have been the right thing to do, but these interventions were suspended, offering an opportunity to Western societies to experience it). Who could have seen this coming? Well, at the very least—everyone who understands the complexity of the world and pays attention. Information isolation could then contribute to the great surprise. In a sense, therefore, such war images were—perversely, since the whole thing was tragic and unequivocally bad—an antidote to this phenomenon. On the other hand, its effect can hardly be expected to last long after the eventual end of hostilities. People may forget, and shift interest elsewhere.

6.4.2 Information bubbles insulate from information, or maybe they don't exist

Information bubbles insulate from undesirable information, but only to a certain extent. Therefore, exaggerating their effect can be misleading. It is worth exercising caution. According to more recent studies, reliably conducted, information bubbles in connection with electronic (social) media may ... not even exist.

Yes, similar mechanisms can foster and solidify polarizations to some extent, at times, but the fact is that while sitting at home in a chair and having access to the Internet, we can reach out to a wide variety of information sources. Not necessarily one-sided ones. After all, no one is forcing anyone to be stuck in a "bubble." It is a choice. What's more, it's thanks to the Internet that it's so easy to interact with people outside the "bubble" (even if only online), with people holding completely different views.[24] It is really wonderful that thanks to the Internet, we have so many different sources of information at our fingertips, we are not limited to any particular one. If only we want to.

6.4.3 Does pluralism combined with social media lead to polarization?

But that is what can contribute to driving polarization. Due to the fact that people like their own worldviews, being exposed to other kinds of information and viewpoints might make one feel uncomfortable. This uncomfortable feeling is related to cognitive dissonance: *wait, what do you mean, so there are other points of view on things? Is it possible for someone to think differently?*

In the face of this, polarizing aggression could occur. "Political wars" where people are "forced" to take sides, adopt some specific viewpoints, or agree or disagree with some arguments.[25] The ideological segregation of offline media was found to be lower than that of online media, and in turn for online media (here the researchers caveat that with the exception of online editions of traditional media, such as newspapers) it is significantly lower compared to the segregation with social network activity.[26] People's differing views can even lead to hatred between them (or of sources of information)[27] and solidify people's opposing views. Here, you can again appreciate the backfire effect,[28] which is the ignorance, suppression, or displacement of the new information. That being the case, perhaps it is better for such people to sit in their safe "bubbles" after all, and not attempt to contact others.

Alternatively: familiarization with differing views or novel information or viewpoints should occur gradually, carefully, and slowly. This can even have propaganda value—if one wants to reach people with completely differing views, it should be done gently, without hammering information into their heads. Unless we are talking about a totalitarian state, such as Soviet Russia or Nazi Germany,[29] where there were no alternatives—but we don't want that! So, on a more serious note: exposure to content with which the viewer strongly disagrees (or has otherwise strong opinions) creates the risk of solidifying people in their own opinions. Because they already know them, they like them. Changing views can be costly (e.g., mentally) and unpleasant.

So, do people even prefer simplified, or false information provided in an accessible way to true, nuanced information? Based on scientific knowledge, the case seems to be clear—yes.

Such may be the practical, possible conclusion from the observation of past events, combined with the modern science of psychology and sociology. Of course, it can be formulated differently, but let's not play with euphemisms, let's be direct and frank. In view of this, people (sometimes) may prefer to live a lie, be wrong, and get their information from unreliable sources of information. They are fine with it. May we call this hypocrisy? No, rather—a lifestyle. So, good luck in combating such falsehoods, disinformation, and so on. One must remember to keep the right proportions and be careful not to end up inciting political violence or undermining the public order.

6.4.4 Polarization and violence

Such methods were used, for example, by the Irish Republican Army (Provisional IRA), whose political goal was liberation from British rule—in practice, what took place were lots of bombings. On the other hand, finances for activities were obtained, for example, in the United States, justifying it with an appropriate propaganda priming.[30] But similar activities can also be identified with many other individuals, many groups, in other countries.

While we consider such paramilitary or para-state groups, one may mention the propaganda activities of ISIS (the Islamic State) in the second decade of the 21st century. Propaganda was efficiently created and directed in various ways. ISIS's "citizens" (rather: subjects) were confirmed in their rationale. Opponents were frightened, in various ways, including by organizing terrorist attacks. Recruits were obtained if only through publicity in connection with the attacks. Western societies were influenced by published violent, cruel videos, including those depicting the destruction of cultural monuments (which was outrageous to some citizens of Western countries). Various digital platforms were used to promote ideas and attract new recruits or money, even the dating app Tinder. For example, first convincing victims to share nude photos, and then blackmailing them with threats of making those photos public if they were unwilling to pay.[31] This was controlled by the relevant structures. ISIS had an entire propaganda department[32] and used a lot of digital media capabilities. But also the traditional ones—content was directed to its "subjects" in the form of a newspaper. ISIS also deliberately used women in propaganda, and even had special brigades (Al-Khansaa Kateeba),[33] made up of Western-educated women,[34] to also undertake information activities and recruit new women.[35]

Palestinian Hamas, too, uses political marketing in its political and militant propaganda, using international law to raise the issue of Palestine internationally—in which, by the way, the Soviet Union helped, successfully supporting the passage of resolutions at the UN.[36] Activities thus consisted of recruiting, building awareness and beliefs in the public, and publicizing real or alleged abuses or massacres (here: perpetrated by Israel). Following the October

2023 attack on Israel by Hamas militants and the associated Israeli defense, Hamas structures successfully planted many propaganda narratives in regional and Western media, which may have contributed to street protests, such as those happening in France, or elsewhere.

6.4.5 Breaking through information isolation bubbles

Assuming that bubbles isolate from some information, even if someone desires to stay in isolation from it (and so—in a "bubble"), varied information content can still reach them. This is due to the fact that digital platforms provide means for advertisers to reach different social groups—on websites, Facebook, Twitter, etc. Such ads can be targeted accordingly.[37]

This is made possible by digital platforms that recognize users' preferences. Do they eat cheese? How about strawberry yogurt? Are they 35 years old? Do they like watching TV series? Are they introverts, or perhaps extroverts? Digital platforms can deduce this information, even determine someone's political preferences. And by doing so, they can better target such people (groups) with tailored content, including ads.[38]

Such methods were also used by professional influence agencies, such as the so-called Russian troll factory[39] but not only that particular one. The cost structure of such "Russian" ads displayed in the 2016 U.S. presidential election was analyzed.

> The most expensive ad cost $5,307 USD. The highest number of impressions generated was 1,335,000 and the maximum number of clicks was 73,060. ... more than 25% of the ads had no impressions, clicks, and cost, suggesting these ads were not launched or ran for a very short period of time. An average ad cost $34.5, was seen by 11,536 users, and received 1,062 clicks ... higher investment (cost) did not always lead to higher return (e.g. impressions, clicks).[40]

The bottom line is this (and it's familiar to PR specialists and advertisers): you have to design ad campaigns well, and things don't always work great. What is interesting, however, is the way in which the message is targeted to specific social groups:

> IRA ads reached audiences that are very biased toward African-Americans and Liberals. More important, we show that ads were overall targeted toward a population that is more likely to believe, and approve and subsequently less likely to report or identify false claims in them.[41]

So, it appears that in addressing these ads, they knew how to select and pick their targeting parameters.

6.4.6 Is the influence of digital platforms on policy decisions exaggerated?

Facebook's informational impact is indicated by studies analyzing this in the context of the 2020 U.S. elections. This research was conducted by Facebook together with outside researchers. The overall tone of this research indicates little (if any) impact of the social platform *itself* on social polarization, at least in the United States. The researchers modulated the content that users saw, such as reducing the number of links displayed to articles on political topics. The result?

In short, the conclusions are that such modifications did not result in changes in user opinions. This, therefore, confirms the observation already noted earlier that the issue of information bubbles seemed somewhat "exaggerated," and that its actual risk severity should be reassessed. Because these opinions were not necessarily driven by social media in the way it was at times portrayed in the public debate, sometimes in a biased manner, and without consideration of the subject. This is because the issue has many nuances, and it is impossible to say "yes" or "no" to it directly. To determine how things work, researchers reduced the frequency of some content for some users. And the existence of problematic "echo chambers" has not been confirmed, that is, information isolation from certain content, a situation when same opinions and theses are repeated over and over again.[42] In addition, shared ("retweet," "share," etc.) content had limited, if any, impact on people's opinions.[43]

Furthermore, the algorithmic recommendation system that promotes displayed content on social media (on Facebook and Instagram) apparently did not affect people's opinions.[44] This was investigated on one group of users, by "turning off" the algorithm (the content was then displayed chronologically). An interesting observation was that it was the non-use of the recommendation algorithm that led to the display of more political content, even of poor quality, from "like-minded" people. Could it be, then, that the lack of a recommendation algorithm has a greater impact on polarization than recommendation algorithms? Such a conclusion would be radical, so we do not draw it—let the Reader decide for himself or herself, in light of the above information. Let's just remind ourselves that people like to stay in their own circles. Including offline. What's more, such a direct conclusion would be slightly awkward, because such modulation of content has resulted in even more moderate content! Whether it appealed to a decidedly non-moderate audience is another matter. On a sample (!) of 208 million U.S. Facebook users, it was also tested how shared political news (articles from websites) can influence people and whether this leads to "ideological segregation." The result was interesting and significant—people with certain views (conservative, liberal) share strongly different content.[45]

6.4.6.1 To have your cake and eat it too?

Recommendation algorithm was able to cut out content from "less trusted" sources of information, that is, moderate content, censoring some sources,[46] for example, limiting the spread of poor quality, false information from fishy websites. Experts and some public officials sometimes desire to have their cake and eat it too: arguing about the harmfulness of algorithms, they may demonize them and would like to restrict them, while at the same time they would like to cut out some content, that is, use algorithms. Where is the sense in that?

6.5 POLARIZATION

Polarization is an interesting phenomenon. In the simplest terms, it is a situation when we have social groups with certain views: some are in favor, others are against an idea, a proposal, a view, or attitude.

The view is for or the view is against—there is nothing in between. Nothing in the middle, and if it appears, one may want to try and suppress it with propaganda methods. This opens the field of activity for many people, companies, and States. One may buy into some view or support such a dispute, division, etc. and, through it, gain, for example, political support, monetary influence, power, and fame. In a sense, adopting some existing view is the easiest way to go, without trying to maneuver, getting into the details, or looking for a "middle ground." To opine—it's so easy! Then, one can adjust views, and actions to it. This way, for example, one does not have to think, what can be difficult, tiring, or even painful.

A polarized society is a kind of an opportunity. For some at least. For others—it is also a threat. It can be considered from various views, both internal (rising tensions, perhaps the risk of violence, etc.) and external (it is simpler from the outside to play up the situation in such a country, to infiltrate, to interfere with it with information activities). Thus, many may gain something from polarization, many may benefit from it. Although for society itself it can be harmful, because it stifles the space for debate.

Can social media "debates" contribute to polarization? Their dynamics are often sharp and emotionally charged. Moreover, the algorithms of digital platforms can support (or even induce) some such tendencies.[47] If, for example, polarizing content is easily amplified (strengthened, shared, spread, promoted)—a frequent criticism against digital platforms that mediate communication—it could reinforce the already existing situation. Digital platforms, in their own interest, promote "popular" content. As we know, popular culture, emotions, etc., sell well. For a healthy society, it could mean a variety of consequences, but we have to live with it.

6.5.1 Natural human predisposition

It is worth maintaining a healthy skepticism about the view that digital platforms are the sole culprit responsible for polarization and radicalization. This is because it is known that people themselves often choose to adopt some and not other sources of information,[48] for example, with a particular political line, and clear social beliefs, specifically "partisan." To establish that, researchers checked what people read, and compared it with the results suggested by the Google search engine. It turned out that people prefer their own preferences. So, it's not so much a technical limitation that bars them from other particular views, but a conscious and deliberate human choice. But actually, why is this the case?

Let's think about it. Some content may appeal more to specific people. People like to confirm themselves in their own beliefs. Watch programs and read articles and books that correspond to their worldview (and reject others). This is an important argument when studying the problem of the so-called "echo chambers" or information bubbles,[49] that is, when social groups are immersed in certain content and isolated from others. In view of this, do people do all this to themselves? After all, there is another way. One can follow a balanced information diet. Draw information from a variety of sources. One can, but why and who would have time for all this? Another conclusion from the work, again, questions the absolutist understanding of information bubbles and echo chambers, namely—a conscious and deliberate human decision is nevertheless important when deciding what content one is confronted with.

6.5.2 Why people share fakes and it doesn't affect their credibility

This brings us to an important question. Why do people share bogus information, sometimes evident hoaxes, such as when someone on social media impersonates a well-known person (e.g., a politician), changing only the profile name, photo, or description, and making an obviously absurd post? Let's refer to the so-called "pizzagate" in the United States, when a story was popularized about important Democratic Party politicians being supposedly involved in the sale of children, a practice that allegedly took place in some pizzeria. This prompted someone to visit that pizzeria, armed with a pistol, and a rifle (shots were fired) in order to "free the children" allegedly held there. Needless to say, no such "activity" took place at the pizza place. This incident is a great demonstration of how propaganda can lead people to take real action.[50]

It would seem that sharing a fake could be costly and involve reputation damage, loss of credibility—obvious losses (cost), but perhaps these may potentially be amortized by a gain, such as a clear signal that one is part of a certain social group, expresses full commitment to a particular option, consistent with a certain position, and views.[51] This would also explain the lack of actual damage to reputation or image within a particular social group (those within other groups can simply be disregarded). If there is social acceptance of this, what is the problem?

The situation of social polarization can also be cleverly and effectively exploited by the methods of information operations using deepfake,[52] so not only in international politics but specifically in domestic politics. This is because in the case of divisions, one party may have especial propensity for easily believing a fake released from that camp, and help making it available to others.

6.6 WHO USES ADVERTISING METHODS IN PROPAGANDA?

"Russian methods"? It is not just Russia that has used advertising infrastructures.[53] Such capabilities and services are simply ordinary advertising, also PR functions that typical candidates in elections[54] or their parties may want to use. If only because it is possible to achieve something through these platforms that is impossible with traditional advertising, that is, TV spots, newspaper ads, and billboards. It's all about reaching the audience more precisely. Not surprisingly, if one wants to reach an audience, one uses the functions at their disposal that make this possible, meeting the audience where they are.

It must be admitted that in the early days of the AdTech industry's development, customer verification on such platforms was either non-existent, residual, or could be foiled easily. Security and abuse problems existed and platforms did not particularly want to deal with this topic. Until they were legally or politically forced to do so. However, even today, it is possible to cleverly circumvent political advertising bans. The easiest way to do this is to target the so-called issue-based targeting, that is, to refer to specific issues, to specific matters. These issues can be considered a political thing and translated accordingly—just indirectly, but in human minds, easily. In view of this, issues of diet, global warming, gender, etc. can be treated as a manifestation of someone's views and act accordingly, targeting the message to such audiences. This is something that no one will ban, because that would be absurd censorship and restriction of freedom of expression.

6.6.1 Moves against manipulation and abuse versus the right to freedom of expression

However, the problem of abuse was so vociferous that online platforms introduced increasingly stringent restrictions against manipulation, misinformation, false information, etc. Until a moment came to relax and normalize operations. YouTube in 2023, for example, was already allowing the mere questioning of the election result (in contrast with some strict previous stances), as long as some specific context is mentioned.[55] This is about the issue of public debate. After the experience of previous elections and the removal of a great deal of content, the YouTube digital platform noted: "We find that while removing this content does curb some misinformation, it could also have the unintended effect of curtailing political speech without meaningfully reducing the risk of violence or other real-world harm."[56]

Of interest in this context may be a report by the U.S. House of Representatives, pointing out at the activities of the (governmental) U.S. Cybersecurity and Infrastructure Security Agency (CISA) and U.S. companies and the actions to allegedly censor Americans under the guise of fighting disinformation.[57] Of course, in the United States, such reports and deliberations were heavily politicized and may be biased. But the very subject addressed from this side is hard to overlook. Matters of propaganda and disinformation can undoubtedly be considered propaganda and disinformation. Or at least as an integral part of politics.

6.6.2 Measurability of Russia's informational impact

People's exposure to the so-called "fake news" websites has been studied in the United States[58] in the context of the 2020 elections. Such "untrustworthy" sites were said to have been accessed (in some way) by as many as 26.2% of Americans. That's a lot. But is it? That doesn't necessarily directly translate into the informational impact on all of them. Mere exposure to information does not equal impact. And such flawed conclusions were sometimes drawn in the public debate. It's an analytical error that stems from a lack of familiarity with previous findings in the field and industry, like scientific research (sometimes even common sense).

Did Russian operations in the information space, on social media, have a measurable impact on the 2016 elections? Not particularly, either, it seems, or at least no evidence has been found directly indicating this. On the contrary, it is argued that such posts were seen by very few people relative to the total size of the electorate—1% of users saw 70% of posts.[59] An interesting conclusion could also be that such propaganda on social media would have no right to exist on a large scale and produce results. Again, common sense—it has to do with campaign spending. Parties in the United States spent hundreds of millions of dollars on official political campaigning and advertising. Compare to this some social media posts made at a much, much smaller scale, at a completely incomparable cost—it conceivably had no chance to be a match. It would be absurd to consider that one can win an election in the world's largest democracy, a nuclear superpower, at a cost of the proverbial pennies. If elections could be rigged or influenced for such proverbial pennies, it would call into question the very meaning of them, the voters, and the quality of democracy too. This leads to the conclusion of the illogicality of such an argument. Naturally, the problem may become more relevant if there is very little difference in support between candidates or votes in the final results, say a few percent, or a fraction of a percent.

But let's also consider how was the evidence sought in the study we consider here? It also has a weakness. The problem is that, as the authors of the study in question acknowledge, it has major limitations: it analyzed data one year after the election, it also examined only a selected month, and, in addition, it analyzed public data after many such posts or accounts had already been deleted (e.g., Twitter did so).[60] This stresses that such research should be done with access to a digital platform, and not from the outside, which will inevitably have much smaller credence. Doing it "from the outside" can impose major limitations. Moreover, the total influence exerted, after all, is also not just about Twitter posts. Because part of the influence is also the sharing of information, its impact on people's opinions, its importance in describing elections in the media, etc. Focusing on the chosen social media alone (here: Twitter) or only social media in general is an oversimplification!

Another thing is that even legitimate information activities in political campaigns may have meager effects (like, zero).[61] However, one cannot overlook the fact that such activities in the information sphere were analyzed and subjected to public discussion in subsequent years as well. Many articles described the situation as if such activities were undoubtedly having an effect. This was also an influence of a kind, because should they not have had an effect, the very fact of describing them as if they had one also constitutes exerting influence,[62] exaggerating the impact.[63]

6.6.3 Informational influence of Russia—methods of hacktivism and information

For what it's worth, the informational impact of cyber attacks was clearly noticed in Russia, when hactivists (individuals without advanced knowledge or skills, taking some sort of action against information systems) belonging to one of the groups favoring Russian war policy in Ukraine launched cyber attacks on various targets in the West. On companies, on parliaments, on government websites, and even on the European Parliament.[64]

The problem? Nearly universally, such covered activities turned out to be of a minor impact.[65] Such activities were limited to distributed denial of service (DDoS) actions, when the attacker floods a server with a huge number of connection requests, causing it to stop handling "normal" visits and become unavailable, for example, for minutes, hours—loss of availability. These are not serious threats, at least not cyber-Armageddon to be worried about. However, such activities were boasted about by such groups, which was eagerly picked up by all sorts of media, sometimes framing these actions absolutely beyond any reasonable proportions. In fact, these were low-profile and low-scale actions, while sometimes they were publicly given prominence as if they were something big and impactful, what-not. This made such meaningless behavior nevertheless as having some effect—an informational one. And perhaps this was precisely the goal of these groups. To create informational, propaganda effects with simple and cheap actions. All this thanks to the media and profiles with a large number of observers, who eagerly publicized them. Sometimes, one can harm oneself in this way, even if it is the pursuit of sensationalism (here: artificially created).

However, it also introduced opportunities for Western politicians to demonstrate that they and their nations, too, are bearing the cost of helping Ukraine, that the West is also a victim. This can help solidify Western publics' belief in support. After all, it is then presented as "Russia's attack on the West." And some readers may be unable to understand its true nature.

6.7 SOURCE CREDIBILITY

Accounts of well-known people: politicians, diplomats, experts, journalists, or celebrities can play an important role in exerting influence. Ordinarily, such people may have big audiences, and people following them. Discreetly injecting various kinds of non-accidental, especially crafted messages can, therefore, be effective. Sometimes indiscreet, expounded directly, in a spoon-feeding manner. If one quotes Joseph Stalin and says that the quote is from Stalin, such content may be perceived differently than if the same words (truthfully or not) are attributed to Einstein, Pope John Paul II, or any other person. The words and content will suddenly be perceived through the prism of the persons and views on them (tactic of appealing to authority). However, if the message "emitted" by a given source deviates too strongly from the views or beliefs of the audience, it may fail and even undermine trust in such a source of information.[66]

The same happens if some words are spoken by a supporter of a certain political option or simply by someone known to subscribe to a certain worldview. This is because media audiences pay attention to the identity of the people who create the content and speak out. Differences have been detected in the perception and acceptance of some words when they were presented as spoken by specific people, compared to when the same content was anonymous (with no identity assigned). It is also faster to accept (or reject) content when it is known who put it forward or promoted it.[67] The idea is that one pays attention to the source of the messages and receives them accordingly. When one has other information besides the message itself, such as name, gender, or skin color—these can then influence the perception of the content. What does this mean?

This means that if you want to reach an audience with your content, you need to know what source to use. If you use the right channel, such as a particular person, to reach his or her supporters, it will have a greater effect than trying to influence "neutral" people. If you want to focus the debate, you can communicate in such a way as to deepen the divide: speaking to supporters and opponents at the same time, which may even result in controversy and even more content propagation. However, if the goal is to reach people opposed to or skeptical of a certain person or option, worldview—it may be better to "mask" the source and use one that is acceptable to this selected social group. Acceptable, that is, for example, one looks upon such a source favorably or at least neutrally. Likewise with releasing leaks to the media—depending on who you want to reach, you can give information to certain media. Some media sometimes like leaks, so there might be no problem with their acceptance and propagation.

Recipients, of course, do not need to be aware that information is being directed to them in this strategic way. They shouldn't even be aware of it and almost never are. Is this ethical? I leave that to the reader's judgment.

6.8 FOREIGN INFLUENCE OPERATIONS—MISCELLANEOUS

Information operations can be considered as methods of warfare, of exerting influence.[68] The European Union service lists 100 foreign influence incidents for only part of the year 2022.[69] Most of the incidents were related to Russia, and slightly fewer to China. In the case of Russia, 42% of the incidents were aimed at distraction and 35% at distorting information and its reception. Many were related to Russia's war in Ukraine, for example, holding NATO responsible for the damage to the Crimean bridge. The second (2024) report by the European External Action Service already identifies 750 incidents (years 2022–2023).[70] Moreover, it notes what was too rarely raised at the beginning of this decade. A very important part of identifying and combating information operations is the decision to prioritize—specifically, which incidents to consider serious, and which to simply ignore so as not to popularize them. There is no point in publicizing niche and meaningless information operations.[71] This is counterproductive: it may help in propagating them. Assessments of the situation should always be made. It is absolutely crucial: if, when, how to publicize. Or not. Another important observation is what I have already pointed out in this book. It is worthwhile in information operations to refer to real events, incidents, and disasters. Taking advantage of the natural interest in them, one can smuggle in information payload. Actors involved in such operations closely analyze incoming information about events (e.g., disasters, elections, political or military events) and get "plugged in" to them.

6.8.1 State context of the precedent of a missile falls on the territory of a NATO Member State (2022)

Now a dangerous precedent. In 2022, for the first time in NATO history—the fall of a missile in the Polish town of Przewodowo happened. Two people were killed. The event electrified the entire NATO, Western world. Was the war inevitable, some asked? There was a big fuss at the time, with some ill-informed analysts and poor-quality social media accounts (including those portraying themselves as "reporters") rallying around the consequences—a hypothetical war with Russia. Although at no time did anything indicate this. Neither does Article 5 of the North Atlantic Treaty[72] about collective defense in the event of armed aggression against one of NATO's Member States work that way.

NATO Article 5 doesn't work that way (there's no automatism involved in taking military actions). But misinformation has been propagated in many Western countries—understandably, to the greatest extent—in Poland. In this case, it can be considered that the adopted information policy of the Polish government at the time was correct. That is, it refrained from giving an immediate diagnosis and waited until it was possible to analyze the case and present the information fairly. The worst thing that could have been done was to present several consecutive versions and thus deepen the information chaos, risking that some of these versions (even if later refuted or amended, updated) would be spread continuously. It is difficult to correct official information once released (and which would have to be straightened out). This topic was also gamed on from the very beginning by Russian media and profiles. In the end, it also didn't help that the West and Poland recognized that it was a Ukrainian missile of the S-300 anti-missile system, launched for defensive purposes that fell, while Ukraine disagreed with this diagnosis. An informational breakout ensued.

Journalists habitually practiced chasing sensational takes. Especially a certain Associated Press journalist who quickly broadcast "a confirmed" information that the missile was (allegedly) fired by Russia. The Associated Press dispatch was brief:

> WARSAW, Poland (AP)—A senior U.S. intelligence official says Russian missiles crossed into NATO member Poland, killing two people.[73]

For a moment, the world stopped.

Driven by this information, many Western media, began to "process" it, writing about a "Russian missile," and even claiming to have "confirmed" these reports locally, in Poland. I wonder with whom and how? It was perhaps about the announcements of local, Polish media, citing the AP's wire, that is, the forming of the so-called "information loop" has been made, when, reporting in good faith, but with questionable content, others confirm a take with following reporting—also made in good faith, though unquestionably. Is this the end of the story? Not quite. The information was ultimately not confirmed, causing the journalist in question to lose his job.[74] Chasing hot news? Why not, but when the stakes are this high, the World War III trigger-event high, verification and integrity are key, and quality media agencies must bear the consequences. To confront the world with the specter of World War III, or at least a major altercation or conflict, is a major achievement in a sense. If confirmed, it would prove the class of this journalist, a major professional achievement. In this case, the risky investment turned out to be misguided.

6.8.2 Wired and moral panic

Nevertheless, in the face of such heated news, some social media users even demanded the triggering of Article 5 of the North Atlantic Treaty—the so-called "moral panic"—which would mean an armed response. Putting it figuratively: "a lot of people spent yesterday calling for war between the world's two largest nuclear powers"[75]—ideal conditions for an accidental miscalculation leading to bad decisions with enormously high stakes. Imagine that someone responds to such a false event with an armed response. But the event in question did not happen. So, there was no legitimate reason to respond, which then might even constitute a category of an armed attack—not a retaliation in defense but an offensive attack. This is also why there are no hasty decisions and automatism in the mechanism of Article 5 of the North Atlantic Treaty—each State assesses the situation for itself and takes action as it sees fit, including not taking any. In the United States, for example, a decision to support a State could even have to be authorized by the U.S. Congress, that is, put to a vote.[76] No automatism.

Fortunately, the moral panic in this case did not affect anything; it turned out to be meaningless. As an aside, as one prominent American journalist from the Associated Press (whom I am not mentioning by name) familiar with the details of the events, said, it was a "bad, very bad day" and he "got headaches" as a result. Poor him.

6.8.3 NATO version, Ukraine version—choose wisely

The confusion described resulted from poor source verification. Ukrainian officials claimed that it was in fact a Russian missile, an example was made by then-Ukrainian Foreign Minister Dmytro Kuleba, accusing Russia[77] of "promoting a conspiracy theory that it was allegedly a Ukrainian air defense missile." This "conspiracy theory" was later adopted by NATO. Also, then-Ukrainian President Zelensky commented[78] that the alleged "Russian attack on collective security in the Euro-Atlantic is a significant escalation."

The West and NATO, however, knew better—although Ukraine did not accept this version, even calling for the establishment of a no-fly zone in Ukraine, which might have demanded for NATO to enter the war to enforce such a ban militarily. However, it was not in NATO's interest to join the war. It would have been even less in Poland's interest to join the war unilaterally, without NATO support. NATO and Poland were not parties to this armed conflict, even though they had interests in it and supported Ukraine. On the other hand, to add a dose of hilarity, it was Russia that denied that it was their missile, claiming that no strikes had occurred in the area. No one addressed their claims, but it's hard not to notice that in this case the Western world, even if not explicitly, or reluctantly, nevertheless adopted a version consistent with Russia's position. Again, the principle that the best propaganda is made with truthful information was confirmed.

6.8.4 Impact and cyber activities in the context of missile fall at Przewodowo

Using cyberoperation methods, in one case an attempt was made to impersonate a Polish official (former chairman of one city council, a local politician) to spread a certain image of the situation—that it was an alleged Ukrainian provocation to draw Poland into the war. This is a dangerous situation and underscores a key propaganda technique—using a credible source can affect the reception of information.

In such cases, the law in effect today may be relevant. These are also important elements of consideration for security and strategic studies. How do such legal security mechanisms work? Let's turn to applicable law. EU Digital Services Act (DSA) provides for crisis protocols to take immediate action, such as removing content. As an aside, however, this is the same law that European Commissioner Thierry Breton later said that it could be used to shut down social media in the event of unrest in France—not how this law was presented originally when it was introduced. And yet such provisions can actually be found there, of course with the so-called customary padding, such actions would only be taken if they were "absolutely necessary, justified and proportionate" (Articles 36 and 51 of the DSA). Well, of course! And, of course, for the public good (Latin: *pro publico bono*). In fairness, it should be noted that, after all, digital platforms are doing a lot to remove and combat problematic content, including in accordance with the EU Code on Combating Disinformation,[79] which provides, for example, for the demonetization of false content so that no money is made from ads displayed next to harmful content, but also for the removal of the disinformation-containing ads themselves. There may be a problem with the latter, because it is not necessary to create obvious disinformation for a propaganda message to be effective. Such is the "code." This law could not have been used during the Przewodowo incident—it was not yet in force.

6.8.5 Source credibility

Returning to the issue of source credibility, it is very important in the information context. It is easier to accept information from a known or trusted source. Also important is the fact that today social media are effective techniques for reaching the masses. In addition, many States also have other channels at their disposal.

To demonstrate this, let's look again at Russia[80] and the means, techniques, and methods it uses. In offensive and informational, influence, psychological operations, and perhaps even information warfare, Russia harnesses a whole spectrum of methods. In use may be true information, false information, fabricated information, manipulated information, unattributed messages using domestic or foreign influencers (well-known individuals, including politicians, as well as non-governmental organizations, and various associations that can be created, but also use existing ones), radio channels, television channels, diplomatic ones.[81] Russia has often and for a long time been attributed to the use of such "active measures" (rus. aktivnye mieroprijatiya), for example, conducted by the KGB, the Committee for State Security, security service of the former Soviet Union.

6.8.6 Operation Infektion

Why are such actions carried out? To gain support abroad (here: for Russia or its goals), to build opposition to a political option or view (to favor the actions of the provocateur, here: Russia). In this context, an interesting operation is Infektion. This is an action by the Soviet services to popularize the idea that the U.S. government was behind the HIV epidemic. The operation was so successful that the theory persisted long after the collapse of the USSR. The greatest damage was to undermine the credibility of official health and sanitary institutions.[82] Some of the logic based on this operation may also have been reproduced during the COVID-19 pandemic and the various conspiracy theories about the alleged state origin of the virus that were popular during it.

In the case of Infektion,[83] the groundwork was laid for skepticism about medications to alleviate the symptoms of diseases. Similar was true of COVID-19, when doubts were expressed about vaccinations and their effectiveness or some supposed "real" targets. Although, in some ways, misguided decisions by States and the World Health Organization, which on its social media profile in 2023 mentioned—in a different context—homeopathy, which may have implied support for it as a treatment method, may have contributed to such skepticism, and may have given credence to this skepticism with these reckless actions.

Disinformation and anti-vaccine propaganda may have contributed to the recurrence of diseases such as measles, mumps, and rubella. This is thanks to the content also promoted by some medical doctors and some well-known people.[84] So, due to some people building popularity on controversy, diseases that seemingly have already been successfully eradicated may return: like measles.[85] Such is the power of information and such can be the results.

Fear of vaccines has been with mankind for a long time, for example, in the 18th century, some maintained that vaccines are a creation of the devil,[86] and in 2020 a judge of South Africa's constitutional court said that the COVID-19 vaccine left the mark of Satan (referring to the devil's name in the Revelation of St. John, the number 666).[87] So, the issue may seem serious to some, since even theological arguments are being raised.

6.8.7 Impact on neighboring States

Today, in the era of the war in Ukraine, States are rediscovering the necessity of psychological operations and information, propaganda activities. Both defense and offense. There will be more on this topic in the next chapter.

After the invasion of Ukraine, Russia, using information methods for political purposes, targeted communications both to its own public and to third countries. The goal was to lay out and present its "own perspective" in this way. These were influence campaigns.[88] Another point is that the view of the war in Europe seemed in 2022–2023 to be very different in countries on other continents, such as South America and Africa, from that views in Western Europe and the U.S. States and societies there showed more understanding of Russia's actions (or less preoccupation in general). However, an interesting trend was observed: the fusion of channeled information and the interplay of official diplomatic channels. This worked coherently and had one goal: to get the Russian message across. It could even have been a stream of activities: *press conference → information in State media → sharing in foreign news agencies*. This was accompanied by social media posts.

There was no shortage of message fabrication. From descriptions of the war situation, including crimes, to alleged Ukrainian work on nuclear, biological, and chemical weapons, not to mention the use of "mutant soldiers" and, for example, "poison-spreading mosquitoes." Did anyone, anywhere, believe this? It's hard to say. There were also diplomatic efforts to build distrust of later allegations against Russia, such as the armed attack on the Mariupol hospital (Russia bombarded it, officially explaining that it was being used as a military depot), which reverberated around the world, since hospitals are given special protection in the laws of war. The same, by the way, was true of bombs and rockets hitting other civilian facilities.

6.8.8 What about digital platforms—one of the arenas of State information activities?

Since many information activities are carried out on digital platforms, it is their personnel who track and combat manifestations of such attempts. Once such an operation is detected and analyzed, posts, accounts, etc. may be deleted. And the whole thing may be voiced in the public. Around the year 2022, this happened with such regularity that there is little point in mentioning all these incidents—let's just say that they were common. An example is the identification and removal of such activity by Google (2022), which affected YouTube channels, clients of the advertising platform, blogs, etc. Such activities were conducted in various languages—Arabic, Farsi, and Russian, but some also promoted the American point of view on international affairs.[89] Yes, American, and more specifically the psychological operations of the U.S. military,[90] because Western States or actors may also perform information operations targeting other States and their societies. These reports[91] mention activities by China, Russia, Burkina Faso, Togo, Iran,[92] Serbia, Cuba, Bolivia, and Ukraine, as well as PR companies (Chinese, American, Arab, Ecuadorian, Ukrainian, Mexican) supporting left and right-wing movements. Sometimes influence companies are hired by governments.

Anyway, shares of China or Russia are not missing from such lists—they make up the majority of announced activities. I could count them in the years after 2020, but this calculation would be of such limited significance that there is no reason to do so. It is companies like Google and Facebook that have full control over the data and the choice of what and how is published. There seems to be no longer any doubt that digital platforms are a (battle) field for such activities, which does not necessarily please the digital platforms, who are skeptical of the idea of them being an arena of influencing or of an interstate conflict or a battlefield. Only with an awareness of these activities can one fully appreciate the reason why I devoted space in this book to the battle in the ether—radio propaganda, something important a century ago. The point was to appreciate this technical evolution.

Shifting attention to Asia, it should be noted that China is modernizing methods of conducting information operations affecting cognition and the so-called three battlefields: psychological, over public opinion, and legal.[93] These are to be methods used against adversaries in the West, perhaps also applied against Taiwan.

6.9 IMPACT ON THE DOMESTIC SITUATION

The information environment within a country determines (or constrains) the ability or vulnerability of influencing the domestic situation. With an adequate understanding of the information environment, one can act accordingly, taking into account, or exploiting the opportunities that come along, knowing how to put events (social, political, international, or natural, such as floods) into an internal context, shaping the content.

In this way, it may be possible to influence people's moods, views, opinions, attitudes and perhaps even actions. Informational influence occurs when people are prompted to take an action. This can be a simple purchase of a product (such as vanilla ice cream) but also casting a vote in an election, throwing a stone at a storefront, causing or joining riots and unrest, putsch, coup d'etats, etc. The possibilities are aplenty and depend on the imagination, ingenuity, and goals of the party designing the information strategy. With the right modulation of information and opinion, it may even be possible to attribute (*put blame on*) the occurrence or consequences of natural disasters—such as floods, pandemics, earthquakes, or asteroid impacts—to specific individuals, political parties, or social groups. This has happened before in history. Various groups of people were *blamed*: Jews, Christians, homosexuals, Freemasons, vegetarians, users of some brand of electronic equipment, members or voters of some political party, cyclists, etc. Scapegoats can be multiplied at will. Or rather—as needed.

Especially today, the flow of information can have a significant impact on the situation inside the country. We have seen the manifestations and effects of this many times. These are, for example, situations where new media, social media, and instant messaging can be used to create or trigger actions or give them momentum or coordinate within those activities. Inter-state coordination of information activities has also been noted in relation to social media content, where one (obvious) goal is greater visibility of messages.[94] Hoaxes spread via instant messaging have contributed to riots in several Asian countries. But perhaps a better example are classic riots.

6.9.1 French upheaval in 2023 and digital coordination

The role of social media and instant messaging made itself known during the 2023 riots in France, when groups of young people massively engaged in the destruction of private property—buildings, cars, when French local administration buildings were set ablaze. When violent and aggressive riots against society, against social property, against the political system, or against the public order were spreading, like when some parts of France were paralyzed for several days, with consequences of financial losses.

It was noted early on that social media was used to spread the content recording the destruction. Videos were popular, depicting a young man driving an expensive sports car into a store through its window, fireworks were shot at the police, an ATM was "opened" with a circular saw, when a motorcycle dragged behind a chainsaw, etc. These videos were spread through channels such as Telegram, Twitter, Snap, TikTok, etc. They rapidly gained an audience, helping to popularize and even promote such activities, advertising violence and riots. Actions were coordinated through instant messaging. It is likely also how the riots began to penetrate Switzerland or Belgium (on a lesser scale).

6.9.2 Tank videos

The impact of new media may also be of a completely different nature. Prior to the intensification of hostilities in Ukraine in February 2022, videos and reports were rampant about Russia's transfer of weapons systems equipment to the border with Ukraine. Such videos were shared for weeks and undoubtedly must have had some psychological effect. When you see entire train cars filled with tanks and rocket launchers heading your way, know that something is going on.

6.10 ELECTION CAMPAIGNS

The election campaign is a peculiar time. Then, we have structures that popularize certain slogans, views, certain people, and a certain vision of the future. Naturally, content appears in information channels: in the media, in newspapers, on TV, on social media, on posters, and on billboards, but it is also raised in personal contacts. The goal of participating in elections is to obtain a good result, and preferably to win.

An election campaign has the dynamics of a social campaign. A lot of people are involved—these are the candidates (sometimes a group of loosely connected people who share a common goal—to get the best possible result) and other people: activists, coordinators, etc. A method of communication is chosen, a catchy slogan about how great the future may be is invented, and it is pushed through all possible routes to the audience. Different channels are used and the message is directed to different types of audiences. It is useful to identify segments of supporters (or possible supporters) and modulate the content in such a way as to induce them to vote for the right people or at least not to vote for the opponents (through negative campaigning). One can also encourage people to go or not go to the elections (increase or decrease voter turnout). In such a situation, harsher issues can also be uttered, because, as the judgments of the European Court of Human Rights indicate, the space for freedom of political expression is very wide.

6.10.1 What to talk about and are there those wishing to get PR training?

But what to talk about and how to talk about it? The choice of what to talk about depends on one's views, the party's program, one's values, one's own inventiveness, and the demand among the electorate (which can be determined by polls and proposals can be tailored to that). So much for content. As for the form, professional politicians, candidates, can benefit from training. Train appropriate and "effective" poses, gestures, behavior, and diction—the way to speak, behave, and act.

This is about public relations training, or PR. People (the electorate) may prefer candidates who look *convincing* and behave "professionally." Since they prefer it that way, it is natural that a candidate who meets their expectations increases his or her chances. However, candidates often are reluctant to admit to using such assistance, preferring instead to give the impression that their behavior is perfectly natural.

Trained moves and prepared statements are something to be benefited from. Public performers, or politicians, have known this for a long time. But how to present it, when politicians are unlikely to flaunt such actions? This is an important element of informational influence—we can't help but discuss it here. Still, they won't admit it for some reason. It's a difficult issue, but there is a solution! To underline how long this phenomenon has existed, we will refer to a certain aspiring German politician from the 1920s. This politician was likely very concerned about his public image and how he presented himself, so he decided to take professional PR advice so that he could more effectively connect with the electorate and perhaps even dream of winning an election. He is depicted during such PR training in Figure 6.1. A curious thing—neither Hitler, Stalin, nor Mussolini ever spoke on the radio before 1939, nor did they broadcast speeches live from their offices.[95] As if they needed

Figure 6.1 Training in political PR. A German political party candidate trains in giving speeches and the art of oratory in 1925. You can see how much work he puts into appropriate and trained poses, behavior, facial expressions. Maybe one day he will win an election? As an aside, it is worth noting that at that time the NSDAP party was denied access to the radio, but still managed to score a good result in the elections.

Source: Bundesarchiv, Bild 102-10460/Hoffmann, Heinrich/CC-BY-SA 3.0.

crowds of spectators to speak effectively. Figure 6.2 depicts another such a campaign. Today means and methods naturally differ, but the basic paradigm is roughly comparable.

Knowing these various tricks and ways to reach voters through various media (now including social media), one carries on until the end of the election campaign, which is marked by the beginning of the electoral silence, the period immediately preceding the election, during which one can no longer actively campaign, in countries where this occurs.

6.10.2 Election silence and its circumvention

Election silence is a mechanism by which the information environment can be stabilized immediately before election day. This is because then almost all information stimuli that accompany an election campaign are suppressed. During election silence, political agitation, encouragement to vote for this or that party, this or that candidate—so, the circulation of

Source gallica.bnf.fr / Bibliothèque nationale de France

Figure 6.2 Example of a door-to-door election billboard "Vote Communist."

Source: Bibliothèque nationale de France, gallica.bnf.fr.

campaign information is disrupted. As an example—publication of polls and broadcasting of election spots may be prohibited some time near the election day.

There are some methods by which the bans associated with election silence can be attempted to circumvent. It's a matter of creativity. For example, one may publish a poll in another country. This was often the case in French elections, for example—polls appear in Belgian or Swiss media. Various kinds of "encoded messages" (indirectly reporting the results) may still be posted on social media. This doesn't mean that electoral silence is a dysfunctional relic. On the contrary, however, most of the public is covered effectively by this silence. Still, those who absolutely have to inform themselves may, if with some effort, get such information, at their own risk, because, after all, it could be completely false or speculative.

To again refer to notable events in France in 2017, an event of a "leak" of stolen information from the staff of the candidate (the future president) Emmanuel Macron occurred. Nothing incriminating was found in there, but the mere fact of the leak reverberated. Moreover, this culminated shortly before the start of the electoral silence, when it would no longer be possible to comment on it. Therefore, the candidate's staff issued an announcement that it was a fake—done a few hours before the election silence. This was the correct thing to do then, as the staff presented their own version and prevented the risk that during the election silence some voters might have their thought processes affected by such possible "last available information" they got (i.e., following the fact of the leak). To preemptively address this risk—the last information directed at voters was the one indicating a disinformation operation. This was the correct action, but it is worth remembering that every election is different. Situations differ, the staff and candidates also differ, the States, their specifics are different, the electorates are different. In view of this, decisions on whether to do something are worth making on a case-by-case basis in each such situation, after considering all the factors imaginable.

There are also countries where election silence does not exist, such as the United States. Some researchers recommend its introduction,[96] while some elements of it are already in place there. For example, in some U.S. States, the possibility of canvassing near voting places is suspended.

Election silence regulations operate in many countries, such as France, Japan, Italy, Ireland, and the United Kingdom. Their details may differ, the silence can last longer or shorter, for example. Let's rejoice and appreciate the benefits of election silence rules. Even if someone doesn't believe in the effects of stabilizing the information space, suppressing division, and minimizing last-minute risks of abuse, then at least they may enjoy the silence. For some people in particular, a walk in the fresh air or a bike ride may do good. Until the next silence, because just a few days after it is over, one may again be immersed in the "fascinating" socio-political information.

6.10.3 Election silence as an element of State information security

The biggest advantage of the election silence is the already mentioned role of stabilizing the information space. It drastically reduces the space for the emergence of falsehoods, disinformation, or propaganda, either internal or externally induced, such as that carried out by foreign military intelligence. So, it's a deliberate suppression of information circulation to build security and resilience—and in an age of possible cyber attacks and information operations, this is invaluable. Pay attention to the voices calling for the abolition of the electoral silence on random pretexts (e.g., citing "modernization," "modernity," and such tricks)—in modern times and understanding the risks, these are not changes for the better. It is worth considering the motivation for making such proposals.

Election silence is a mechanism that was created long before the acceleration of information circulation, of information technology rise, of the emergence of digital platforms, and social media. And it turns out to be an excellent remedy for some potential digital risks that could not have been foreseen in the past. So, it's a fascinating case where *previously created rules* have beneficial effects when new technologies emerge. This builds cyber-resilience of the State. It may be worthwhile to detail more such methods and practices and maintain and strengthen them accordingly. States that take cyber-resilience and information resilience seriously would certainly benefit.

Disinformation in an election campaign can also be legal if it is within the bounds of the law. Note, however, that in 2018 the European Commission issued guidelines due to concerns about "hacking" of the 2019 European Parliament elections, out of fear of deepfakes and so on. However, the communication and concerns failed to note that, first, deepfakes back then were not a real problem. Second, European Parliament elections are generally quite systemically resistant to disinformation and their "hacking." That's because they are distributed—held in 27 EU countries simultaneously, with campaigns held in different languages. It may be difficult for cyber and info operators of a foreign country to be able to effectively handle all such venues at once. Any operations are, therefore, limited by the very nature of European Parliament elections (unless an influence structure allocates a lot of resources to the action).

Prior to the 2024 elections to the European Parliament, the European Commission once again released guidelines. But his time not as soft guidelines. Rather—legally anchored in the Digital Services Act. In 2024, the elections were still held in a distributed fashion, but the situation was quite different from 2019. This change was due to technological progress

(specifically, emergence of generative AI). But also the introduction of certain, as it turned out, divisive themes resulting from proposed policies (such as concerns over the costs placed on citizens to implement green policies, like the so-called Green Deal), which sparked controversies and public protests. Let's analyze some of the recommendations. The quoted content below comes directly from the guidelines,[97] and is annotated with explanatory comments.[98]

- Provide official information about elections process, like popups or banners on websites. The European Commission apparently interpreted the Digital Services Act as justifying efforts to increase voter turnout.
- "Tools and information to help users assess the trustworthiness of information sources, like trust marks focused on source integrity." This recommendation is potentially problematic. Assessing source trustworthiness, especially for politically inclined news sites, is challenging. Furthermore, not all users may trust such "trust labels," possibly leading to perceptions of manipulation or social engineering.
- "Establishing measures to limit the amplification of deceptive, false, or misleading AI-generated content in elections via their recommender systems." This is a fair recommendation, as Very Large Online Platforms (*VLOPs*) are well-positioned to combat such harmful content, provided they can identify it and assess when action is warranted. Recommender systems and moderation can reduce its reach through de-promotion or censorship.
- A note on influencers posing risks: "Influencers can significantly impact the electoral choices of service recipients." The European Commission urges VLOPs to label influencers sending political advertising content.
- Demonetizing disinformation content—good idea. Ad-supported funds may cut the financing of bogus websites.
- "Implement procedures to detect and disrupt service manipulation," including bot detection and impersonation (like: of election candidates), preventing deception via impersonation, manipulated media, and fake engagements.
- VLOPs' Information Operations teams should cooperate and share information—a crucial point.
- Concerning generative AI creations—labeling such created (e.g., deepfake) audio and video content is crucial, but requires detection, which guidelines suggest should be done "to the extent technically feasible."
- Watermarking generative AI-created images is also recommended, though watermark removal tools could easily undermine this effort. Metadata-based solutions won't work, and cryptographic marking could embed a signal throughout the image to withstand format changes. Provenance tracking is important but attackers could not use widely available tools that would mark the creations accordingly.

In the end, similarly to 2019, no siginficant propaganda or disinformation activities were identified in use in 2024.

6.11 DIPLOMACY

State structures can issue messages to the outside world—directed at audiences based in other countries, to the societies of those countries, aimed at foreign States, etc. This can be executed in a variety of ways: posting a message on the foreign ministry's website, sending formal correspondence (e.g., a letter) to such a country, using the ambassador to a State to say something in public, or directly to a policymaker, or via national press. It can be made through social media, such as sending tweets or posting on Facebook—sometimes in provocative manners. The channels have always been used to the advantage of the States, which is, after all, natural—it's their job. As a rule, ambassadors do not act against the interests of their States, even if in some cases this may have been the case.

Diplomatic activities may also involve actions within blocs of States, within organizations: European Union, NATO, Shanghai Security Organization (SCO), G7, and others. Such messages can be reproduced through electronic and traditional media, including social media, to reinforce or enrich the message.

It is also a field for action, for example, in the United Nations or within its agencies. For example, in 2023, Pakistan put forward a draft resolution condemning the burning of the "Quran and other holy books", described as religious hatred.[99] This was met with skepticism from the Western States, where the commitment to freedom of expression is strong and perhaps even outweighs the right to freedom of religion, at least when it comes to the protection of materials linked to religious orders. Said resolution was adopted—against the preferences of the West. A message was then sent out, obviously reproduced by media all around the world. What's more, perhaps some kind of process was set in motion at the UN. The future will tell. When a State understands how the complex structure of the UN functions, and knows how to navigate within its framework, it may be a powerful asset.

With regard to activities of impact, a point should be made that the information environment can be affected by actions taken by States. The expulsion of a diplomat, such as an ambassador, at a certain time and justified in a particular way, can bring about an informational impact and send a message; recalling an ambassador, even when temporarily ("on consultations") may send a message as well. Both internally and externally, that is, in the State of the expelled diplomat, in allied States, but also in neutral ones.

6.12 PROPAGANDA AND INTERNATIONAL POLICY

An important peculiarity of modern interstate relations and influence[100–101] is PR. Influence can be exerted through these methods as well. Such as what happened in the United States when a 15-year-old girl testified as a witness about the Iraqi massacres in Kuwait, when Iraqi soldiers were said to have committed atrocities, including stealing incubators—previously throwing babies out of them on hospital floors—what was then widely[102] disseminated through the media (press, television, etc.), which shocked the public and enhanced public sympathy for the armed response. Only later was it revealed that the hearing was organized by a PR firm. The girl received professional training,[103] and her testimony ultimately turned out to be, suffice it to say, stretched, in fact fictitious. In addition, she was not exactly an independent witness, as it turned out that she belonged to the Kuwaiti royal family.[104] For what it's worth, the future military intervention was real, and the PR activity,[105,106] perhaps contributed to building support for it.

6.12.1 How many years after the war are relations returning to "business as usual"?

I am not taking a stand here on whether the Iraq intervention was justified or not. There's a different argument to be made. I am merely showing the mechanism of influence that many analysts and researchers believe played a role in convincing the public of this military intervention. Since then, engaging PR firms to either improve the image of States or assist in formal diplomatic processes has been more popular—in fact a standard. It was used by smaller States like Angola but also larger ones like China,[107] and Russia. If only to build the perception that "Russia is a safe and profitable country to invest in."[108] Although naturally, especially around 2022, some reasonable doubts in the public domain arose about this. But who knows what will happen a few years "after the war"? Is it even possible to predict the future? It is not. However, it is worth taking past experience into consideration.

One may be convinced that after significant divisions, or wars, there may never be a return to "business as usual," that is, normalized relations (or any) with some aggressive State. However, it is worth pondering what happened in such situations in the past. World War II was full of some of the most brutal events in history of mankind. Now hear this—just a few years after World War II, biographies of German Nazis involved in the occupation of Paris, in battles on the Eastern Front, and perhaps even in war crimes, began to appear in the West.[109] This allowed the Western world to learn about the "*dilemmas and intellectual hardships*" of a Wehrmacht soldier. Readers could purchase such a book just four years after World War II. Will there be willing publishers to publish memoirs of the "hardships" of Russian (or other) soldiers in Russia's war with Ukraine (or others) after the war in Ukraine (or others) as well? Inevitably.

6.12.2 Exaggeration in PR and its effects—the case of Iraq

Sometimes, however, one can overdo with the influence or ambiguity. Saddam Hussein's Iraq did just that. After the first U.S. intervention and peace was established in 1991, stockpiles of weapons of mass destruction were destroyed—complete and verifiable disarmament in this regard was a condition of peace. But after that, the Iraqi government deliberately built up information ambiguity: do they still have these weapons? Or do they not? Maybe they haven't gotten rid of them yet? Iraq's problem was that they failed to convince[110] Western countries that disarmament had actually taken place. This ambiguity may have also contributed to the later decision to invade in 2003, if only because the intelligence services were unable to interpret the information correctly.

Iraq was not credible,[111] and there were reasonable suspicions that it was violating UN Security Council resolutions,[112] with stockpiles of weapons of mass destruction. The conclusion? It's better not to lie when the stakes are high. If one wants to lie, it is better to do so only when the lie cannot be discovered.

In the case of Iraq, internal friction has also contributed to its unreliable information policy.[113] So, domestic politics can cause problems in international politics. If an official or politician says one thing and someone else and his or her entourage says another, it complicates the situation for the entire country, State. It may be smarter, or safer, to have one unified communication policy that is clear and coherent. Especially if the world is carefully paying attention.

6.12.3 Rumors, gossip, unofficial information

All this underscores the need for a responsible information policy and to be careful about what signals (including information) are sent through real actions, not just through announcements, speeches, etc.

It is worth considering, however, that the manufacture of rumors or gossip can be a propaganda method to defend one's own societies, strengthen allies, and discourage enemies, opponents, and belligerents. This is what British propaganda did during World War II, when, for example, the information about the deaths of enemy officers was publicized in the British press. Suicides of officers were reported, including falsely. It was at one time reported that a German general committed suicide, which was officially denied by the German political services. Then, it so happened that this general actually did commit suicide, which lent credence to the earlier false rumors.[114] These are methods of political warfare using propaganda.

6.12.4 Information on the illness of the leader of the enemy State

Since 1941, rumors of Hitler's poor health have appeared frequently,[115] reaching various media outlets around the world.[116] This is reminiscent of press "reports" in 1945 about Stalin's poor health condition, and even his death.[117] The same was true of Deng Xiaoping (China's leader) after the Tiananmen Square massacre (1989). This one was even said to have died, twice (all of this was debunked).[118]

Reports of poor health and "imminent death" of leaders of various States—enemies or rivals of other States, for various reasons—have never been in short supply. Therefore, the intelligence services of various States are engaged in determining the veracity of such reports.[119] For example, there were rumors that the CIA managed to seize the secretions of two world leaders (including Khrushchev, during a visit to Washington in 1959).[120]

What does this have to do with propaganda? Namely, that establishing the veracity of rumors can be laborious, difficult, and complicated, and such information (including in the public) can cause confusion. Or expectations, including those false ones. Curiously, during Russia's war with Ukraine in 2022, 2023, and 2024, there were quite regular reports of Vladimir Putin's ill health.

6.12.5 Information operations in the service of diplomacy

Information operations can be used to support State policy,[121] in all dimensions: economic, scientific, political, diplomatic, and military. This means, however, that other States may also undertake such actions. In view of this, it is necessary to detect such attempts, analyze them, draw conclusions, and, when necessary, take action, and respond. Sometimes, this does not have to be done overtly, loudly, and radically.

6.12.6 Public and silent cyber attribution

The same is true of attributing responsibility for cyber attacks on States. Some States have a policy of announcing such cyber attacks officially, assigning responsibility to some entity, perhaps a foreign State. But this does not always have to happen openly.

Some States may do this stuff unofficially, silently, including through diplomatic channels. This can be done for example by summoning the ambassador of such a State and giving him or her official information, but without announcing it publicly.

6.12.7 When opinion shaping fails

The channels and methods differ. Sometimes the conduct can also fail, as happened in the case of the 1982 Falklands War, when apparently Great Britain did not communicate its intentions to Argentina clearly enough beforehand, specifically, its determination to defend the island.[122] In the face of Argentina's attempts to retake the islands, it was necessary to "send a message" through military action.

A different response using more contemporary methods came within 24 hours of the downing of Malaysian Airlines flight MH17 by the Russians in Ukraine in 2014. More than 60,000 posts appeared on Twitter at the time. Written en masse, and in a partially automated fashion, with content blaming Ukraine. Similarly, during the seizure of Crimea, Ukrainian broadcasting stations were turned off (Russian ones were launched, with their content).[123] With that said, there is no doubt that social media can be an arena or even a tool used in information warfare (the audience is there, so there is someone to influence).[124] Of particular interest to Russian information operations in cyberspace is the Central and Eastern European region. One of the necessary measures is not to give up the field, for which it is necessary to have one's own State media and institutions active in electronic and social media.[125]

This may not appeal to some legal activists (e.g., those in Europe, oversensitive about alleged support of U.S. companies by the EU or EU Member State services), but plenty of real people use social media. So, the active presence of state institutions is absolutely a must (e.g., profiles of state institutions). If they weren't there, it would mean giving up the field to external actors looking to fill such voids with their own information. There is no choice or alternative here.

Sometimes, however, niches emerge in other ways.

6.12.8 Blocking and cutting channels of information influence of the Russian Federation

The West was susceptible to Russian propaganda content, especially when it came to techniques for gaming problems that actually already existed in the minds of societies.[126] Let's emphasize that it may not have been so much about *creating* issues but about exploiting the existing ones. After all, creating a popular topic from scratch is difficult, and costly. It is more effective to insert messages into something that already exists—a type of bandwagon. There will be no shortage of recipients for such content in a pluralistic society, if only those individuals and groups that are by definition skeptical (contrarians) of any mainstream information, such as those supported by States—if only because they are supported by official state stances. Here's an example of this (flawed) logic: since everyone believes in the moon landing and it's a line supported by States, it certainly didn't happen. It's also about the posing of the so-called inconvenient (supposedly) questions that suggest doubt, e.g., "*who benefited from something*"—without providing any corroborating evidence or credible arguments.[127]

But in Europe, there is freedom of expression, freedom of speech. What a bummer, nothing can be done about the broadcasting stations. Or is it the lack of motivation that plays a role here? Strong blockades became acceptable in the European Union only after the Russian aggression against Ukraine in 2022. That's when RT (Russia Today) broadcasting was shut down, something the EU General Court also agreed with under the circumstances of the case *RT France v. Council of the European Union*.[128] In this case, the strong guarantees of freedom of expression in Europe were not used against Europe:

> Against that background, on 1 March 2022 the Council adopted, on the basis of Article 29 TEU, the contested decision and, on the basis of Article 215 TFEU, the contested regulation, in order to prohibit continuous and concerted propaganda actions in support of military aggression against Ukraine by the Russian Federation, targeted at civil society in the European Union and neighbouring countries, channelled through a number of media outlets under the permanent direct or indirect control of the leadership of the Russian Federation, since such actions constituted a threat to the EU's public order and security.

The proceedings explicitly pointed to the propaganda activities of these media: "activity of disinformation or manipulation of information in which the applicant is engaged."[129] It is a rare contemporary case where EU States have effectively blocked a broadcaster on the grounds that it spreads hostile propaganda that destabilizes States. This was performed by demonstrating and arguing that RT is "a media outlet under the permanent direct or indirect control of the leadership of the Russian Federation, for having engaged in propaganda actions justifying and supporting the Russian Federation's military aggression."[130] Therefore, a temporary prohibition on broadcasting was imposed.

Such blockades have reduced the effectiveness of Russian influence operations, propaganda, or disinformation, in unprecedented ways. At some points and for at least some parties—perhaps reduced that impact to negligible levels, or nearly zero.[131] Western societies even organized a kind of self-influence campaigns (likely unintentional; we speak of practical outcomes). Statements by Russian leaders, politicians, propagandists, and various entries at Telegram-type media were publicized, and conclusions were drawn from them, sometimes beyond healthy proportions, given too much importance or credence to them. It is possible that in Russia it was noticed, and therefore acted just so, pumping up certain content. Fear sells, doesn't it?

It is worth noting that the "Russian point of view" has managed to be promoted elsewhere, such as in South American countries.[132] The views of the "non-Western" world were manifested in the statements of their leaders, in the results of polls made in these societies, also in the votes of some States in the UN. In many cases, they were inconsistent with the position of Western countries.

States can create analytical units that study the information space, with the possibility of conducting activities in it. They can also influence information circulation.

6.13 COMMUNICATION CONTROL AND CENSORSHIP

Once upon a time, States strictly controlled the circulation of information, on a standard basis. Newspapers or media were under control. If necessary, the population was "protected" (isolated) from "bad" information by simply blocking it. Content was censored. Necessary from whose point of view? Typically, the ruling circles had a monopoly on such decisions. Information control was an integral state prerogative.

Today, at least in Western societies, things have become more complicated. There are free media, many points of view. The public is skeptical and even hostile to information blockades.

Still, even today, States reserve the right to block information, including in peacetime, as I mentioned in the previous chapter. They have the legal authority to do so. Technical capabilities are another matter. Tests to "disable" the Internet are not carried out by anyone in Europe, Russia being an exception. One can imagine that the possible introduction of an information blockade could be a challenge. It is not that simple to *turn off the Internet*, including technically. Such networks are distributed and redundant (there are many of them). However, the goal need not be a perfect and universal blockade but one that is "good enough." Such a one may be achievable. Crisis protocols introduced in 2022 at the EU level through the Digital Services Act could in certain situations serve as a legal mandate to shut down certain services or platforms, such as social media, both nationally and in the European Union. After the 2023 riots in France, politicians had had enough, and ideas to introduce the ability to block content or entire platforms were routinely floated. And again with social media posts during Israel's armed conflict with Hamas (October 2023), in the context of the posted content.

Various decisions to ban the installation or use of smartphone apps can also be viewed through the prism of censorship, and such decisions were made by various States in the 2020s, such as India's ban on Chinese apps. Or, like in 2024, Chinese bans of American apps (such as WhatsApp). Or attempts in the U.S. to ban apps (such as TikTok). If such events are not necessarily a testament the of censorship, then perhaps of geopolitical competition?

6.13.1 Content moderation as a form of censorship

Also important are issues of content moderation, sometimes equated with preventive censorship. Moderation is often important, if only so that digital platforms can be used pleasantly at all. Consider, however, terrorist content. The issue may be more difficult to resolve, as the content moderation policy makes clear. Admittedly, at one point, Facebook claimed that it was quick to remove terrorist content, even more than 99% of it, but one must remember that a lot depends on how one defines it.[133] And of course, some parts of the audience or policymakers may still complain about that 1%, or even a few images, when identified or found.

6.14 DIVERSION AND INFORMATIONALLY UNDERMINING THE CONFIDENCE IN A STATE—SUBVERSION

Trust in the State can be undermined through informational means. This can be done in multiple ways. Imagine the following scenario of an information diversion where a number of public services, perhaps including banks, are shut down by a cyber attack:

- Unauthorized content, such as anti-government content, perhaps targeting specific social groups or other countries, appears on government websites. For contemporary examples: prior to the war in Ukraine, there were some messages and cyber-activity implanted that funneled messages critical of the government and trying to bolster historical resentments between neighboring nations;
- That's when information about relevant content comes out of nowhere—distributed on social media, electronic media, and social media profiles followed by significant audiences—whether the information was from hacking operations, or not;
- The so-called fifth column of subversion, agents of influence, people who for some reason favor the aggressor, become active. Not much can be done about it. Inevitably, various messages, narratives, and reports may reach and appeal to some audiences, perhaps fostering their radicalization or countering (defensive) attitudes against the subversives;
- That's when leaks of correspondence between politicians occur. They are presented in the appropriate light that the attacking party modulates;
- Perhaps some diplomatic or political correspondence surface is disclosed or leaked, such as that from 10 or 15 years ago—old, outdated, but put in the context of events happening much later, even contemporary, by twisting arguments.

What then? Then, there's a problem, especially when the information campaign coincides with other crises. It may be hard to say how to straighten things out, to clean it up.

It is possible to defend against subversion and the induced disintegration of the State. In particular, this is what a State that is the victim of aggression must do. For example, in Ukraine, after the 2022 aggression, a policy of total resistance was introduced. All policies and resources were geared toward resisting, surviving, and fighting the enemy, with the support of the entire society, at every level.[134] Total resistance is a "national effort to regain sovereignty after an invasion and occupation by an aggressor nation. It is a whole-of-society effort encompassing a total resistance posture."[135] This envisages, among other things, setting aside current disputes (this can be clearly seen, for example, from the surge in support for the incumbent President Zelensky, including from people who previously voted for his rivals), including—in defense of their own business attempts—to force or impose unfavorable economic decisions on allied States. Of additional help in maintaining such attitudes are some positive views of the future. These must exist. The situation must not look hopeless or desperate, even if it could in fact be an extremely difficult one, or less openly, indeed dire. In the case of Ukraine, for example, it was about the vision of joining NATO and the European Union, which had to be credibly communicated to the public. These are important goals of communication and defensive political propaganda.

6.15 NEW TECHNOLOGIES AS METHODS OF ORGANIZING OR EXECUTING REVOLUTIONS, RIOTS, UPHEAVALS

This may sound provocative but let's face it. With new methods of processing, acquiring, and propagating information, it is possible to reach audiences instantly and with bypassing of traditional channels, such as those more closely monitored by States. In view of this, it has become feasible to address communications to selected groups, perhaps enthusiasts of unorthodox, alternative, non-standard (e.g., conspiracy) theories or views on the world, or those susceptible to believing them. These groups may be too small to constitute a sufficient seed to initiate significant movements, but one has to start somewhere.

6.15.1 Just engage 3–5% of the population

Let's revisit the diagnosis indicating that it was at times sufficient to organize the support of about 3.5% of a country's population to bring about a successful coup, and ultimately the overthrow of the government. At least in an autocratic system.[136] That is, not necessarily in liberal, democratic States.[137] The idea here was to stage a coup peacefully. Although the analyses of historical data indeed indicated that it was rare to mobilize as much as 5% of the population, the level of 3.5% may have been obtainable and enough. That at least according to data from 1945 to 2006. In rare cases, even less was enough. For example, 0.05% of the population, but let's put that aside as exceptional.

Let's stress an important aspect: the 3.5% rule referred to peaceful demonstrations, not violent coups or armed conflicts.[138] So, without an active cooperation of forces having access to weapons, and similar. Still, the theory of sufficient 3.5% support in the population is alluded to by contemporary radical movements concerned with climate change, and demanding that States and companies take action; for example, among Extinction Rebellion's goals is to "[mobilize] 3.5% of the population to achieve system change—using ideas such as 'Momentum-driven organizing' to achieve this."[139] Now, let's move away from the assumption of peaceful methods.

6.15.2 Starting a coup in a State—it's complicated

The issue of coups is a complex one. Much depends on the internal conditions of the State, although one thing seems to be understandable. It is necessary to control to some extent a fragment of the (armed) forces, such as military or otherwise armed units, like police. It is also important to take control of the flow of information. Formerly the mass media. This is an absolutely necessary consideration.[140] The rationale is to limit opposing sides and drive one's agenda. Today, it would also be necessary to disable telecommunications networks to prevent the organization of defense, resistance, etc. (I have already written about censorship as a means of preserving "public order" above, in the present context here, however, "public order" refers to the view of the spheres carrying out subversive actions).

The problem is that if cooperation from the force apparatus were needed for a successful coup beyond peaceful demonstrations, this would place constraints on such operations or plans. People in control of such services or military units would have to be involved. This would require more than merely informational influence on the general society. One would have to take the risk of communicating with such people in the hope that they would want to "join in," risking serious responsibility if things do not turn out as planned. The instigators would also need to assume that they would not report such attempts to conspire for purposes of illegally undermining state and public order—anywhere, to anyone. In other words, the instigator would have to convince some people to commit a crime of treason—one that would surely be prosecuted should the coup fail, naturally. How difficult this may be was seen in 2023 during a (simulated?) pseudo-putsch organized by Yevgeny Prigozhin, head of the Private Military Company "Wagner" mercenary group. It did not succeed. Let's put that aside. What view clearly emerges? Systematic issues arising from these events.

Perhaps it's not so simple? Perhaps it does not suffice to have some weapons and a bunch of people to take control of a State where distributed, armed force structures of various kinds are not in short supply? Especially when these structures do not join the conspiring movement. If only to wait and see what happens, not to mention—actively oppose it. Then, such or similar quasi-coup actions can be considered in terms of artistic performance rather than serious challenge to the established order. Eventually, everybody moves on and all forget about such failed attempt. Unless it succeeds for some reasons: then it becomes an evolution of the country and the State, perhaps historically rationalized, etc.

However, in the 20th century, in Africa, coups were often successful, and there were many such coups there at that time—including several attempts also in 2023, 2022, 2021, 2020, and 2019. In contrast, the attempts carried out in France (Algiers, 1961) were unsuccessful. Fortunately, staging a coup is not all that easy, especially today and in stable States. One of the system recommendations for building safeguards and resilience against coups into the political-state system is precisely the existence of a variety of armed structures.[141] Then, even if the revolting parties manage to take control of a part of one of such force structures, others remain to fight back. Today, distributed information sources are also very relevant. Even if control over state media is seized, policymakers tend to have social media presence with significant follower count—those could be used to issue information. In other words, hijacking a modern, Western State government structure is much more difficult than, say, 200, 100, even 50 years ago. It all still depends on the circumstances, so there are never guarantees. One can only scale the acceptable risk accordingly. I do not recommend trying out making a coup d'etat—the available data shows there is a good chance that it fails, and the consequences can be rather unpleasant.

6.15.3 Arab Spring

On the other hand, it is also worth recalling the so-called Arab Spring and the demonstrations, some of them riots, that were organized as part of it—we won't go into how, because why would we do that, what matters is the visible process and subsequent effects. In some places of the region, it may have contributed to the replacement of governments, to coups, although, of course, this was not done only by the public taking to the streets. That is a separate matter. And another is what, in retrospect, these changes led to. Did the changes in Egypt or around go the way the protesting people believed they would? What did consumers of information in Western countries, whose understanding of these events was built through media means, believe about the movement of events? Still, it was then that the power of the Internet and social media was widely recognized. In the exchange of information, organization, coordination, bringing support, etc. That was clearly a momentous effect, visible to all. From then on, any such action had to coincide with information management performed over social media and other new channels.

6.15.4 Media control and propaganda through artists, creators, writers

The importance of the media was well known to the Committee of Public Safety in the late 18th century during the French Revolution. Evidence of awareness of the power of newspapers and caricature as a vehicle for political propaganda has survived to this day. Artists have to make a living out of something. So, even if something is not in line with their views, after all, a paid commission has to be fulfilled. Those commissioning paid work naturally expect delivery of the results of the work. Consider, for example, the famous painter David, who was issued a commission to produce "pictures and caricatures suitable for awakening the public spirit and revealing how awful and ridiculous the enemies of freedom and the republic are."[142] Many such caricatures were also aimed externally, at England, at Russia, while others were for internal uses—those with anti-Catholic themes, for example. Caricatures were also created in the context of the events of World War I—this was done in Great Britain, their blade aimed at either the Kaiser of Germany or the soldiers of Prussia depicted as obese,[143] which was a reason to ridicule them.

The role of propaganda during the French Revolution was significant. Its vehicle was culture, but also formal documents, almanacs. Because of the high level of illiteracy in the rural population, it was also necessary to send "missionaries," or agitators, to extol the virtues of the new system of rule, the new principles. Such a content had to be shorter, written in simpler language—and it was. According to the so-called *d'Herbois method*, content should be comprehensible to someone who has finished primary education, to include anecdotes and humorous elements.[144] That is: the *form is entertaining, the content is completely political.* Masked by the format. In one such campaign, a major argument was used—money. The idea was to explain that thanks to the revolution, the lower classes would save money. Under the previous system, income was siphoned off through various taxes.[145] Such proselytizing of the new political system had to work—it was referring to the typical, daily issues of importance to all.

Here, it is also worth noting that the government of Nazi Germany issued a full instruction manual for the media explaining how to report on events. This was very effective, the idea being that the media themselves "know" what to do and how to do it. What to write about, in what way; and what to omit.[146] These directives were confidential. The documents were written by very competent people. For example, on the anniversary of Goethe's birth, directives were issued indicating that the propagandists had an advanced knowledge of the works of this author and of Goethe himself—they even tried to juxtapose him (Goethe, the great author) with Hitler, because they both disliked coffee![147]

6.16 CASE STUDY—ENCRYPTION

At a certain stage in the development of technology, it became possible for any user to use strong encryption. One that cannot be easily or even at all broken (since encryption takes place on the user's device, such as a smartphone, and decryption on the recipient's; it does not take place on intermediary servers—so the intermediary cannot simply reverse it—which was the previous standard); these technologies gained popularity in the second and third decades of the 21st century, becoming a standard. However—back to the 1990s—there was extensive debate in the United States on this topic, the so-called *crypto wars*. Some desired to eliminate encryption capabilities and the "export" of ciphers was even banned. To little avail, other than weakening the cybersecurity of systems, such vulnerabilities could be exploited and may even have been. The debate went quiet—only to return in the second and third decades of the 21st century.

Many arguments against encryption can be said. For example, they hinder law enforcement investigations or police work. However, there has never been a situation where a person's entire life record was on a single device (smartphone). Like it is today. Making this data available, for example, at a routine traffic check, seems absurd. It must be secured, and strongly.

Another argument pointed out that encryption is used by terrorists—indeed, they can use it too, but it does not mean that every user is immediately a terrorist. Encryption supposedly makes it impossible to prosecute abuses against children. It is, therefore, a play on the fears of the public. People fear terrorists, terrorists use encryption, and so one may be induced to think that [*feel free to end this simplistic sentence yourself*] ... But it would obviously be absurd to suggest that using encryption makes one suspicious. Anyway, such suppositions have at times appeared to be expressed by politicians and some opinion leaders in the media. Like: encryption is problematic, video games are problematic, artificial intelligence (AI) is problematic. With encryption, the debate is still ongoing. Since there is strong encryption in instant messaging, which cannot be stripped during content delivery, at some stage (at least in 2024, still) there emerged ideas of scanning content and messages before they were sent, on the user's devices—scanning without the user's knowledge or consent; scanning that can ring a "false positive" alarm, that is, casting suspicion, for example, baselessly. The problems are numerous. But the constructed narratives and informational efforts are having some effect. For a sufficient evidence take the following, for example: the issue is being discussed or debated for over 30 years, and is still being considered. Since the problem has been on the political agenda for so long, it is unlikely to disappear by itself. If only because of a simple mechanism. Debates and explanations are directed at the current generation of experts and politicians. Policymakers of today may eventually receive honest and merit-based explanation of the factual situation. But when those leave—and they will, (changing the industry, interests, retirement)—new ones will come in. The debate will have to be conducted from scratch. And perhaps indefinitely. Such is our fate.

I believe that technology is for the people. Sadly, abuses are possible and must be pursued and prosecuted. But is it a good idea to undermine security infrastructures on a large scale? This poses a tough nut to crack.

6.17 CASE STUDY—5G, CORONAVIRUS, PANDEMIC

It's hard to say where it originated, but there was an interesting synergy of conspiracy theories in the coronavirus pandemic. Some people, skeptical of the very existence of the pandemic (or the effectiveness of vaccines, or something else), apparently at some stage began to link these issues with other "controversies"—with the 5G telecommunications standard, which supposedly had some inducing effect on the development of the pandemic, and perhaps even activated some substances in the vaccine. It sounds absurd and it is.

The information was spreading. On social media, in articles on websites, in the face of this it was also raised in media debates and even began to be considered seriously. It was a so-called disruptor—a meaningless topic on which the involved parties were wasting their efforts. The introduction of this topic may have been done seriously, or perhaps as a joke, which is difficult to conclusively judge today. No matter. We may assume that the very fact of the appearance of this topic could have been used and played up by various participants in information interactions, and perhaps even by the so-called foreign services interested in information diversion.

This is because it is one of the very effective propaganda techniques: using current events, referring to them, writing in their context in some way, and developing them. This fulfills an important premise that determines the effectiveness of propaganda. The idea is to refer to an already existing topic. By doing so, one immediately benefits from the fact that there exist sides promoting some point of view on such issues. For such a side, of course, this would be the "correct point of view." And by the way, info operators would perhaps be able to "plug in" to the topic to give credibility to other things, theses, topics as well. So, it's also the use of the information "jumping on the bandwagon" approach. As a side note, in Europe around 2020, 5G telecom masts were set ablaze (others probably too) in many places.[148,149]

6.18 CASE STUDY—KOREAN POP AS A THREAT TO STATE SECURITY?

In 2022 in China, skepticism about Korean pop music reached a crescendo and K-pop was considered a national security problem, complicating the lives of fans of music bands,[150] deleting the accounts of influencers[151] or censoring them; digital platforms helped enforce such "consequences."[152] Is this a joke? That was the third decade of the 21st century, and these were formal decisions of Chinese authorities. One can get used to it.

To what point was the prohibition enacted? The point is that Korean pop had many fans around the world. These fans organize themselves into groups, and through social media and instant messaging they can exchange information and even organize activities. This was demonstrated when a fundraiser was held to raise money for a gift for a member of a certain K-pop group. In a State like China, this could be a cause for concern—some sort of rival center emerged, a center bringing people together, organizing their lives, themselves too. Capable of leading to a coordinated action. Perhaps challenging, by its very existence, the state organization itself, and therefore the so-called socialist values. From a State point of view, this may seem a risk.

Furthermore, state authorities in China were not impressed with the content itself,[153] or the "values," popularized,[154] and "ideology" spread by K-pop artists and their music. In line with the recommendations of the Central Propaganda Department of the Communist Party of China to carry out comprehensive management in the field of culture and entertainment aimed at countering the activities of "illegal and immoral artists," and worthy of implementing the spirit of General Secretary Xi Jinping's lectures and instructions on literary and artistic creation.[155] It was stressed that the problem is

> inflated salaries, tax evasion, the pursuit of audience numbers, abnormal aesthetics and chaos in the 'fan circle' [that] have also appeared in the entertainment field, which has seriously damaged the atmosphere of the literary and artistic community, tarnished the image of literary and artistic workers and affected the healthy development of the literary and artistic industry.[156]

For example, it was about promoting an "effeminate image of men," like using cosmetics. These are standards that were difficult for the Chinese authorities to accept at the time. Therefore, the decision was made to consider K-pop a threat and use the full scale of the state apparatus against the trend. Here, it is worth noting that some of the restrictions put in place against K-pop were lifted a few months later. However, it is a fact that the introduction of the campaign against K-pop also had social overtones, and there were situations when ordinary citizens on the streets or in stores spoke out loudly against K-pop, condemned people listening to this music, etc.

6.18.1 Can a popular influencer lead to riots in a State?

Imagine an opinion leader or a popular influencer. They may have thousands, some even millions of followers on their profile. Fans are ready to take action. Let's assume that 5% of these, say, 10 million, or 500 thousand, or even 10 thousand, are dedicated enough that after a suggestion or command is issued—they will be ready to take practical action offline, "in real life," such as going to a protest, and some of them—engaging in activity such as the proverbial throwing a stone. Then, we have significant groups of people ready to act. This could already constitute a real internal security risk. Of course, I'm not suggesting that fans of K-pop or other artists might be capable of such actions. This is merely a thought experiment. Now, what is some 70-year-old state bureaucrat supposed to do when he or she conducts such a thought experiment? Backed up, for example, by a think-tank composed of a group of 30-, 40-, 50-, and 60-year-olds who will offer him or her an analysis and recommendations. Well again, what should the bureaucrat in power do? Is he or she to—as in Russia—criminalize, punish, and ban the spread of certain concepts, for example, "LGBT propagation"[157] (while using the subject to play up Western societies)? Or send prosecutors or forces outright?

A separate issue entirely is how perfectly South Korea was using its K-pop stars as asset. Members of a popular K-pop band were even sent to the United Nations General Assembly to speak there. This, then, is the use of K-pop in diplomacy. Hats off to such a high level in the Korean Foreign Ministry.

6.19 CASE STUDY—CULINARY PREFERENCES AND CONSUMPTION OF INSECTS

An interesting extension of Overton's window on culinary or food issues is the introduction of the topic of eating insects, the so-called bugs, or worms, into the public debate. Once unthinkable, in recent years it has been talked about more often—this is what the expansion of the debate space is all about. This is how to construct the right conditions for the adoption of certain ideas—by simply introducing the topic. One such example is the vegetarian or vegan diet, which is, after all, quite typical today, perhaps even fashionable, in good taste, or laudable.

But can one actually use the topic of insect consumption for political purposes, political communication? By all means, yes. Just to name a story popular in some niche circles (by some, sometimes called conspiracy theory enthusiasts) that "*someone*" worked on getting people to (allegedly) switch to eating "bugs." In 2023, it seemed to have its origin somewhere in 2022 discussions on online boards. It's hard to determine this precisely—the concept itself originated in the second decade of the 21st century but was very niche initially. A renaissance of sorts occurred in 2023.[158] It has been attributed to the interest in this topic by the so-called right-wing circles across Europe,[159] who of course were to blame the "Eurocrats from Brussels" for everything, which has even been made easier by European Union policies introducing phrases like "The New Normal" on the occasion of the COVID-19 pandemic.[160] In view of this, can the slogan "If you don't vote for us, our opponents will force you to eat meat" (or bugs, or whatever) be effective? And what to do in such a situation? How to explain it properly?

6.20 A CASE STUDY OF THE ACTIVITIES OF THE INTERNATIONAL COMMITTEE OF THE RED CROSS (ICRC)

There are also examples of operations openly targeting humanitarian organizations such as the International Committee of the Red Cross (ICRC). In 2020, it emerged that the Burkina Faso government was to contract a PR firm for an information operation against the ICRC. As part of this campaign, articles were published in the press, including in Europe, which could then be reprinted locally in Burkina Faso. Harmful narratives were spread that supposedly the ICRC employees were collaborating with terrorists (they weren't). This PR firm realized the high stakes contract—successfully combating a well-known organization like the ICRC is something that they may add to its advertising portfolio. It did just that: "Our client had a real problem with a specific NGO that really was not objective ... The question is, how do you take this NGO out of the negative ball game and put them on the sideline?"[161]

This was done either without the slightest consideration of the specifics of the work of a humanitarian institution such as the ICRC, or simply business-cynical. This company used the methods of the so-called unattributed campaigns, that is, with a hidden background, true sponsors and goals concealed. One can create a special NGO for such purposes, and this was done. Profiles of non-existent people (deep avatars, in their parlance) were created and constructed to look real. How is this done? One can simply set up fake social media profiles and websites. One may also build some "cover stories" for such profiles to look more credibly, such as publishing something under their names in the media. Create some trace of activity bearing the hallmark of being maybe-real, so that possible verifiers can more easily believe that someone like this exists. In this case, it is about the services of propaganda (disinformation) on demand. Such methods can be used widely by many organizations around the world.

In fact, the International Committee of the Red Cross is by definition a neutral and impartial organization. This is the only way it can effectively help in armed conflicts, where there are many sides, and taking sides of any particular one of them can make the work more difficult or dangerous—the other side will stop recognizing such an organization as impartial, which can hinder operations, and even put personnel under a risk, for example. So, one has to remain neutral no matter who is right. Such is this work. Propagandists, or people who have difficulties (or refuse to) accepting such complex realities, may exploit such limitations or constraints.

6.20.1 Criticism of ICRC activities in Ukraine (2022)

During the Russian war in Ukraine from 2022 onward, it was at a time difficult for some Ukrainians to accept that the ICRC had contacts with Russia at all (remember, this is a requirement of impartiality; this was also done by some Ukraine supporters—maintaining contact is the standard thing to do in armed conflicts). A campaign against the ICRC was unleashed in some online media (and social media), openly criticizing the fact that it did not take a particular side (here implicitly: the Ukrainian side). But wait a minute—just what could an organization like the ICRC do? It has no battalions, no tanks, no armed forces. Its effectiveness is based on it being recognized—by everyone—as impartial. This can be difficult to portray in a world of social media and rapid information sharing, where people with partizan-like attitudes casually take sides and segregate themselves in strictly for or strictly against. And yet, this was the only way the ICRC could mediate the release of Ukrainians (Azovstal captives[162]) in 2022 and in general many other captives in many other places.

However, it must be admitted that the ICRC apparently may have had some trouble figuring out how to find its way around the new media channels environment during full-scale hostilities in the 21st century. During World War II, information flow occurred on a much smaller scale. During modern wars, this is no longer the case (actions are taken instantly, everything happens in real time, extremely fast pace), and therefore one can suddenly become the target of a strong informational influence resulting from the actions of many people (inspired in some way). It apparently took a while for the ICRC to find its way in navigating in this environment, although in 2023 it still appeared as if full awareness or preparedness was not assimilated in this area of activity in the organization—let's hope this happens in the future. For example, while the ICRC must remain neutral and impartial, after all, nothing compelled the then-president of the organization to smile while posing for a photo with Sergey Lavrov (Russian Foreign Minister) in 2022. A trifle issue, and yet no one informed the ICRC leader about it, or the leader ignored such a recommendation, which effectively has the same outcome. With all due respect, but who instructed him to smile then in such a situation? In March 2022, when the magnitude of the humanitarian catastrophe was already emerging (even if the images from Ukrainian Bucha were not yet widely known at the time), it had to look terrible and shocking. And I say this as a former employee of the International Committee of the Red Cross.

Evidently, however, "disinformation" targeting the ICRC was noted, as a devoted message was issued[163]: "The ICRC does not ever help organize or carry out forced evacuations. Building and maintaining a dialogue with parties to a conflict is essential to get access to all people affected, by obtaining necessary security guarantees for our teams to deliver life-saving aid". It is clear that working in such an environment of an armed conflict is dangerous. This may not be clear to everyone sitting in front of a computer or sitting on their couches. Although it is understandable that the public of an attacked country wants and expects all organizations to support their side, which is imaginably why there have been criticisms in Ukraine.[164] In the case of the ICRC, however, the traditional requirements of neutrality make such taking sides impossible. A misunderstanding of this fact has also led to misunderstandings when confusing the ICRC with another organization, namely the Ukrainian Red Cross (similarly separate organizations are the British Red Cross for example). Notably, such humanitarian organizations are not capable of stopping a war. In the same way, also, as the Vatican, which has no armies. To reiterate: an organization like the ICRC must be credible to both sides of the conflict. This means not advocating for either side, which can be difficult. It also means not speaking out on certain topics or speaking out on certain issues. This may sound difficult, maybe even cruel, but that's how this business works.

Turning to other international organizations, the UN applied information operations understood as using information channels for peacekeeping. This was already the case, for example, in the stabilization missions in Africa in the 1990s—while then the challenge would be to maintain the image of an impartial institution.[165] Personnel such as former journalists or mere PR people are not sufficient for such tasks.[166] But it should be clear that a general understanding for conducting information activities exists, and there was more of that kind of operation—such as during the Kosovo mission—activities that were not sufficiently well coordinated at the time between the various coalition countries (e.g., the U.S. and France).[167] So, this is another challenge, to synchronize activities in information sphere. Actions can also be made on broader scales—Africa is sizeable—as shown by the experience of the military mission organized by the African Union in Somalia and the informational fight against the influence of the Islamist radical group Ash-Shabab (Mujahideen Youth Movement).[168] These were carried out during the conflict, as well as during the transition to peacetime operations.

6.21 PROPAGANDA IN ELECTIONS

One of the more interesting potentials of propaganda is to create in the public message (in the public consciousness, in public opinion) a sense of the existence of some kind of problems or issues. The existence of concepts that should be identified as something to be worked on, remedied, or addressed, or solved.

This doesn't necessarily have to be based on facts—the idea is to create, in groups of audience, a sense of the existence of some issue, perhaps never before known. The perception of the existence of a problem poses a serious challenge.[169] Such problems can be popularized and one can portray oneself as someone who understands the issue and is able to act on it, that is, solve the problem, and save the day.

It could be the issue of separation of State and church, immigrants, gender equality, food issues, vegetarianism, overpriced stores, unemployment, global warming, problems with the healthcare system, and many others, also those not very significant or exciting. Actually, any social or political problem fits the bill. The problems to be considered may objectively exist—or not. If they don't exist, they can be completely artificially created if needed.

However, once they do exist in the consciousness of many people, they will cease to be artificial and contrived, and become as real as possible, as any others, shaping the debate, having consequences. Such issues need not be useless. So, is this propaganda?

Propaganda can mean informing or educating. It does not necessarily have to be a fishy, nefarious method, exploitation of people, or abuse. But is the application of the term "propaganda" to election campaigns and politics justified then? In some cases, however, propaganda is referred to directly. The electoral codes of States define such issues as limits on financial expenditures on election campaigns, etc. In French law, the matter of acquiring advertising services is defined as follows: "During the six months preceding the first day of the month of the election and until the day of the ballot in which it is acquired, the use for election propaganda purposes of any form of commercial advertising in the press or by any other means of audiovisual communication is prohibited" (Art. L52-1 Code Électoral).[170] In addition, because France is a mature country with well-established legislation: "the provisions of the law of July 29, 1881 on freedom of the press apply to propaganda" (Art. L307 Code Électoral). That is a very old, established law. The phrase "electoral *propaganda*" is also in use. The word "propaganda" itself occurs 102 times in this Electoral Code. This should probably suffice to recognize that propaganda is being referred to explicitly, but not in any demonic, Goebbelsian-like sense, any pejorative sense. It is the ordinary use of the word in its concrete meaning. In view of this, it can be said that political messages or advertisements may or may not be propaganda activities.

6.21.1 Memes in the service of politics and diplomacy

What kind of activities or messages? The content may comprise speeches, advertisements, as well as things like memes or even trolling, which politicians also engage in. For instance, presidents Trump or Biden did some but so did others all around the globe. Why not apply it to discourse, as memes are also used by the U.S. government in influence operations?[171] Similar techniques—humor, memes—are also used by the Russians (including state organs, in disinformation operations).[172] Naturally, not only by them. After all, activists supporting Ukraine in its war with Russia also use memes as a means of conveying information or expression. And this is fine.

What can memes be used for? To spread funny messages, offer insightful remarks. To popularize concepts within the State. To strengthen the State, the morale of the public, and state services. They can be aimed at the enemy—ridiculing them, or their actions. One may direct propaganda or disinformation in this way, and also fight it. In use are irony, sarcasm, and other rhetorical tricks, which may not be understood by all audiences these days, but this is not necessarily an obstacle. How does it work? As explained previously, memes take advantage of social, cultural, political (etc.), or humorous situations, alluding to them through short, concise, but relevant content.[173] They can be applied to other media, such as images. Nowadays, this is a widely used, popular, and effective form. When effective, memes are widely shared, modified, and recycled, being adapted to new situations, and framed in new contexts. In terms of expressing views, opinions, and judgments, they are similar to earlier concepts of caricature or satire. See the mock-up example meme in Figure 6.3.

6.21.2 Astroturfing

Astroturfing is a way of popularizing a message that has a great broadcasting capacity. It can be a process prepared in such a way that it looks normal, like "grassroots" or "independent" of external influence. For example, an issue may be described by a certain well-known person, a journalist, an influencer, a celebrity, or thousands of real users, including individuals, just

Figure 6.3 Serious cat meme. A meme is a template for creating a meme "popular image," here using a cat-theme. Creating a meme requires inserting a short textual content. Popular or viral images are often selected, such as the famous keyboard cat. In this case, serious cat is serious.

ordinary people, can be active in the propagation of information lines (by writing, speaking, and sometimes even waving a flag in public).[174] If a message gains sudden popularity and is widely shared, however, it may sometimes, somehow be "aided"—and this may be astroturfing.[175] In the digital age, the process is made particularly easier. There are many information channels with a large number of users. If we have some very popular profiles, for example, on social media, these can artificially, in a coordinated way, support some messages.[176] This can include political content, such as that which is hot, outrageous, controversial, or scandalous. When such content suddenly becomes popular, it can become viral, something that spreads like a virus. More and more people subjected to this message decide to share it, and at a certain stage everything is already "spinning on its own" and working like an automaton. However, these are not natural, grassroots campaigns, yet they are meant to look like such. A good example are the many astroturfing campaigns on Twitter.[177]

How to verify if something is astroturfing? Sometimes, it may be possible. If only by determining whether, at the initial stage of such a message, it was shared by many people in a similar category: several celebrities (perhaps they cooperate, the action is coordinated), politicians of a certain option, that is, by circles that have something in common. By examining (using network analysis) the relationships among those sharing the content, one may determine which groups of people are doing so. As the message is spread more widely, however, such artificial origins can become obfuscated, or obscured, so the chronology of interactions plays a role. This masking, moreover, is the point. Astroturfing doesn't have to involve bots (automatons), it can, and maybe even should, use normal people.

But beware: not everything that gains sudden popularity has to be created artificially. Some content is simply popular because it is interesting, like pictures of cute kittens.

6.21.3 Identity communication

Let's discuss two simplistic methods of creating a political movement. The first is simple: a political party is formed with a program and views that correspond or respond to the challenges of reality, and voters either like it or not. The second method involves doing some prior research—checking the popularity of various types of issues among the public and creating statements and a program that corresponds to these beliefs, lines of programs or proposals, or candidates selected for this. The second method involves creating things tailored to existing people, the electorate, and voters. Once such "maps" are identified, one moves on—activity (politicians, activists) is kept up within different fields. Various approaches are used here, using traditional and social media, purely in-person activities, like meetings with the electorate, with voters, with people, in different environments and circumstances. Everyone knows and is familiar with this. However, in an election campaign, one may need to create a staff and strategy, coordinate communication, and direct the message. Communication can occur between members of a political movement (by email, SMS, instant messaging, or directly, in person). Communication must also be directed toward the voter, and here the important channels are where the voters are. Voters used to get their information from television, from the radio, from other people, and from newspapers. Today, these traditional forms remain relevant, but the role of the Internet and social media is growing, will be growing, and is very important. Various new formats are being introduced, and consequently being used. It is possible to reach the public and, above all, voters through them. One can use advertising campaigns based on algorithms that direct the message to the right audience. Here, strategists should set the message and outline the design of the appearance, graphic designers creating this content and formats, and platforms used for broadcasting.

If we consider TV or radio, the matter is clear—one contracts an ad campaign, a spot, and it's being aired. If it's an Internet platform, such as Facebook, Twitter/X, advertising on websites—similarly. The important thing is to effectively reach out with a message. For example, it is possible to target ads profiled according to the gender of the recipient.[178] One may present as a defender of women, men, animals, the environment, etc. and offer specific solutions, somehow presenting this, promoting, popularizing, and convincing the audience that this is what they themselves desired.

This is *identity-based* targeting, when one does not so much talk about political options as about *issues*, e.g., gender equality, abortion, coal burning, veganism, global climate change, model airplane gluing. In the case of gender, for example, it is possible to build effective communication and even divisions, because the issue here is clear—it is possible to roughly divide society in half, into men and women (for simplicity's sake, we do not take into account fluid gender identity; I leave it to willing Readers to conduct this analysis with such criteria as an exercise in combinatorial optimization). Targeting messages in terms of identity can be effective, because these are messages that the voter believes in and supports or does not believe in and opposes. One can then talk about purely political issues without even mentioning party names or politicians' names—this the voter will figure out for himself or herself. One talks about an issue. About an issue on which a certain political option has a view, perhaps even has it on the agenda.

In general, a voter may feel that he or she is a member of some social group, and then such people can also be reached with appropriate messages.[179] For example, the elderly can be told about improvements for retirees or health care. To vegetarians with children—about the choice of a variety of meals at school. To students—about internship programs but also about various worldview issues (these are usually young people). To parents—about extending maternity and paternity leave. To teachers—about pay increases.[180] In general, one can distinguish identity issues and direct the message in relation to them, to the topics. In this way, it may even be possible to legally "circumvent" election silence to a certain extent (even if one has to get a little creative to do so; use at your own risk). But beware, because too much party bias can affect cognitive issues, memory—the brains of people,[181] one needs to be careful, so as not to unnecessarily create cognitive dissonance in the voter. Content, therefore, should be rather pleasant.

6.21.4 Reverse use of search engines for political purposes

Another interesting phenomenon is the reverse traffic method—from politicians' speeches to the Internet. Politicians may include certain specific words or phrases, terms in their speeches or addresses with the hope that these will later be searched for on the Internet. However, this involves uttering such lines of messages that already appear in Internet search engine results. The procedure is about convincing a person (a voter) that such a politician knows what he or she is talking about, that he or she is right.[182] This can be persuasive—it can be aided or constructed, crafted, manufactured, a certain thought process can be induced intended to lead to a particular conclusion (without saying it explicitly), which can result in support for a particular political party or a politician (possibly leading to a change in thinking about them). Why? Because the voter would come to that conclusion himself or herself (or so he or she thinks, at least). Very sophisticated.

Establishing an understanding of specific phrases in people's minds can lead to the fact that when these people search for these specific phrases in an Internet search engine, they will get specific results. If those phrases were to be subtly changed or negated—the result might be different. The trick, then, is to pinpoint the exact phrase someone would be looking for. He or she may not get into the idea of searching for information on a particular topic in a more general way, without such support. He or she will search for the desired specific information, in the desired context. For example, search results for the keywords "the history of cats" and "history of the cat" may differ (the first keyword is the title of a book). Looking at this mechanism from the other side: a voter, reading the other side's media (skeptical or opposed to his or her preferred political option, or preferences), may even be reinforced in the view that these other media skew what the politically preferred option actually says. That is, what Politician X or Politician Y actually said is attacked in Media 1 or Media 2, and the voter perceives that the representation of reality, for example, of the words of Politicians X or Y, is untrue. In view of this, such a voter automatically reaffirms his or her views. This is an interesting effect, although currently underexplored. Basic psychological effects, for example, strain, cognitive dissonance, and confirmation, can justify and drive it.

6.21.5 Technologization of politics, neurotechnology

Ochlocracy (mob rule) is a degenerate form of democracy, a "government by the populace; mob rule; a state, etc., ruled or dominated by the populace".[183] The question arises whether the technologization of society has the side effect of approaching this form of rule,[184] where it is all about controlling and influencing the sentiments of the masses, and exploiting the mass effects of crowd psychology[185] on large scales. Technologization, automatization, and a kind of dehumanization of the political and democratic process may carry broader, bottom-up risks.

If a political leader creates policy in response to posts by segmented, isolated individuals[186] on social media (or interprets them to make decisions desired by such an individual), isn't that already dangerously close to a system of degenerate democracy? Just keep in mind that the previous large-scale ochlocratic system was implemented by Lenin in Soviet Russia in the 1920s. What this ended with—we know (slaughter, genocide, mass suffering, and unfortunately much more unpleasant things). But back then, people could not communicate and organize as easily as it is possible today and will be even more possible tomorrow. The "power of the crowd" and the rules that emerge in this way can also have other effects, such as prohibiting the utterance of thoughts or the dissemination of content deemed iniquitous, according to somehow developed doctrinal assumptions. Thus, it is also the possibility of imposing a blockade, censorship,[187] removing people from social debate, from the job market, etc.—sometimes manifesting itself under the name of cancel culture, potentially reinforced by rapid information circulation, although it should not be confused with the usual meaning of ostracism.[188,189] Cancel culture is sometimes referred to as delegitimizing people with whom one disagrees, and can lead to intimidation of others not to speak out on a topic.[190] On what topic? On a variety of topics, it can be a matter of simple 2 + 2 = 5, but mostly they are socio-political issues. Drifting under the influence of news coverage affecting social groups could have dangerous effects if such truncation concerned matters relevant to national security. Thoughts, of course, can be hidden, not expressed in the open. In 2023, it was still not possible to inspect human thoughts straight from the human brain—this was merely being worked on, with very limited results known. On the other hand, such neurotechnologies are something to watch closely. It's doubtful that they will be easy to implement before 2030, perhaps even by 2040. Still, it is difficult to predict progress in this field. However, if it were to occur to forces under ochlocracy to subject even unspoken views to inspection, it would pose a major threat to the future social order—potentially preventing any change in the States, and therefore any development, including social development. Happily, the emergence of such technical capabilities is not on the horizon, for at least the next 10–20 years. People are still protected by constitutionally guaranteed freedoms of thought, conscience, and opinion. At least for now.

However, if user interfaces were at a time being put into use that would allow us to control devices or computer programs or smartphones with our thoughts—we must be aware that we are already approaching that mind-reading stage, at least of technological capability to do so in some form. Why "put into use"? It's usable, practical deployment. Only that would signal that such technology is gaining reliability, repeatability to some degree, and simply usability. So, it's not just about scientific development but about deployments.

6.21.6 Political marketing

This is not a book about PR. This will be short and to the point. Political PR is the popularization of ideas or candidates, for the purpose of winning elections, increasing or maintaining support, by means of promoting a certain vision of the future to appeal to the voter.[191] It is perhaps more of an art and practical activity than an academic discipline. It's about designing communications and distributing the emphasis appropriately. According to some, political marketing is a form of propaganda.[192] Or rather: of information and education? Probably it depends on the distribution of accents and the methods and techniques used. However, if it were to be the presentation of a candidate in an election "on par" with a product such as soap, we would rather call it advertising.[193]

A slight difference: soap, even the nice-smelling one, however, does not later decide the fate of States and their citizens. The latter requires intellect, some consideration.

6.22 ARMIES OF TROLLS

Since people reside at, and are using social media—including people such as opinion leaders, journalists, and politicians—the public debate happens there, at least in part. Naturally, all sorts of actors have noticed this—including security services of States. For instance, Cambodia was said to be using a so-called troll army.[194] Such structures can inject certain content into the debate, suppress other, mislead, create confusion, promote certain narratives as actually existing or popular, etc. The so-called Russian troll factory was already mentioned in Chapter 3. Active since 2012 (so a long-term investment),[195,196] the structure executed procedures targeting other States. Such structures can cause a mild stir.

Such structures can be internal-looking and attempt to influence sentiment, debate, or elections. But they can also be more offensive—directed externally, targeting electoral or political processes in other States. One can suppress debate on certain topics, and induce discussion on other topics. One can oppose some specific candidates, some specific issues, ideas, questions, and problems. One can discredit individuals, products, brands, countries, and views. It can be done on a mass scale. Although in recent years, awareness of the problem has increased, and it is no longer so simple to inspire such activity in the media as to make them write an article. This does not mean that it is not possible and that it no longer takes place. It may. It all depends on quality, not quantity. People are needed for such practices: strategists, content creators, developers, and operators of systems such as bot farms. Perhaps emerging opportunities due to AI/LLM will affect efficiency and reduce the cost of operations. For example, such tools are able to adopt certain styles of expressions, such as, writing as French, English, German native speakers, and so on. If digital platforms can't keep up with these risks, a problem may surface eventually—to the surprise of none, let's hope so. To none, because the possibilities clearly exist. There's no sense in not taking advantage of such capabilities, so the capabilities will be put in use. In 2024, this was already being noticed gradually.

Of course, it would be wrong to consider that such a troll or fake profile has views on issues, political inclinations. Some may be expressed, others discredited. But as a rule, such non-state actors are doing it for money, and not for pleasure or out of activism. The assumption, however, is that thanks to the many people who do not tone down their statements, trolls can build on the views or disputes that exist in society. Use them to fuel arguments, "flamewars": wars of words, bickering, the so-called shitstorms.

6.23 BRINGING ONLINE EXPRESSION TO THE STREETS—DIVERSION

How to evaluate the effectiveness of propaganda efforts? One of the main measures, I repeat, are the effects. Actual effects. Actions performed by people subjected to propaganda. For example, taking to the streets in protest, setting fire to a car, or, sure, voting. Russian troll factories have been known to exploit (or reinforce) worldview and racial divisions in the United States. For example, one group of trolls strengthened one side of an argument, while another group strengthened the other side. Manufactured street protest events were created, and to some extent it worked. An example of the topic could have been attempts to strengthen divisions on issues of race in the United States, such practices were attributed to Russia.[197,198] And these are already concrete effects of propaganda—people brought to the streets. Who knows, perhaps it could have been inflamed even more, leading to riots? Or maybe that is yet to come. So, these are actions of which a source may be the Internet or social media, and which target is the physical world. Actions demonstrated to be successful, though not on a grand scale. In 2022, a Chinese PR firm was contracted to create *de facto* artificial but real-looking protests in the United States (in Washington).[199] Later, images from such protests can be secondarily used on the Internet to amplify messages, already based on "real" events that took place—once they do take place, they, well, take place.

The flow in the other direction is also possible—from existing protests to the Internet, social media. The same was true of Russian operations to fabricate Western societies' support for Russia in the war in Ukraine or calls for peace. This was done by attempts to "plug" into existing protests. All it takes is a few or a dozen individuals with a banner expressing support for some cause—like the Russian side or its goals (of the "Free Donbas" type). To increase chances of being noticed, one may stand in front of the press cameras, which may be somewhere on the spot. One can also take a photo of such a diversionary group, later to be spread on social media directly. And in this way an illusion may be built that a lot of people supposedly are taking part in a demonstration supposedly supporting Russia—in reality it may be only a few people or even no one. Such situations have occurred in protests in France,[200] as well as in many other places.

Europe is compact. Travel is easy. In the case of simulated (sham) pro-Russian demonstrations, the same people appeared several times in different places[201] and countries. Content critical of Ukraine was presented at demonstrations devoted to completely different issues. The goal, of course, was to create propaganda material on which to build messages and narratives on the Internet. In several European cities (Berlin, Vienna) "grassroots" demonstrations happened by local communities, likely of the Russian origin. Russian flags were waved. Such background details are not necessarily clear to a viewer from another country, watching the coverage on social media or television. Then, it's easy to oversimplify and conclude that someone there actually might have been protesting or supporting Russia (to be more specific: almost all Western European governments sided with Ukraine).

In the case of the 2023 unrest in France, a certain amount of coordination through social media, instant messaging was noted early on. Such coordinated riots on such a scale (communicative) and with such speed were not possible, for example, in 1791 (French Revolution) or even later. This is a novelty of modern times and societies are not yet adapted to such reality, phenomena, effects, and risks to come. Societies are not ready, but they want to be, which is why there have been ideas in various countries (e.g., France, Belgium) to block social networks during riots, to block the propagation of "terrorist content," etc. No one can deny the usefulness of social media and instant messaging communication in various protests, like dissent. Decades ago, it was possible to exert influence through radio broadcasting[202] on a more widespread scale. Today, the matter is simpler, one can act much more faster and more effectively, with a much greater reach, but also precision.

There are also known cases where spreading a rumor, gossip, or hearsay (i.e., spreading disinformation or misinformation) on the Internet (via instant messaging) has led to real lynching,[203] cases of physical violence, and killings. This has happened, for example, in India.[204–205] And all this via instant messengers, such as WhatsApp Messenger, but others could have been used. The reason why WhatsApp stood out is that it was widely used—large number of users—and the simplicity of sharing "outrageous content" with their contacts. Such content spreads akin to a forest fire, and when we have hundreds, or thousands of people in quick succession spreading calls for violence, the situation becomes dangerous. Thus, for example, in 2018 several people were stigmatized as "child kidnappers". The information was spread by instant messaging,[206] shared massively (which was technically easy). As a result, the persons in question were killed in a brutal manner. And this is just one such a case, as there were many, many more. Furthermore, there were more events of the kind, including beyond India, just to name Israel,[207] not to mention the riots in France in 2023 which had a slightly different nature. Although it was in India that the problem was substantial enough that the state authorities issued a warning to WhatsApp,[208] demanding that it take action and curb such opportunities, for example, to make it harder to share messages on a massive scale or introducing other forms of restrictions. In general, the problem is that giving audiences the ability to communicate en masse on social media and through instant messaging has certain dangers involved. This is a social problem. Resulting at least from the psychological composition of certain people, perhaps social groups and social-communication dynamics. Some people in their nature can furthermore have a propensity to take nefarious actions, involving themselves in disgusting, or nasty affairs. And thanks to technologies, such people are given an opportunity to act that they did not have before. And this nature of theirs is then subject to externalization, sometimes with effects observable on the scale of society, cities, even entire nations. Before the Internet era, it was difficult to see how many people were affected by such mental-intellectual issues.

6.23.1 Industrial-scale content creation—deepfake, generative AI

Artificially created statements made by substituted people was also one of the methods of describing the world in some Chinese media. Specifically, this involves describing the situation in the United States (how bad it is there) or China's actions on the international stage (how great they are). One can say that this is normal. One may engage actors to say what they have scripted on a given topic. And now such persons can also be created automatically, using AI, applying generative AI (deepfake). So, they are persons that do not exist but read what they need to.[209] How about creating a political party whose leader does not exist, but is an AI-created avatar? Who knows what the future holds!

Who knows, perhaps someday it will also be possible to create political spots in a mass manner. With the help of generative AI, given a scenario, sentences to say, a product will be created without the involvement of a real person. Perhaps speaking about hyper-local issues, such as building a local road in a small neighborhood in a small city. Because then such a "politician" will be able to speak on absolutely any topic. This is still nothing, after all, he or she may not even be alive anymore.[210] Having technical source data (voice samples, photos), it is possible to produce material such as videos with people who are no longer alive. This is a thing of the future, of course. There are companies that are already able to create such products—deepfake—on demand, do synthetization, voice cloning. Soon, it may be much simpler and available to everyone.

It is worth noting that historically, however, information was fabricated by many States, by various actors or persons, in various contexts. For instance, a special cell in the services of Great Britain, aimed at producing propaganda that could not be attributed to anyone. The media in various States were inspired by these materials, with the important hint that instead of selecting general targets (such as "communism" or "Russia"), the messages should be aimed at specific individuals or organizations.[211] The motivation was not given, but one can guess that the idea was to be precise and act in such a way that the recipients can more easily understand what is at stake, realize who (specifically) is the "bad guy." On the other hand, it is important to emphasize the need to mask the source.[212] With deepfake all this will be even easier. But it will also enable a paradox when content that is actually true, but inconvenient for someone, is referred to as alleged deepfake (synthetically created content). The importance of the source will remain relevant. In other words—who posts the manufactured, deepfake material? Is it some random Internet user, or some well-known public person? The effect, such as credibility, may depend on that.

6.24 POLITICAL AND PROPAGANDA ISSUES IN BIOLOGY, GEOGRAPHY, AND AGRICULTURE

The COVID-19 pandemic created a very interesting opportunity and conditions for observing how information spreads, and of various currents and nature of information dissemination in the modern world. One could see the existence of four social groups.

The first was made up of people who "*believe the science*," also more likely to favor policy decisions such as lockdowns (restrictions on movement, closure of restaurants, cafes, stores, cultural centers, etc.) and other restrictions, including remote work requirements.

The second group includes skeptics—more or less opposed to messages about the epidemic or to decisions taken (such as lockdowns or their extent). In Belgium, for example, "lockdowns" have been made by taking such actions as taping benches to visibly mark them as out of use to discourage people from sitting on them. This probably came out of a highly publicized, quite unfortunately in retrospect, study about how long the virus survived in laboratory conditions on various types of surfaces—such as wood or aluminum. Well, a scientific career involves writing scientific publications, and this was an excellent time to publish on this very topic—COVID-19. Another issue is the reception of such work by the public, or experts, or advisors to governments. With unfortunate results and long-term impacts on tampering with human behavior. The topic of pandemics occupied a lot of space in the information environment. Where information spreads instantly, such research fell on fertile ground, its results were popularized and publicized, perhaps not necessarily in fortunate ways. There was no lack of absurd restrictions, for example, in Brazil the use of pillows during air travel was banned, in Poland, authorities prohibited entering forests.

The third group were the "people in the middle," accepting to some extent the arguments of both sides, without extreme opinions or decisions. They did see some absurdities, but this was not the moment to listen to moderate voices, an interesting observation about social dynamics in the information age.

Obviously, there were also (fourth group!) fringe groups, arguing that "there was no epidemic" or that "vaccines were unnecessary" or even "harmful". Here, we do not get into that conversation—that's in the past and let others worry about it. However, it is worth noting the various types of disinformation activities conducted.[213]

6.24.1 Propaganda targeting vaccines

The event of hacking of employee email accounts of the European Medicines Agency to later propagate (leak) the non-public data about the details of the vaccine made by the manufacturer Pfizer is an interesting case. The viewers were looking for incriminating things there, for example, about the ineffectiveness or harmfulness of the vaccine. To no avail. But the attempt to find anything of notice was very interesting because such medical information is by its nature extremely difficult to interpret by laypeople—it is very specialized, one needs a very advanced knowledge of biochemistry or biology to understand it. There is no way that a typical viewer of content on the Internet could correctly interpret this topic. And yet, disinformation campaigns, including those using this particular fact, have had some effect—if only that the content have spread. Why? Perhaps they could have considered an example, or incriminating "evidence," in the very fact of the leak happening at all. If there is a leak, then something must be in there, right? Or maybe not, but why delve into it.

The fact is that at one stage, digital platforms intensively filtered content, cutting out things deemed disinformation or fake. They were urged to do so by States. The platforms felt obliged to do *something*, pressed by public opinion. Afterward, it was admitted that the moderation put in place was at times too harsh and that some removed content later turned out to be true—that is, true information was subjected to censorship, interpreting it as false,[214] taking it down. Why all the fuss? Humanity then experienced the first global pandemic under the conditions of the information age, where information flows instantly, things happen at a fast pace, having immediate impact. No one had the experience here, and it was likely to be feared that even innocuous debates on a certain topic could harm a vaccination campaign that was supposed to help bring an end to economically damaging restrictions, self-imposed by most States. In view of this, perhaps it was better to cut out some of the statements at the time, even if justified, true, factual, or regardless of not being false? Or not. That's for the reader to decide. In the end, the vaccination campaigns had a positive effect.[215] Still, there is no way to fully compare with the situation if there was no vaccine—mankind has only one timeline. Therefore, some people may not be satisfied with such scientific results, and not much can be done about it—it's their opinion or beliefs.

The problem of disinformation and information circulation in general with epidemic disease was also noted in the previous (2002) SARS coronavirus epidemic in the early 21st century. More specifically, it was noticed by the Propaganda Department of the Chinese Communist Party Central Committee, issuing guidelines and a circular letter on how to behave in this crisis, which noted that it was necessary to conduct propaganda in accordance with the spirit of the "16th Congress of the Communist Party of China".[216] It may sound like party-bureaucratic gibberish, but the idea is to spread the word about the effective control of the epidemic, to which communist ideology was supposed to contribute. Information centers should "adhere to the principles of unity, stability, encouragement, and positive propaganda; stress politics, the overall situation, stability, and science; firmly grasp the correct direction of public opinion".[217] That is what later happened everywhere in the world during the (later, more serious) SARS-CoV-2 epidemic in 2020. It's as if this circular letter following the 2002 epidemic in China was copied. But perhaps nowhere—except in China—it was even known about? Subsequently, post-pandemic, exactly like any government of any State, China was also able to portray itself as a "winner," arguing that the right policies led to "victory" over the pandemic. The proof here would be that the pandemic had ended. This is, of course, not an appropriate logic.

In other words, it is adapting official versions of information to affairs that have already occurred, and explaining what happened—in some way. Other actions in other natural disasters can be similarly justified, and this is because after the fact, in retrospect, it is easier to adapt explanations to a situation that one already knows well, or at least much better than when it was occurring. Since the public, and people in general, have it in their nature to rationalize reality, to seek explanations, so some information must be provided to them, this is understandable and justified. People need it, as many scientific studies also show. That is human nature. It is sufficient that such explanations should be satisfactory, that is, in some ways rational and reasonably acceptable. Still people will eventually move on to other activities anyway.

In essence, this was the situation in many countries after the pandemic crisis operations. Many leaders during and after the SARS epidemic (in the early 2000s) showed themselves to be holding the reins, leading the fight, etc. Like China's then-leader Hu Jintao, whose visits, oversight, and advice were dissected in the Chinese media.[218] It is essentially a very similar mechanism, if not exactly the same, because who would have the nerve and time to go into the details. I point out that the SARS (2002) epidemic in China occurred around 20 years before the global SARS-CoV-2 (2020) pandemic, and the mechanisms of political-information-propaganda handling were very similar (especially in Asia, it is understandable—they had previous experience and procedures that were lacking in Europe or the US, for example). Similar, if not in some cases, exactly the same—regardless of time, place, type of events, political system even. This was not always noted correctly by some media outlets, writing about how *someone wins or loses with an epidemic*, and that certain political systems were supposedly better or worse in such situations. Such takes only added to the information chaos.

6.24.2 Decisions amid widespread moral panic are difficult

A completely different problem is to what extent this dynamic of information confusion could have even forced the world's governments to impose restrictions. This is a different, unexplored problem. When things were happening fast, it was challenging to assess what needed to be done—there was a lack of information. However, *some action* had to be taken, even if fraught with the risk of mistakes. Decision-making in the absence of available, quality information is extremely difficult. In addition, there may be accompanying pressure (or criticism) from the public, and at some stage perhaps some sides with vested interests. The role of a decision maker or politician in a crisis may be particularly difficult. Especially because when the situation calms down, there may be reckoning—already from a position of being wiser (retrospectively after the fact, having information unavailable previously!). The issues surrounding pandemic and vaccines have become an integral part of politics. Technically—health policy. But also the so-called pure politics—when a party supports the measures, and another party is against and spreads skepticism for political gain from it. There were voices in societies questioning the existence of pandemics, the effectiveness of vaccines, etc. And these could be expected in democratic pluralism.

A separate problem is the fact, as pointed out by researchers, of discrimination against people who have not been vaccinated. Manifestations of exclusion and even prejudice against unvaccinated people.[219] Vaccination has become an integral part of politics and quite a strictly political issue in the pandemic, sometimes a divisive issue—not just a matter of medicine or science.

Even after the restrictions were lifted, messages began to tentatively break through in the press around the world, indicating that the approach of States to the construction of policy toward the pandemic challenge was not based on facts, and even, according to some, were based on "lies" and "unscientific".[220] Let me repeat: everyone is always wiser after the fact. Another problem is that it can be natural to want to hold someone responsible—after the fact, preferably others.

6.24.3 Biological names

Propaganda can also be done with biology. An example is that a beetle was named after Adolf Hitler—*Anophthalmus hitleri*. The name was given in 1937 by an Austrian biologist, best known precisely for giving the beetle such a name. It is perhaps his greatest achievement in life. However, it can be said that such naming of fauna or flora is propaganda. The same may be true of comets, planets, etc. For example, the asteroid 1283 Komsomolia is named after the Kommunisticheskiy Soyuz Molodiosiya, an organization of youth in the Union of Soviet Socialist Republics. Similarly, the beetle *Demonax fochi is named* after the French Marshal Foch. Naming can also be used to express disapproval, as was the case with the name *Khruschevia ridicula*, given to an insect by a scientist not fond of USSR leader Khrushchev.[221]

6.24.4 Geography, cartography, maps, and geopolitics

Today, environmental issues can be the subject of propaganda, an element of political debate—so not just scientific and not understood as policy-making in response to scientific results. Then, there are questions about financial considerations, political considerations, or others.[222] So much for biological or chemical issues. But there can also be propaganda value in things of a geographic, or rather cartographic, nature. Like maps, which is related to the fact observed by German geopoliticians that the public gives credence to content presented graphically. And this can be exploited by presenting real data in such a way as to create a certain impression. For example, German maps indicated the size of the German minority in Latvia, symbolizing it in such a way that it visually looked larger than it actually was.[223] Similarly, with the portrayal of Czechoslovakia as a threat—the map concentrically placed planes "aimed" at German territory, with the range of the planes circled to include Germany's distant territories.[224] The aim was to have a psychological effect so as to build support for armed aggression and annexation of Czechoslovakia, which was successful. The significance of the maps remains important. For example, consider the double name of the islands: the Malvinas Islands (Spanish: Islas Malvinas), and the Falkland Islands. The two names operate side by side, reflecting a dispute over the territory between Argentina and Great Britain.

More contemporary to us was the dispute over Crimea and how to depict it on maps, including digital maps, on map services like Google Maps. Is it Ukrainian territory, Russian territory, or perhaps disputed territory? Similarly, Donbas and Luhansk. Legally, these areas belong to Ukraine territory, although Russia held an effective control (as of 2024) in parts. If a Western map service attributes these areas to Russia, however, they are making a mistake—accepting a version of sides in the armed conflict, perhaps with a psychological impact on public perception and negative public response. So, they don't do it (as of 2024). Russia's Yandex had to find another solution, because in Russia, the territories are treated as Russian. The found solution was to remove the borders from the maps. One can try to circumvent such a dilemma in various ways as it seems. No borders—no problem? According to an old joke, the question "with whom Russia borders" could be answered: "with whom it wants".

6.24.5 Agricultural propaganda, potato beetle attacks

Agricultural propaganda is also an interesting area of application. Farmers have historically been numerous in society—a sizable group to whom information messages can be directed. This was performed, for example, during the communist era in Europe (1945–1989) when communist governments spread fear among the people with the potato beetle threat. A type of beetle (*Leptinotarsa decemlineata*) that wreaks particular havoc on agricultural crops—precisely on potatoes. According to Communist propaganda, the beetle was supposed to be the responsibility of "American capitalists," who dropped it[225] on East Germany, Poland, Czechoslovakia, and throughout the Eastern Bloc. So, there was fear propaganda in use there ("the evil capitalists are attacking us"), as well as defensive propaganda ("we are under attack—we must defend ourselves"—hence the manual beetle harvesting campaigns gathering populations of said countries). This was a real problem in the agricultural sector—it involved significant crop losses. In view of this, "defense" could also be a manifestation of patriotism, but also of building an atmosphere of fear, and looming danger could only help such a cause.[226] That's not all. The beetle had been a popular topic even before. During World War II in Great Britain, the appearance of potato beetle was explained by German attempts to destroy British agriculture (potato crops). The first potato beetle "bomb" was to be dropped in 1943 on the British Isle of Wight.[227] So, it seems that multiple States had a potato beetle problem, and all of them portrayed it as an external, deliberate "attack". Conclusions? Draw them on your own.

In our modern times, one could get the impression that States were flip-flopping over allegations of being the source of the SARS-CoV-2 virus, for example, that it leaked from laboratories or came from a wet market in China; on the Internet, it was sometimes joked that "someone ate an undercooked bat," etc. According to the version that emerged in China, the United States was to blame. According to the World Health Organization, however, the most likely cause of the outbreak was the transmission of the virus from animal to human.[228]

6.25 POLITICAL BUZZWORDS, NEUTRON BOMB, AND CONCLUSION

Several books could be devoted to the topic of political propaganda. The subject can be analyzed from many sides. For example, do some key words in resolutions or regulations of the European Parliament appear by accident? Phrases such as "virtual worlds," "quantum technologies," "blockchain," "web 4.0," "*Acheta domesticus*," and other so-called buzzwords.[229]

Is this a coincidence, a grassroots action, or is it actually a natural pick up of them (because they are spoken of publicly, there is some hype)? Or is it some kind of popularization of these terms due to some strange lobbying effect or promotional action? After all, this is a further solidification of a said term, perhaps linked to a technology or even products, their popularization, aiding in their credibility. It could be an absolute coincidence, or it could be an ordinary process of cause and effect (I am not looking for any hidden agenda here; something is said, some problem worthy of regulation is perceived, so the idea of regulation arises). The fact is that when one EU institution uses a term or a word, often others start using it as well. Is this a deliberate positioning of a product, solution, sector, or issue? Or rather, a normal, ordinary, and natural diffusion of terms and information—because after all, some terms must be used to name things and concepts? I offer this for the Reader's consideration as an interesting case study to analyze over the next years.

In 1977, there was a political dispute in the U.S. Congress over the decision of whether or not to build a neutron bomb. President Carter had a problem with the decision and wanted NATO to support it. There was a problem with this, because social movements opposed to the nuclear bomb were growing in strength in West Germany. These fears did not come from nowhere—they were inspired by Soviet propaganda.[230] The lessons are the following: sometimes it's hard to make difficult decisions individually. These can be contested from many sides. Perhaps the best solution is to politically dilute causation through collegial decisions—one could wonder. For example, by arguing that "this is how it was decided in the NATO alliance". Or at such a level "as the European Union," even though each EU country has representatives in the European Council (prime ministers of Member States). This may not be common knowledge among the public in EU Member States. What was used, for example, in the campaign to promote Great Britain's exit from the EU (effectively, as it led to exiting of the United Kingdom from the EU). The fact of "democratically unelected EU bureaucrats" was cited numerous times during the anti-EU campaign. Against the truth that they in fact were democratically elected; moreover, the democratically elected UK policymakers had a great deal of influence on the work going on within the Union.

The great changes in communications are having an unequivocal impact on state operations, but also on military operations. This is no longer the 19th century or the beginning of the 20th century, when state powers could turn off the information circuit and quietly determine the details of state and interstate policy, modulating what their societies know and thus influencing what they should think. What they should favor and what they should oppose. What they are supposed to know and what they are not supposed to know. Today, in a pluralistic society, it is not so easy to turn off the information circuit. Quite surprisingly, Russia learned this in practice in 2022 and 2023. Reports, photos, and videos depicting massacres, crimes, and killings could not escape the attention of Western public opinion, as well as the broad public. Simply put, everyone could see it, which must have resulted in effects on public perception. This brought increased pressure on Western governments to support Ukraine. Even if some Western States weren't initially eager to help Ukraine with arms supplies, they would still have been forced to do so by the pressure of public opinion, which, according to any poll, was very moved by the war and supportive of their own governments in the aid. This underscores why the rapid and broad circulation of information has such a great impact today.

NOTES

1 J. Yourman, Propaganda techniques within Nazi Germany, *The Journal of Educational Sociology* 1939, vol. 13, no. 3, pp. 148–163.
2 M.M. Dundon, S.C. Houck, Adversarial propaganda: How enemies target the U.S. to fuel division, *Journal of Applied Security Research* 2023, vol. 18, no. 4.
3 E.C. Tandoc Jr, Z.W. Lim, R. Ling, Defining "fake news": A typology of scholarly definitions, *Digital Journalism* 2018, vol. 6, no. 2, pp. 137–153.
4 House of Commons, Digital, Culture, Media and Sport Committee, *Disinformation and 'fake news': Interim report: government response to the Committee's fifth report of session 2017–19*, October 23, 2018, https://publications.parliament.uk/pa/cm201719/cmselect/cmcumeds/1630/1630.pdf.
5 European Commission, *Final Report of the High Level Expert Group on Fake News and Online Disinformation*, March 12, 2018, https://digital-strategy.ec.europa.eu/en/library/final-report-high-level-expert-group-fake-news-and-online-disinformation.
6 L.J. Martin, Disinformation: An instrumentality in the propaganda arsenal, *Political Communication* 1982, vol. 2, no. 1, pp. 47–64.
7 L.W. Doob, Goebbels' principles of propaganda, *Public Opinion Quarterly* 1950, vol. 14, no. 3, pp. 419–442.
8 E.M. Rogers, Theoretical diversity in political communication, in *Handbook of Political Communication Research*, ed. by L.L. Kaid, Routledge 2004, pp. 21–34.
9 E.M. Rogers, J.W. Dearing, D. Bregman, The anatomy of agenda-setting research, *Journal of Communication* 1993, vol. 43, no. 2, pp. 68–84.
10 Oxford English Dictionary, s.v. "narrative (n.), sense 2.a," September 2023, https://doi.org/10.1093/OED/1161337353.
11 UK Ministry of Defence, *Influence Wargaming Handbook*, July 2023, p. 125, https://www.gov.uk/government/publications/influence-wargaming-handbook.
12 UK Ministry of Defence, *Influence Wargaming Handbook*, July 2023, p. 125, https://www.gov.uk/government/publications/influence-wargaming-handbook.
13 P. Polak-Springer, 'Jammin' with 'Karlik': The German-Polish 'radio war' and the Gleiwitz 'provocation', 1925–1939, *European History Quarterly 2013*, vol. 43, no. 2, pp. 279–300.
14 G.P. Jan, Radio propaganda in Chinese villages, *Asian Survey* 1967, pp. 305–315.
15 C. Saerchinger, Radio, censorship and neutrality, *Foreign Affairs* 1940, vol. 18, no. 2, pp. 337–349.
16 C. Saerchinger, Radio, censorship and neutrality, *Foreign Affairs* 1940, vol. 18, no. 2, p. 13.
17 J.B. Whitton, War by radio, *Foreign Affairs* 1941, vol. 19, no. 3, pp. 584–596.
18 J.B. Whitton, War by radio, *Foreign Affairs* 1941, vol. 19, no. 3, pp. 584–596.
19 F. Chalk, Radio propaganda and genocide, 1999, "MIGS: Occasional Paper Series," September 4, 2015, https://spectrum.library.concordia.ca/id/eprint/979957/1/A-MIGS__Occasional_Paper_Series__RADIO_PROPAGANDA_AND_GENOCIDE.pdf.
20 T. McKinney, Radio jamming: the disarmament of radio propaganda, *Small Wars and Insurgencies* 2002, vol. 13, no. 3, pp. 111–144.
21 T. McKinney, Radio jamming: the disarmament of radio propaganda, *Small Wars and Insurgencies* 2002, vol. 13, no. 3, pp. 111–144.
22 S. Erlanger, Crisis in the Balkans: Reporter's notebook; Serbs seem to be blaming U.S., not Milosevic, *The New York Times*, April 6, 1999, https://www.nytimes.com/1999/04/06/world/crisis-balkans-reporter-s-notebook-serbs-seem-be-blaming-us-not-milosevic.html.
23 L. Eko, Bombs and bombast in the NATO/Yugoslav War of 1999: The attack on Radio Television Serbia and the laws of war, *Communications and the Law* 2002, vol. 24, no. 1.
24 P. Törnberg, How digital media drive affective polarization through partisan sorting, *Proceedings of the National Academy of Sciences* 2022, vol. 119, no. 42.
25 P. Törnberg, How digital media drive affective polarization through partisan sorting, *Proceedings of the National Academy of Sciences* 2022, vol. 119, no. 42.
26 M. Gentzkow, J.M. Shapiro, Ideological segregation online and offline, *The Quarterly Journal of Economics* 2011, vol. 126, no. 4, pp. 1799–1839.
27 S. Iyengar, G. Sood, Y. Lelkes, Affect, not ideology: A social identity perspective on polarization, *Public Opinion Quarterly* 2012, vol. 76, no. 3, pp. 405–431.

28 B. Nyhan, J. Reifler, When corrections fail: The persistence of political misperceptions, *Political Behavior* 2010, vol. 32, no. 2, pp. 303–330.
29 J. Yourman, *Propaganda....*
30 M. Tugwell, Politics and propaganda of the provisional IRA, *Studies in Conflict & Terrorism* 1981, vol. 5, no. 1–2, pp. 13–40.
31 ISIS uses fake tinder profiles to scam South Africans, finance terrorism, *The Jerusalem Post*, November 16, 2022, https://www.jpost.com/international/article-722566.
32 A.M. Fernandez, *Here to stay and growing: Combating ISIS propaganda networks.* in *The Brookings Project on U.S. Relations with the Islamic World*, Washington 2015, https://www.brookings.edu/wp-content/uploads/2016/06/is-propaganda_web_english.pdf.
33 R. Zakaria, *Women and Islamic militancy*, *Dissent* 2015, vol. 62, no. 1, pp. 118–125.
34 A. Mah-Rukh, ISIS and propaganda: How ISIS exploits women, in *Reuters Institute Fellow's Paper*, Oxford 2015.
35 *ISIS all-female hacking group looks to recruit more women*, The Foreign Desk by Lisa Daftari, April 19, 2017, https://foreigndesknews.com/lisas-desk/isis-female-hacking-group-looks-recruit-women/.
36 R. Schleifer, Propaganda, PSYOP, and political marketing: The Hamas campaign as a case in point, *Journal of Political Marketing* 2014, vol. 13, no. 1–2, pp. 152–173.
37 M. Ali, A. Goetzen, A. Mislove, E.M. Redmiles, P. Sapiezynski, *Problematic advertising and its disparate exposure on Facebook*, 2023, https://www.usenix.org/system/files/usenixsecurity23-ali.pdf.
38 L. Olejnik, *Real-time bidding. Your data sold for $0.0005, in less than 100 milliseconds*, July 31, 2018, https://prywatnik.pl/2018/07/31/real-time-bidding-twoje-dane-sprzedawane-za-0-0005-w-mniej-niz-100-milisekund.
39 F.N. Ribeiro, K. Saha, M. Babaei, L. Henrique, J. Messias, F. Benevenuto, O. Goga, K.P. Gummadi, E.M. Redmiles, *On microtargeting socially divisive ads: A case study of russia-linked ad campaigns on Facebook*, in *Proceedings of the Conference on Fairness, Accountability, and Transparency, January 20–31, 2019*, Atlanta, pp. 140–149, https://arxiv.org/pdf/1808.09218.pdf.
40 F.N. Ribeiro, K. Saha, M. Babaei, L. Henrique, J. Messias, F. Benevenuto, O. Goga, K.P. Gummadi, E.M. Redmiles, *On microtargeting socially divisive ads: A case study of russia-linked ad campaigns on Facebook*, in *Proceedings of the Conference on Fairness, Accountability, and Transparency, January 20–31, 2019*, Atlanta, p. 3, https://arxiv.org/pdf/1808.09218.pdf.
41 F.N. Ribeiro, K. Saha, M. Babaei, L. Henrique, J. Messias, F. Benevenuto, O. Goga, K.P. Gummadi, E.M. Redmiles, *On microtargeting socially divisive ads: A case study of russia-linked ad campaigns on Facebook*, in *Proceedings of the Conference on Fairness, Accountability, and Transparency, January 20–31, 2019*, Atlanta, p. 10, https://arxiv.org/pdf/1808.09218.pdf.
42 B. Nyhan, J. Settle, E. Thorson et al., Like-minded sources on Facebook are prevalent but not polarizing, *Nature* 2023, vol. 620, pp. 137–144.
43 A.M. Guess et al., Reshares on social media amplify political news but do not detectably affect beliefs or opinions, *Science* 2023, vol. 381, pp. 404–408.
44 A.M. Guess et al., How do social media feed algorithms affect attitudes and behavior in an election campaign?, *Science* 2023, vol. 381, pp. 398–404.
45 S. González-Bailón et al., Asymmetric ideological segregation in exposure to political news on Facebook, *Science* 2023, vol. 381, pp. 392–398.
46 A.M. Guess et al., *How do social media....*
47 S. Milli, M. Carroll, S. Pandey, Y. Wang, A.D. Dragan, *Twitter's algorithm: Amplifying anger, animosity, and affective polarization*, 2023, https://www.arxiv-vanity.com/papers/2305.16941/.
48 R.E. Robertson, J. Green, D.J. Ruck, K. Ognyanova, C. Wilson, D. Lazer, Users choose to engage with more partisan news than they are exposed to on Google Search, *Nature* 2023, vol. 618, pp. 342–348.
49 M. Cinelli, G. De Francisci Morales, A. Galeazzi, W. Quattrociocchi, M. Starnini, The echo chamber effect on social media, *Proceedings of the National Academy of Sciences* 2021, vol. 118, no. 9.
50 M. Fisher, J.W. Cox, P. Hermann, Pizzagate: From rumor, to hashtag, to gunfire in DC, *Washington Post*, 2016, vol. 6, pp. 8410–8415.
51 M. Fisher, J.W. Cox, P. Hermann, Pizzagate: From rumor, to hashtag, to gunfire in DC, *Washington Post*, 2016, vol. 6, pp. 8410–8415.

52 D.L. Byman, Ch. Gao, Ch. Meserole, V.S. Subrahmanian, *Deepfakes and international conflict*, January 2023, https://www.brookings.edu/articles/deepfakes-and-international-conflict/.
53 M. Crain, A. Nadler, Political manipulation and internet advertising infrastructure, *Journal of Information Policy* 2019, vol. 9, pp. 370–410.
54 E.F. Fowler, M.M. Franz, G.J. Martin, Z. Peskowitz, T.N. Ridout, Political advertising online and offline, *American Political Science Review* 2021, vol. 115, no. 1, pp. 130–149.
55 *An update on our approach to US election misinformation*, June 2, 2023, https://blog.youtube/inside-youtube/us-election-misinformation-update-2023/.
56 *An update on our approach to US election misinformation*, June 2, 2023, https://blog.youtube/inside-youtube/us-election-misinformation-update-2023/.
57 *The weaponization of CISA: How a 'cybersecurity' agency colluded with big tech and 'disinformation' partners to censor Americans*, June 26, 2023, http://judiciary.house.gov/media/press-releases/new-report-reveals-cisa-tried-cover-censorship-practices.
58 R.C. Moore, R. Dahlke, J.T. Hancock, Exposure to untrustworthy websites in the 2020 US election, *Nature Human Behaviour*, April 13, 2023, pp. 1–10.
59 G. Eady, T. Paskhalis, J. Zilinsky, R. Bonneau, J. Nagler, J.A. Tucker, Exposure to the Russian Internet Research Agency foreign influence campaign on Twitter in the 2016 US election and its relationship to attitudes and voting behavior, *Nature Communications* 2023, vol. 14, no. 1, p. 62.
60 "[T]he authors acknowledge a number of limitations: the available data are from a year after the 2016 US election occurred, cover a short one-month time window, and were collected after Twitter removed many Russian foreign influence accounts from its platform," G. Eady, T. Paskhalis, J. Zilinsky, R. Bonneau, J. Nagler, J.A. Tucker, Exposure to the Russian Internet Research Agency foreign influence campaign on Twitter in the 2016 US election and its relationship to attitudes and voting behavior, *Nature Communications* 2023, vol. 14, no. 1, p. 62.
61 J.L. Kalla, D.E. Broockman, The minimal persuasive effects of campaign contact in general elections: Evidence from 49 field experiments, *American Political Science Review* 2018, vol. 112, no. 1, pp. 148–166.
62 E. Nakashima, Overstating the foreign threat to elections poses its own risks, U.S. officials and experts say, *Washington Post*, October 29, 2020, https://www.washingtonpost.com/national-security/foreign-interference-threat-elections-overestimated/2020/10/29/387d4640-17e7-11eb-82db-60b15c874105_story.html.
63 Wilde, G. From Panic to Policy: The Limits of Foreign Propaganda and the Foundations of an Effective Response.
64 C. Stupp, Hackers temporarily take down European Parliament website, *Wall Street Journal*, November 23, 2022, https://www.wsj.com/articles/hackers-take-down-european-parliament-website-11669230991.
65 Vu, A., Thomas, D., Collier, B., Hutchings, A., Clayton, R., & Anderson, R. (2024, January). Getting Bored of Cyberwar: Exploring the Role of Low-level Cybercrime Actors in the Russia-Ukraine Conflict. In *WWW The ACM Web Conference 2024*.
66 C. Sherif, M. Sherif, R. Nebergall, *Attitude and attitude change*, Philadelphia 1965; C.W. Sherif, N.R. Jackman, Judgments of truth by participants in collective controversy, *Public Opinion Quarterly* 1966, vol. 30, no. 2.
67 S.J. Taylor, L. Muchnik, M. Kumar, S. Aral, Identity effects in social media, *Nature Human Behaviour* 2023, vol. 7, no. 1, pp. 27–37.
68 M.R.J. Nussio, Sherman and Nimitz: Examples of modern information operations, *Potomac* 2014.
69 *1st EEAS Report on foreign information manipulation and interference threats*, February 7, 2023, https://www.eeas.europa.eu/eeas/1st-eeas-report-foreign-information-manipulation-and-interference-threats_en.
70 *2nd EEAS Report on Foreign Information Manipulation and Interference Threats|EEAS*. (n.d.). Retrieved January 29, 2024, from https://www.eeas.europa.eu/eeas/2nd-eeas-report-foreign-information-manipulation-and-interference-threats_en.
71 *2nd EEAS Report on Foreign Information Manipulation and Interference Threats|EEAS*. (n.d.). Retrieved January 29, 2024, from https://www.eeas.europa.eu/eeas/2nd-eeas-report-foreign-information-manipulation-and-interference-threats_en.
72 North Atlantic Treaty, drawn up in Washington on April 4, 1949, OJ. 2000, no. 87, item 970.

73 A senior U.S. intelligence official says Russian missiles crossed into NATO member Poland, killing two people, *AP News*, November 15, 2022, https://apnews.com/article/nato-ap-news-alert-europe-poland-government-and-politics-ba48101fd25c86e68e57dc56fe2adf80.
74 P. Farhi, Associated Press reporter fired over erroneous story on Russian attack, *Washington Post*, November 22, 2022, https://www.washingtonpost.com/media/2022/11/21/james-laporta-associated-press-poland-russia-missile/.
75 C. Echols, *How a lightly-sourced AP story almost set off World War III*, Responsible Statecraft, November 16, 2022, https://responsiblestatecraft.org/2022/11/16/how-a-lightly-sourced-ap-story-almost-set-of-world-war-iii/.
76 C. Echols, *How a lightly-sourced AP story almost set off World War III*, Responsible Statecraft, November 16, 2022, https://responsiblestatecraft.org/2022/11/16/how-a-lightly-sourced-ap-story-almost-set-of-world-war-iii/.
77 *Russia now promotes a conspiracy theory that it was allegedly a missile of Ukrainian air defense that fell on the Polish theory*, D. Kuleba, Twitter Post, November 15, 2022, https://twitter.com/DmytroKuleba/status/1592632386751434752.
78 V. Zelenski, Twitter Post, November 15, 2022, https://twitter.com/ZelenskyyUa/status/1592629863349129217.
79 *2022 Strengthened Code of Practice on Disinformation*, Shaping Europe's Digital Future, June 16, 2022, https://digital-strategy.ec.europa.eu/en/library/2022-strengthened-code-practice-disinformation.
80 S.G. Jones, *Going on the offensive: A U.S. strategy to combat Russian information warfare*, October 1, 2018, https://www.csis.org/analysis/going-offensive-us-strategy-combat-russian-information-warfare.
81 S.G. Jones, *Going on the offensive: A U.S. strategy to combat Russian information warfare*, October 1, 2018, https://www.csis.org/analysis/going-offensive-us-strategy-combat-russian-information-warfare.
82 F.M. Burkle, Political intrusions into the International Health Regulations Treaty and its impact on management of rapidly emerging zoonotic pandemics: What history tells us, *Prehospital and Disaster Medicine* 2020, vol. 35, no. 4, pp. 426–430.
83 D.V. Gioe, R. Lovering, T. Pachesny, The Soviet legacy of Russian active measures: New vodka from old stills?, *International Journal of Intelligence and Counter Intelligence* 2020, vol. 33, no. 3, pp. 514–539.
84 A.S. Bradshaw, S.S. Shelton, A. Fitzsimmons, D. Treise, 'From cover-up to catastrophe': How the anti-vaccine propaganda documentary 'Vaxxed' impacted student perceptions and intentions about MMR vaccination, *Journal of Communication in Healthcare* 2022, vol. 15, no. 3, pp. 219–231.
85 O. Benecke, S.E. DeYoung, Anti-vaccine decision-making and measles resurgence in the United States, *Global Pediatric Health* 2019, no. 6.
86 A. Hussain, S. Ali, M. Ahmed, S. Hussain, The anti-vaccination movement: A regression in modern medicine, *Cureus* 2018, vol. 10, no. 7.
87 B.B. Senokoane, The devil, 666 and the COVID-19 vaccine, *HTS Theologiese Studies* 2021, vol. 77, no. 1.
88 T. Burt, *Nation-state cyberattacks become more brazen as authoritarian leaders ramp up aggression*, Microsoft On the Issues, November 4, 2022, https://blogs.microsoft.com/on-the-issues/2022/11/04/microsoft-digital-defense-report-2022-ukraine/3.
89 *TAG Bulletin: Q3 2022*, Google, October 26, 2022, https://blog.google/threat-analysis-group/tag-bulletin-q3-2022/.
90 *Meta's adversarial threat report, third quarter 2022*, Meta, November 22, 2022, https://about.fb.com/news/2022/11/metas-adversarial-threat-report-q3-2022/.
91 *TAG Bulletin: Q3 2022…*; *Meta's adversarial…*.
92 *Meta's adversarial threat report, first quarter 2023*, Meta, May 3, 2023, https://about.fb.com/news/2023/05/metas-adversarial-threat-report-first-quarter-2023/.
93 *China Security Report 2023: China's quest for control of the cognitive domain and gray zone situations*, http://www.nids.mod.go.jp/english/publication/chinareport/.
94 X. Wang, J. Li, E. Srivatsavaya, S. Rajtmajer, Evidence of inter-state coordination among state-backed information operation, *Scientific Reports* 2023, vol. 13, no. 1, p. 7716.

95 C. Saerchinger, Radio as a political instrument, *Foreign Affairs* 1937, vol. 16, p. 244.
96 N.E. Petrosky, Election silence: Revisiting Mills v. Alabama in the modern context, *University of Dayton Law Review* 2022, vol. 47, p. 135.
97 European Commission (2024). COMMUNICATION TO THE COMMISSION Approval of the content of a draft Communication from the Commission on Guidelines for providers of Very Large Online Platforms and Very Large Online Search Engines on the mitigation of systemic risks for electoral processes pursuant to the Digital Services Act (Regulation (EU) 2022/2065). https://digital-strategy.ec.europa.eu/en/library/guidelines-providers-vlops-and-vloses-mitigation-systemic-risks-electoral-processes.
98 *Analysis of European Union election interference guidelines (2024)*. (2024, March 27). Security, Privacy & Tech Inquiries. https://blog.lukaszolejnik.com/analysis-of-european-union-election-interference-guidelines-2024/.
99 Human Rights Council resolution 53/1 Countering religious hatred constituting incitement to discrimination, hostility or violence, 12.07.2023, A/HRC/53/L.23.
100 A. Willert, Publicity and propaganda in international affairs, *International Affairs* 1938, vol. 17, no. 6, pp. 809–826.
101 R.T. Newman, Propaganda: An instrument of foreign policy, *Columbia Journal of International Affairs* 1951, pp. 56–64.
102 B. Ellis, *Contemporary legendry: A fundamentally political act*, Contemporary Legend 2017, vol. 7, pp. 1–19.
103 J.E. Grunig, Public relations and international affairs: Effects, ethics and responsibility, *Journal of International Affairs* 1993, pp. 137–162.
104 D. Walton, Appeal to pity: A case study of the argumentum ad misericordiam, *Argumentation* 1995, vol. 9, no. 5, pp. 769–784.
105 D. Walton, Appeal to pity: A case study of the argumentum ad misericordiam, *Argumentation* 1995, vol. 9, no. 5, pp. 769–784.
106 J. Darda, Kicking the Vietnam Syndrome narrative: Human rights, the Nayirah testimony, and the Gulf War, *American Quarterly* 2017, vol. 69, no. 1, pp. 71–92.
107 J.E. Grunig, *Public relations....*
108 G. Simons, Russian public diplomacy in the 21st century: Structure, means and message, *Public Relations Review* 2014, vol. 40, no. 3, pp. 440–449.
109 E. Jünger, *A German Officer in Occupied Paris: The War Journals, 1941–1945*, New York 2018.
110 M. Braut-Hegghammer, Cheater's dilemma: Iraq, weapons of mass destruction, and the path to war, *International Security* 2020, vol. 45, no. 1, pp. 51–89.
111 M. Braut-Hegghammer, Cheater's dilemma: Iraq, weapons of mass destruction, and the path to war, *International Security* 2020, vol. 45, no. 1, pp. 51–89.
112 N.D. White, R. Cryer, Unilateral enforcement of Resolution 687: A threat too far, *California Western International Law Journal* 1998, vol. 29, p. 243.
113 M. Braut-Hegghammer, *Cheater's dilemma....*
114 M. Argemi, G.A. Fine, Faked news: The politics of rumor in British World War II propaganda, *Journal of War & Culture Studies* 2019, vol. 12, no. 2, pp. 176–193.
115 T. Brooks, *British Propaganda to France, 1940–1944: Machinery, Method, and Message*, Edinburgh 2008.
116 T. Brooks, *British Propaganda to France, 1940–1944: Machinery, Method, and Message*, Edinburgh 2008.
117 E.H. Zerner, Rumors in Paris newspapers, *Public Opinion Quarterly* 1946, vol. 10, no. 3, pp. 382–391.
118 J.D. Clemente, CIA's Medical and Psychological Analysis Center (MPAC) and the health of foreign leaders, *International Journal of Intelligence and CounterIntelligence* 2006, vol. 19, no. 3, pp. 385–423.
119 J.D. Clemente, CIA's Medical and Psychological Analysis Center (MPAC) and the health of foreign leaders, *International Journal of Intelligence and CounterIntelligence* 2006, vol. 19, no. 3, pp. 385–423.
120 J.D. Clemente, In Sickness + in Health, *Bulletin of the Atomic Scientists* 2007, vol. 63, no. 2, pp. 38–66.

121 R.W. Barnett, Information operations, deterrence, and the use of force, *Naval War College Review* 1998, vol. 51, no. 2, pp. 7–19.
122 R.W. Barnett, Information operations, deterrence, and the use of force, *Naval War College Review* 1998, vol. 51, no. 2, pp. 7–19.
123 D. McCrory, Russian electronic warfare, cyber and information operations in Ukraine: Implications for NATO and security in the Baltic States, *The RUSI Journal* 2020, vol. 165, no. 7, pp. 34–44.
124 J. Prier, Commanding the trend: social media as information warfare, in *Information Warfare in the Age of Cyber Conflict*, edited by Ch. Whyte, A.T. Thrall, B.M. Mazanec, Routledge, 2020, pp. 88–113.
125 T.C. Helmus, E. Bodine-Baron, A. Radin, M. Magnuson, J. Mendelsohn, W. Marcellino, A. Bega, Z. Winkelman, *Russian Social Media Influence: Understanding Russian Propaganda in Eastern Europe*, Rand Corporation, 2018.
126 I. Yablokov, Russian disinformation finds fertile ground in the West, *Nature Human Behaviour* 2022, vol. 6, no. 6, pp. 766–767.
127 I. Yablokov, Russian disinformation finds fertile ground in the West, *Nature Human Behaviour* 2022, vol. 6, no. 6, pp. 766–767.
128 Judgment of the General Court (Grand Chamber) of July 27, 2022, T-125/22, ECLI:EU:T:2022:483, para 21.
129 Judgment of the General Court (Grand Chamber) of July 27, 2022, T-125/22, ECLI:EU:T:2022:483, para 125.
130 Judgment of the General Court (Grand Chamber) of July 27, 2022, T-125/22, ECLI:EU:T:2022:483, para 142.
131 A. Chandra, R. Ferreira, How to lose influence and alienate people, *Graphika*, February 23, 2023, https://graphika.com/reports/how-to-lose-influence-and-alienate-people.
132 J. Brandt, V. Wirtschafter, Working the Western Hemisphere, *Brookings*, December 2022, https://www.brookings.edu/articles/working-the-western-hemisphere/.
133 R. Gorwa, R. Binns, C. Katzenbach, Algorithmic content moderation: technical and political challenges in the automation of platform governance, *Big Data & Society* 2020, vol. 7, no. 1.
134 Ch. Miller, J.P. Rathbone, Ukraine's civilian army takes aim at Russia as Moscow steps up strikes, *Financial Times*, October 21, 2022, https://www.ft.com/content/a8e21e65-d3e6-4f96-b287-126c01a0acbe.
135 J. Friberg, *SOCEUR and the Resistance Operating Concept (ROC)*, SOF News, July 19, 2019, https://sof.news/uw/resistance-operating-concept/.
136 E. Chenoweth, M.J. Stephan, *Why Civil Resistance Works: The Strategic Logic of Nonviolent Conflict*, New York 2011.
137 K.R. Matthews, Social movements and the (mis)use of research: Extinction rebellion and the 3.5% rule, *Interface: A Journal for and about Social Movements* 2020, vol. 12, no. 1, pp. 591–615.
138 E. Chenoweth, *Questions, answers, and some cautionary updates regarding the 3.5% rule*, April 20, 2020, https://carrcenter.hks.harvard.edu/publications/questions-answers-and-some-cautionary-updates-regarding-35-rule.
139 Extinction Rebellion UK, *About Us*, https://extinctionrebellion.uk/the-truth/about-us/.
140 E.N. Luttwak, *Coup D'État: A Practical Handbook*, Revised Edition. Harvard University Press 2016.
141 E.N. Luttwak, *Coup D'État: A Practical Handbook*, Revised Edition. Harvard University Press 2016.
142 H. Dupre, Some French revolutionary propaganda techniques, *The Historian* 1940, vol. 2, no. 2, pp. 156–164.
143 D. Huxley, Kidding the Kaiser: British propaganda animation, 1914–1919, *Early Popular Visual Culture* 2006, vol. 4, no. 3, pp. 307–320.
144 J. Maciak, Learning to love the republic: Jacobin propaganda and the peasantry of the Haute-Garonne, *European Review of History: Revue européenne d'histoire* 1999, vol. 6, no. 2, pp. 165–179.
145 J. Maciak, Learning to love the republic: Jacobin propaganda and the peasantry of the Haute-Garonne, *European Review of History: Revue européenne d'histoire* 1999, vol. 6, no. 2, pp. 165–179.

146 G. Mathieu, A Nazi Propaganda Directive on Goethe, in Publications of the English Goethe Society, *Cardiff* 1952, vol. 22, pp. 129–137.

147 G. Mathieu, A Nazi Propaganda Directive on Goethe, in Publications of the English Goethe Society, *Cardiff* 1952, vol. 22, pp. 129–137.

148 E. Harbinja, M.R. Leiser, [Redacted]: This article categorized [harmful] by the Government, *ScriptED* 2022, vol. 19, no. 1, p. 88.

149 P. Ball, A. Maxmen, The epic battle against coronavirus misinformation and conspiracy theories, *Nature* 2020, vol. 581, no. 7809, pp. 371–375.

150 E. White, China's Xi Jinping faces off against fan armies in crackdown on celebrity culture, *Financial Times*, September 10, 2021, https://www.ft.com/content/ceb9b60e-c78d-4b1f-9fa0-210a1a099671.

151 China's Weibo bans BTS fan account for illegal fundraising, *AP News*, September 6, 2021, https://apnews.com/article/entertainment-business-music-china-arts-and-entertainment-0b10738629ebaf5d0ad17ab5dfceb910.

152 Chinese content platforms pledge self-discipline—industry group, *Reuters*, September 11, 2021, https://www.reuters.com/world/china/chinese-content-platforms-pledge-self-discipline-industry-group-2021-09-11/.

153 关于进一步加强娱乐明星网上信息规范相关工作的通知, Weixin official accounts platform, http://mp.weixin.qq.com/s?__biz=MzAwMjU0MjIyNw==&mid=2651396582&idx=2&sn=c95f002b538c5adba654499cbd7f4b35&chksm=8135661ab642ef0cbf39dcb0c9496c52eb9ce9f8dfdd67fc5922cb55305ad2169cc53dd18551#rd.

154 China targets celebrity online information in ramp up of fan culture crackdown, *Reuters*, November 23, 2021, https://www.reuters.com/world/china/china-says-will-more-tightly-regulate-celebrities-online-information-2021-11-23/.

155 Notice of the Central Propaganda Department to Conduct Comprehensive Management in Culture and Entertainment, 文化和旅游部召开加强文娱领域综合治理工作电视电话会议_部门政务_中, 国政府网 https://www.gov.cn/xinwen/2021-09/09/content_5636510.htm.

156 Notice of the Central Propaganda Department to Conduct Comprehensive Management in Culture and Entertainment, 文化和旅游部召开加强文娱领域综合治理工作电视电话会议_部门政务_中, 国政府网 https://www.gov.cn/xinwen/2021-09/09/content_5636510.htm.

157 T. Jones, Double-use of LGBT youth in propaganda, *Journal of LGBT Youth* 2020, vol. 17, no. 4, pp. 408–431.

158 J. Huo, From 4chan to international politics, a bug-eating conspiracy theory goes mainstream, *NPR*, April 2, 2023, https://www.npr.org/2023/03/31/1166649732/conspiracy-theory-eating-bugs-4chan.

159 Want flies with that? EU critics have a new conspiracy theory, *Bloomberg.com*, March 6, 2023, https://www.bloomberg.com/news/articles/2023-03-26/eating-insects-is-anti-eu-new-conspiracy-theory-for-european-populists.

160 *After the New Normal: Scenarios for Europe in the post COVID-19 world*, April 4, 2022, https://research-and-innovation.ec.europa.eu/knowledge-publications-tools-and-data/publications/all-publications/after-new-normal-scenarios-europe-post-covid-19-world_en.

161 C. Andrzejewski, *The 'masters of perception', Burkina Faso and the International Committee of the Red Cross: Anatomy of a manipulation campaign*, February 16, 2023, https://forbiddenstories.org/story-killers/percepto-icrc-burkina/.

162 Ukraine: ICRC registers hundreds of prisoners of war from Azovstal Plant, *International Committee of the Red Cross*, May 19, 2022, https://www.icrc.org/en/document/ukraine-icrc-registers-hundreds-prisoners-war-azovstal-plant.

163 Ukraine: Addressing misinformation about ICRC's activities, *International Committee of the Red Cross*, March 26, 2022, https://www.icrc.org/en/document/ukraine-addressing-misinformation-about-icrcs-activities.

164 Evacuation challenges and bad optics: Why Ukrainians are losing faith in the ICRC, *The New Humanitarian*, May 3, 2022, https://www.thenewhumanitarian.org/news-feature/2022/05/03/the-icrc-and-the-pitfalls-of-neutrality-in-ukraine.

165 E. Paddon, *Taking Sides: Impartiality, Norm Contestation and the Politics of UN Peacekeeping*, doctoral dissertation, Oxford 2013.

166 D. Lindley, Untapped power? The status of UN information operations, *International Peacekeeping* 2004, vol. 11, no. 4, pp. 608–624.

167 O. Mentes, C. Browne, *Case studies on UN information operations: Ethiopia, Liberia, and Kosovo*, doctoral dissertation, Monterey 2012.
168 P.D. Williams, Strategic communications for peace operations: the African Union's information war against al-Shabaab, *Stability: International Journal of Security & Development* 2018, vol. 7, no. 1.
169 J. Ellul, *Propaganda: The Formation of Men's Attitudes*, New York 2021.
170 See https://www.legifrance.gouv.fr/codes/article_lc/LEGIARTI000023883001.
171 V. Zakem, M.K. McBride, K. Hammerberg, Exploring the utility of memes for US government influence campaigns, *CNA*, 2021.
172 I. Manor, The Russians are laughing! The Russians are laughing! How Russian diplomats employ humor in online public diplomacy, *Global Society* 2021, vol. 35, no. 1, pp. 61–83.
173 R. Rogers, G. Giorgi, What is a meme, technically speaking?, *Information, Communication and Society* February 2023, pp. 1–19.
174 N. O'shaughnessy, The limitations of persuasion?, *Journal of Political Marketing* 2003, vol. 2, no. 1, pp. 117–124.
175 M. Kovic, A. Rauchfleisch, M. Sele, C. Caspar, Digital astroturfing in politics: Definition, typology, and countermeasures, *Studies in Communication Sciences* 2018, vol. 18, no. 1, pp. 69–85.
176 D. Pacheco, P.M. Hui, C. Torres-Lugo, B.T. Truong, A. Flammini, F. Menczer, *Uncovering coordinated networks on social media: Methods and case studies*, in *Proceedings of the International AAAI Conference on Web and Social Media*, Palo Alto 2021, vol. 15, pp. 455–466.
177 F.B. Keller, D. Schoch, S. Stier, J. Yang, Political astroturfing on twitter: How to coordinate a disinformation campaign, *Political Communication* 2020, vol. 37, no. 2, pp. 256–280.
178 M.R. Holman, M.C. Schneider, K. Pondel, Gender targeting in political advertisements, *Political Research Quarterly* 2015, vol. 68, no. 4, pp. 816–829.
179 L.M. Huber, Beyond policy: the use of social group appeals in party communication, *Political Communication* 2022, vol. 39, no. 3, pp. 293–310.
180 A. Horn, A. Kevins, C. Jensen, K. Van Kersbergen, Political parties and social groups: New perspectives and data on group and policy appeals, *Party Politics* 2021, vol. 27, no. 5, pp. 983–995.
181 J.J. Van Bavel, A. Pereira, The partisan brain: An identity-based model of political belief, *Trends in Cognitive Sciences* 2018, vol. 22, no. 3, pp. 213–224.
182 F. Tripodi, Searching for alternative facts, *Data & Society*, May 16, 2018, https://datasociety.net/library/searching-for-alternative-facts.
183 N. Ochlocracy, *Oxford English Dictionary*, Oxford UP, September 2023, https://doi.org/10.1093/OED/8113501604.
184 G. Wills, Ochlocracy: Are we there yet?, *Marquette Law Review* 2019, vol. 103, no. 2, p. 681.
185 *The Crowd: A Study of the Popular Mind*, London 1897.
186 Y. Kamitake, From democracy to ochlocracy, *Hitotsubashi Journal of Economics* 2007, vol. 48, no. 1, pp. 83–93.
187 B. Zelizer, Mob censorship, *Digital Journalism*, June 23, 2023, pp. 1–7.
188 A. Zhang, Ostracism and democracy, *New York University Law Review* 2021, vol. 96, p. 235.
189 P. Norris, Cancel culture: Myth or reality?, *Political Studies* 2023, vol. 71, no. 1, pp. 145–174.
190 H. Berghel, A collapsing academy. Part II: How cancel culture works on the academy, *Computer* 2021, vol. 54, no. 10, pp. 138–144.
191 N. O'shaughnessy, The marketing of political marketing, *European Journal of Marketing* 2001, vol. 35, no. 9–10, pp. 1047–1057.
192 P.R. Baines, N.J. O'shaughnessy, Political marketing and propaganda: Uses, abuses, misuses, *Journal of Political Marketing* 2014, vol. 13, no. 1–2, pp. 1–18.
193 A. Marland, Marketing political soap: A political marketing view of selling candidates like soap, of electioneering as a ritual, and of electoral military analogies, *Journal of Public Affairs: An International Journal* 2003, vol. 3, no. 2, pp. 103–115.
194 S. Woolley, Some of the worst troll armies are gaining ground. Just look at Cambodia, *The New York Times*, July 11, 2023, https://www.nytimes.com/2023/07/11/opinion/cambodia-elections-hun-sen-hun-manet-facebook.html.
195 R. DiResta, K. Shaffer, B. Ruppel, D. Sullivan, R. Matney, R. Fox, J. Albright, B. Johnson, *The tactics & tropes of the Internet Research Agency*, October 2019, https://digitalcommons.unl.edu/cgi/viewcontent.cgi?article=1003&context=senatedocs.

196 A. Dawson, M. Innes, How Russia's internet research agency built its disinformation campaign, *The Political Quarterly* 2019, vol. 90, no. 2, pp. 245–256.
197 D. O'Sullivan, D. Byers, Exclusive: Fake black activist social media accounts linked to Russian Government, *CNNMoney*, September 28, 2017, https://money.cnn.com/2017/09/28/media/blacktivist-russia-facebook-twitter/index.html.
198 R. Lucas, How Russia Used Facebook To Organize 2 Sets Of Protesters, *NPR*, November 1, 2017, https://www.npr.org/2017/11/01/561427876/how-russia-used-facebook-to-organize-two-sets-of-protesters.
199 R. Serabian, D. Kapellmann Zafra, C. Quigley, D. Mainor, Pro-PRC HaiEnergy Campaign exploits U.S. news outlets via Newswire services to Target U.S. audiences; Evidence of commissioned protests in Washington, D.C., *Mandiant*, July 24, 2023, https://www.mandiant.com/resources/blog/pro-prc-haienergy-us-news.
200 T. Eydoux, M. Farran, How Russia is staging fake protests in Europe to discredit Ukraine, *Le Monde.fr*, May 7, 2023, https://www.lemonde.fr/en/international/article/2023/05/07/how-russia-is-staging-fake-protests-in-europe-to-discredit-ukraine_6025808_4.html.
201 K. Shakir, F.H. Ledegaard Thim, L. Quass, N. Fastrup, *Falske demonstranter dukker op flere steder: Russisk efterretningstjeneste kobles til ti aktioner i Europa*, DR, May 8, 2023, https://www.dr.dk/nyheder/indland/moerklagt/falske-demonstranter-dukker-op-flere-steder-russisk-efterretningstjeneste.
202 C. Saerchinger, Radio as a political instrument, *Foreign Affairs* 1938, vol. 16, no. 2, p. 244.
203 S. Banaji, R. Bhat, WhatsApp vigilantes: An exploration of citizen reception and circulation of WhatsApp misinformation linked to mob violence in India, November 11, 2019, https://blogs.lse.ac.uk/medialse/2019/11/11/whatsapp-vigilantes-an-exploration-of-citizen-reception-and-circulation-of-whatsapp-misinformation-linked-to-mob-violence-in-india/.
204 V. Atram, Lynching crimes and its effects on India, AGPE. *The Royal Gondwana Research Journal of History, Science, Economic, Political and Social Science* 2019, vol. 1, no. 1, pp. 61–67.
205 T. McLaughlin, How WhatsApp fuels fake news and violence in India, *Wired Magazine*, December 12, 2018, https://www.wired.com/story/how-whatsapp-fuels-fake-newsand-violence-in-india/.
206 P.Dixit,R.Mac,HowWhatsAppdestroyedavillage,*BuzzFeedNews*,September10,2018,https://www.buzzfeednews.com/article/pranavdixit/whatsapp-destroyed-village-lynchings-rainpada-india.
207 B. Pereg, Three Jewish suspects indicted in attempted lynching of Arab driver in central Israel, *Haaretz*, May 24, 2021, https://www.haaretz.com/israel-news/2021-05-24/ty-article/.premium/three-jewish-men-indicted-in-attempted-lynching-of-arab-driver-in-central-israel/0000017f-ea57-d639-af7f-ebd7f1aa0000.
208 *WhatsApp warned for abuse of their platform*, July 3, 2018, https://pib.gov.in/newsite/PrintRelease.aspx?relid=180364.
209 A. Satariano, P. Mozur, The people onscreen are fake. The disinformation is real, *The New York Times*, February 7, 2023, https://www.nytimes.com/2023/02/07/technology/artificial-intelligence-training-deepfake.html.
210 *European Union regulating AI - allowing the use of deepfakes*. (2021, April 15). Security, Privacy & Tech Inquiries. https://blog.lukaszolejnik.com/european-union-regulating-ai-allowing-the-use-of-deepfakes/.
211 R. Cormac, Techniques of covert propaganda: The British approach in the mid-1960s, *Intelligence and National Security* 2019, vol. 34, no. 7, pp. 1064–1069.
212 R. Cormac, Techniques of covert propaganda: The British approach in the mid-1960s, *Intelligence and National Security* 2019, vol. 34, no. 7, pp. 1064–1069.
213 J. Tollefson, The race to curb the spread of COVID vaccine disinformation, *Nature*, April 16, 2021, https://www.nature.com/articles/d41586-021-00997-x.
214 B. Bernstein, Mark Zuckerberg says Facebook censored 'true' Covid claims at request of health establishment, *National Review*, June 12, 2023, https://www.nationalreview.com/news/mark-zuckerberg-says-facebook-censored-true-covid-claims-at-request-of-health-establishment.
215 O.J. Watson, G. Barnsley, J. Toor, A.B. Hogan, P. Winskill, A.C. Ghani, Global impact of the first year of COVID-19 vaccination: A mathematical modelling study, *The Lancet Infectious Diseases* 2022, vol. 22, no. 9, pp. 1293–1302.

216 Department of Propaganda of the Central Committee of the Chinese Communist Party, *SARS-related propaganda*, Beijing 16.04.2003, transl. M.E. Sharpe, *Chinese Law & Government* 2004, vol. 37, no. 1, pp. 28–42.
217 Department of Propaganda of the Central Committee of the Chinese Communist Party, *SARS-related propaganda*, Beijing 16.04.2003, transl. M.E. Sharpe, *Chinese Law & Government* 2004, vol. 37, no. 1, pp. 28–42.
218 Department of Propaganda of the Central Committee of the Chinese Communist Party, *SARS-related propaganda*, Beijing 16.04.2003, transl. M.E. Sharpe, *Chinese Law & Government* 2004, vol. 37, no. 1, pp. 28–42.
219 A. Bor, F. Jørgensen, M.B. Petersen, Discriminatory attitudes against unvaccinated people during the pandemic, *Nature* 2023, vol. 613, no. 7945, nos. 704–711.
220 S.W. Atlas, *America's COVID response was based on lies*, Newsweek, March 6, 2023, https://www.newsweek.com/america-covid-response-was-based-lies-opinion-1785177.
221 S. Horenstein, Paleontology and evolution in the News, *Evolution: Education and Outreach* 2012, vol. 5, no. 1, pp. 171–178.
222 K. Crowley, Environmental propaganda, *Journal of Mass Media Ethics* 2014, vol. 29, no. 2, pp. 134–135.
223 L.O. Quam, The use of maps in propaganda, *Journal of Geography* 1943, vol. 42, no. 1, pp. 21–32.
224 L.O. Quam, The use of maps in propaganda, *Journal of Geography* 1943, vol. 42, no. 1, pp. 21–32.
225 U. Nowakowska, H. Ignatowicz, 'Crops for the state!' Agriculture and the countryside in 1950s propaganda posters of Central and Eastern Europe, *Folk Life* 2014, vol. 52, no. 1, pp. 62–81.
226 U. Nowakowska, H. Ignatowicz, 'Crops for the state!' Agriculture and the countryside in 1950s propaganda posters of Central and Eastern Europe, *Folk Life* 2014, vol. 52, no. 1, pp. 62–81.
227 B.C. Garrett, The Colorado potato beetle goes to war, *Chemical Weapons Convention Bulletin* 1996, vol. 33, pp. 2–3.
228 *WHO-Convened Global Study of Origins of SARS-CoV-2: China Part*, March 30, 2021, https://www.who.int/publications-detail-redirect/who-convened-global-study-of-origins-of-sars-cov-2-china-part.
229 Well, okay, the latter is not a techno-buzzword, but the Latin name for the domestic (edible) cricket.
230 S.D. Symms, E.D. Snow Jr, Soviet propaganda and the neutron bomb decision, *Political Communication* 1981, vol. 1, no. 3, pp. 257–268.

Chapter 7

Propaganda and military affairs, war propaganda, and information warfare

The propagation of information, or conducting educational or information campaigns aimed at different audiences, has applications also in military affairs—including crucial importance when conducting armed conflicts, or wars and related affairs. Propaganda has long accompanied wars and has many applications. It can be directed at one's own society or military, if only for defensive purposes, such as to illuminate the methods—including propaganda of the enemy, of the adversaries. Offensive uses against external actors, or States, are possible. It may find application before, during, and after war and in its contexts.

That's also when the uses of the magical keyword *information warfare*—when the actions are related to some ongoing armed conflict (i.e., war)—are fully justified, without stretching things. And that's where we must start.

7.1 INFORMATION WARFARE—PEACETIME, ARMED CONFLICT, WAR

Cyber warfare is the use of digital tools, means, and methods of warfare in cyberspace (tools for using information systems, information and communications technology (ICT) as part of an armed conflict.[1] Similarly, I adopt here the established, strict binary division with thresholds. One that leaves no room between states of peace and of war. No room—for the so-called gray zone. This will simplify the analysis and is furthermore especially justified when events in early 2022 have shown that major wars can happen and are not, in fact, things of the past. There is no need to amend or stretch analytical paradigms just to talk about some special times in between war and peace. Either there is an armed conflict or there isn't. Any other approach would at least question the principles of humanitarianism, risking a return to pre-1945 customs (we will leave such attempts to others). The advantage of such an approach is that it is in line with recognized principles of international law, with the approach of States to the problem, and simply with reality. Such architecture is relevant, and the rules or laws did not change; nobody attempted to reform them. For good reasons. We follow reality, and objective rules—we are on the right track.

Propaganda activities during peacetime are possible and rather typical—including those conducted by the military—but then happening outside of an armed conflict (war). Then, it is more precise to refer to them as *information operations*, information *activities*, *influence* operations, etc. There is no shortage of possible terms. Such a division makes a lot of sense.

Still, even during peacetime, one may hear people using the term "*information war*," as well as other war-themed expressions: "*war on drugs*," "*war on traffic pirates*," and other such names with no connection to the state of an armed conflict. Instead, these may be various columnist, commenters', pundits', journalistic takes, and, sometimes, political expressions,

DOI: 10.1201/9781003499497-7

overloading the term "war". The use of such a war-themed terminology may then be meant to emphasize the expressed opinions, lending a certain gravity to those uttering them. After all, someone talking about war may look serious. Real wars are serious affairs. And this perception remained in times of *peace dividend* after the year 1989, when during the long times of peace the term "war" used to be overloaded. But there is no *need* to resort to that following 2022 and a traditionally understood armed conflict (of high intensity, between two States) in Ukraine, simply put—a war. In view of this, it is worth keeping expressions in right proportions. There's no need to pretend that wars do not exist, that they are supposedly some things of the past, that "in the modern times" the term "war" has "changed its meaning." They have not. Those who want to see it like that can have a look at Ukraine. Events in Eastern Europe have restored the meaning and proportion of the word "war."

After 1945, the matter is clear—there has been a shift away from the use of the term "war"[2] to the more precise phrase "armed conflict,"[3] less prone to ambiguity. To refer to the Geneva Conventions, an armed conflict occurs whenever there are acts of violence between two States, "even if one of the Parties denies the existence of a state of war."[4] Referring to it with some other, perhaps creative term does not change the facts. It *doesn't matter how these actions are defined by those two States*, or any other. What counts are objective actions. Some actions result in an armed conflict and that is that. The advantage of this formulation, then, is that it is undeniable and objective.

7.1.1 Precision

Why is this so important? Precision is insanely important. Especially due to the very subject matter of this book—because of propaganda and issues of truthfulness and falsity of information, of misinformation or disinformation. Precisely because the phrase "war" may be misused, and "overloaded,"—creatively used to call things that in fact are not wars (it is then a false term)—perhaps as some kind of processes or campaigns. To regain precision and the correct lens of seeing things through, let's simply put them in objective terms guided by the Geneva Convention: does violence occur within activities, are people killed, and is property (objects) destroyed? Are weapons systems used routinely? If so, well, that's an armed conflict.

But as pointed out here, the very word "war" itself is very susceptible to use in propaganda, especially in political propaganda. The word is familiar to everyone, it perhaps suffices to finish elementary school, or possibly expand one's knowledge by playing computer games, to get to know it. Nevertheless, something does not add up here. By uttering a word of such gravity, one can play up emotions, fears, and anxieties of the recipients—or assign someone or something a false seriousness. By doing so, the word "war" loses meaning. It becomes an empty shell, without substance. Thus, especially in this chapter, war will be understood traditionally.

7.1.2 Attack and propaganda

The definition of an *attack* is "acts of violence against the adversary, whether in offence or in defence."[5] It is debatable whether by itself an "*information attack*" or "*propaganda attack*" could in itself constitute the beginning of an armed conflict (attaining the level of an armed attack). Perhaps so if it would be a declaration of war, properly presented—that said, in modern times, declarations of war work best in computer games like "Civilization" franchise. However, information attacks can lead to an armed conflict, so the outbreak of war could be triggered—if indirectly. They could also hint at impending hostilities, exactly as things unraveled prior to the start of intensified military operations in the Ukraine war in February 2022.

7.1.2.1 The ugly word "hybrid"—or PMESII-PT

Similarly, the so-called *hybrid methods* are not wars, since—to simplify a bit for our needs and keep the proportions—virtually all actions taken in an armed conflict constitute just that: actions taken in war. Concepts of *hybrid methods*, on the other hand, foresee, by definition, an operation below the threshold of war. So, logically, they cannot constitute war, since they are to happen below the threshold of war, without crossing it. Such paradoxes and challenges to logic are also dealt with by the terminology of an armed conflict explained below. Therefore, such terms as "interstate conflict" and even "information conflict" are not necessarily equated with wars. On the other hand, information operations and propaganda activities (both political and military propaganda) may fall under the so-called hybrid methods, if one desires to use this, at times fashionable, "hybrid" terminology. Here, I point out that the so-called PMESII-PT framework, meaning the fusion of political, military, economic, social, information, infrastructure, physical environment, and time aspects (PMESII-PT)[6] is a useful classification of complex conflicts, and may encompass the so-called hybrid methods, below the threshold of war. It is simply an analytical approach, where the actions taken are placed into classification boxes in tables to infer the nature of the escalation. If the activity goes beyond a certain threshold, then we may be dealing with an armed conflict, and then it makes no sense to use terms like "hybrid methods" or "hybrid war," because it's just war, or the more precise term: armed conflict.

7.2 PROPAGANDA BEFORE, DURING, AND AFTER THE ARMED CONFLICT

Now that we've got these necessary preliminaries out of the way, we can move on. This chapter will deal with propaganda during the war, as well as before or beyond it. This is because information methods can be used at many levels. In this sense—in addition to activities strictly related to war (armed conflict)—these will potentially be concepts close to those considered in the previous (political) chapter as well. These issues have been separated, but for completeness in places presented in this chapter as well. Wars need not be waged all-out.

7.2.1 Limited war, communication channels

Conflicts may be limited. Sometimes, limited only to the cyber and information layer. Then, it is useful to keep in mind Schelling's wisdom that "[l]imited war requires limits; so do strategic maneuvers if they are to be stabilized short of war. But limits require agreement or at least some kind of mutual recognition and acquiescence. And agreement on limits is difficult to reach, not only because of the uncertainties and the acute divergence of interests but because negotiation is severely inhibited both during war and before it begins and because communication becomes difficult between adversaries in time of war,"[7] which is a challenge, since communication between two adversarial States is a problem, especially in wartime.

However, such "emergency" channels of communication are important assets. They can stabilize the conflict and lead to the avoidance of possible misunderstandings leading to escalation (i.e., an increase in either the intensity or scope of the conflict[8]), as well as prevent the crossing of "thresholds, considered significant,"[9] for example, *thresholds* such as:

- disruption of critical infrastructure using cyber operations,
- armed attack,
- indiscriminate bombardment,
- use of nuclear weapons.

Essentially, it is a decision-making problem. Communication in such a mode should not be confused with ordinary diplomatic communication or with diplomatic or political relations between such States. In general, however, it is better for well-equipped and armed States to be able to talk to each other to avoid the risks of misunderstandings—so that there is at least a chance of avoiding things going really wrong ways. There must be some channels of communication, even between hostile parties—because of the need for stability.

This has often been the case in history. It is the case today. We know this well, if only from public messages. The hotline—communication between Russia and the United States on the use of nuclear weapons, established in the 1960s—is a perfect example.[10] The same is true of relations with France and the United Kingdom, Russia–China, United States–China, China–India, and other channels.[11] Similar channels (although not nuclear-related) existed between Turkey and Greece,[12] or between the United States and Russia during the war in Ukraine. It turns out that talking is necessary. This goes somewhat beyond the issues of propaganda and information influence operations. Nonetheless, these are security and diplomatic considerations strictly linked to information exchange.

Badly phrased, or interpreted information and misinterpretations are something better to be avoided if one has an arsenal of nuclear weapons. When one side sees something appearing on the radar, it may be better to consult the other side first, before giving orders of retaliation. If only to avoid an accidental skirmish. Especially in the information age, when groups of people can succumb to moral panic, a reference source of reliable information is indispensable.

7.3 INFORMATION OPERATIONS ENABLED BY CYBER ATTACKS

Cyber-enabled information operations are a mix of the two methods. These are cyber operations with information-impact goals. Or, rather, information operations aided by cyber operations. Cyber operation is the method employed to lead to informational impact, such as delivering information payloads and content.

Of more active cyber activities such as taking over accounts, passwords, and access to IT systems or infrastructure, and using them to implant information payload, narratives, messages, and broadcasts. This fusion enables more effective information influence. It is a form of diversion and deception.

The information layer can be carried out by military operators, but also by, for example, front companies and even public relations (PR) firms. An interesting example was the so-called VULKAN,[13] operation of an actor linked to the Russian military intelligence GRU involving information operations. The Russian company developed solutions (software) for monitoring the information environment and designing information campaigns, enabling the manipulation of audience opinions. The information was leaked to journalists and analyzed by the U.S. cyber security company Mandiant. Thanks to this, we learned about the fact of creating and using advanced frameworks, at least for Russian purposes. Is that it?

It is very easy to imagine that similar capabilities could be developed by other States as well. These are solutions for monitoring, information retrieval, trend discovery, and interference capabilities. The former resembles rather typical, ordinary PR tools for observing information and trends, such as whether a particular keyword, term, or name appears in various channels like websites, news headlines, and social media. These are the basics of online PR. And, unsurprisingly, information warfare and propaganda departments in military units borrow the expertise to do the same—with similar or identical methods. What else should they be doing? One has to get information from somewhere, and it so happens that such units are specialized for exactly these activities. Not just active operations but also monitoring.

7.4 FIVE FUNDAMENTAL CRITERIA FOR MEASURING SERIOUSNESS OF OPERATIONS

When can an influence operation be considered serious? Several criteria can be distinguished that indicate professionalism, and consequently—risk that an influence campaign will be carried out successfully. So, when should such operations be considered serious, and malicious? This is determined by:

- **Transparency**—whether it is known who is initiating the activities, whether they are transparent;
- **Content quality**—resulting in the potential for results;
- **Payload**—and whether, for example, it is intended to lead to some action.[14]

This may not suffice to appreciate the true seriousness of the activities. It is also worth considering the *mode of* reaching the audience—what medium is in use, how widely propagated these information payloads are. An information operation is meaningless if it falls on stony ground. Only by finding the audience, it can bring about the consequences in the form of actions taken by them.

These four criteria are, therefore, appropriate for analysis. But it may also be worth determining whether the information payload meets the level identified, or even prohibited by national or international law. So, the fifth may be *legality* (or policy aspects). Such prohibited practices could involve the publication of content calling for actions inspired by ethnic or religious hatred or incitement to war, sowing terror, and inciting prohibited actions such as crimes against humanity or genocide (though it must be verified for any following, actual actions, if any). Interpretations of the seriousness of influence operation activities in these five dimensions can be helpful in determining the malice of the activities. Such an assessment may be used to decide how to respond to such actions. Which is reasonable, especially if their illegality is established. For example, it is illegal to incite war. But what about building the ground for it? This is not necessarily so clear-cut.

7.5 PREPARING SOCIETY FOR WAR

Calling for war and incitement to war—are formally forbidden. However, States sometimes go to war—offensively, defensively, joining the fight within the framework of alliances. In view of this, there at times may be a need to properly justify these goals to their own society (and others). This is the problem of how to "sell" war to the public. In other words—propaganda that builds the atmosphere prior to war.

Societies in their mass are not necessarily aware of the details of the complex international and even domestic situations. People may not know what's going on because they have other priorities, such as watching TV series, entertainment programs, or breakfast TV. Nobody can blame people for their hobbies. There is nothing wrong with that, that's just a part of life. Hence, it may be difficult for decisions to enter a war to be made purely from the bottom up—which applies to both World War II and more contemporary armed conflicts. Somehow, a picture of reality may be molded or formed by public opinion leaders. When the pace of events accelerates, this image can be more easily assimilated by the broad public.[15] Then, too, political leaders can gain more room for decision-making—with public support, they can push the right button, decide to redeploy troops, boost arms or ammunition production, etc.

Of course, this does not apply in such a way to a State that is unexpectedly attacked, and so the needs may be more immediate. Here, however, it is worth making a caveat. It is not the case that events develop suddenly and arise out of nothing. It is a series of events that make up the process potentially leading to aggression (from the aggressor State point of view) or being the victim of aggression (in the case of the victim State). By its nature, this issue cannot be facile, and I do not consider it appropriate to ignore the wisdom of adapting to current circumstances, or the wisdom of the people.

7.5.1 The wisdom and preferences of the people—and Talleyrand

However, people are capable of determining that something is or is not in their interest. For, as Talleyrand used to say, the people (public opinion) may hold more wisdom than rulers (he mentioned Napoleon), wisemen (he mentioned Voltaire), or many a minister, now or present. So, what may people or public opinion know collectively?

We would all prefer that there be no wars—that there be no conflicts, no aggression, no fighting. Unfortunately, people and States have it in common that they sometimes fall into conflicts, including interstate armed conflicts, and the history of the previous thousand years—unfortunately—attests to that. Sometimes, affairs may be more peaceful in certain geographic locations or historical periods, which allows people and generations living in such conditions to form views or opinions—for example, such that the time of wars is over, that other times have come, that things are different now—even if "just because." To some extent, this characterized post-1945 Europe (certainly Western Europe), and specifically post-1989. The sobering events in 2022 came quite unexpectedly to many. I do not claim here to be able to capture this complex problem holistically, and that is not the purpose of this book anyway. Therefore, I make use of relevant analyses, studies, and scientific publications—as in the other chapters of this book on security.

Here, however, it seems particularly important. The times of the first half of the third decade of the 21st century (2020s) were particularly conducive to deliberation and expert treatment of the subject matter. Affairs since 2022 are far from theoretical deliberations, even if earlier (a few years back) consideration of the prospect of war outbreak would have been ridiculed (or ignored) by the majority part of the public, experts, and politicians (as there is a right time to consider specific threats). Exactly like the concept of propaganda itself—it is now a unique moment to create such an analysis and the book you are now reading. It would have been much more difficult to write this chapter of the book in particular if we had not experienced the war in Ukraine. Let's say that in 2015, it would have been a great hassle to cover this topic at all, who would have cared about it anyway? With polls being taken in 2022–2024 about military support (or not) for Ukraine, as well as support for military action by some States in the event of a potential defense of Taiwan—and in China, support for military seizure of the island—it all may sound ominous. Luckily, we don't have to resort to predicting the future. And we won't—what is to be, will be. Let's get back to the essence.

7.5.2 Preparing for war from the top, such as in statements by state leaders

In a memorable speech by Vladimir Putin in February 2022, he explained that, in his view, Ukraine was not in fact a separate State and that, in addition, "*Lenin made a mistake*" by leading to actions resulting in the transfer of lands to Ukraine. Putin explained that the West also allegedly violated an unclear and alleged principle of the "indivisible security" in that NATO, by approaching Russia's borders, supposedly reduced Russia's security. "Historical Essays" on the subject of Europe have been published earlier, in 2021. They were either ignored or ridiculed in the West. Perhaps erroneously, given that they apparently led directly to what the West in question did not want to believe until the very end—the aggression and war.

We know that preparing official, or facade, justifications for war in the information age can be of little value. We know this thanks to the unprecedented decision made by the United States, which since the fall of 2021 has been revealing intelligence information to States, and the public, about the impending war. As a result, there was little room for surprise—everyone should have reckoned with what was to happen, and what did eventually happen. Everyone is always wiser after the fact, in this case. However, much was known and even discernible to everyone—we are talking about the redeployment of troops on a grand scale. If some States doubted this, they made a big mistake. A telling example was the necessity for the immediate evacuation of the head of German BND (intelligence) when he went to Kiev at the last possible moment, in fact, when it was too late, perhaps highlighting German analytical capabilities or convictions. As a result, he had to be transported back. The United States undoubtedly *constructed* ground and *awareness* in Western societies of the impending possibility of war. This forms an example of excellent recognition and use of information. However, even before World War I, a kind of similar action was also being made through the press and the issuance of ultimatums to States. World War I did not break out all of sudden. Similarly, prior to World War II, German leaders in the 1930s were rather honest and straightforward about their intentions, and from a certain point in time—what they were even doing. It sufficed to treat it seriously. No one could be surprised. In the 1930s and especially in 1939, the inevitability of war was already often discussed, or written about. So, it sufficed to receive signals correctly, interpret them, and make decisions. Unfortunately, acting is costly, and the outbreak of war is never certain anyway. So, perhaps it may be worth taking the risk and doing nothing (World War II itself was, of course, much more costly than any preparations to prevent it)?

7.5.3 Pro-war PR—why die for the State?

If state leaders are convinced of the inevitability of war, before anything happens, it may be necessary to rally the public and justify the potential coming sacrifices. Why should citizens risk their lives, their health, and their property? The atmosphere may be built precisely with propaganda, or PR of war, and this has been happening since time immemorial.[16] There are many examples, such as the time when the administration of U.S. President Roosevelt began preparing (or convincing) the public for the risk or inevitability of entering World War II, before the United States entered the war by being attacked. In the United States, polls in the 1930s measured public support for various ideas, for example, allied support for war in Europe, war with Japan.

In addition, preparedness (or even desirability) for war is something that those seeking to resort to war may have to build in their societies. So, how does one build awareness and readiness for war in a society using propaganda measures? One may start subtly, creating the right stories, narratives, messages, and public comments (i.e., to shape sentiment)—directed at the targeted State—that *something is a threat*, that the situation needs to be "corrected." In Nazi Germany, an entire narrative of expanding the "living space" (German: Lebensraum) was built around this. The leader of the State could speak about war—in public gatherings or over radio. In Soviet Russia of the 1920s this happened often, though it is unclear whether the leaders of the State believed and desired to resort to war, or just intended to motivate (by fear) the public to work. Such manipulation with the risk (fear) of war is intentional and can be used to justify, for example, hardship in life, economic, and financial.[17] For example, fluctuations in parameters such as economic growth or inflation—regardless of the real sources. Although, of course, it does not have to be a real risk; however, if one can profit from the mere creation of risk awareness—it was sometimes done. Convincing to increase defense spending—including when these are in fact justified and reasonable things to do—is a related manner. Increased spending on defense means shift in priorities, including public spending. It is all but natural that such intention must be communicated to the public to build public awareness, understanding, or support. This may be done using warning signals, expressing merit-based arguments, and/or fear.

In 1930s Germany, however, it went further—propaganda was conducted to convince the public of the necessity of the genocide of the parts of society—Jews, presenting extermination in terms of defense.[18] When a State is armed to the teeth and militaristically aggressive and suggests or even openly talks about the necessity of exterminating certain groups of people, it cannot be taken frivolously. This is why the world intervened in the Balkans in the 1990s. Then such propaganda was spread through state and media channels, as well as interpersonal channels—in conversations between people. Also used in its reassertion was what the foreign press wrote about Nazi Germany.[19] This is a warning not to treat politicians' statements during certain historical periods as speeches without consequences.

7.5.4 Absurd war scare versus pluralism

Sometimes, this can take a caricatured form. For example, from our perspective, the propaganda of North Korea, building in its own society a constant sense of threat of war by "imperialists" (the U.S.), may sound hilarious, or absurd. It's probably less laughable to people in North Korea, including those who believe this propaganda, because they are immersed in a totalitarian information system and may have no choice, or even awareness of the actual form. With totalitarian propaganda, everything is subordinated to a unified political, informational line. There is only a single point of view (or several, amounting to the same thing), and propaganda content is "injected" into various areas of life. At school, at work, at the health clinic, on the streets, and in the media, there is one goal, one opinion.[20] According to the principle that:

> Propaganda has no meaning and hence no effectiveness except in terms of life conditions of people-their needs, fears, hatreds, loves, aspirations, prejudices, and tradition ... National Socialist propaganda [was] based on the hatreds, fears, aspirations, and traditions of the German people.[21]

When there is no pluralism, when there is only one source of information (the so-called truth), then societies can be controlled, and people have no real alternatives. Their opinion may be steered. Such a situation does not exist in pluralistic societies. There are different media and different sources of information, including foreign ones. Examples from the past may help explain this point. One cannot limit oneself to only selected manifestations of the present to show trends and processes. Thus, more than 60% of Americans supported the war (referred to as a "police action"[22]) in Korea (1950)[23]—so not all, despite the obvious educational campaigns about the necessity of such action. Pictures of public protests in the United States opposing U.S involvement in World War II in Europe are known. Though perhaps from protests held before 1942, when Soviet agents induced such activities—activities stopped after the USSR ceased cooperation with Germany, following the German attack on the USSR. The increase in support for U.S. participation in World War II did occur only around 1942—from about 20% to over 80%. This means that there are always some groups that may oppose taking some action, such as engaging in war. That's pluralism.

It is relevant to make some distinctions between attitudes. One can publicly oppose war and even be friendly to a particular State but actually favor war, the so-called friendly hostile attitude.[24] In other words: to say the opposite of what one thinks—and this is not hypocrisy, because that would be mixing orders. Societies may begin to favor war, for example, in response to an act of aggression directed against them (the attack on Pearl Harbor in 1941, the attack on the World Trade Center and other facilities in 2001). In turn, this support may diminish in response to some turn of events and fate—such as the rising human casualties.[25] State services know this. In view of this, some things can be publicized (being subjected to attack, aggression, casualties, massacres, but also successes, positive prospects for the future, etc.), while others muted (e.g., human casualties of warfare, including those accidental or collateral, failures, destruction, the dire economic state, negative prospects for the future). Here, at the same time, changes (attitude switch) in public support can occur very quickly. And these are the conclusions from the last 70 years about the fluctuation of public support and perception of attitudes *for or against* a war. Reliable data from the earlier years is not available—it was not customary then to compile polls and publish them—besides, we must also limit ourselves to a period, if only due to practical considerations. In view of this, let us point out that it is not known what public support there was among the people for, for example, the Thirty Years' War (1618–1648), although, importantly, then the voice of the people counted less, nor did public opinion exist. And this is also why going back too far makes limited or no sense.

7.5.5 The illuminating examples of pandemic or COVID-19 events

Provocatively, one may consider whether the circulation of information regarding the COVID-19 pandemic (to be clear: a real, genuine health problem) cannot be evaluated in context of events as happening in totalitarian-like circumstances where there was only one point of view.

So, same content, information, or message in most if not all media with a significant audience—regardless of political option. The information was promoted by public figures and by influencers, the state system, school system, etc. The activities were visible in practice: regular and broad publications of disease levels or counts, social restrictions, the need to wash hands, disinfect, wear masks, etc. It was a fairly closed information circuit. The pursuit of sensationalism and clicks even fueled the spiral of seeking these sensations (sometimes a spiral of fear). Every shred of information and every emerging scientific publication was publicized (especially in the early days of the pandemic). I don't consider the question of whether all the restrictions were justified, whether they made sense, whether there was room for abuse, fraud, etc. That is not the point. As I pointed out, this was a real health and sanitary issue. Pointing out the informational issues cannot be avoided, though. Indeed, the single point of view and shunning of questioning of practices was justified by considerations of public health emergency and safety. Let others be the judge.

7.6 SITUATION DURING WAR—TARGETING COMMUNICATIONS TO AUDIENCE GROUPS

And what is it like during war? Much has been written about the role of the media in the United States in shifting opposition sentiments to the Vietnam War in American society. More contemporarily, as Fallujah came under siege in 2004, information about exaggerated civilian casualties was distributed in the Arab media in order to build pressure on the United States to cease operations.[26] Such information could not be ignored and competent commanders had to be aware of its impact—those more astute even paid attention to the tone of sermons in local mosques.[27] Because it is useful to have many sources of information to develop an overview of the situation. This is also how it happens in situations of tension before or during armed conflicts; we saw this clearly in 2022 and 2023, and in different parts of the globe, in addition, in the "live coverage" mode, that is—in real time. This is a key difference from how things were done 100, 50, or even 10 years ago.

Military information services directing communications to the public[28] are tasked with building a favorable or friendly portrayal of military activities. Biased descriptions of military activities can result in undesirable consequences. This is true of both domestic and foreign media. This can be seen even during the Russian war in Ukraine, where some Western countries devoted space to presenting Russia's point of view. How were decisions to do this reached?

No one in the Western sphere doubts reports of civilian casualties among Ukrainians due to the war unleashed by Russia. In fact, the war in Ukraine is so widely publicized, and information comes from so many sources, that such records could potentially function as evidence for a hypothetical future tribunal to determine alleged (in the legal sense) war crimes in the future, if one were ever to be established.

An interesting example is the targeting of propaganda to specific social groups. Specifically, to women to foster public understanding of the war. That is, to "sell the war,"[29] which may require popularizing the idea that women may perform any job, including physical work in factories (to be more precise—this happened during World War II), or also—as in the memorable "women on tractors" campaign—referring to agricultural work (in the communist bloc 1945–1989). Such jobs must be filled when people are sent to the front, to fight. Today such campaigns may be viewed differently but needs of war times have their specific considerations.

During the war in Afghanistan, the United States used psychological operations extensively.[30] Analyses have found that arguments like "the war on terror justifies U.S. intervention in Afghanistan" are ineffective, while messages like "democracy will help Afghanistan" may work better[31] (although from the perspective of 2023, the effects of such actions may need to be re-evaluated). Messages considering intervention must be crafted in a certain way. The typical Western citizen probably has little or no actual idea about the Taliban, Afghanistan, and the local conditions.

Societies in the West may have been formatted in specific ways—culturally, also naturally, by processes taking decades. Stereotypes and thought clichés may have been formed, but an existence of similar ones elsewhere cannot be counted on—like in Afghanistan. For understandable reasons:

> [M]ost Afghans have never seen a terrorist training camp and have had little or no contact with al-Qaeda. When [the U.S. military] labeled the Taliban as terrorists, the effort lost credibility because it seems that most of the target audience, the Pashtuns, do not consider the Taliban to be international terrorists and do not accept the premise that the Taliban had anything to do with the September 11 attack on New York.[32]

They may not even have known what happened on September 11, 2001, in New York! In view of this, any attempt to speak to local populations in a language originally intended for use at other societies is pointless. For that, the societies of Western countries have "directly" and "with their own eyes" seen both terrorist training camps and assassinations. In news services, in TV series, in movies, for example.

On the other hand, it is interesting to note that in Afghanistan, at that time, the role of radio was very important—much more important than in Western societies. People in Afghanistan listened to the radio and used it as a source of information, so the U.S. military bought air time and sponsored local stations to get the message out to local communities.[33] In 2005, the U.S. military even dropped leaflets from helicopters there.

7.7 DECEPTION

As Sigmund Freud wrote,

> groups have never thirsted after truth. They demand illusions, and cannot do without them. They constantly give what is unreal precedence over what is real; they are almost as strongly influenced by what is untrue as by what is true. They have an evident tendency not to distinguish between the two.[34]

He claimed so a very long time ago. Can it be considered inapplicable today?

Strategic deception can be used to conceal or mask the intentions or capabilities of States or their armies,[35] including military capabilities and albeit armaments. With deception itself understood as "deliberate misrepresentation of reality done to gain a competitive advantage,"[36] two types can be distinguished:

1) causing confusion, and
2) misleading.[37]

These are psychological methods.[38]

One of the simpler examples of creating *illusions* or deception are military parades, where armaments and weapons are on display: from tanks to intercontinental missiles. In countries that isolate themselves from others, such parades are closely watched by analysts. Until the actual capabilities of weapons are verified in practice on the battlefield, parades and the presentations of weapons systems themselves may be received uncritically. In this way, they help create the illusion of strength. Actual combat capabilities are not, after all, based solely on the type of weapons—even when these reliably work as advertised.

Alternatively, and on the contrary, it may be possible to create the illusion of the weakness of some specific goals or objectives, or lack thereof. Establishing an image of the factual situation can be difficult, especially when a State chooses a strategy of deception as its policy and strategic approach of choice. For example, Hitler's Germany spread false information about its military strength,[39] and the Soviet Union spread false information about the strength, or weakness, of its nuclear forces—depending on the situation, one or the other can be pretended, as needed.[40] In this way, for example, deterrent means can be created to dissuade potential States interested in an offensive attack, or other types of interventions. Test launches of space rockets officially for purely scientific purposes can also have such an effect. Rocket technology has a dual use. Launching rockets with a vertical (approximately) trajectory demonstrates that these trajectories can also be "flattened out" and this "scientific" equipment can be used as military—ballistic missiles to carry explosive charges. The Soviets often emphasized the "scientific aspect" of their space programs, but it was noted in the Soviet media that this also meant a missile range reaching the United States.[41] The same was true of North Korea,[42] when missiles were still being launched "into space." The fact of dual-use means that these missiles may be capable of carrying payloads over medium and long distances. So, these are military demonstrations, and not necessarily just "scientific" ones. Similarly, there was the regular repetition in Soviet Russia that the country has missiles that cannot be shot down, including claims about the design of the so-called fractional orbital bombardment systems—based on partial circling of the Earth's orbit, capable of entering Earth's orbit, moving around it, and setting a trajectory to some specific target on Earth surface.[43] Messages also have propaganda significance. In the Soviet and Russian case, methods of deception and concealment of information are sometimes called "maskirovka."[44,45]

Deception, therefore, is the sending of signals of information to be picked up by the other (or *some*) party and leads to errors and fatal mistakes. Let's repeat the classic again. Gustave Le Bon maintained that

> [t]he masses have never thirsted after truth. They turn aside from evidence that is not to their taste, preferring to deify error, if error seduces them. Whoever can supply them with illusions is easily their master; whoever attempts to destroy their illusions is always their victim. An individual in a crowd is a grain of sand amid other grains of sand, which the wind stirs up at will.[46]

But he asserted this more than 100 years ago, so perhaps things are different today? Let the readers decide for themselves.

7.8 PSYOP—PSYCHOLOGICAL OPERATIONS AND ACTIVITIES

Psychological operations are the use of psychological (scientific; theoretical, practical) knowledge in influence operations. They have been used for a long time, but a solid scientific foundation in this area has only existed since the 20th century. According to the U.S. military, psychological operations are defined as

> [p]lanned operations to convey selected information and indicators to foreign audiences to influence their emotions, motives, objective reasoning, and ultimately the behavior of foreign governments, organizations, groups, and individuals. The purpose of psychological operations is to induce or reinforce foreign attitudes and behavior favorable to the originator's objectives.[47]

According to Chinese doctrines, psychological warfare can disrupt adversaries' understanding of reality, leading decision makers to make mistakes—so, it is meant to influence the political decision-making process.[48]

The goal of PSYOP is to influence the recipients in such a way that they take actions that favor the goals of the PSYOP initiators.[49] An interesting example of PSYOP are terrorist actions—the use of intimidation or violence to induce the population (the audience, public, politicians) to take *some* action in the terrorists' favor. In this sense, the propagation of such terrorist events is important. How to do this? By bringing about spectacular events and incidents so that the mass media broadcast and widely propagate them[50]—this is one imaginable, most obvious method, of course not the only one. Wide broadcasting of shocking events or depictions may only help the terrorists to achieve their goals of terrorizing audience and causing support for adopting an action. At least in the traditional politically motivated terrorism. As is well known, fear sells well, and appeal to fear is the persuasive technique of choice here. Terrorists exploit this element of how societies function, namely susceptibility to fear. So effectively, in fact, that in spite of the actual decrease in terrorist incidents since the 1960s—there has been a paradoxical increase in the sense of threat regarding these issues in societies. Perhaps proliferation of mass media had something to do here. This hypothesis is that this fear grew due to informational reasons. The contents or events are disseminated often and widely—in this way, awareness of the problem becomes exaggerated (availability bias!) in the eyes of societies and the public. The above definition of PSYOP comes from the U.S. military but has a broader meaning. Russia also undertakes such activities, although it has a smaller budget.[51] However, it is not always money that determines the effectiveness of actions. Finesse and quality of techniques may have significant impacts. Part of unconventional methods to cause destabilization or even government changes (i.e., overthrowing) tend to be rather consistent over decades and involve supporting parts of populations adhering to a particular sentiment, with a view to construct the support of specific persons—circles, groups, "elites," or just politicians. Opting for perfected results—like convincing the "majority"—is not the actual point.[52]

7.8.1 PSYOP—from the Mongols to "DAS BOOT SINKT"

Returning to PSYOP, war, and psychological warfare are of great importance during armed conflicts. During peace, psychological operations have been used for centuries.[53] Genghis Khan had a method—before the arrival of the Mongol army people were sent to spread rumors about the size of the incoming army. This was supported by the actions of the army, performing rapid maneuvers to give credence to earlier rumors,[54] reinforcing them, an early example of combined arms.

If the methods of the Mongolian barbarians using an antiquated approach to spreading information seem like something obsolete (because they are), here are the British radio messages directed (via the BBC) to the German troops during World War II, worded flawlessly in German[55]:

> [A]nd so it will be best if you learn a few useful phrases in English before visiting us. For your first lesson, we take:
>
> DIE KANALUEBERFAHRT. Crossing the [English—L.O.] Channel.
>
> Now just repeat after me: DAS BOOT SINKT. The boat is sinking. The boat is sinking.
>
> DAS WASSER IST KALT. The water is cold. SEHR KALT. Very cold.
>
> Now I will give you a verb that should be very useful. Again, please repeat after me. ICH BRENNE. I am burning. DU BRENNST. You are burning. ER BRENNT. He is burning. WIR BRENNEN. We burn. IHR BRENNT. You are burning. SIR BRENNEN. They are burning.

From today's perspective, it may be difficult to comprehend what this is all about. The message was addressed to German soldiers who may have known the relevant context. The message fit into the context. It's about false information (rumors) about a miracle weapon allegedly developed by Great Britain, which supposedly had the ability to cover large areas of water surface (sea) with a burning substance, that is, to "set the sea on fire." This information was spread in Germany. The above transcript from the BBC communicates these capabilities in a highly suggestive manner and may have achieved an effect, assuming that the recipient of this content had prior knowledge of these rumors about the new weapon.[56]

7.8.2 Why the Internet was created—the untrue version, even if harmless

Naturally, not all rumors and gossip are necessarily harmful. For example, the widespread, albeit mistaken, view that the Internet network was designed to withstand a nuclear attack may be plausible at first glance. After all, it is true that it was also military agencies in the United States that funded research on computer networks. It's just that they did so in spite of their core activities, rather than intentionally. The idea was to develop a redundant fault-tolerant network to efficiently use the then-expensive, rare equipment (computers, memory, etc.) geographically located in different locations.[57] So that in places where the expensive computers were lacking, there would have been access to them via the network.

Linking this to stories about nuclear explosions may sound exciting at a glance, but it is incorrect. It is sensationalist. Finding connections between unrelated events, stories, and things is in human nature, which likes to find explanations to rationalize some events. However, this erroneous story related to the Internet only emerged in the 1990s and has been living its own life ever since. Of note, the work on the World Wide Web system (the one we browse using web browsers, which is what makes the Internet so useful) was carried out by Tim Berners-Lee at CERN by accident, so to speak. CERN as an organization accepted the result but quickly got rid of the project and turned custody over to the outside. CERN's focus on the actual purpose of their existence—fundamental research in particle physics, the physics of accelerators—is understandable. However, it's hard to shake the suspicion that CERN may have underestimated Web's, potential and, with the information it has today, would prefer to play some role, such as keeping custody of the system to itself. Luckily, no one is trying to tie the nature and history of the World Wide Web to historical and social events happening before or during.

And yet, I could make up a story that this opening to information exchange is on the cusp of the collapse of the U.S.S.R. and the opening up of the world in the 1990s (I just made that up; it's not true). By the way, when writing R&D projects and applying for funding, one may need to signal compliance with the directions of grant programs—somehow refer to them. For example, in the second and third decades of the 21st century, the so-called "green technologies" played a very important role. So, it may be worthwhile to indicate in grant application that the project, for example, will contribute to green development and is in line with it (add some buzzwords, too). This may lead to truisms or absurdities: even when applying to expand a data center and put in new computers, it may be argued that it is a "green," "eco-friendly" project because the new computers have new processors that are more energy efficient than the old ones. However, new processors are usually always more efficient than the previous generation. However, this natural fact can be emphasized as being in line with the "green" policy—on paper, all is true and fine. Such tricks were recommended when writing grant applications to increase the chances of being successful. This example is true, and the project was naturally accepted, and successfully completed. The server room was expanded, and officials were satisfied. That is to say, it all adds up in the spreadsheet, although, of course, in no way did it contribute to ecological or "green" development. Such is the peculiarity of grant proposal writing, much does not change here—it is the same nowadays, only the topics, terms, and themes evolve.

7.8.3 Psychological impact of events

We consider the psychological impact of propaganda and information. But it is worth noting that practical actions or their effects may also have a propaganda or psychological impact. For example, if the weather is very cold in winter and there is a shortage of heating and food, who is to blame? The simplest target could be the current ruling option. It is their responsibility, even if not their fault. Such is their fate—that's also why the authorities are elected, so that there is someone to hold responsible, to blame, when necessary.

7.8.3.1 PSYOP and superstition

One of the other interesting methods is to use superstitions in PSYOP.[58] Since people in different societies and cultures are susceptible to interests in the supernatural, like astrology, this can be exploited. State leaders can also be susceptible. Hitler, Goebbels, or Hess were. Furthermore, during World War II, Goebbels noted that the Allies dropped leaflets on Germany with horoscopes intended to indicate Germany's imminent demise. On this occasion, he acknowledged that German propaganda was familiar with these methods—and used them too, both against external enemies and for internal use in Germany.[59]

7.8.3.2 Psychological effects of weapons used—night bombardment, lack of food

The psychological effects of the weapons used are another. Invasions, aggressions, detonations, and explosions definitely must carry psychological effects on individuals as well as on whole societies. There is plenty of evidence for such a thesis.

The U.S. Army has studied the psychological impact of air operations—including effects such as demoralization and even desertions in enemy forces.[60] This can be easily imagined. If soldiers in bunkers or in trenches are subjected to massive bombardment, and there is no indication that reinforcements and support are to come, what to do then? What to think? How long to hold the positions? And what when food begins to run out? The U.S. Army's observations show that multi-week bombardments against enemy belligerents work best when food is in short supply (supply lines have been interrupted) and people are targeted by ground attacks after earlier bombardments.[61] These are observations based on practice, so I don't enter into discussion with them. That's the way it was. Probably better not to experience it in practice, either. For instance, during World War II, Great Britain deliberately bombarded targets in Germany at night—precisely to lower their morale[62] and their will.

PSYOP and information operations can have a real impact. Practical events may also influence people's perceptions and opinions. When both are in action—the synergistic effect further strengthens the message. Think about it—if it's raining and there's a flood, and there's no support or help coming from anywhere, it's easy to form an opinion about the ineptitude of "the government" and more generally of the people in power—the politicians, perhaps all of them. Similar processes may be relevant for battlefield events, including events that are happening—the ineptitude of the command can negatively affect the mental condition of the military. However, the operations of the "enemy" can bring about an effect. Militaries knows this, and psychological analyses and studies have long been conducted to determine the consequences of military maneuvers, or the very impact of the use of certain weapons on those against whom these weapons are used.[63] How can a researcher determine such an impact? For example, by interviewing people who have had experiences with weapons use and the ensuing effects. This could be the wounded on both sides of the war, captured soldiers of the other side (prisoners of war), also civilians. As a result of such interviews, it was possible to determine that, for example, 36% of soldiers feared bomb shrapnel, 22% mortars, and 6% grenades[64]; 38% feared the sound of a falling airplane bomb, 3% feared the sight after a bomb explosion, and for 10%, there was no difference. In contrast, thoughts of desertion (motivated, after all, psychologically) were most strongly triggered by the use of aerial weapons and artillery.[65] The greatest fear was attributed to the use of artillery—a greater effect compared to incendiary substances such as napalm. Thus, perceptions can be established as to the effectiveness of weapons, the fear of using any type of weapon, and the effect on soldiers experiencing the use of weapons on themselves. Armed conflicts are also an opportunity to conduct unique psychological research. At least in the 1960s—until the ones made later will eventually surface.

7.8.3.3 PSYOP versus use of nuclear weapons—psychological effects of detonation

What about the use of nuclear weapons (a nuclear maneuver)? I admit it openly: this topic is very niche. Furthermore, such weapons are better not to be used in practice.

The psychological consequences of the use of these weapons have been analyzed by the U.S. Army on soldiers observing nuclear test explosions.[66] Interestingly, army soldiers did not draw many conclusions from their own experiences, that is, visually experiencing the explosion and feeling the tremors caused by it. They also shared, on their own initiative, the information with other members of their units (who did not experience the explosion). It is difficult to translate this into practice, as it is easy to imagine that soldiers or civilians against whom such a weapon would be used would also definitely share their observations. But today, in a reality where, for example, there are plenty of YouTube videos depicting actual nuclear explosions, these observations are likely of limited value (except personal feeling of light, shocks, or tremors). In the past, it was a more elitist experience. In preparation for the eventuality of nuclear warfare, the psychological effects of the use of tactical (limited in range and detonation power[67]) nuclear weapons were also estimated[68]—such studies are difficult to conduct—after all, in the history of mankind, these weapons have been used only twice (and let's hope this number won't expand). In addition, it was experienced mostly by civilians.[69]

What may be surprising today, but is quite rationally explained, after the detonation at Hiroshima and Nagasaki in 1945, there was no mass panic in society. How come? At that time, the weapons were completely novel, there was no information about them—meaning also no awareness of the effects, and therefore—no widespread fear and panic. That cannot be said about the world today.[70] Commanders, however, may be interested, for example, in whether there would be immediate and widespread desertions or a catastrophic decline in the morale of soldiers. Or whether human beings are so accustomed to dealing with extreme situations that if something like this were to happen, they would somehow cope despite the extreme stress. There is no doubt that soldiers would cope better here than civilians.[71] This is what motivates the desire to study such effects, not just the experience of the detonation itself, but also the consequences of receiving a dose of radioactive radiation.

Imagine soldiers in a detonation zone. They survive the explosion itself. Will they want to continue fighting? *I have no idea!* I doubt anyone would be much wiser today. It's also not merely a question of how would the army act after such a detonation—but also society, including how would the information environment be affected in state and international media? Today, information about such an event would spread instantly, and around the world. So fast that such an event could imaginably overwhelm servers of news sites. After the detonation, "the experience of being exposed to a nuclear attack can be expected, in the short run, to be an intensely traumatic emotional stimulus, capable of rendering individuals temporarily ineffective in performing routine military duties."[72] Apart from the fact that people may then be focused on other things, primarily survival, it might be unreasonable or impossible to expect them to take action. However, public order may be preserved—without any social breakdown—provided, of course, that government and state structures survive. In such extreme situations, people prefer to act as a group and respect the authority of leaders, even in the dark—without evaluating the decisions (even when they are wrong).[73] Prior to any eventual nuclear detonations, therefore, soldiers and the public might benefit from preparedness. Soldiers can be trained, for example, in stress management. The public should be given information about the basics of survival in such a situation. To reduce panic, one can try to introduce the topic of the possibility of nuclear detonation into the information space, to raise the public debate beforehand. To prepare the public for this—not to sow fear. Practical advice, not fear would be relevant. Whether this would be of any help—I do not know, and in my view–probably no one knows! It is better not to test this in practice. A manifestation of such activities in our modern times was, for example, a series of articles in the press in 2022 and 2023, in which more space was devoted to this topic than in the preceding 30 years.

So, what does it involve to prepare people for the eventuality during and after an "incident" (detonation)? Information should be given in an understandable, factual way but also gradually.[74] This sounds like a truism in such a situation. And, of course, it assumes that there will be someone to give such information to. And by what means? Through social media? Or would radio be more effective? If so, the public would have to be equipped with radio, a thing that may not be fashionable to have in one's home in the 2020s.

Let's recall the response to the governments' crisis actions during the pandemic caused by the SARS-CoV-2 virus: decisions were, especially in the early stages, respected, even if the situation was mildly chaotic or not perfectly organized (questioning may have begun once the public realized that the authorities clearly had rather limited understanding of the situation nor a clear, coherent plan of action—that is another aspect entirely, but with a nuclear detonation, the event would not be as prolonged as the pandemic was; it's in fact pretty instantaneous).

The good news is that nuclear weapons are universally not used—not even test detonations are carried out, North Korea perhaps being an exception in this regard. On the other hand, the fact of past U.S. threats against China on the occasion of the Korean War in 1950 (in that war the U.S. even threatened China with a nuclear attack, which could have contributed to an accelerated ceasefire[75]), the Cuban Missile Crisis in the 1960s, and information through various channels about such a potential moves by Russia on the occasion of the war in Ukraine in 2022 are notable. Yes, they may be chilling, though the public at large in the 2020s rather forgot about the nuclear threat—with respect to the awareness of the risk during the Cold War.

The use of nuclear weapons remains a taboo subject in 2023. The use of this technology alone would undoubtedly have a significant psychological impact—worldwide. Paradoxically, it would lower the threshold for the use of such weapons. By such moves, it could become normalized (in line with the principle of the Overton's window), unless the world would choose to rewind the change, as they attempted to do after World War II to make it a taboo. Currently, nuclear weapons function as elements of deterrence—military but also psychological. For this reason, it is better not to use them. The power of such deterrence lies precisely in the fact of the potential capability to use the weapon, but not doing so in practice—just keeping this as an option. If someone actually chooses to use it, then the effect of deterrence, and nuclear restraint, will be nullified—in favor of practical counteraction by other means (including nuclear). On the other hand, after the first detonations, a shocked public may not even want to bring about a ceasefire, what may potentially be the case in a (hypothetical) nuclear conflict between nuclear states like India and Pakistan.[76] To stress—it's better not to test such scenarios in practice.

After the detonation, information chaos could occur on a scale unknown before, both in the affected and external (allied, neutral) countries. Everywhere! This is a purely hypothetical scenario—it has not been tested in practice. And again, it is better not to do so.

7.8.4 Information warfare versus ceasefire or achieving peace

Information warfare methods can complicate the process leading to a ceasefire (or peace) between States, which is due to the fact that the political leadership in States is not necessarily static, and monolith. There may be factions, or interest groups willing, but also others—unwilling—to make some specific decisions, concessions, or changes, such as peace or the establishment of cooperation,[77] including decisions on economy or industrial policies. In such a situation, State communication (information) can lose coherence, become ambiguous, take undesirable directions, and even lead to difficulties in drawing conclusions about what such a State really wants or intends. This may cause problems internally but also externally, against allied States.

If there are several factions in power (in the government, in the state elite) and one, for example, wants to pursue a ceasefire, or cooperation, with a third country, and another faction does not want a ceasefire—or is otherwise placing obstacles, creating problems (if only on economic grounds)—this may cause misunderstandings and make work difficult. Even impossible. For example, there was no substantial challenge to finish World War II—Germany was completely defeated and the opinions of any political-military factions did not matter, as the only available outcome was unconditional surrender. With Japan in World War II, this was not the case—some preferred to fight until the end.[78] In the information age, information and opinions expressed publicly by policymakers, ambassadors, public figures, and perhaps even the broader masses of society can play a role. These lines of messages may support either option without having a complete picture of the situation, which can constrain the decision-making situation, such as limiting the decision space or imposing additional conditions.

How will the war in Ukraine unfold after 2024? While the results of public surveys in Western Europe varied relating to such things as the preference for negotiated settlement, opinions that Russia or Ukraine wins, etc., to speculate is pointless. Instead, what matters is what's actually to come, so to observe the flow of events. One thing is certain: information issues will continue to play a significant role in ending this conflict, including after it's finished.

7.8.5 What does it feel like when a "Peacemaker" arrives?

Returning to kinetic weapons, another interesting information trick is the use of euphemism. Euphemism is a process of not calling things by their names—including using words or expressions creatively. Certain situations, methods, products, and technologies may thus be described euphemistically. For example, a surrender may be called an '*organized technical back-wards maneuver*'. The names of weapons systems can also carry such information. For example, the U.S. MX missile was renamed "*Peacekeeper*." "Collateral damage" may mean damage done to civilians (e.g., civilian casualties),[79] even if unintentionally—without specifying things directly. When a "Peacekeeper" flies toward us, do we feel less threatened than if a "Giga-destroyer" or "Shark" did?

7.8.6 PSYOP and commercial products, gadgets

Another vehicle for PSYOP can be commercial products, as well as gadgets and gifts that convey propaganda content in some way. These can be inscribed T-shirts, some kind of tags, pins, lighters, or even soap.[80] There will always be a place for some kind of message—if only on the box. The important thing is that such products should be useful for something.[81] Products "with a message" have been used on many occasions, by various armies and underground movements, insurgent movements, also terrorist movements. It is necessary to do it with a head firmly on one's shoulders, targeting certain social groups, such as young people: "PSYOP personnel should target the youth, as their opinions are not as ingrained. When passing out handbills and novelty items, PSYOP personnel should take care to adhere to cultural nuisances."[82] Undoubtedly, products may carry some propaganda value, disinformation potential, useful in influence psychology. This is probably why North Korea was careful to remove any content informing about the origin of food aid to the country.

We know from studies of the military and war propaganda that commercial products have an undeniable impact on people's psychological condition.

7.8.7 Good advice from Uncle Sam

And now a handful of selected quotes straight from the U.S. Army's PSYOP manual:

> Newspapers and magazines are extremely powerful means of transmitting a PSYOP message ... Newspapers produced by PSYOP should provide timely, truthful news and entertainment ... The printed word has a high degree of credibility, acceptance, and prestige

> ... a persuasive product attains its objective through use of reason. ... Facts are presented so that the audience is convinced that the conclusions reached by the author are valid. The informative product is factual. [PSYOP writer puts aside all personal prejudices and biases when writing for enemy consumption. ... Truthful, credible, and accurate news reporting is the best way to gain and hold attention.[83]

Of course, this does not apply only to the United States or even only to PSYOP. Treat it as remarks of a more general nature of propaganda, about persuasion.

7.8.8 PSYOP to defend IT systems against cyberattacks

Psychological methods can also be used to frustrate attempts at cyber attacks, deliberately hindering activities in information systems in such a way that attackers lose, waste time, and thus mental cycles.[84] Operators are human beings, and unproductively spending many hours indeed may be frustrating and can, therefore, act as a barrier, as a defense, slowing down operations.

7.8.9 Harry Potter and Woland versus propaganda

We will conclude our consideration of PSYOP with magic. More specifically—the application of techniques relating to magical thinking, divination, superstition, zodiac signs, etc. in psychological operations.[85] As Behemoth (the Cat) explained in Bulgakov's *Master and Margarita* during a performance at the *Varietes Theater*, such phenomena are total hogwash, but (according to the Cat) some perhaps take them seriously. And others may exploit it. Like creators of such content—to make money on the naive. Or the military—to control people. And this is what the United States noticed during military operations in the Congo in the 1960s. Paramilitary groups have used "magical" terminology to motivate local people to fight and even convince them that they magically become bulletproof. The use of such worldview conditioning, however, requires caution—for where one tribe recognizes that a certain product or amulet promotes good luck, others may consider the same product harmful. This is not a joke—such observations and analyses were actually made by the U.S. military and intended to be put into practice.[86] So, this may require specific recognition among social groups, for example.

This can be difficult for us to understand in modern times, perhaps an analogy with zodiac signs and horoscopes might be useful here. I have already pointed out earlier in this chapter their uses in propaganda. The basics of how these products work are probably familiar to everyone. So, in this case, the activities would have to be coordinated to fit, for example, into certain phases of the Moon, hence the so-called astrological conditions. But in relation to true, false, or imaginable future events (depending on the objectives).

For example, when Venus enters the sign of Capricorn, then do "*something*." Or this "*something*" is to be justified by "the entry of Venus into the sign of Cancer." One can imagine the adoption of some bill in parliament due to "the conjunction of planets: or a solar eclipse." "Under the influence of favorable astrological aspects, including the conjunction of Venus with Jupiter, we are adopting a law on the protection of personal data. The harmony of the heavens inspires action in the name of privacy and balance. Amethyst, a protective stone, further enhances this energy." If this sounds like gibberish to you, it is an apt observation.

7.9 RESPONSE TO THE INFORMATION WARFARE

States are announcing options for military responses to information operations. France is an example of a State that sounded this explicitly and officially. Various responses are foreseen.

Unsurprisingly, none were stated explicitly and precisely (ambiguity is the goal). Responses may foresee the neutralization of information operations, such as blocking them, paralyzing operations, the media channels and technology used, cutting off funding, and banning information measures/media. In the latter case, it could likely be, for example, the banning of television broadcasts. In Europe, the most famous contemporary move of this kind is the blockade of RT (Russia Today) in France. During wars, responses may include bombing of centers manufacturing information operations, or stations broadcasting it—when warranted.

Another response can involve imposing sanctions—on individuals, companies, institutions, and state structures. Such responses have been taken by the United States, the European Union, and the United Kingdom, culminating in the time during the Russian war with Ukraine. Frequent reason for sanctions was, for example, the spread of misleading or untrue information about military aggression.

Sometimes, however, blockades are not possible in principle, because a certain informational influence is created by legal means that cannot be blocked. Such a situation occurs, for example, when internationally recognized treaties are used.

7.10 INFORMATION OPERATIONS UNITS FORMATION—ATTACK AND DEFENSE

All States resort to such activities, both civilian and military structures. The question then is, how to develop effective capacity? We begin with a preliminary remark. Under peacetime conditions in democratic States at least, where pluralism is the standard, creating a coherent information system as working in modern times is a challenge. Societies may have legitimate doubts and even concerns about the formation of such entities. If only due to the fact of formation under conditions of openness. One potential solution is again the use of euphemism. One may, for example, call such centers as simple as *information centers*.

Another manifestation of the difficulty is highlighted during the years of developing the information operations doctrine of the U.S. military. Today positioned close to cyberwarfare[87] but not identical to it. The development of a modern configuration and understanding took decades and did not come out of nowhere. Counterintuitively, this may be important especially due to the hierarchical structure of the military. The proper definition of the spectrum of interests and activities, standards, and even organizational culture—it is important for the object of work. And by extension, it is important for the security of the State. And so, in the Western system, a division can be distinguished. Operation domains: cyber and information. These need to be positioned somehow, and one possibility is to place them in a same structure, in order to be able to take advantage of synergies when needed (like during cyber-enabled information operations to achieve effects). And this is not difficult to imagine. In view of this, despite specific references here to the organizational culture of the U.S. military, the conclusions apply broadly—overall. Naturally still—military and civilian centers must be kept separate.

Cyber activities target IT—information systems, and may involve cyber operations and attacks, hacking, activities against confidentiality, integrity, availability, etc., system disruption, denial, degradation, and destruction.

Activities may be thought of as a more soft approach—not involving hacking, no cyber attack tools used, unless at a stage, which is not to say that effective operations are trivial or unproblematic. It is worth quoting again the U.S. military's definition of propaganda. It is "[a]ny form of communication in support of national objectives *designed to influence the opinions, emotions, attitudes, or behavior* of any group in order to benefit the sponsor, either directly or indirectly."[88]

7.10.1 Continuous conflict

It is possible to speak of a continuous conflict in the cyber and information issue—that is, occurring not only during an armed conflict. Operations may take place below the threshold of war. Proper deployment is, therefore, absolutely crucial (if only to avoid crossing of the thresholds). These are not missile troops, which are naturally—aside from training or parading—reserved for use only during actual war. If such artificial barriers were put up—barring the uses of info or cyber operations when below the threshold of war—cyber and info units would have much more limited use, perhaps even questioning their existence in such a narrow-minded State. To the satisfaction of adversaries with a different approach. It would be a shame to spend taxpayer money on it then.

Therefore, it is not a surprise that military cyber and information units may, must, and are used actively during peacetime, that is—without hostilities. Then, their activities include maintaining and supporting their own forces, situational orientation, detection of adversary activity, incident detection, analysis, investigation, and response to incidents, among others. Also offensive activities—without crossing the thresholds.

Cyber-enabled information warfare is a serious risk[89] in a world where information spreads rapidly and may suddenly find many recipients, for example, through social media, or even traditional media. Imagine that *someone* successfully impersonates the leader of a nuclear State and sends a public message with threats of a nuclear attack.[90] And that *someone who got the message*—takes it seriously, deciding to respond (militarily). Destabilization is done. However, it takes time to determine the veracity or falsity. That is why it is necessary to have analytical units within the State and the military—to detect such actions, or even attempts, to bring them to the attention of state leaders, to publicize them when necessary, and to prevent their dissemination. To disarm them. Especially when the situation is unstable. To rob state services of structures capable of such activities today would be harmful, even diversionary and suicidal for the State. Hence, the concern is justifiable when, during election campaigns, some political parties would take up the banner of cyber security slogans in purely political terms, proclaiming: "Today everything is bad, we must improve by doing everything from scratch." What does that mean? Make everything from the start? That's risky—if one were to really think that way and want to implement it. Although it may be a matter of poetics during elections, it necessarily needs to, or at least should, change during the practicalities of managing the state. And that's fortunate.

7.10.2 Information dominance

Effective control of the information environment, including in the area of enemy territory or systems, makes it possible to achieve information dominance to be able to achieve operational superiority and prevent the enemy from doing so.[91] This explanation comes from American terminology, but similar, analogous, studies are being made for the armed forces of the People's Republic of China.[92] From which it is clear that this is one of the necessities when conducting conflicts—defeating the enemy in the information domain, preventing the enemy from functioning. It is also interesting to note cases where such effects (information dominance) have not been achieved to any extent, as was the case with Russia and the war waged against Ukraine.

Such units should have a strong analytical arm, but also an operational one.

7.11 STRATEGIC COMMUNICATIONS—STRATCOM

States being serious about the sphere of strategic communication establish special *StratCom* (strategic communication) centers. These are structures that monitor incoming information

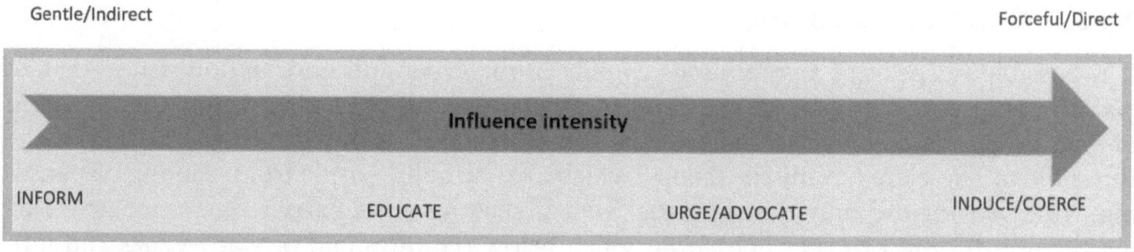

Figure 7.1 Influence spectrum: from subtle and indirect to explicit methods.

Source: Adapted from Department of Defense, *Strategic communications joint integrating concept*, October 7, 2009, https://www.jcs.mil/Portals/36/Documents/Doctrine/concepts/jic_strategic communications.pdf.

and enable consistent, timely responses or even influence. StratCom activities can include PR, advertising, propaganda, information, and partly diplomacy. Such a structure can work in peacetime and can be invaluable during war, directing messages inward (domestically), to the adversary, to allies (externally), via, and to the media, etc. The U.S. Department of Defense's definition, which is "[f]ocused United States Government efforts to understand and engage key audiences to create, strengthen, or preserve conditions favorable for the advancement of United States Government interests, policies, and objectives through the use of coordinated programs, plans, themes, messages, and products synchronized with the actions of all instruments of national power,"[93] describes the role of StratCom well. This is a pretty concise and good definition. Possible actions could be to strengthen one's own messages and weaken hostile ones ("sensitive" propaganda). The related influence spectrum showing varying levels of activities is depicted in Figure 7.1.

7.11.1 StratCom and impact

StratCom is about decoding foreign messages. But it's also about exerting influence. It's the whole spectrum: from sensitive information through persuasion to intimidation and threats.[94] Achieving such effects requires clear and lucid communication. So that the addressee can perceive it, interpret it appropriately, appreciate the seriousness of the situation, and respond accordingly. Preferably in ways expected by the sender of the message. This works most effectively when there are arguments of an appropriate weight, of a certain nature, for example—regarding money, a significant number of weapons like tanks, howitzers, fighter jets and bombers, or even nuclear weapons. It's harder to ignore the voice of someone wielding ballistic missiles with payloads of a few megatons (strategic nuclear weapons, capable of destroying entire cities and neighborhoods) and even kilotons (tactical nuclear weapons).

StratCom should be able to evaluate the effects of its communications. When there is only one sender and one recipient, this can be easy. But what if there are multiple recipients, and they draw information from multiple sources? Then assessing impact (effectiveness) can be more complex. Therefore, depending on the targets, the defined recipients may be, for example, state leaders, media in the target country (or international), influencers, and opinion leaders. They will distribute these signals, albeit in their understanding— so in altered forms. StratCom must be a flexible structure—responding to changes in the environment and even undergoing changes itself. This can be a challenge for State institutions that prefer strict bureaucratic, hierarchical structures. Information is part of exerting influence and power, and with the actions taken beforehand. Some end result (state) is assumed and pursued. They are not unplanned, chaotic, pointless actions.[95]

7.11.2 Operation scheme

For the purposes of efficient narrative construction, the following simplified template of activities can also be adopted according to NATO.[96]

StratCom scheme:

- **Current state**—a description of the issues to be addressed or the desired state to be maintained;
- **Justification**—why the proposed change in the current status quo or maintenance of the status is better than the alternatives—it is the justification for the path taken;
- **The chosen path**—how to reach the end goal;
- **Future state**—description of goals, maintenance of the *status quo* or some kind of change.

Many supporting or identical messages may be built around communications that fit into the points of the StratCom scheme. Nowadays, these can be supported on many levels—politically, internally, such as sending politicians or officials to the media, posting on social media. If this works well, a communication fusion may be attained to reinforce a main message. But I point out: *if it works*. Because it involves people. People may: lack understanding, have their own (hidden?) goals, be unable to communicate, or even cause harm (perhaps intentionally).

An example of a (not very cleverly) arranged narrative from the point of view of 1930s France could look like this:

- Germany is a threat, so we need to do something about it;
- If we do nothing, we are in danger of another invasion, as in World War I;
- So, we will build a wall and a fortified line (Maginot) to prevent the Germans from invading.

Using this narrative, for example, the public may be persuaded to spend money on the defensive effort—but also to build the illusion of state security. As we know from history—to put it mildly—this was not entirely successful, as the Germans bypassed the fortifications by invading through neutral States. It is worth noting that the possibility of bypassing these fortifications was raised publicly in the press long before 1939. So, the problem was elsewhere, certainly not at the narrative level. The problem sat in some offices or staffs. On the chairs. Perhaps previously receiving promotions and appointments.

7.11.3 StratCom levels below

Strategic communications activities can also benefit from the bottom-up activity, by ordinary people able to communicate through contemporary, social media, through individual creativity. This is not a comprehensive, or typical StratCom, but it is possible to have an impact in this way. As was seen in the situation of many crises in the Middle East—when individuals were able to impose an interpretation of certain events and influence their view of them in Western countries, for example.[97] This was the case, for example, in the Syrian crisis in 2011.[98] Such methods have expanded—since then they have been and are being used on a wider scale. Similar attempts seemed to have been made during the 2023 war between Israel and Hamas, although at that time, the flood of bogus or misleading information, photos, and video recordings (e.g., even real but old ones—not current during the events) was considerable, and it was difficult to establish any information distribution centers in the early days of these activities. The problem, then, is at a different level: when one refuses to believe the depicted scenes, even considering the *real ones as fakes*. Or distributing some past scenes unrelated to the events but put in its context. In a situation of sudden developments, this may introduce an element of confusion and even undermine confidence in truthful reports. Verifying such content in a short period of time can be especially difficult. It is not conducive of today's news coverage pace, which is very fast.

This culminates in the use of communication during the war in Ukraine, where any civilian may report on the situation—and even contribute to the imposition of interpretation of events. It is much more difficult, perhaps impossible today to "effectively" hide massacres and genocide. What was possible during World War II and before—when Western governments knew about systemic genocide in occupied terrains but chose to ignore it—would be extremely difficult today. There is greater transparency. It is more difficult to hide such practices. Obviously, we are not complaining about it here. To some extent, this is an "asymmetric" activity—in the sense that information resources are used in ways surprising for a major actor (e.g., the State).[99] Interestingly, however, this apparently came as a surprise to Russia, which was seen as a State that knew how to wage information warfare.

States have caught up a lot in this regard and are able to apply methods of informational influence through modern means of communication. They may always be slightly behind due to a certain inertia, resulting from bureaucratic limitations or personnel approaches. Perhaps there shouldn't be a significant backlog anymore—cyber or info military formations are, after all, a standard. But there is still room for faster development and movement outside of rigid structures, at least for selected States. So one has to take into account that it is not only the role of public opinion in individual States that is important. There are also grassroots activities, even when quasi-organized. We no longer deal with a situation like that of the 19th century, even of World War I or World War II, where military and information state actors played the main, superior, actually unique role.

7.12 STATES AND UNIQUE POWERS—CENSORSHIP AND ABSURDITIES IN NEWSPAPERS DURING WAR

State actors may still have the upper hand where access to information or certain information is lacking. When censorship has been imposed, blockades have been put in place, or there is no access to information for any other reasons. For example, in the case of major events, crises, conflicts, or descriptions unfavorable to the government, various (probably all) States may censor the press, information—even if by granting selective information, confirming, or debunking some statements. An excellent and direct example is the strong censorship of French newspapers during World War I.[100] It is excellent because it is now historical—not prone to debate, interpretations, or denial, unaffected by the current political contexts. Meanwhile, more recent events could be perceived not so much as historical, objective, but political, subject to interpretation, or through the prism of some particular views. The passage of over 100 years since the events seems to limit the field for such interpretations and the events can be treated as purely historical.

7.12.1 France during World War I

During World War I, the French press stood in solidarity with the Nation and agreed to the suspension of press freedom (guaranteed by law decades before). Censorship was often very strict, even absurdly noticeable, as shown in Figure 7.2. In the "Journal des débats politiques et littéraires", an entire article about the situation at the Battle of Verdun was erased—"white-space" is left—and the afternoon edition carried a laconic official government communiqué that "there was some activity in the north" (in fact, it was a huge artillery activity).[101] At other times, single words were cut out, which has the effect that there is a full sentence, but with a white area in the middle of it.

DERNIÈRE HEURE

La Guerre Européenne

COMMUNIQUÉ

Voici le texte du communiqué officiel de cet après-midi :

15 heures

Nuit calme dans toute la région de Verdun.

Une attaque allemande, qui se préparait hier en fin de journée vers nos positions de la côte 304, n'est pas sortie des tranchées.

Les tirs de barrage de notre artillerie et le bombardement dirigé par nos batteries du secteur voisin sur les colonnes ennemies rassemblées dans le bois de Malancourt paraissent avoir fait avorter cette opération.

Aucun événement important à signaler sur l'ensemble du front.

L'Allemagne et les Etats-Unis

La note américaine

Le Conseil des ministres aurait décidé l'envoi à l'Allemagne d'une nouvelle note, sorte d'ultimatum, qui exigerait la cessation immédiate des attaques contre les vaisseaux neutres ou non armés et déclarerait que toute récidive entraînerait *ipso facto* la rupture des relations diplomatiques.

Le Torpillage du "Sussex"

Les faux de la propagande allemande

On sait que la propagande allemande a

néral d'Allemagne à Rotterdam, qui a lancé le bruit d'un ultimatum anglais à la Hollande. »

Le problème alimentaire en Hongrie

(*De notre correspondant particulier*)

Genève, le 13 avril. — Le gouvernement hongrois vient de décider la majoration à des prix maxima pour le maïs, les haricots, les petits pois et les lentilles de la récolte de cette année. Pour les denrées de la récolte précédente, le tarif actuel reste en vigueur.

Cependant ces mesures n'autorisent en rien les personnes possédant des stocks de légumes et de céréales de se soustraire à la réquisition et profiter ainsi des nouvelles dispositions. Les autorités compétentes veilleront à l'observation du présent règlement et s'efforceront de subvenir aux besoins de la consommation. En outre, la récolte de 1916 est frappée de séquestre : défense est faite aux propriétaires fonciers d'en disposer sous peine d'un emprisonnement pouvant s'élever à 6 mois et d'une amende pouvant atteindre 2,000 couronnes.

La santé de Gabriele d'Annunzio

Nous avons eu aujourd'hui même des nouvelles du poète. Condamné à l'immobilité absolue et à l'obscurité depuis quatre semaines, il commençait à aller beaucoup mieux lorsqu'une complication est intervenue.

La guérison, qui semblait devoir être prochaine, est de nouveau reculée. M. d'Annunzio fait preuve de la plus grande patience et du plus grand courage.

Figure 7.2 An example of press censorship. The content of the article has disappeared.

Source: "Journal de débats politiques et littéraires", 14 avril 1916. Public domain; https://gallica.bnf.fr/ark:/12148/bpt6k4859845/f4.item.zoom.

The relevant law allowing strong censorship—*Loi reprimand les indiscretions de la presse en temps de guerre (Law to punish press indiscretions in wartime)*—was introduced on August 5, 1914. It banned information about military activities, mobilizations, etc. Hence, the subsequent emerging public assurances that "*the war would be short*"[102] (it lasted five years). But the fascinating thing about this system is that it involved the press, reporters, and military experts or scholars—all making statements despite their lack of actual knowledge of the actual situation![103]

In public discourse, the enemy was described as "weak," said to be "retreating," "tired," etc. Emblematic is an article from "Le Miroir" of August 23, 1914, under the title *Germany is fighting without conviction*.[104] In August, "La Croix" wrote that an "eyewitness" saw German prisoners of war: "the bewilderment, softness and indifference of the men; the vanity, cruelty and stupidity of the officers, these are the virtues they offer us." On top of this, there were articles about German barbarism, exemplified by the execution of prisoners of war, about the German army being inefficient and obsolete (again, "La Croix"),[105] the artillery being poor, shooting inaccurately, etc. All this five years before the end of the war. On the other hand, on December 20, 1914, the cover of "Le Petit journal" showed the execution of a spy, as a reminder that it is not worth betraying the homeland. Other covers demonized the German Kaiser, depicted the Germans as arsonists of the countryside (it's another matter that they actually leveled cities, such as Leuven), etc.

By the way, France introduced a similar law on August 27, 1939, a few days before the outbreak of World War II.[106] The relevant and specialized legal provisions were passed in early 1938 and 1939. They had a good sense of what was going on, didn't they? The French ambassador, after all, had been sounding the alarm throughout 1939 about Germany getting along with Soviet Russia. He was ignored.

On September 2, 1939, the French newspaper *Le Grand Écho du Nord de France* reported on the German aggression against Poland and the mobilization of France and Great Britain, and the bombing of many Polish cities—Warsaw, Krakow, Gdynia, Vilnius, and Grodno. On September 3, the same newspaper reported on Polish military actions—the destruction of 33 aircraft, 16 tanks, and the taking of prisoners of war. On September 17, this newspaper considered "hypotheses" about the intervention of the USSR: will it enter the war with Germany, or will it occupy the territories of eastern Poland? On September 19, there was already a mention of "the fight of the Polish soldier against the Russian-German invader."

7.12.2 September 1939—Poland, the first victim of World War II

All this seems to have been trumped by the content directed to the public of the country attacked in September 1939. At the beginning of World War II, the military-controlled press directed pure success propaganda to the public—including assurances about the bombing of Berlin. How did the Polish press write about it? Here are examples from September 1939: reflections on whether Germany would rebel against the war, and the optimistic reports themselves, such as "After panic and fright, gloom in Berlin—Reich Capital bombed by English, French, and Polish squadrons" (It didn't happen). On September 7, 1939, French and English troops supposedly captured "all bridges over the Rhine" (German). In reality, they did not cross the border. So, how was it in reality? Well, the war lasted until 1945 and then came the decades of communism. What was the purpose of this propaganda? To maintain the spirit of the nation and the soldiers, of course. Some might add that perhaps it was helpful in maintaining a certain social order, to enable the immediate evacuation of high politicians and military command—and conducting defense to the very end. Such propaganda activities lead nowhere. Another handful from newspaper articles: "The experts calculate that four more days will be needed for complete control … Only then will it be possible to launch a lightning offensive. The army will not give up Warsaw!", "Everything the Germans preach is nonsense and falsehood." This was false information—propaganda. What is shocking today is the massiveness of this phenomenon, which probably covered most if not all of the media. The public at the time could not verify any of this information—there was a lack of the kind of access to information that we have today. Today, it would unlikely work this way.

Perhaps similar was the case of Iraqi government spokesman Mohammed Saeed al-Sahhaf when U.S. troops were already approaching Baghdad in 2003. He memorably claimed that U.S. soldiers were "committing suicide by the hundreds." One may laugh, but that was his job, and apparently he did it to the very end. When the U.S. tanks were just a few miles away from his office.

When the law allows for control of the means of information, then the exclusive right to provide information is given to whoever has access to it: state structures, the military, or possibly private structures with access to satellite imaging, etc.

7.12.3 Breakthrough of modern times—satellite imaging

It is satellites that may give further impetus to such asymmetric actions—widespread access to satellite Internet (such as through the Starlink system) means limiting the ability of States to impose information isolation. This is because access to information means the inability to impose a "single, reference version" of events. In the past, States were able to impose one particular point of view. When this is not the case, "strategic communication" is only one of many methods or parties conducting communication. Just one of many.

This genie, luckily, has been let out of the bottle, and this process will not be reversed. Cat is out of the box, and it won't be put back in it. However, is it really for the good? Which is better? It depends on one's point of view, whether one is a city dweller (civilian), a policymaker, or a military commander.

Precisely as with many other processes that have taken place over previous centuries and could not be reversed, neither can this one. However, this may be a challenge for States in a situation of conflict or crisis, when there is a need to establish one version of events, and various speculations could destabilize the situation and lead in the wrong direction.

7.13 CONTENT DELIVERY

Any method of delivering information can aid in spreading propaganda. So it's radio, television, leaflets, newspapers,[107] billboards, posters, word-of-mouth, rumors, and writing on walls, social media, and never-ending streams of information on news sites of choice, including those of poor quality. While before the battles of the early 19th century, the voice of a leader like Napoleon spread in a limited way (audible perhaps by soldiers in divisions only physically near to the speaker),[108] later, loudspeakers and radio have completely transformed the possibilities of reaching an audience. Napoleon could be heard by a division. Hitler, 100 years after him—by every soldier and citizen (radio). However, it's still similar content, although accessible to a mass audience.

What could be next? Social media has enabled a whole new quality—precisely reaching a specific person. Micro-targeting can become a tool in the information warfare.[109] Not a weapon. A tool. Just like flyers. With generative techniques (AI), it will also be possible to create content precisely created and tailored for a specific audience, not just for some target group. This will be a shift from creating content for thousands, hundreds, and dozens—to content for individuals. Unprecedented in world history.

7.13.1 Leaflet bombs

Armed activities like bombardment during the Korean War—and many others—were accompanied by the dropping of propaganda leaflets from planes.[110] One has to be careful of local cultural or religious sensibilities with this approach. For example, when the military dropped leaflets printed with peaceful quotations from the Quran, societies may have considered it blasphemy because the holy verses, touching the ground, could be stained.[111] Leaflets? Nowadays, you might consider this an outdated method—there is the Internet, after all. Sure, there is the Internet. As long as one has access to network—or electricity, and during wars, power plants and electricity distribution centers also became targets.

We are familiar with leaflets urging people to vote for a particular candidate or political party or advertising products. Leaflets have long been used in warfare. For example, during World War I, leaflets were dropped by the Italian army on Austro-Hungarian troops.[112] Flyers can also be used, for example, to urge civilians to take certain actions, such as leaving areas where military operations are to be conducted, as has been done on many occasions, most recently during Israel's 2023 war with Hamas. Propaganda may try to convince the audience to see a way of reasoning (like calling for resistance), and direct it also to the soldiers of the enemy side (calling for surrender). This has been used for decades. Since leaflets in military operations may be necessary, it may be worthwhile to improve the process of delivering them.

Leaflet dropping can be done with special bombs. The U.S. Army stocks 52-kilogram leaflet bombs M129E1, M129E2, M129E2 (100-kilogram when loaded), PDU-5/B—and they can hold up to about 300,000 standard-size leaflets.[113] The leaflets are rolled; there are dozens of rolls, stacked side by side. These are placed in a tube and then in a bomb. The drop is followed by a swarm of leaflets. These, falling, may form clouds that take on various geometries depending on the wind.[114] Such bombs can be dropped from B-52 Stratofortress strategic bombers. Leaflet dropping can also occur from lower altitudes, from turboprop aircraft or from helicopters. These activities can also be combined with armed attacks. For example, kinetic bombs are dropped first, causing shock and destruction. Then, bombers are sent with leaflets saying something like "Well, how was that? You just experienced *<type of weapon used>*. It will be back soon. Perhaps you prefer to surrender?" Of course, the same can be done through other channels, such as radio.

7.13.2 Unmasking the leaders of hostile States

In a campaign against the morale of soldiers or civilians of an enemy State, one can talk of negative actions of their leaders—about the scams, corruption thievery, etc., including their ineffectiveness in wartime. Thus, BBC radio communicated to the Germans:

> And now, about Goebbels. ... You know that modest way of his? This probably accounts for the fact that he has told you too little about his castle ... on the Bergensee, the walls of which are decorated with marble, and also a country house ... on the Langensee, and also a 50-room mansion in Berlin. ...
>
> Similar opulence was charged against Goering, Himmler, Ley and Ribbentrop, who, it was alleged, were making a rather broad interpretation of the Lebensraum slogan.[115]

In wars, chain letter scams were also used. They consisted of sending letters that were supposed to ward off harmful future mischief or bad luck, but only if one addressed the same ones to many people. During World War II, such paper letters were sent. And it was also a vehicle for propaganda or simply disrupting the functioning of systems: such activities take up people's time, and also hinder the work of the postal service.[116] The U.S. military of modern times, for example, knows this, as well as the European Commission do—only that today e-mails are sent.[117] What to do to avoid spreading such paralysis? It's simple: don't forward them!

7.14 MILITARY INFORMATION OPERATIONS

Military propaganda has many roles to play, among them are control of opinion within one's own State, control of opinion in allied States, control of opinion of neutral (or impartial) States, control of enemy opinion, counterpropaganda, and counteraction.[118,119]

An exemplary approach would be the deliberate positive shaping of attitudes of the public toward war, convincing it of its justice, and leaving the impression that everything is going smoothly.[120] This is propaganda of optimism, while at the same time undermining the morale of the enemy, that is, promoting pessimism, even defeatism in them. In this case, one can even check the quality and effects of such propaganda, if only by questioning prisoners of war. When a State loses, its military and society become more susceptible to propaganda.[121]

Today, much of such activity follows people on social media. Digital platforms, however, may not want to be such an information battle arena. The U.S. military, for example, has found this out the hard way, with psychological activities targeting audiences in Afghanistan, Algeria, Iran, Iraq, Kazakhstan, Kyrgyzstan, Russia, Somalia, etc.[122] detected and publicized by Twitter and Facebook platforms in 2022.[123] Messages sent via Russian social networks (e.g., VKontakte) were also used. Such activities included, for example, posts with anti-Russian narratives, arguing, for instance, about the "imperialist" nature of the war against Ukraine.[124] This was done through specially prepared fake persona accounts. As a Pentagon spokesman put it, information operations support U.S. priorities. Not surprisingly, States are conducting such operations. However, one must be careful not to get caught. This is, therefore, not just limited to China and Russia. The revelation of French information operations, or more specifically, the actions of the French military directed at exerting influence in Africa (Central African Republic, Mali, Burkina Faso, Niger, Algeria, Chad, etc.) and the Middle East is another. In doing so, the units competed with analogous Russian information operation. Finding this out and publicizing has also had a great impact.[125] There were even situations where "information operators" interacted by commenting on each other's posts. That is, operators of one side were "talking" to operators of the other side.

The United States paid ($540 million to a PR firm) for activities supporting its own operations in Iraq, and targeting al-Qaeda.[126] It is hardly surprising to support one's own military operations, although such an amount for an outside PR firm seemed large at the time. In fact, it was one of the costliest PR operations of those years (2007–2011). The PR firm's employees also worked on the ground, taking part in psychological operations. It required several hundred people locally in Iraq. The work created messages targeting al-Qaeda, as well as false content that could be attributed to al-Qaeda. CDs with the materials were deliberately left during U.S. military raids on homes.[127] Someone would later review the CDs and execute the planted content. Because they contained tracking elements, it was possible (for the military) to determine the approximate location of where someone was viewing such content.

7.15 DECODING PROPAGANDA BEFORE AND DURING THE WAR

Vladimir Putin's essay[128] published in the summer of 2021 has caught the attention of historians and political science researchers. It contains a certain vision of the past, as well as such theses: "what Ukraine will be—it is up to its citizens to decide."[129] Is that so? Because it was also written that "true sovereignty of Ukraine is possible only in partnership with Russia."[130] In February 2022, Putin gave a speech that, in retrospect, can be considered an ideological primer for the coming war.

Can conclusions be drawn from events and propaganda information about ongoing (and upcoming), political and military decisions? Perhaps yes, although this would require careful and insightful analysis, while determining effectiveness would not be obvious. In how many cases would the correct conclusion be drawn? In how many would it be false? This is quite a problem, because to be meaningful and useful, analysis and conclusions must be justified and preferably somehow verifiable. During World War II, for example, U.S. services tried to draw conclusions from German propaganda[131] intended to indicate future developments. This can make sense, because with propaganda, one can shape the information space and conclusions of the audience, for example, to prepare the audience for hardships and defeats or upcoming actions,[132]—that is, to "handle" in advance, pre-emptively, failures and successes in the military or political fields. In this way, one may limit losses by causing incoming information not to appear suddenly, to prepare recipients to receive it. It is also possible, of course, to blame some event or person in this way, and for the societies or armies of the enemy—to mask the coming actions.[133] Reading up on such material may allow the other side to draw conclusions, too.

In an analysis of media information since the early 1900s, it is also clear that before the outbreak of war, there was a significant increase in media coverage of military affairs, war, and conflict—information influx. In the case of World War II, this increase was noticeable as early as 1935.[134] Predicting the future is difficult. Some have made analytical predictions on conflicts likely to occur by 2050 (one of the valuable indicators is the State's population dynamic),[135] and not at all with the help of a glass ball but mathematical models. Sometimes, in the case of conflicts and wars, it was possible to predict them[136] (if retrospectively). We won't get into such predictions here, but it indicates the potential of interpreting information to draw general conclusions about conflicts of various scales. How? For example by inspecting certain media of choice for the appearance of certain pre-defined keywords. Counting these, somehow normalizing, finding proper metrics, and drawing conclusions. Signals of impending events may be residing or emerging somewhere.

7.15.1 The transmitted message must be received

Speaking of signals—according to the Royal United Services Institute report on Russia's actions in Ukraine in 2022, it was noted that Russia may not be capable of reading subtle signals, such as NATO sending fighters with certain armaments, in a certain configuration.[137] These signals may be overlooked, and this is no laughing matter, but an important problem. If one side wants to send a signal to the other side, it only makes sense if the other side receives the signal. When this does not occur—there is no communication. There are no effective information signals then—military, propaganda, deterrence—none. Moreover, if the party sending the signal is convinced that it was received (interpreted), and it was not, analytical errors, miscalculations, misunderstandings, and mistakes may occur. It's important to be able to correctly assess incoming information and to keep in mind the possibility of mistakes in judgment.

This is especially important in situations of tension and instability, such as the activity near Kaliningrad (Königsberg)[138] and the so-called Suwalki Gap—potential crisis spots in Russia-NATO relations. This should also include sending and receiving signals during the artificially provoked Belarusian migration crisis in 2021, when significant Belarusian and Polish forces were near the border—as such situations are potential conflict hotspots.[139] At the time, potential violations of the NATO border occurred there, According to reports, including by armed individuals, potentially by officers of the Belarusian State. There was simulated shooting and flashing with laser beams there.

7.16 ATROCITY PROPAGANDA

Once a war is underway, internal as well as external influence may be exerted through propaganda methods—including influence impacts on external countries, allied ones, and neutral ones. One of the historically (not only that) used methods is atrocity propaganda,[140] that is, propaganda efforts encompassing the publication of crimes and atrocities committed by aggressors against civilians, for instance. One of the functions of *atrocity propaganda* may be to spread fear (offensive side). The other is to strengthen the fighting spirit and defense of the defensive side and the civilian population. The World War I era dates as the source of the widespread use of this method. At that time (and since then), the use of this technique was widespread.[141]

The following definition of the term is worth quoting. Atrocity propaganda involves the "reports of cruel or shocking acts, circulated widely, and intended to produce an inappropriate martial response" (political, military).[142] So, for instance, spreading of content like shocking images, videos, depictions, stories. Using such material may aim to cause a reaction or influence opinion. This is a method that appeals to the emotions of the audience. Especially today, when everyone has access to current information (verified, unverified; including raw content), and information spreads quickly—it can be especially effective in influencing the audience (e.g., public opinion). These, in turn, may put significant pressure on decision makers in their own States, to either put a stop to it (in some ways), provide support, or take action directly—such as by funding aid or even joining an armed conflict, through an intervention.

Is the use of this method in defensive ways to impact domestic and external parties ethical? That is beside the point. One cannot be surprised that an attacked State uses all means or methods of influence for defensive purposes. Even when at times we may see similar deliberately made manifestations of the uses of such propaganda methods today—it should not be surprising. Remember: the attacked State has a well-defined goal: to defend itself. Outside assistance may be necessary for such a cause. Such actions can also assist later investigations to establish issues such as crimes against humanity, genocide (in the strict, legal meaning), etc. Hence, quasi-public records of actions (to limit ourselves to contemporary conflicts; similar may be identified in many other wars during the 20th century) in Syria, the Republic of Congo, or Ukraine are understandable and could even be helpful. Propaganda of atrocities, in some form, might accompany just about any armed conflict. There is no lack of historical evidence. Russian brutality has been described more than once in history as an "invasion of Asian hordes," and the such, which from the perspective of 2022–2023 remains understood. Such descriptions may have been shocking to an unaccustomed viewer based in Western regions at the time, where governments are scrupulous in taking down some forms of brutal depictions, calling them "terrorist content" or "hate content" or such. So were the situations in 2022 and 2023, but at least at times the content trimming appears to have been put on hold.

If such modes of communication affect political and society audiences, all the better for the purposes of that information campaign.

It should already be clear to the Reader of this book that if something is described as propaganda or such methods are in use, it does not necessarily equate with things being untrue, or correspond to any moral valuation. I must emphasize this again—specifically in this subsection on atrocity propaganda. Spreading content is not necessarily involving the categories of truth and falsehood. However, it must be admitted that sometimes such methods use simplifications, overload certain legal terms, or even omit certain facts. For example, when hospitals or churches are or have been used for military purposes, they cease to be viewed (if they were so at all in the first place) by the belligerent side as sanctuaries to be spared or protected. Furthermore, their destruction may even be used in propaganda for defensive purposes. For a perverse argument, let's consider the positioning of military supplies (including ammunition) at or near churches by Nazi Germany forces in 1944 in such a way as to make them targets for attack by approaching Russian troops. Then, Germany can direct a message to its military and civilian citizens about the "exceptional barbarism" of Russia, which deliberately attacks such facilities—disseminating messages that Russians then don't even spare faith sanctuaries, like churches, perhaps hospitals. Without adding that little detail about the fact that the object in question was in fact used for military purposes by the "spreader of the later messages"—effectively making it a military target. The Reader should reflect here on the cynicism of using such methods deliberately—the audience typically lacks full context and may be faced solely with that part of the object becoming bombarded. Such lines may work until the details and context about them are revealed—then they may even result in losses to the party engaging in such actions, including potential loss of credibility.

Verification by bystanders may be very difficult during wars, as access to independent, information may be impossible. Controlling information and shaping reception can support military objectives. But a different thing is that some mobilized soldiers may not exactly be of greatest moral qualities, so some soldiers may also be "interested" in plundering and stealing for their own use, harvesting the spoils of war, and looting. The responsibility then falls on the armed forces and the State having control over them.

Atrocity propaganda functioned most effectively in a situation of total state control over the media—with no so-called other-side perspective or the possibility of verifying facts. Returning to the placement of military materials next to churches during World War II—awareness of these facts was probably only limited to the people in the direct area at the time. The message, on the other hand, was directed more broadly, and on a wider scale. Those located far off simply could not verify it—regardless of whether they accepted it or not, they still got the message.

Atrocity propaganda is a particular, specific field of application. There are many flavors of propaganda. Let's mention them here: enlightenment propaganda, despair propaganda, partisan propaganda, revolutionary propaganda, integration propaganda, agitation propaganda, sociological propaganda, political propaganda, vertical propaganda, and horizontal propaganda.[143] These are mentioned elsewhere in this book, even when not by formal names—as this is not necessary. The German National Socialist Party (NSDAP) used atrocity propaganda to terrorize the German public and get them to support the invasion of Poland, starting World War II.[144] An element of this was the Gleiwitz Incident, that is, a sham "attack on Germany" (feigned attack, under a false flag) carried out by German SS officers dressed in uniforms of Polish soldiers. This was one of the events that built acquiescence for the war in German society—by creating a situation where sober judgment could be suspended. This was publicized at the Nuremberg trial, and one member of the groups of people responsible for that, the group of German soldiers (Alfred Helmut Naujocks), confessed to the mystification.[145] Evidence of alleged (untrue) attacks by Poles on Germans was also fabricated, using the bodies of German concentration camp convicts who had been killed—to show the "bodies" to the foreign press as "evidence." On September 1, Hitler accused Poland of committing these acts and decided to "respond" to them.[146] Thus, a pretext was created. Today, the knowledge of this falsehood is broadly available and clear—it is common knowledge. However, prior to September 1, 1939, it did not have to be so, for example, for the Germans. Attempts at similar justifications were made many times in future conflicts or wars, and even in our not-so-distant past.

Prior or during World War II, making fun of leaders of enemy States was also practiced. Specifically, of Adolf Hitler. Films were made, and radio productions were prepared, to name a famous film with Charlie Chaplin, "The Dictator." This led to a debate as to whether it was appropriate to laugh at war activities. After all, wars are fraught with atrocities.[147] In the case of the war in Ukraine, there is a general consensus: it is not only appropriate but even necessary to laugh at the leaders and decision makers of enemy States.

7.17 USE OF INTERNATIONAL TREATIES IN PROPAGANDA—THE CASE OF RUSSIA

States may conduct propaganda activities via their diplomatic services arms.[148] Against this background, the 2020s case of Russia attempting to use international disarmament treaties to target propaganda information is very interesting. In Russian terminology, it is predicted that in the 21st century, information confrontation will be one of the main fields of interstate rivalry,[149] and an important tool of information warfare may be the spread of false information about radiological, biological, and chemical threats.[150] In this sense, information activities can be carried out at many levels and by many state structures. One manifestation of such conduct could be the policy at the level of the United Nations, where Russia is a member of the UN Security Council. Disarmament and arms control treaties are a great asset—they introduce an element of stability in the case of weapons such as nuclear, biological, and chemical. The related treaties are signed by many States (parties to them). The treaties typically provide for a mechanism for consultation when one of the parties develops doubts, concerns, or desires to present information signaling a kind of threat.

Can it be that Russia is in fact treating their opinions about information operations as a prescription—not precaution—as a playbook for conducting activities? Because exactly these mechanisms were used by the Russian Federation in the course of hostilities against Ukraine. Recognized mechanisms under the Biological, Chemical, Radiological Weapons Convention were used. So, it was done in the most formal mode possible.

7.17.1 Exploiting Biological Weapons Convention

Article 5 of the Biological Weapons Convention,[151] which defines the consultation and cooperation mechanism, reads:

> The States Parties to this Convention undertake to consult one another and to co-operate in solving any problems which may arise in relation to the objective of, or in the application of the provisions of, the Convention. Consultation and co-operation pursuant to this Article may also be undertaken through appropriate international procedures within the framework of the United Nations and in accordance with its Charter.

The provisions are clear. Consult and cooperate on "*any problems*." These *problems* are to be signaled by the signatories to the Convention, and the rest of the signatories must listen to them with seriousness. Moreover, according to Article VI of that convention:

> Any State Party to this Convention which finds that any other State Party is acting in breach of obligations deriving from the provisions of the Convention may lodge a complaint with the Security Council of the United Nations. Such a complaint should include all possible evidence confirming its validity, as well as a request for its consideration by the Security Council.

Now about the exploitation of the Convention. According to Russian documents filed in 2022, the United States was allegedly funding 30 weapons development centers in Ukraine. Developments on weapons that could supposedly be carried by animals and insects such as bats and mosquitoes. It was even claimed that Ukrainian drones with canisters for spraying biological pathogens were intercepted.[152] Furthermore, this was juxtaposed with a (real) 2015 U.S. patent for an "unmanned aerial vehicle for aerial release of infected mosquitoes,"[153] building such a multi-tiered theory on some supposedly credible elements.

7.17.2 What needs to be done? What has been done?

Since it became evident that Russia is building "stories" and narratives about alleged Ukrainian attempts to create or use biological, chemical, and radiological weapons—it may sound very serious. If it is considered that a State is making such allegations seriously, someone may credibly consider that this may be (later) used for some kind of action, such as military, large-scale, even unprecedented. It may be used to "respond." What to do about it, then? Diplomats of Western States had no doubt: one must act. The stories must not be ignored with hopes of the situation magically resolving itself—the process left to itself may lead to aggravation. It is necessary to address the arguments, rebut and refute them, and put forward one's own arguments—strongly point out that this is a fabrication and there is no basis for taking such "consultation" materials seriously. Indeed, for some States it was too much. Typically, firm language is not used in diplomatic settings, but UK diplomacy sent a strong message of the kind: "we've had enough," and "how much more of this can we take." It stated outright that Russia was instrumentalizing provisions and mechanisms in (biological) arms control treaties, misusing them, and directing unbelievable and unfounded accusations to Ukraine or the United States.[154] Russia has also been accused of presenting public documents and content from the online encyclopedia Wikipedia—as evidence or valid information corroborating the accusations. Similarly, the United Kingdom and France (i.e., two countries on the UN Security Council) issued a joint communiqué that the alleged allegations of preparing dirty bombs (radiological weapons) were unfounded,[155] and that they were nonsense. A communiqué with similar overtones, a response to a letter with questions containing the claims,[156] was put forward by the United States[157] and the relevant United Nations commission.[158]

Propaganda-wise, however, the material such as the one Russia produced and put forward itself, may have tangible potential for uses. This is because regardless of whether anyone accepts it externally (like in the UN meetings), it can still be "truthfully" reported in the domestic media (i.e., Russian in this case), or allied States, and perhaps it may still also reach people in other countries, like the neutral ones. The story is partly based on truthful elements in the sense that the process within the UN mechanism actually happened, at least diplomatically, "formally." Even if it may be considered diplomatic trolling.

The public and typical citizens, such as social media users, have no way to verify the claims of either side. That's why it may be so serious. It may sound more serious than the absurd claims about Ukrainian testing of specifics allegedly to transform their soldiers into mutants (lines propagated in Russian media at a time in 2022), or attempts to use "combat mosquitoes" to carry biological weapons. Let's leave aside the details propagated by the Russian military command—unmanned drones to be used in the transportation of mosquitoes. Still, at the same time, this was mixed with the truth, as Russia's defense minister actually warned of disease-carrying mosquitoes that allegedly could multiply at the site of the blown-up dam on the Dnieper river. Still, as the Norwegian representative in the United Nations put it: this was a theater of disinformation. The Albanian representative called it "Security Council information about nothing." In general, to Russia's disappointment, there was no desire to continue the conversation on this issue. The Security Council rejected Russia's request to establish a commission to study the issue—Russia and China were in favor.[159] This was likely the most exciting happening regarding the Biological Weapons Convention, because aside from such informational fireworks—believe me—the framework and the related process is really boring.

Similar (insinuating) accusations have been made before, in 2013,[160] and actually in some forms even in the 1950s.[161] They could be considered part of a political "operation"—but I advise against using the word "combat" or "warfare" here, though enthusiasts of the phrase "hybrid warfare" would classify it into just such activities. Returning to the activities—it's another operation with elements that could even be justified in some ways before 2014, and still—before 2022. Such political methods can discredit the target in the eyes of other states, their citizens, and others. Undoubtedly, propaganda can be "pulled up," and classified under the framework of "hybrid tactics."

Similar accusations have been made against the U.S. laboratories in Georgia.[162] As is well known, Russia was also militarily involved in Georgia. This is emerging as a consistent, deliberate, and repetitive political propaganda tactic, in use below the threshold of war as well as in contexts of operations above the threshold. In view of this, it may be reasonable to expect a similar nature of accusations, charges, and insinuations against other States that may fall within the Russian Federation's scope of interest. This can be considered a yardstick, an indicator, or a signal. States should prepare responses. The use of multilateral mechanisms, including disarmament or arms control treaties or the treaties on the control of dangerous weapons for this, is a kind of "innovation."

7.18 WAR IN UKRAINE

7.18.1 The beginning—information activities toward Georgia and Ukraine

Russia has a rich "tradition" of using propaganda and information warfare—one that dates back to the communist and even tsarist era.[163] Such methods were involved during the annexation of Crimea in 2014, preceding the event, and during the following actions. For a number of reasons, the Western world was receptive—susceptible—to such "informational" framing of the issue. Perhaps it was thought that it was better not to mention it and hope that the issue would resolve itself? Informationally, Russian channels began accusing Georgia and Ukraine of committing "genocidal" acts and abusing this legal term as early as the beginning of the 21st century.[164] Since then, there may have been a kind of permanent, or continuous conflict,[165] and even attempts to create the impression of the occurrence of a kind of *bellum omnium contra omnes*[166] (Latin phrase for: war of all against all). With a key role in information activities, carried out through various channels: state, media, and, when they were created, online, including through social media. Informational use continued to be made of real (or not) events, tailored to the accepted theses—and so they were reported.

7.18.1.1 Dehumanization and denial of statehood

Materials with dehumanizing content have been broadcast for a long time (not just since 2022) as have assertions that Ukraine is "part of the Russian world" (or even that it does not exist as a State).[167] This was more widely recognized in the West only in and after 2022. Understanding the totality of this complex matter is beyond the scope of this book.

It may be difficult to determine in what proportions the recipients of such content were to be Russian-speaking residents of Ukraine (including those based in Lithuania, Estonia, and

Latvia), and in what proportions Russian citizens. Where, then, does the truth lie? This is not an appropriate framing.

Informational impact led to intensification of activities.

7.18.2 Pre-invasion situation (2022)

The Russian invasion of Ukraine in 2022 is the first high-intensity armed conflict in a long time. Information issues have played and are playing a key role in it. It's not just about cyber attacks on information systems, security breaches, hacking, and paralyzing systems.[168] But these also comprise interesting activities conducted before and during the war. Arguably, they will be conducted after the war ends.

7.18.2.1 Recordings of traveling depots with weapons visible to anyone

Before the war began, the initiative in the information layer was almost entirely outside Ukraine. A "historical essay"[169] was published (its authorship attributed to Vladimir Putin) basically justifying that, in essence, Ukraine is part of Russia, and there are virtually no differences between the peoples of Russia and Ukraine.

The troop surge in the spring of 2022 was clearly noticeable, through satellite imaging, but also social media videos, although such cases had occurred in earlier years. However, this one was exceptionally huge, taking place on a large scale. Importantly, this arms transfer was noted, almost live, via publicly available videos on the Internet, and on social media (Telegram, TikTok). There were traveling train sets with a huge number of military equipment of various kinds—missile launchers, tanks, etc. It must have been impressive. None of these weapon depots were covered with a tarp or anything; none were camouflaged. It was as if the goal was to create an opportunity for them to be seen, recorded on film, and for the material to be published. This is a huge information pressure, even if unintentional.

7.18.2.2 U.S. disarms pretext-potential with early warning of what may approach

Information pressure was also exerted by Western countries, led by the U.S. intelligence determined that war could occur. From late October and early November, it passed this information to the European governments, met with skepticism by some of them (who refused to accept it). The information eventually surfaced to the public and to the societies. In this way, Russia's attack lost the element of surprise, the information release pre-empted a possible foray with "being attacked" (and the "need to defend" in "response"). Everyone saw what was happening. Everyone knew what was coming—perhaps except those few policymakers in selected capital cities in Europe.

7.18.2.3 Russian diplomatic ultimatum—NATO to turn back the clock to 1997

But prior to military moves, Russia upped the ante diplomatically—giving the West an ultimatum so that NATO would retreat to the pre-1997 lines. That is, to the situation before the Central and Eastern Europeans joined the NATO alliance. And that it would guarantee NATO's permanent push back from Russia's borders—that is, also the non-admission of Ukraine to NATO (although Ukraine had previously declared no such intentions).

7.18.2.4 Television speech

Vladimir Putin repeated the theses from the "historical essay" shortly before the invasion, in a televised speech. Informationally important was the so-called meeting of Russia's Security Council, where Putin briefed members of the government and heads of the security forces, "asking" on "what should be done." This was a signal sent internally but also clearly noted externally. The theatre has been televised internationally, and covered live.

From today's perspective, it may be concluded that these signals led directly to war. Although they didn't have to—if the war hadn't happened, we would draw different conclusions. That's just the way it is. And that's that for geopolitical analysis based on limited sources. What matters are the facts, and the facts are that the war happened, and the assessments of "unlikely," "likely," or "very likely" got to be verified. After the event, everyone is wiser and everyone can tell each other what they did or didn't predict beforehand.

7.18.3 Prelude to the armed conflict—cyber and information operations

A prime example is the cyber operation activity prior to the intensification of the armed conflict in Ukraine in January 2022. At the time, a series of Ukrainian websites were hacked, including government websites. Some of the sites had an image inserted with specifically crafted content in three languages. Content perhaps intended to play up historical resentments between the societies of Poland and Ukraine (in connection with true historical issues in the 1940s). This image is shown in Figure 7.3.

The content in Polish language reads like this (with spelling errors due to machine translation):

> *Ukrainian! All your personal information has been uploaded to a common network. All data on your computer is destroyed, it cannot be recovered. All information about you has become public, be afraid and wait for the worst. This is for you for your past, present and future. For Volhynia, for the [OUN-UPA] Ukrainian Insurgent Army, Galicia, Polesie and for the historical territories.*

An attentive reader could notice that this was not a text written by a person whose native language is Polish. It seems obvious that this text was machine-translated, such as in an online translator. The Polish text accompanies texts in Ukrainian and Russian—aimed at the Ukrainian public. This is one of the activities of Operation Ghostwritter,[170] associated with a Belarusian actor (UNC11511), which undertakes such actions targeting Central and Eastern European countries in the context of these events.

If increase of resentment was the goal, then it didn't work. Polish society welcomed war refugees with open arms, Poland supported Ukraine in a humanitarian manner, economically and militarily. But that's not the end of the story, information-wise. The picture contained metadata. Someone (behind the operation) must have put that data there. The image itself was manipulated to contain artificially added information potentially pointing to the location (GPS: 52.208630, 21.009427) of the Polish General Staff (of the Armed Forces) in Warsaw.[171] Coincidence? Definitely not. This is just an additional, less obvious, element of the information payload in this message. As if someone attempted to draw attention to the Polish military, or perhaps even try to blame Polish army on this operation, or send a signal to Poland—the intention is not clear. But such signaling may be seen as consistent with other information elements in the war—like the insinuation that Poland would allegedly send troops to occupy western Ukraine, and others.

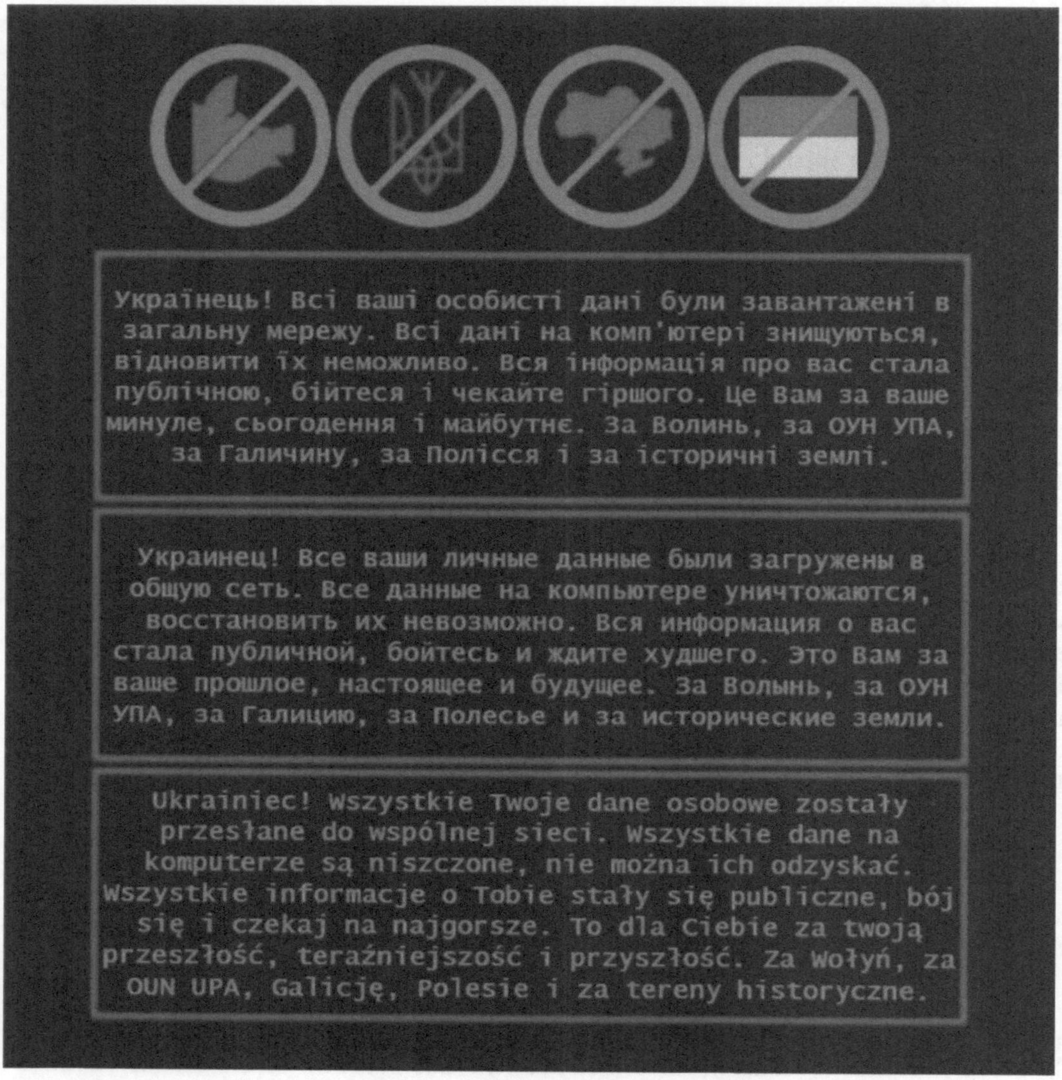

Figure 7.3 Message inserted on hacked Ukrainian sites in January 2022. Text in three languages (Russian, Ukrainian, Polish—machine translated with spelling errors).

Source: Author's private archive.

Very curiously, but unfortunately, it so happened that some major Western media outlets, more specifically the *Financial Times*,[172] had difficulty correctly weighing, analyzing, and perceiving the incident and the informational content. Specifically, the article covering the event contained the paragraph: "It was not immediately clear if the hackers were Polish or if this was an attempt to incite divisions between Ukraine and Poland, one of Kyiv's strongest European allies in the face of Russian aggression."[173] A rather unfortunate point. I must point out that I have a full understanding of the needs of the media to give voice to multiple sides, to present different points of view. Really. However, giving credence and making available to the public, without any commentary, communications from potential perpetrators of later military aggression as a "party to the dispute" (what party? who is the other party? military services?), perhaps coming from the military intelligence of a State planning a major armed aggression, sounds a bit eccentric. So, it's a representation of Ukraine's rationale on the one hand, and a potential (in January 2022) aggressor on the other. I leave this to the judgment of the Reader.

The signal sent in the posted graphic on the hacked websites indeed touched on history and played up resentments between Poland and Ukraine. Hard and difficult facts, historical events. In this case, however, the crux of the matter lies entirely elsewhere. Given that Poland is the *de facto* distribution center (hub) for aid to Ukraine, through which aid from the West (military, humanitarian) flows, the gravity of the issue increases significantly. An attempt to inject negative information or narratives early on—perhaps to sow divisions, or reinforce them—may have been one of the goals. Or at least it cannot be excluded. I have pointed this out publicly several times.

Fortunately, the above content was later removed from the said article. Very well. And at this point, the editors and authors at the *Financial Times* are to be commended for this subsequent change. However, in the future, accounts with large numbers of followers or large media outlets with significant audiences should be wary of such risks of being instrumentalized in attempts at military-style information operations. There is also an upside. Some journalists, like those of French "Le Monde," remained cautious, reliably covering the event.[174]

In the described case, the use of the term "information warfare" can be justified by the fact that, around a month later, military operations were intensified. A war erupted.

7.18.4 Fog of war, information blockade—attention to erroneous conclusions

The reality of this war is brutal and aggressive. But from the beginning, it was also being broadcast around the world in an unprecedented manner. Sometimes even "live." Both sides, Ukraine and Russia, published multimedia records (videos) showing military operations, material naturally often prepared in specific ways. Since the beginning, Ukraine has been conducting information operations—like publishing videos,[175] which showed the successful destruction of enemy vehicles and units. They depicted the dropping of grenades and the use of drones. There were so many of them that some Western observers (journalists, analysts, ex-military) even committed a collective analytical error at a time, concluding that this is what a modern war would look like, even sometimes assuming that drones are so forward-looking and effective, that armored troops (like tanks) are losing or have even lost their reason for existence. This was happening at a time when the importance of artillery and armored units (so, tanks) was absolutely crucial in this war—but perhaps there were fewer videos of the kind, and perhaps less exciting for the general public, at the same time.

And that is why it was an *analytical error*. How did it unfold? Availability bias was induced by the bias in the nature of watched videos. Likely, very simple: after watching dozens or hundreds of drone videos (not knowing the actual scale and true proportions and context to draw conclusions), one could come to the mistaken belief that only drones matter. However, these are conclusions made on the basis of incomplete information.

Content influences what is spread, so what is viewed. More spectacular footage spreads more easily, for example, the destruction of a tank by a missile may be shared more often than a tank being hit by a missile when there was no explosion and destruction.[176] Another analytical error made by some was the belief that cyber operations in this war were unused, or even that Russia allegedly proved weak, overrated, and unsuccessful here.

Fortunately, good quality analysts did not commit such mistakes. But too often, the most sensationalist takes were promoted or covered. Contributing to the reinforcement of bad conclusions.

7.18.4.1 Caution not to believe your own propaganda

In part, however, the "demand" for information about Russia's failures and weaknesses was useful for propaganda supporting Ukraine or the Ukrainian cause. Which is natural—because it is about acting in favor of one's own struggle and goals, or that of the side one supports. So, it is then less about factual issues, because these, for example, can be kept low or secret, and information can be revealed selectively. The time for transparency will come later, like after the war. However, it is prudent not to believe in such "own, one-sided" propaganda by accident, because this can lead to wrong decisions.

7.18.4.2 Caution about premature conclusions

When it comes to military action and conclusions, one must be wary of premature ones. As the Royal United Services Institute think-tank noted, a great deal has been said about the capabilities, or lack thereof, of both Russia and Ukraine. Such information may be propagated by both—but a great deal of the data was and is non-public. An ordinary observer without proper visibility or access to information is simply unable to (and cannot) draw full, appropriate conclusions about the disposition of armies, the quality of the actions taken, and the state of armaments or weapons. Such conclusions may come in the future. Thus, there is a great risk of drawing incorrect conclusions and, consequently, of making a mistake if one makes political, military, or defense decisions on the basis of manipulated or inaccurate views.[177]

7.18.4.3 Falsehoods about weapon damage—when the math doesn't add up

Examples of bogus Russian content included propaganda reports that Russia had destroyed more HIMARS missile launchers than Ukraine actually possessed. The same was true of the information about the number of aircraft destroyed, which was communicated as being three times more than the equipment actually possessed by Ukraine.[178] Russia also communicated that it was to destroy more Bayraktar TB2 drones than Ukraine had in stock.[179] Thus, there was a miraculous multiplication—when one event was reported several times as if they were separate incidents. These are obvious slip-ups in the information provided, easily corrected, and undermining the credibility of the communication.

However, war propaganda was and is used on both sides, as well as in third countries. Earlier I explained that Soviet propaganda emphasized the supposed impossibility of shooting down their missiles. A quick jump to the 2020s indicates that modern Russia, too, was repeating similar theses—the Kinzhal (Kh-47M2) hypersonic missiles were supposed to be impossible to shoot down. This is pretty obvious propaganda and informational influence, but is it based on facts? The problem arose when U.S. PAC-3 (Patriot) systems actually, supposedly, shot down (or at least so it was claimed) these super-missiles over Ukraine in 2023. Here, an important note: this was according to the Ukrainian side and press reports, to some extent confirmed by the United States,[180] though the details of the mode of employment of those shot missiles were not known. Still, this had a big informational impact—so much so that the Chinese envoy to Kiev even refused to see the remains of the downed hypersonic missile, expressing a thesis that shooting down such a missile is impossible.[181] (What did this say about China's hypersonic weapons programs?) The Russian side stubbornly stood its ground and described any information about the destruction of its weapons as propaganda.[182] However, there is a lot of talk, but at some point there is a verification of the information, which is what happened when Ukraine demonstrated photos that were purported to show the downed warheads.

During a war, information can have propaganda value. So, how to determine the truth? There will probably be room for that—at another time.

7.18.5 Winning narratives, information dominance

With the exception of the area of Russia itself and perhaps a few other places, Russia has failed to dictate to the media how to portray the events, despite the fact that in the war with Georgia, Russia was very conscious of the need to informationally shape the picture of the events. And sometimes it worked, helping to promote understanding of the 'Russian point of view' in Europe and elsewhere. This facilitated the purchase of gas and other products from Russia, without losing face.[183] Despite the fact that the aggression of a small country against a nuclear power seems an absurd idea—if that's the point of view taken! Most European leaders or States had full understanding—or ignorance, or 'appeasement' of the situation. In the case of aggression in Ukraine in 2022, it was impossible to maintain such a political-diplomatic-media line. Nobody bought it, including due to the prior pressure from the United States and other European States. Information was flowing in a wide stream—from politicians, journalists, and other visitors to the country, the military, and the Ukrainian State. Undoubtedly, by the end of 2023, Ukraine was winning the information war, although various kinds of missteps or cracks were noticeable.

Nevertheless, let us remember that many images and information from this war were or are still not shared, presented, published, or spread. They don't exist in the information space. This, however, cannot be a hindrance to a global audience—because there is so much information (even if much of it is of a similar type) that one can, so to speak, "be content" with what was available out there. Due to this information deluge, some may not even feel the need to think about the potential information asymmetries, or unavailability. After all, plenty of information is still available, although some content of specific types—are not, or become underrepresented, dimmed. The feeling is "smoothed out" because there is still a lot of information (quantitatively) available—even too much of it, an overload. This could distort some analyses or even the way facts were presented or interpreted. Similar was true of the Iraq war in 2003: some quality media did not necessarily verify the data they got, at least to the standard degree—although at that time, at the beginning of the 21st century, there was dramatically less information[184] than during the war in Ukraine. Still, the war in Iraq also—for the time—had an unprecedented openness to the press, but the situation in Ukraine undoubtedly trumped that.

Naturally, it is impossible to foresee how this war will be judged, perceived, and understood in the future. Much depends on its outcome (Win? Lose? Settlement? To what degrees or ends?), and the decisions taken, in other States too. Nobody has a crystal ball.

7.18.6 Psychology in a conflict situation

Psychological actions are important—including when directed "inward," to the citizens of the State, to own military. Properly conducted, they can help sustain morale and willingness to fight (defend).[185] Ukraine's morale and willingness to fight were understandably influenced by fear of Russian occupation, justified by publicized cases of crimes.[186] But probably also by a sense of support from the entire Western world, including the publicly presented visions of the future, including the talk (vision) of joining the European Union. In June 2024, the EU started the membership negotiation process, NATO also held some talks and expressed messages about forms of future association. So to speak—this constituted a vision of a (positive) future. The willingness to fight cannot be reduced to the mere prospect of a monthly paycheck or even an obligation (this is in the context of countries where men or women are subject to compulsory service during wartime and can be drafted). Having something to fight for (a future) is a helpful factor, for example, when one may consider the needs of the (current) sacrifices. And these messages of vision for the future can be effectively communicated to the public and allies.

Allies, too, can direct signals to the public of such a country, lending credence to the assurances of local governments. A dilemma arises with regard to potentially disseminating discouraging information—like a picture of possible destruction, the economic situation, demographics, human casualties (demography), and impacts in the long run. These can be given selectively, justifying (quite sensibly in some cases) the need to keep this information secret for the sake of state stability. In a sense, such information initiatives can be considered indoctrination, but this depends on the actual intensity of the action taken. Besides, a State under attack is reasonably struggling with many challenges—this is all but natural and understandable.

In totalitarian or authoritarian societies, indoctrination certainly occurs, moreover, even outside of wartime. In essence, everything can be reduced to a consequences-of-war calculus.[187] This can be communicated to the public accordingly—including in distorted ways, selectively, for example by making some of the information secret, or giving less attention to it. The informational overtones can also be influenced by the fact that today losses can be calculated very precisely. This is a starkly different situation than during World War I, where the precise number of human casualties has not been established to this day (there are only estimates). Losses are undoubtedly the kind of information that can discourage, frighten, or even deter—influencing the decisions of States.

7.18.6.1 Diversionary train with Lenin and its consequences

It may be challenging to hide the truth about the length of the war being waged, as this can also affect the fatigue of societies—as evidenced, for example, by the collapse of the Russian Empire during World War I. This, by the way, was significantly contributed to by the deliberate German diversion. At the right moment (a situation of public fatigue, mistakes of command and political leadership, hardships of the people, the disintegration of the public order), high-rank German general Ludendorff sent a sealed train to Russia with the "carriers of the revolutionary bacillus," that is, with Lenin and other revolutionaries. Ultimately, this diversion was so effective that not only did the existing order in Russia completely disintegrate, but it set in motion a course of events leading to World War II, the Cold War, and communism in the Eastern Bloc, and who knows, perhaps aggression against Ukraine in 2014 and 2022? When you wonder that all of this can be traced back to an information diversion—the sending of a revolutionary-propaganda group at the right moment—it must be very impressive. Of course, the whole thing is not based solely on psychological and propaganda activities, but these were very important considerations at the beginning of the process.

7.18.6.2 Holding a hostile society under occupation is difficult, though some don't fight back

Sociological studies of non-violent resistance methods to occupation show that population control is highly dependent on social group cohesion, internal polarization within them, divisions within the nation, etc. Having access to information, to the media, fosters the formation of attitudes of resistance to occupation.[188] Such a situation exists especially today, with widespread access to information resources on the Internet and the ability to connect to the network under almost any conditions. It may be more difficult to keep a country under occupation under such circumstances, especially when its population universally opposes the occupier. This is not the 16th century, when national borders were fluid.

However, there are situations, societies, and countries that did not put up a fight (despite training and having weapons)—the contemporary example is likely the society of Afghanistan. After the U.S. troops left the country, there was no apparent resistance to the newly established (by itself) Taliban authority, and thus to the adoption of the social and life standards that came with them.

7.18.7 Russian propaganda—inside and outside Russia

Network censorship measures were introduced in Russia that blocked access to content.[189] Russian propaganda worked inside Russia—including involvement of teachers, fears of an alleged nuclear threat from Ukraine were spread or were given credence. Such narratives were used to justify a "special military operation" in Ukraine.[190]

7.18.7.1 Social media view

The Russian propaganda campaign during the hostilities was very extensive,[191] mostly inward, domestic. But it also aimed to influence Ukraine or its allies (EU, NATO), and countries of the Global South (Africa, India, South America, etc.)—where understanding of Russia's actions was greater than in the Western world. This was evident, for example, in network analyses of content spread through social media. Social media analysis can be done in many ways, if only by checking the use of selected hashtags or keywords in published or shared messages.[192]

When analyzing the use of hashtags like '#istandwithrussia' ('*I stand with Russia*') or '#istandwithputin' ('*I stand with Putin*'),[193] it can be assumed that content so labeled is favorable to Russia—analyzing such posts may aid in establishing the rates of propagation of such message content. Messages of this kind appeared more frequently at certain times, such as on the day the UN General Assembly voted on a resolution condemning Russia's aggression. If there were many more such messages than there were in the days before or after the vote, and if they came from India or Pakistan, this may suggest a correlation—even when such accounts, at least in part, may have been bogus or artificial. On the contrary, it may signal a coordinated effort, their intentionality.[194]

7.18.7.2 Measure of impact

One is support in the societies of the Global South, as measured by surveys. The other is the effects of actions.

Here again, I point out that determining the actual effectiveness of information activities (their impact) is difficult,[195] as it requires defining and measuring effectiveness, and how to measure taking of some action in response to message content. The decision on the choice of methods lies with the propaganda operators. However, even injecting messages into the debate can have some effects on many levels, albeit sometimes subtle. It normalizes at least the framing of certain issues. However, it certainly cannot be said that the effectiveness of propaganda can always be objectively measured by purely scientific methods of natural science, with mathematical precision. For mundane reasons. Even if there is an impact, an objective comparison would have to be relative to an identical process—without propaganda interference. Effects can also affect the cognitive layer, and therefore the thinking[196]—about the decisions made. Even if the effect of influence would be indirect, or non-obvious. Then, the effect might not even be measurable and analysts could find themselves in the realm of assumptions or guesswork. Sometimes, a layered model may be distinguished, where actions occur in the following spheres: physical (kinetic attacks, such as tanks), cyber (cyber operations, attacks, defense, targeting information systems), informational, or cognitive. Models are being created; diagrams are being drawn. It might be useful; it may also be an overkill. We're not getting into that—let's keep it serious.

7.18.7.3 A practical measure?

If one measures effectiveness by a measure of specifics—such as the aid provided to Ukraine in 2022 and 2023 by third countries—then one might be tempted to make the risky assertion that a discouraging or dissuasive effect of Russian propaganda operations has not been demonstrated here as effective. At least considering Western countries, which provided a huge aid, even if some of it took time or was stalled at times. In the West, the dynamics were quite different from those of, for example, in the Global South, or Africa. Causality, reasons—these are different.

But perhaps efficiency has been demonstrated after all? Precisely manifested by this intensive assistance and aid, which could also be related to the information propagated on the so-called Western side of things, as well as reports of massacres of civilians in Ukraine. Inferring this is quite pointless in the ongoing war situation—this will (maybe!) be possible after the situation has stabilized. There are complications for such surveys; the situation is highly dynamic.

First, it is not possible to establish a state of eventuality with an assumed situation of no working propaganda or agents of influence, without working propaganda or agents of influence. Here, we return to the issue of the timeline. It's not a physical experiment; it's impossible to conduct an "experimental test" of the same situation, but with a differently shaped information environment, for comparison purposes, to determine whether something worked or not. Relying only on the statements and judgments of experts to resolve the effects is also not appropriate; it is not an adequate measure. It may be some partial explanation, or even a clue, and estimate—but it would be hard to treat it as a certain hard result.

Second, there was a very strong influence from political-military circles convincing their governments or societies to provide military support, and on a large scale. Even before the invasion took place, that is, when the destruction, casualties, etc. were not yet visible or foreseeable on such a scale as they happened. There were political circles opposing aid at the time, but their voices ceased to be treated as serious, after the war began, the voices then ended as obscurities.

I would venture to say that informational influence did exist. There was certainly a propaganda influence inside Russia, where there seemed to have been significant public support for the actions of the authorities (or at least—a lack of meaningful opposition). External influence was exerted as well, determining what kind of influence is difficult still in a wartime situation and without a full view of the information environment and classified information, although it's reasonable to consider that causing divisions and pitting some social groups, even nations, against others—would certainly be in Russian interest. Someone may know partial answers, but this information is not necessarily public. It is certainly not a sign of efficiency that some content has been viewed by a certain number of people. For a mundane reason: such viewers may have watched many material like videos, including those claiming the opposite—this cannot be easily determined. A researcher, observer, or propaganda analyst cannot know this, at least on a large scale and accurately. They can't and that's that. Some knowledge may be available to digital platforms, but again only as to issues within their platform, with no insight into others. Inferring intent is also difficult.

We come to the fractious, frustrating outcome: that it is impossible to determine the clear impact of the viewed war-related or propaganda content. Or really difficult to determine this conclusively (without significant error bars). And then it all hinges on exceptional qualities of analysts, interpretation, and communication.

In addition to the above deliberations, the presence of propaganda can be used in Ukraine and allied States for political-military purposes—depicting a conflict situation in which one must defend oneself or even attack. Evidence of conflict activity may contribute to building support. In fact, the very information about the fighting Ukrainians has a positive influence on support. If there were none, it would be straightforward to deny aid. After all, why support militarily a State that is not willing to defend itself?

Now, getting back to the substance.

7.18.8 New technologies in use

New technologies were used on a very large scale during the war, enabling real-time transmission of tactical information, for example, Instant Messaging. New media were also used in information operations,[197] both defensively and offensively. There are a great many lessons to be learned from this by countries and their militaries around the world. Not even speaking about the increased pace of developing new weapons and the shortened time from design or test, to fielding. Not even speaking of the dramatic changes in warfighting technologies, AI assisted, including with uses of various types of unmanned vehicles, like drones.

7.18.8.1 The need to draw conclusions—they better be correct

Failure to draw correct conclusions poses an outstanding risk with the emergence of full-scale armed conflicts and rapid change in the 21st century. This could lead to taking the wrong development direction. However, it is worth noting again that Ukraine dominates informationally—the favoring narratives were at a time the main if not the only messages, at least in the Western world. This has also happened through an unprecedented openness to the media—an awareness of how the modern information and media environment works, and favorable conditions—Western public opinion favored Ukraine, when the war happened—mistakes were passed over.[198] Overlooked, or muted, as was the case of missile or drone fallings on the territory of NATO countries.[199]

7.18.8.2 Moral panic and fears of World War III—a mental drift

This coupled with the information threat, when at least twice false information was spread in information space of NATO States, about the alleged risk of entering a war that would start due to missile fall—in Poland, such as the Russian one in December 2022. Fortunately, military and political treaties don't work that way, and outbreaks of war don't happen all of sudden and automatically—they are decisions made by States. The best evidence of this is the assassination of Archduke Franz Ferdinand in 1914, which is pointed to as the reason for World War I. In fact, there was no shortage of tensions in Europe during the period preceding World War I, and the lead-up to war itself in this case was also not sudden—it took weeks.

However, the view of automaticity has become so deeply entrenched that when the United States killed an important Iranian general Ghasem Solemani in 2020, a tag related to the archduke trended on U.S. Twitter. It was as if an escalation was expected or inevitable due to the automatic repetition of history. Nothing pointed at the eruption of World War III, but the informational inertia of human nature on social media, combined with insufficient historical and military knowledge, led to a short-lived moral panic (soon everyone forgot about it and got busy with other topics). With the war in Ukraine, it also had to be decided by someone in Russia. It did not happen on its own.

7.18.8.3 Information overload? Attention to copy-paste analysis

The influx, flood even, of information in the war in Ukraine highlighted a challenge. It's a challenge to analyze it all, to establish veracity, to put it into specific proportions. To leave out irrelevant information. A challenge not to draw hasty or mistaken, inaccurate conclusions. The challenge is to conduct the analysis sufficiently fast, but nevertheless reliably and effectively. To avoid uncritical *copy-paste analytics* from random sources (e.g., social network accounts, from messengers like Telegram) and propagate this uncritically. Such an approach has tricked selected individuals, or circles, on several occasions.

For example, during Yevgeny Prigozhin's quasi-putsch, when he was "*moving on Moscow*" but didn't get there, eventually, and afterward everything ended "happily" (if not for everyone) and the matter was simply forgotten as if it had no impact—and removed from information space.

Or when Russia renewed threats to attack ships sailing for Ukrainian grain in 2023, when a *public analyst* popularized the idea that Israeli ships were ignoring the blockade at that time, and were just sailing for that grain—which turned out not to be true but was previously treated as a sensation in the media, and given space.

There could and may be more untruths, misguided analyses, and deliberate misinformation. How to avoid them?

7.18.8.4 Recipe for defense against false information in an environment of rapid change

One approach is to follow events in stages, rather than hour by hour or even more frequently—an approach of *measured media intake*. After days, a week, or weeks, more can be determined, trends can be seen more clearly, and it's harder to succumb to moral panic on the moment's feelings or hopes. For most public audiences, such a slow-news approach should suffice. Unless one treats war reporting as infotainment. But if so—since it's entertainment, it's clear that it doesn't have to be accurate, serious, and truthful—so, keep it in the right proportions and apply the right weight to reports.

Such an approach is obviously limited, and for some, it cannot be seen as appropriate or even serious. Actual analysts (i.e., professionals), such as those in state-run centers or intelligence agencies (including private ones), have it slightly worse. For them, the weekly timeframe is not precise enough. Especially when events happen fast, and stakes are huge—such was the case in February and March 2022. So, how should they cope? Let me answer this way: hopefully as best as possible! I wish them *good luck* in any such circumstances! Simply speaking, it's about the ability to assess correctly based on flows of incoming information from multiple sources, and applying the right methods to that. Refer to sources about the art of analysis, assessment, or foresight.

It appears that analytical tools like data processing with the support of AI/LLM models may support analyses, where there is a lot of data incoming. However, much depends on the quality of the information and judgment. AI/LLM may still not be adequate for ambiguous situations, taking into account abnormal events. And the world is aplenty in ambiguity.

7.18.9 Influence via the media

During the war, TV stations were hacked, leading to the display of propaganda material, such as Russian stations broadcasting material on the Ukrainian counteroffensive instead of, for example, the ballet "Swan Lake."[200] Through the hacked radio, information was spread about the threat of a missile attack on Russian regions.[201] Thus, it was an information diversion. In turn, the actions of Russian GRU cyber operatives were expected to have psychological effects.[202]

A number of groups suspected of ties to Russian services were also formed—they directed messages via social media or messengers like Telegram. Information was taken from those sources by many Western media or analysts, and spread further—in good faith, even when either uncritically or for profit or popularity, regardless of content veracity.

Unsuccessful attempts at cyber attacks can also be publicized,[203] which is, after all, information without any significant meaning and of unclear relevance to the general outcome. An attempt to do something insignificant—how exciting is that? But it is possible to try to create the impression of taking actions, and a sense of constant danger, some kind of psychosis. The feeling of being the target of impending attacks. If furthermore, one encounters a journalist, reporter, or analyst who does not understand these things, they may be unable to keep the right balance, and proportions. As a result, some legitimate medium then becomes an element in the information dissemination, perhaps also a transmitter of psychological operations content. Such situations have occurred in many States in Europe and the United States multiple times. This tactic is brilliant in its simplicity. And it was successful if the intention of these groups was to propagate some lines of information. Then, the effect is actually a measurable spread of the message. It seems that sometimes the goal was indeed exactly that.

For example, while unrelated to the war in Ukraine (in this case), but still worth considering, cyber threat groups are sometimes interested in hacking industrial control systems. And sometimes they just claim so over open channels. However, there is a difference between *being interested* and being able to act. What is claimed one-sidedly is not necessarily true. So, one has to be careful. It can be an exaggerated boast, a kind of information operation even—propaganda. Just because someone says something doesn't mean it's true, or significant. In the case of the activities I refer to, a group was "interested" in industrial automation systems, but in most cases, the claims were exaggerated or unfounded.[204]

Diagram of exploiting media outlets in the information operation by cyber operation methods:

- Creating messages (background information) that are technically credible;
- Disseminating them in various places, such as social media; Some previous "credibility" helps, but it does not have to be built on spectacular actions, such as hacking industrial systems;
- An attempt to get media attention (maybe some will take the bait, if they do—it's a success).

This was being done on multiple occasions—including during war in Ukraine. Russian hacktivist groups were sometimes interested in such easy gains. Publicizing insignificant actions or even desires, or unsuccessful attempts.[205] Just an information operation, not a significant cyber operation. To function, it had to be read and shared. If that suffices because there will be receipt and willingness to transmit it, then why bother with making a more substantial effort? It's whatever works.

7.18.10 Bot farms

Bot farms (botnets) have been neutralized in Ukraine[206] on several occasions. These are infrastructures for transmitting propaganda content, including on social media. In practice, it's a lot of computer devices, smartphones, SIM cards (for mobile telephony)—proxy devices with which operators may mask the origin of network traffic. In this way, information and psychological operations can be carried out—including the such with political or military objectives. Technically, creating such a hardware and software environment is not difficult (I explained it in Chapter 3). But it has to be placed somewhere, such as in someone's house, like one used by foreign services, or by renting space from citizens who do not necessarily know what it will be used for (or such is their version of events).

7.18.11 Unconventional activities

British think-tank RUSI analyzed unconventional operations in the Russian-Ukrainian war and highlighted the importance of information and psychological operations.[207] Russian influence agents have conducted operations both from Ukraine and from third countries, such as in Western Europe.

Similarly, the goals of publicizing corruption in Ukraine, including corruption in connection with the transfer of Western weapons—to reduce the support of Western countries,[208] have also been pointed out. It may be exploited informationally. Also noteworthy is the information activity in the early days of the war.

7.18.11.1 What to do after receiving a "surrender!" message?

During the first three days of the war, many senior Ukrainian commanders received text messages, or phone calls, often from their counterparts in Russia, urging them to desist taking action in order to "avoid bloodshed."[209] In other words: to surrender. Another interesting manifestation of the information warfare noted by RUSI think-tank was calls on social media to report suspicious symbols and markings placed on buildings. Were they meant to be set up by Russia's agents for targeting? In effect, the reporting overloaded the Ukrainian police's lines of communication. And that may also have been the goal, as these turned out to be insignificant, false reports.

The activity extended to the network infrastructure. In the occupied territories, it was switched so that network traffic went through Russia rather than Ukraine, which could allow monitoring of network traffic. This is what happened, for example, in the Ukrainian city of Kherson—the Internet was turned off, cables were rewired, and then the network flow was restarted.[210] In general, however, the resilience of the information and telecommunications infrastructure during this war was at a high level.[211] This surprised many, and in fact was quite, remarkable. It suffices to imagine that repairs to such an infrastructure often involved great risks for technicians[212] when working in areas near armed activity. Working internet connectivity allowed war coverage to flow in a wide stream. For this conflict, this is crucial—so that the interest of Western societies, on which Western governments depend for support, can be maintained. It is, therefore, a strategic necessity. Something that became one of the priority requirements and activities during this war.

7.18.11.2 Soldier, civilian, unlawful combatant—consequences and risks

Modern technology enabled an unprecedented blurring of the distinction between soldiers, combatants, and civilians—reporting information through systems provided by the Ukrainian government.

Such systems—smartphone applications—allow reporting the positions and types of enemy weapons or spotted military units, and their movements. If such an application-based infrastructure, however, contributes to, or is used to direct attacks—such as by Ukrainian artillery—this has certain consequences. Such that then a civilian using such a smartphone application ceases to be formally a civilian—he or she becomes part of a warning system, akin to an anti-missile system. In the sense of international law, such someone is no longer a civilian. They lose the Geneva Conventions protections, which guarantee the protection of civilians.[213] Via the use of such digital tools, they may effectively become an *unlawful combatant*. Reporting of troop movements by civilians may have happened in previous wars, but not on this scale, actually in real time. This novelty will be studied for years and may even influence international norms and law in future or their interpretation. In 2023, the International Committee of the Red Cross announced an initiative to reduce the practice of blurring the distinction between civilians and legitimate combatants.[214]

It is perfectly understandable that the population under attack wants to defend and support the military of their country. The problem is that if it is universally accepted that every civilian is potentially a node in the information system of weapons systems, this could have unpleasant consequences in practice—for civilians. If, or when, for example, the (aggressor) military begins to suspect or treat every citizen with a smartphone as a potential combatant taking part in the battle. This would, of course, be unacceptable—giving up the protections of the Geneva Conventions can last at most while such persons are taking action—but during an armed conflict people are already rather interested in survival. These are not easy decisions. Furthermore, mistakes or miscalculations may happen.

Indeed, there have been situations when Russian soldiers subjected devices of Ukrainian civilians to an "inspection." In view of this, there is a need to have devices properly "cleaned" and pruned out of suspicious content, but nevertheless ones looking credible (i.e., not completely restored to factory settings, which is completely not credible).

It's not that I condemn this attitude—aiding a military with information, via smartphone apps. Whoever has such a preference—it is their choice. However, it is worth being aware of the risks or potential consequences, and how this issue stands under international humanitarian law. And let everyone make their own decisions—as long as they are properly informed. States should be aware of this and at least inform citizens of the risks.

7.18.11.3 Throwing Molotovs at the recruitment center—via retirees

Insofar as anything can be surprising in the case of Russia, events have occurred there that can be considered somewhat extraordinary. For example, a retired woman tried to set fire (with a Molotov cocktail or similar tools) to a military recruitment office in the northern Russian city of Usinsk.[215] She was convinced that she was taking part in a secret FSB mission. There were more events of this kind, the whole phenomenon being complex in nature. It seems that some of such activities may have been a manifestation of civilian resistance to military action and military draft in Russia. How could this be taking place? There were suspicions that it may be the Russian FSB fabricating calls (allegedly—of Ukraine) to take such actions. Some may have been provoked by people riding the trend and, for example, interested in profit when a bank is targeted. Some could be scams and such manipulations. In most cases, fraud was involved—such people were tricked or misled into taking action. The background is less relevant to our analysis. What is important is that from February 28, 2022, to October 2023, more than 125 such actions were counted. Sometimes exceeding 10 on a single day, and in various places in Russia. So, this was a clear trend. Here are a handful of examples, but keep in mind that they are all from Russian media. An attempt to set fire to a military registration and enlistment office in Nizhny Tagil. After arriving at the office, a pensioner tried to set it on fire using acetone and Molotov cocktails. A resident of the Moscow region threw a Molotov cocktail into a bank branch. The scammers forced him to take out a loan. They then convinced him to set fire to the bank branch.

7.18.12 Ukraine, PR, information and propaganda activities, and memes

In the context of Ukrainian information efforts, an efficient information machine was created consisting of activists, enthusiasts, as well as PR professionals. They regularly created memes—images with short and pertinent content relating to current events. According to the principle that "[r]idicule is man's most potent weapon,"[216] such informational activities can be "weaponized" and used against the enemy—including a common enemy.

People from outside Ukraine, such as those gathered in the informal group '#NAFO' (standing for *North Atlantic Fellas Organization*; the similarity to the NATO abbreviation is not coincidental, logo on Figure 7.4), joined the activities. The movement was designed to counter Russian propaganda but also directed information messages supporting Ukraine. Formally, humor techniques also take a trolling approach. Russia, its leaders, officers, military, and diplomacy are being trolled. This is the use of humor to laugh at and ridicule the opponent.[217]

NAFO's activities have been officially supported by former and current politicians in the Central Eastern Europe region, such as former Estonian President Thomas Hendrik Ilves, or the current Lithuanian foreign minister. Such information activities may be effective, as can be the popularization of the legend of the so-called Ghost of Kiev (a pilot who was said to have high efficiency; actually: a myth or war propaganda), or the supposedly fallen, but actually captured soldiers on Ukraine's Serpent Island, who issued a refusal to surrender to a Russian warship (the cruiser "Moskva") in the words: "russkiy voyennyy korabl, idi na khuy." It's also a legend that helps to aid defense, boost morale, and even garner support from foreign audiences. It matters not that at first it was claimed that the island's crew was killed, and later it turned out that they were captured. What matters is the informational effect, and this one was significant, in such a situation the details are secondary—it is war, after all!

SUCHO, an initiative archiving Ukrainian war memes, in 2023 already had nearly three thousand of them.[218] Rather unsurprisingly, the person who appeared most often in them was Putin (the second most common was Zelensky).[219]

Figure 7.4 NAFO logo, without the additional overlay of the shiba inu doggies.

Source: https://en.wikipedia.org/wiki/File:NAFO_OFAN_brain_damaged_cartoon_dogs.jpeg.

7.18.13 Making fun of Western politicians

Trolling techniques were also used on the Russian side, including by official institutions such as embassies.[220] Trolling, making fun of, and screwing over interlocutors—such as politicians of Western States—was also the approach of the so-called Russian comedians/satirists Alexei Stolyarov and Vladimir Kuznetsov, known as Vovan and Lexus. Is it possible to make leaders of States a laughing stock? Seems that it sure is. They have punked many. "These satirists" have played at the expense of many European politicians: the mayors of Berlin, Vienna, Warsaw, British Prime Minister Boris Johnson, and Polish President Andrzej Duda (twice). What did they punk them to do? To disclose information, to make statements about Ukraine, etc. The way it worked is that they impersonated foreign politicians and government officials, such as the mayor of Kiev, Vitali Klitschko. Employees of the offices of those politicians unfortunately failed to verify the callers—they let themselves be punked. It seems that all the 'satirists' needed was a phone number and a convincing story. This does not speak well of these important figures in the targeted States, or their staff. How did these pranksters-jokers get accurate contacts to the politicians of other States, having the cognizance of the likely course of the conversation to know what to expect, which lends credence to the conversation? Who knows. Can 'Vovan and Lexus' be considered a threat group in an influence operation? Probably yes.[221] But this in no way excuses the state leaders who let themselves be approached in this way. Is this propaganda, or perhaps humoresque or satire for television? Well, as Goebbels used to say, "[p]ropaganda becomes ineffective the moment we are aware of it."[222] Even if it uses humor—if these are not grassroots activities, it may be "more effective" to conceal them, to mask their true motive or source.

7.18.14 Targeting Western States

Influence and manipulation campaigns were also conducted against third countries. Like in Europe—NATO, and European Union Member States—such as Germany, Poland, and France. Misinformation about Russian aggression was amplified and spread in such a way as to try to undermine support for Ukraine. This was done through the creation of profiles and pages on social media or fake sites purporting to be informative,[223] but in reality actively channeling disinformation. France attributed such actions to the Russian State. It was a multi-channel campaign with the participation of Russian embassies, cultural centers (actively participating in reinforcement, including through social media accounts), bogus websites, and further activities—popularizing them via search engine optimization.

The campaign accused European States of Russophobia and barbarism, while Ukraine was accused of Neo-Nazism. It was argued about the "negative effects of accepting refugees from Ukraine."[224] Real and respected media outlets were impersonated, as well as government websites, such as of the French Foreign Ministry, or the German Interior Ministry. In this way, the bogus websites "informed" about supposed "new taxes" to fund aid to Ukraine. Images and memes with anti-Western content were published. One of the techniques of the Russian media was also—this perhaps on the heels of the West's fascination with the subject of disinformation and the so-called fact-checking—to pretend to verify true reports and depictions. But *decode them as false*. That is, the essence of fact-checking was misrepresented, which also highlights the problems of the approach itself. Someone always has to establish the "*truth*" or the "*facts*." Although it gets scary if someone's social media account ends up blocked because of posting satire and a joke that fact-checkers "verify" as "untrue." This is how trust in such activities may be lost, unfortunately.

At the same time, "protests" "in support of Russia" were organized in Western Europe. In fact, they often involved not so much Western societies, as Russians, because national diasporas can also be a great instrument for propaganda.[225] And not everyone needs to delve into the background details of such activities. If the demonstration takes place in Vienna, some may take it for granted that "the Austrians" organized it, right? Well, it turns out that not exactly. The situation may be similar with joining public protests of other kinds.

A protest is organized. It gathers a lot of people. Among them, several people appear with pro-Russian, anti-Ukrainian slogans, or simply—some slogans, etc. They ostentatiously stand in front of the cameras of media correspondents, demonstrating their slogans, waving flags, showing posters, with messages, shouting, etc. In reality this may be a few individuals (provocateurs, inciters) in legitimate groups of several thousand people protesting for completely different issues! And there it is. There is an informative content for Western media, of the kind: "*Western societies against supporting Ukraine*." But perhaps more so for the Russian media? Like: "*The West is tired of Ukraine*." Similar diversionary-propaganda methods were used in the publicized graffiti against Zelensky, which supposedly appeared on the streets of many European cities from the end of 2022. Only in fact they didn't appear anywhere—they weren't physically there—contrary to what was attempted to be shown. Neither in Zurich nor in Paris, or other cities. They were only graphically superimposed on photos of streets. Posted to social media like Instagram. In reality, they did not appear.[226] These are psychological operations.

7.18.15 Influence and social engineering methods

In the case of the events surrounding the war in Ukraine, it is worth noting of the influx of war refugees. Of course, this could have led to social tensions. We are talking about the sudden arrival of hundreds of thousands of people, people suddenly clearly noticeable, visible in the streets, etc.

Therefore, some have decided to act pre-emptively, using the method of pre-bunking. That is, pre-emptively straightening out potential misinformation or disinformation lines. As part of such actions, the idea is to instill in people "immunity," to "inoculate" them against disinformation before people are even subjected to such information exposure presenting events in ways inconsistent with the established view, perhaps distorted. Technically it is, therefore, a kind of information influence activity. In this case, it involved refugees, for protective measures. It may, however, be considered a kind of social engineering—such actions must be made with care.

The American company Jigsaw (a subsidiary of Google) performed such activities through ads on the YouTube platform.[227] The activities were conducted from September 2022—in the fall and winter. They provided for the proactive display of short videos "straightening out" *possible* false or untrue ideas—for example, that "*these Ukrainians*" are associated with (*causing*) "social problems" in the places they reach. According to Jigsaw, the informational messages reached a really broad audience—one-third of the public in Poland, Slovakia, and the Czech Republic. The ads were displayed 38 million times, reaching 80% of Facebook users in Poland, 68% of Twitter/X users, and 50% of TikTok users.[228] When reporting on the measurements of effectiveness, it was determined that the effectiveness was rather limited—just a few percent. In Slovakia, efficiency was found to be particularly low (about 2%). Perhaps it would be possible to increase it by reaching people through other channels as well, or over a broader timeframe.

As the initiators of the action noted, the groups most susceptible to this campaign appeared to be young people. At the time of writing these words, the results from similar actions taken at German and Indian societies have not been disclosed. Of course, one can understand that the goals of these actions are well defined and positive. Nevertheless, the methods used are methods of influence. Similar actions in principle are possible, especially when performed by digital platform operators. For example, Facebook had an "*I Voted*" button, the role of which was to spread the word about election day, therefore, increasing voter turnout[229]—which may have influenced millions of users as well as their families and friends, to decide to vote.[230] This survey was conducted on a sample of 60 million people.

7.19 SUMMARY

7.19.1 OODA

Information is a key element of the so-called OODA (observe, orient, decide, act) loop,[231] a process considering observation, orientation, decision, and taking action. The faster the right information is acquired or analyzed—the faster and better the decision is made to act, and the results achieved. This depends on the quality of the information acquired. Hence, the drive to reduce uncertainty, the so-called *fog of war* during conflicts, when—in simple and figurative terms—one does not know what is going on and how to interpret the incoming information or lack thereof. Thinning this fog of war—or thickening it—can also be done with informational measures. By acquiring information that can be relied upon, disrupting this process in the adversary (increasing ambiguity, etc.). In this way, informational actions can even be revolutionary.[232] Certainly, these tools and measures are absolutely indispensable today.

7.19.2 Strategic culture

Activities in the information sphere are part of what is known as *strategic culture*, which should be understood as

> the sum total of ideas, conditioned emotional responses, and patterns of habitual behavior that members of a national strategic community have acquired through instruction or imitation and share with each other with regard to [nuclear] strategy. In the area of strategy, habitual behavior is largely cognitive behavior.[233]

This is in reference to the values held in the societies in question, including values of humanitarianism, European values, national values, and socialist values (this in China). Strategic culture refers to things derived from military, social, historical conditions (including military history).[234]

Today, this definition needs to be broadened to include technological issues. That is, strategic culture should also be defined through the prism of the function of technological issues, advances in this field (taking into account scientific developments), and methods of applying such technological solutions.

As it happens, information operations and warfare require a good awareness of all these elements, so they are conditioned by them. Even though it can sometimes be instrumentalized, such a broad background is important. The war in Ukraine was a shock to the strategic culture of European States. It turned out that the previously used or accepted concepts, or models of thought or reasoning, and intellect, proved to be completely inadequate with respect to reality. How does this testify to the political leadership of such a structure? Luckily, changes were made quickly—under the influence of the crisis.[235] Perhaps this must be so, and it is crises that shape the strategies, tactics, and actions of States and such blocs, and we should not expect a different approach in normal situations, when there is the so-called peace and tranquility.

Information operations (warfare) are integral to propaganda before, during, and after an armed conflict. Propaganda can be used to shape public views, modulate fears, and even arouse emotions favorable to war. Propaganda also makes it possible to shape the information environment during war. These are defensive issues (such as maintaining high morale, willingness to defend one's country), as well as offensive (demoralizing, demotivating the enemy). Propaganda comprises also of activities that support specific military actions—such as kinetic ones. They can shape the situation before, during, and after battles.

In crises, information deficit is something one must reckon with. This can cause unease, even social uncertainty, perhaps unrest—it may be a gap waiting to be filled. Who will fill it and with what? Failure to fill it is a risk. Someone (an adversary) or something (a natural phenomenon or a drift of opinion) may introduce content of its own, in a way that is unfavorable to a State, social groups, even individuals.

The question arises as to how modern information operations capabilities should be constructed. Times are changing. Staffs, tactics, and means to fight today fundamentally differ from, say, the reality of 100 years ago. The range of weapons systems is greater. But so is the reach of information means. While in 1924 radio systems—wide broadcasting to entire populations—were in their infancy, then in 2024 capabilities are available to reach even small groups of people, with highly targeted messages, soon created by generative methods (AI), perhaps with highly personalized content. Skillful use of such solutions appears to be a key challenge (perhaps also advantage) as the elements of content generation themselves are known quite well—many psychological effects are so well understood that it is known how to create effective communication.

It is this element of "outreaching audiences" and content generation, that will change. These are the main conclusions of this book.

However, technology alone is not enough, because it is necessary to know the psychological, sociological, cultural, situational, and even historical background. Even if it doesn't have to be a deep recognition—technocrats and narrow specialists may only need some elements—hence the importance of transdisciplinary competence of the "X in one" kind will be emphasized. So, what counts is the competence of people who have a wide range of knowledge and skillset, even if not deeply specialized in all of these topics, although they should be specialist in at least one particular field; as opposed to: groups of people with separate specializations acting together. Not so much interdisciplinary teams but teams composed of multidisciplinary people. This seems to be where the future lies in taking practical action, and AI/LLM aids will only help.

The biggest problem in crisis situations, such as during military crises, is therefore the lack of adequate information. Especially today, this can lead to inertia and chaos. However, information cannot be provided just for the sake of saying something, or anything. Once official information is given, it can be difficult to correct it, especially if the data necessary to analyze and update the situation keeps coming in. These are difficult decisions. It is worthwhile for the State to have the resources to make them.

NOTES

1 L. Olejnik, A. Kurasinski, *Philosophy of Cybersecurity*. CRC Press, 2023.
2 Greenwood Ch., *The Concept of War in Modern International Law*, "International & Comparative Law Quarterly" 1987, 36(2), 283–306.
3 J.S. Pictet, *Commentary of the First Geneva Convention for the Amelioration of the Condition of the Wounded and Sick in Armed Forces in the Field*, Geneva 1952.
4 Article 2 of the Geneva Convention of August 12, 1949, for the Amelioration of the Fate of the Wounded and Sick in Active Armies, OJ. 1956, no. 38 item 171, app.
5 Article 49(1) of the Protocol Additional to the Geneva Conventions of August 12, 1949, Relating to the Protection of Victims of International Armed Conflicts (Protocol I), done in Geneva on June 8, 1977, OJ. 1992, no. 41, item 175, app.

6 B.M. Ducote, *Challenging the Application of PMESII-PT in a Complex Environment. A monograph*, Fort Leavenworth, 2010, p. 3, footnote 8.
7 T.C. Schelling, *The Strategy of Conflict*, Cambridge 1980, p. 52.
8 F.E. Morgan, K.P. Mueller, E.S. Medeiros, K.L. Pollpeter, R. Cliff, *Dangerous Thresholds: Managing Escalation in the 21st Century*, Santa Monica 2008.
9 F.E. Morgan, K.P. Mueller, E.S. Medeiros, K.L. Pollpeter, R. Cliff, *Dangerous Thresholds: Managing Escalation in the 21st Century*, Santa Monica 2008.
10 Y. Nadtochey, Staying in Touch During Escalation, *The Fletcher Forum Of World Affairs*, October 27, 2022, http://www.fletcherforum.org/home/2022/10/27/staying-in-touch-during-escalation.
11 S.E. Miller, Nuclear hotlines: origins, evolution, applications, *Journal for Peace and Nuclear Disarmament* 2021, vol. 4, pp. 176–191.
12 S.E. Miller, Nuclear hotlines: origins, evolution, applications, *Journal for Peace and Nuclear Disarmament* 2021, vol. 4, pp. 176–191.
13 A. Wahlstrom, G. Roncone, K. Lunden, D. Kapellmann Zafra, Contracts identify cyber operations projects from Russian company NTC Vulkan, *Mandiant*, March 30, 2023, https://www.mandiant.com/resources/blog/cyber-operations-russian-vulkan.
14 K. Yadav, M.J. Riedl, A. Wanless, S. Woolley, What makes an influence operation malign?, *Carnegie Endowment for International Peace*, August 7, 2023, https://carnegieendowment.org/2023/08/03/what-makes-influence-operation-malign-pub-90323.
15 A.J. Berinsky, Assuming the costs of war: Events, elites, and American public support for military conflict, *The Journal of Politics* 2007, vol. 69, no. 4, pp. 975–997.
16 R.G. Herbert, In search of the virtuous propagandist: The ethics of selling war, *Journal of Military Ethics* 2021, vol. 20, no. 2, pp. 93–112.
17 M. Rush, The war danger in Soviet policy and propaganda, *Comparative Strategy* 1989, vol. 8, no. 1, pp. 1–9.
18 R.L. Bytwerk, The argument for genocide in Nazi propaganda, *Quarterly Journal of Speech* 2005, vol. 91, no. 1, pp. 37–62.
19 R.L. Bytwerk, The argument for genocide in Nazi propaganda, *Quarterly Journal of Speech* 2005, vol. 91, no. 1, pp. 37–62.
20 J. Yourman, Propaganda techniques within Nazi Germany, *The Journal of Educational Sociology* 1939, vol. 13, no. 3, pp. 148–163.
21 J. Yourman, Propaganda techniques within Nazi Germany, *The Journal of Educational Sociology* 1939, vol. 13, no. 3, p. 14.
22 *NSC-68 and the Korean War*, Office of the Historian, https://history.state.gov/departmenthistory/short-history/koreanwar.
23 J.T. Campbell, L.S. Cain, Public opinion and the outbreak of war, *Journal of Conflict Resolution* 1965, vol. 9, no. 3, pp. 318–329.
24 J.T. Campbell, L.S. Cain, Public opinion and the outbreak of war, *Journal of Conflict Resolution* 1965, vol. 9, no. 3, pp. 318–329.
25 A.J. Berinsky, Assuming the costs of war: Events, elites, and American public support for military conflict, *The Journal of Politics* 2007, vol. 69, no. 4, pp. 975–997.
26 E.V. Larson, *Understanding commanders' information needs for influence operations*, Santa Monica 2009.
27 E.V. Larson, *Understanding commanders' information needs for influence operations*, Santa Monica 2009.
28 W.C. Garrison, *Information Operations and Counter-Propaganda: Making A Weapon of Public Affairs*, Carlisle Barracks 1999.
29 M. Honey, The "womanpower" campaign: Advertising and recruitment propaganda during World War II, *Frontiers: A Journal of Women Studies* 1981, pp. 50–56.
30 A. Munoz, *US military information operations in Afghanistan: Effectiveness of psychological operations 2001–2010*, Santa Monica 2012.
31 A. Munoz, *US military information operations in Afghanistan: Effectiveness of psychological operations 2001–2010*, Santa Monica 2012.
32 A. Munoz, *US military information operations in Afghanistan: Effectiveness of psychological operations 2001–2010*, Santa Monica 2012.

33 A. Munoz, *US military information operations in Afghanistan: Effectiveness of psychological operations 2001–2010*, Santa Monica 2012.
34 S. Freud, *Group Psychology and the Analysis of the Ego*, London-Vienna, 1922, p. 8. Freud took this claim from Gustave Le Bon (*Psychology of the Crowd*).
35 M. Mihalka, Soviet strategic deception, 1955–1981, in *Military Deception and Strategic Surprise!*, ed. by J. Gooch, A. Perlmutter, Routledge 1982, pp. 48–101.
36 D.C. Daniel, K.L. Herbig, Propositions on military deception, *The Journal of Strategic Studies* 1982, vol. 5, no. 1, pp. 155–177.
37 D.C. Daniel, K.L. Herbig, Propositions on military deception, *The Journal of Strategic Studies* 1982, vol. 5, no. 1, pp. 155–177.
38 B. Whaley, Toward a general theory of deception, *The Journal of Strategic Studies* 1982, vol. 5, no. 1, pp. 178–192.
39 B. Whaley, Covert rearmament in Germany 1919–1939: Deception and misperception, in *Military Deception and Strategic Surprise!*, ed. by J. Gooch, A. Perlmutter, Routledge 1982, pp. 11–47.
40 M. Mihalka, *Soviet….*
41 M. Mihalka, *Soviet….*
42 H.R. Park, North Korea's nuclear armament strategy and deception, *Defense Studies* 2023, vol. 23, no. 1, pp. 126–147.
43 M. Gyűrösi, *The Soviet Fractional Orbital Bombardment System Program. Technical report APA-TR-2010-0101*, January 2010, pp. 1–1, https://www.ausairpower.net/APA-Sov-FOBS-Program.html.
44 M. Maier, *A little masquerade: Russia's evolving employment of Maskirovka. A monograph*, Fort Leavenworth 2016, https://apps.dtic.mil/sti/citations/AD1022096.
45 T. Thomas, Russia's reflexive control theory and the military, *Journal of Slavic Military Studies* 2004, vol. 17, no. 2, pp. 237–256.
46 G. Le Bon, *The Crowd. A Study of the Popular Mind*, Mineola 2002, p. 67.
47 Department of Defense, *Strategic Communication Joint Integrating Concept*, October 7, 2009, Appendix B, p. B-8, https://www.jcs.mil/Portals/36/Documents/Doctrine/concepts/jic_strategic communications.pdf.
48 N. Beauchamp-Mustafaga, *Chinese next-generation psychological warfare. The military applications of emerging technologies and implications for the United States*, Santa Monica 2023, https://www.rand.org/content/dam/rand/pubs/research_reports/RRA800/RRA853-1/RAND_RRA853-1.pdf.
49 M. Maharaj, B. van Nikerk, The information warfare lifecycle model, *South African Journal of Information Management* 2011, vol. 13, no. 1.
50 T. Ramluckan, B. van Niekerk, The terrorism/mass media symbiosis, *Journal of Information Warfare* 2009, vol. 8, no. 2, pp. 1–12.
51 L.T. Timothy, *Dialectical Versus Empirical Thinking: Ten Key Elements of the Russian Understanding of Information Operations*, Fort Leavenworth 1998.
52 *The Threat from Russia's Unconventional Warfare Beyond Ukraine, 2022–24*. (n.d.). Retrieved 21 February 2024, from https://rusi.org.
53 S. Narula, Psychological operations (PSYOPs): A conceptual overview, *Strategic Analysis* 2004, vol. 28, no. 1, pp. 177–192.
54 S. Narula, Psychological operations (PSYOPs): A conceptual overview, *Strategic Analysis* 2004, vol. 28, no. 1, pp. 177–192.
55 E. Rouse, History of PSYOP, https://www.psywarrior.com/psyhist.html.
56 E. Rouse, History of PSYOP, https://www.psywarrior.com/psyhist.html.
57 *Silicon folklore*, https://siliconfolklore.com/internet-history/.
58 J.M. Hungerford, *The Exploitation of Superstitions for Purposes of Psychological Warfare*, Santa Monica 1950.
59 J.M. Hungerford, *The Exploitation of Superstitions for Purposes of Psychological Warfare*, Santa Monica 1950.
60 S.T. Hosmer, *Maximizing the psychological effects of airpower: Lessons from past wars*, January 1, 1996, https://www.rand.org/pubs/research_briefs/RB38.html.

61 S.T. Hosmer, *Psychological effects of U.S. air operations in four wars, 1941–1991: Lessons for U.S. commanders*, January 1, 1996, https://www.rand.org/pubs/monograph_reports/MR576.html.
62 S.T. Hosmer, *Psychological effects of U.S. air operations in four wars, 1941–1991: Lessons for U.S. commanders*, January 1, 1996, https://www.rand.org/pubs/monograph_reports/MR576.html.
63 R.A. Terry, *Toward a psychological index of weapons effectiveness. Part 1: Field studies*, Technical Report, December 1964, https://apps.dtic.mil/sti/pdfs/AD0609089.pdf.
64 R.A. Terry, *Toward a psychological index of weapons effectiveness. Part 1: Field studies*, Technical Report, December 1964, https://apps.dtic.mil/sti/pdfs/AD0609089.pdf.
65 R.A. Terry, *Toward a psychological index of weapons effectiveness. Part 1: Field studies*, Technical Report, December 1964, https://apps.dtic.mil/sti/pdfs/AD0609089.pdf.
66 R. Snyder, E. Saltz, *Spread of Information Following an Atomic Maneuver*, vol. 2, Washington 1954.
67 J.T. Cappello, G.M. Hall, S.P. Lambert, *Tactical nuclear weapons: Debunking the mythology*, Report, August 2002, https://apps.dtic.mil/sti/pdfs/ADA435014.pdf.
68 G.R. Sessions, *A summary of the psychological effects of tactical nuclear warfare*, April 1984, https://apps.dtic.mil/sti/pdfs/ADP003256.pdf.
69 G.R. Sessions, *A summary of the psychological effects of tactical nuclear warfare*, April 1984, https://apps.dtic.mil/sti/pdfs/ADP003256.pdf.
70 S.M. Becker, Psychological issues in a radiological or nuclear attack, in *Medical Consequences of Radiological and Nuclear Weapons*, ed. by M.K. Lenhart, Fort Detrick 2012, pp. 171–194.
71 R. Vineberg, *Human factors in tactical nuclear combat*, January 1965, p. 97, https://apps.dtic.mil/sti/tr/pdf/AD0647838.pdf.
72 R. Vineberg, *Human factors in tactical nuclear combat*, January 1965, p. 97, https://apps.dtic.mil/sti/tr/pdf/AD0647838.pdf.
73 R. Vineberg, *Human factors in tactical nuclear combat*, January 1965, p. 97, https://apps.dtic.mil/sti/tr/pdf/AD0647838.pdf.
74 R. Vineberg, *Human factors in tactical nuclear combat*, January 1965, p. 97, https://apps.dtic.mil/sti/tr/pdf/AD0647838.pdf.
75 R. Dingman, Atomic diplomacy during the Korean War, *International Security* 1988, vol. 13, no. 3, pp. 50–91.
76 R. Dingman, Atomic diplomacy during the Korean War, *International Security* 1988, vol. 13, no. 3, pp. 50–91.
77 S.J. Cimbala, Information warfare and nuclear conflict termination, *European Security* 1998, vol. 7, no. 4, pp. 69–90.
78 S.J. Cimbala, Information warfare and nuclear conflict termination, *European Security* 1998, vol. 7, no. 4, pp. 69–90.
79 "[E]uphemisms as a propaganda technique in military discourse. As examples, the MX-Missile was renamed the 'Peacekeeper,' and 'collateral damage' often means civilian casualties," R.S. Rodgers, *Propaganda in the Information Age*, Soldier-Scholar, Fall 1996, 20, after W.C. Garrison, *Information operations and counter-propaganda: Making a weapon of public affairs*, Carlisle Barracks 1999, p. 13, https://apps.dtic.mil/sti/tr/pdf/ADA363892.pdf.
80 Department of the Army, *Psychological Operations Tactics, Techniques, and Procedures*, Washington 2003, https://irp.fas.org/doddir/army/fm3-05-301.pdf.
81 Department of the Army, *Psychological Operations Process Tactics, Techniques, and Procedures*, Washington 1994.
82 Department of the Army, *Psychological Operations Process Tactics, Techniques, and Procedures*, Washington 1994, p. 10–7.
83 Department of the Army, *Psychological operations…*, 2003.
84 J. Dykstra, K. Shortridge, J. Met, D. Hough, *Sludge for Good: Slowing and Imposing Costs on Cyber Attackers*, 2022, https://nsarchive.gwu.edu/sites/default/files/documents/rmsj3h-751x3/2022-11-29-arXiv-Sludge-for-Good-Slowing-and-Imposing-Costs-on-Cyber-Attackers-Cornell%20Tech.pdf.
85 J.R. Price, P. Jureidini, *Witchcraft, Sorcery, Magic, and Other Psychological Phenomena and their Implications on Military and Paramilitary Operations in the Congo*, August 8, 1964, https://apps.dtic.mil/sti/citations/AD0464903.

86 J.R. Price, P. Jureidini, *Witchcraft, Sorcery, Magic, and Other Psychological Phenomena and their Implications on Military and Paramilitary Operations in the Congo*, August 8, 1964, https://apps.dtic.mil/sti/citations/AD0464903.
87 S.P. White, The Organizational determinants of military doctrine: A History of Army information operations, *Texas National Security Review* 2023, vol. 6, no. 1.
88 Department of Defense, *Strategic communication...*, p. B-8.
89 H. Lin, The existential threat from cyber-enabled information warfare, *Bulletin of the Atomic Scientists* 2019, vol. 75, no. 4, pp. 187–196.
90 H. Lin, The existential threat from cyber-enabled information warfare, *Bulletin of the Atomic Scientists* 2019, vol. 75, no. 4.
91 Department of the Army, *Information operations: doctrine, tactics, techniques, and procedures*, November 2003, https://irp.fas.org/doddir/army/fm3-13-2003.pdf.
92 U.S. Department of Defense, *Report on military and security developments involving the People's Republic of China*, November 29, 2022, https://www.defense.gov/Spotlights/2022-China-Military-Power-Report/.
93 Department of Defense, *Strategic communication...*, p. 54.
94 Department of Defense, *Strategic communication...*, p. 54.
95 Ministry of Defense, *Allied joint doctrine for strategic communications*, NATO standard AJP-10 (with UK additions), March 2023, https://assets.publishing.service.gov.uk/media/6525459d244f8e00138e7343/AJP_10_Strat_Comm_Change_1_web.pdf.
96 Ministry of Defense, *Allied joint doctrine for strategic communications*, NATO standard AJP-10 (with UK additions), March 2023, https://assets.publishing.service.gov.uk/media/6525459d244f8e00138e7343/AJP_10_Strat_Comm_Change_1_web.pdf, p. A-2.
97 M.E. Price, Strategic communication in asymmetric conflict, *Dynamics of Asymmetric Conflict* 2013, vol. 6, no. 1–3, pp. 135–152.
98 A. Shadid, Exiles Shaping World's Image of Syria Revolt, *The New York Times*, April 23, 2011, https://www.nytimes.com/2011/04/24/world/middleeast/24beirut.html.
99 M.E. Price, *Strategic communication...*
100 A. Flandrin, *"En 1914, la presse accepte la censure parce que la France participe à l'effort de guerre". Pour l'istorien de médias Christian Delporte, le bourrage de crâne ne relève pas d'une volonté délibérée d'instaurer une propagande, mais plutôt d'une succession de dérapages de la presse*, Le Monde, 18 juillet 2014, https://www.lemonde.fr/centenaire-14-18-decryptages/article/2014/07/18/la-presse-accepte-la-censure-parce-que-la-france-participe-a-l-effort-de-guerre_4458959_4366930.html.
101 J.P. Moreux, *Verdun 1916: quand la presse était censurée*, Le Blog de Gallica, mars 4, 2016, https://gallica.bnf.fr/blog/04032016/verdun-1916-quand-la-presse-etait-censuree?mode=desktop.
102 J.P. Moreux, *Verdun 1916: quand la presse était censurée*, Le Blog de Gallica, mars 4, 2016, https://gallica.bnf.fr/blog/04032016/verdun-1916-quand-la-presse-etait-censuree?mode=desktop
103 J.P. Moreux, *Verdun 1916: quand la presse était censurée*, Le Blog de Gallica, mars 4, 2016, https://gallica.bnf.fr/blog/04032016/verdun-1916-quand-la-presse-etait-censuree?mode=desktop
104 *En août 1914, La Croix publie la lettre d'un lecteur qui a pu observer des prisonniers allemands: "au total, ahurissement, mollesse et indifférence des hommes; vanité, cruauté et niaiserie des officiers, voilà les vertus qu'ils nous offrent". On lit dans L'Homme libre du 19 août que" la barbarie allemande ne veut plus connaître aucune borne. Aucun sentiment humain ne retient leur soif de massacre"*, I. Copin, *La propagande dans la presse au début de la Grand guerre*, 26 avril 2019, https://gallica.bnf.fr/blog/print/1057?mode=desktop.
105 *En août 1914, La Croix publie la lettre d'un lecteur qui a pu observer des prisonniers allemands: "au total, ahurissement, mollesse et indifférence des hommes; vanité, cruauté et niaiserie des officiers, voilà les vertus qu'ils nous offrent". On lit dans L'Homme libre du 19 août que" la barbarie allemande ne veut plus connaître aucune borne. Aucun sentiment humain ne retient leur soif de massacre"*, I. Copin, *La propagande dans la presse au début de la Grand guerre*, 26 avril 2019, https://gallica.bnf.fr/blog/print/1057?mode=desktop.
106 Décret-loi du 27 août 1939 Controle de la presse et de publications en temps de guerre, JORF du 28 août 1939.
107 A. Munoz, *US military information...*

108 C.R. Miller, Radio and propaganda, *The Annals of the American Academy of Political and Social Science* 1941, vol. 213, no. 1, pp. 69–74.
109 J. Dawson, Microtargeting as information warfare, *The Cyber Defense Review* 2021, vol. 6, no. 1, pp. 63–80.
110 J. Dawson, Microtargeting as information warfare, *The Cyber Defense Review* 2021, vol. 6, no. 1, pp. 63–80.
111 A. Munoz, *US military information…*
112 I. Zaharia, For God and/or emperor: Habsburg Romanian military chaplains and wartime propaganda in camps for returning POWs, *European Review of History: Revue européenne d'histoire* 2017, vol. 24, no. 2, 288–304.
113 Department of the Army, *Psychological operations…*, 2003.
114 Department of the Army, *Psychological operations…*, 2003.
115 J.B. Whitton, War by radio, *Foreign Affairs* 1941, vol. 19, no. 3, p. 7.
116 J.B. Whitton, War by radio, *Foreign Affairs* 1941, vol. 19, no. 3, p. 7.
117 The Army officer email chain that caused pandemonium, *Military.com*, February 9, 2023, https://www.military.com/daily-news/opinions/2023/02/09/army-officer-email-chain-caused-pandemonium.html.
118 H.M. Horne, Propaganda in war, *Royal United Services Institution Journal* 1930, vol. 75, no. 499, pp. 524–533.
119 E. Kris, Some problems of war propaganda: A note on propaganda new and old, *The Psychoanalytic Quarterly* 1943, vol. 12, no. 3, pp. 381–399.
120 E. Kris, Some problems of war propaganda: A note on propaganda new and old, *The Psychoanalytic Quarterly* 1943, vol. 12, no. 3, pp. 381–399.
121 E. Kris, Some problems of war propaganda: A note on propaganda new and old, *The Psychoanalytic Quarterly* 1943, vol. 12, no. 3, pp. 381–399.
122 Meta's adversarial threat report, third quarter 2022, *Meta*, November 22, 2022, https://about.fb.com/news/2022/11/metas-adversarial-threat-report-q3-2022/.
123 E. Nakashima, Pentagon Opens Sweeping Review of Clandestine Psychological Operations, *Washington Post*, September 20, 2022, https://www.washingtonpost.com/national-security/2022/09/19/pentagon-psychological-operations-facebook-twitter/.
124 E. Nakashima, Pentagon Opens Sweeping Review of Clandestine Psychological Operations, *Washington Post*, September 20, 2022, https://www.washingtonpost.com/national-security/2022/09/19/pentagon-psychological-operations-facebook-twitter/.
125 Removing Coordinated Inauthentic Behavior from France and Russia, *Meta*, December 15, 2020, https://about.fb.com/news/2020/12/removing-coordinated-inauthentic-behavior-france-russia/.
126 *US said to have paid $500m for fake al-Qaeda-style propaganda videos*, October 2, 2016, http://www.timesofisrael.com/us-said-to-have-paid-500m-for-fake-al-qaeda-style-propaganda-videos/.
127 A. Fielding-Smith, C. Black, *Fake news and false flags. How the Pentagon paid a British PR firm $500 million for top secret Iraq propaganda*, October 2, 2016, http://labs.thebureauinvestigates.com/fake-news-and-false-flags/.
128 V. Putin, On the Historical Unity of Russians and Ukrainians, *President of Russia*, July 12, 2021, http://en.kremlin.ru/events/president/news/66181.
129 V. Putin, On the Historical Unity of Russians and Ukrainians, *President of Russia*, July 12, 2021, http://en.kremlin.ru/events/president/news/66181.
130 V. Putin, On the Historical Unity of Russians and Ukrainians, *President of Russia*, July 12, 2021, http://en.kremlin.ru/events/president/news/66181.
131 A.L. George, Prediction of political action by means of propaganda analysis, in *Alexander L. George: A Pioneer in Political and Social Sciences*, ed. D. Caldwell, Springer 2019, pp. 75–87.
132 A.L. George, Prediction of political action by means of propaganda analysis, in *Alexander L. George: A Pioneer in Political and Social Sciences*, ed. D. Caldwell, Springer 2019, pp. 75–87.
133 A.L. George, Prediction of political action by means of propaganda analysis, in *Alexander L. George: A Pioneer in Political and Social Sciences*, ed. D. Caldwell, Springer 2019, pp. 75–87.
134 T. Chadefaux, Early warning signals for war in the news, *Journal of Peace Research* 2014, vol. 51, no. 1, pp. 5–18.

135 H. Hegre, J. Karlsen, H.M. Nygård, H. Strand, H. Urdal, Predicting armed conflict, 2010–2050, *International Studies Quarterly* 2013, vol. 57, no. 2, pp. 250–270.
136 H. Hegre, H.M. Nygård, P. Landsverk, Can we predict armed conflict? How the first 9 years of published forecasts stand up to reality, *International Studies Quarterly* 2021, vol. 65, no. 3, pp. 660–668.
137 M. Zabrodskyi, J. Watling, O.V. Danylyuk, N. Reynolds, *Preliminary lessons in conventional warfighting from Russia's invasion of Ukraine, February–July 2022*, Royal United Services Institute for Defence and Security Studies, November 30, 2022, https://www.rusi.org/explore-our-research/publications/special-resources/preliminary-lessons-conventional-warfighting-russias-invasion-ukraine-february-july-2022.
138 S. Charap, A. Lynch, J.J. Drennan, D. Massicot, G.P. Paoli, *A New Approach to Conventional Arms Control in Europe. Addressing The Security Challenges of the 21st Century*, Santa Monica 2020, p. 21.
139 L. Olejnik, *Belarus is Risking Crisis on the Polish Border*, FP, November 9, 2021, https://foreignpolicy.com/2021/11/09/belarus-poland-border-migrant-crisis/.
140 W.C. Garrison, *Information Operations and Counter-Propaganda: Making A Weapon of Public Affairs*, Carlisle Barracks 1999.
141 G.S. Jowett, V. O'Donnell, *Propaganda & Persuasion*, Beverly Hills 2018.
142 P. Morrow, A Theory of Atrocity Propaganda, *Humanity: An International Journal of Human Rights, Humanitarianism, and Development* 2018, vol. 9, no. 1, p. 6.
143 P.R. Baines, N.J. O'Shaughnessy, Political marketing and propaganda: Uses, abuses, misuses, *Journal of Political Marketing* 2014, vol. 13, no. 1–2, pp. 1–18.
144 M.B. Debney, *Atrocity tales, propaganda and the Nazi invasion of Poland*, https://www.academia.edu/50086023/Atrocity_tales_propaganda_and_the_Nazi_invasion_of_Poland.
145 B.M. Debney, Modelling patterns of scapegoating, in eadem, *The oldest trick in the book: Panic-driven scapegoating in history and recurring patterns of persecution*, Singapore 2020, pp. 59–72.
146 B.M. Debney, Modelling patterns of scapegoating, in eadem, *The oldest trick in the book: Panic-driven scapegoating in history and recurring patterns of persecution*, Singapore 2020, pp. 59–72.
147 B. Webb, Hitler must be laughed at!: The PCA, Propaganda and the perils of parody during wartime, *Historical Journal of Film, Radio and Television* 2019, vol. 39, no. 4, pp. 749–767.
148 K. Yadav, M.J. Riedl, A. Wanless, S. Woolley, *What makes an influence operation malignant*, August 7, 2023, https://carnegieendowment.org/2023/08/07/what-makes-influence-operation-malign-pub-90323.
149 M. Grisé, A. Demus, Y. Shokh, M. Kepe, J.W. Welburn, K. Holynska, *Rivalry in the Information Sphere: Russian Conceptions of Information Confrontation*, Santa Monica 2022.
150 M. Grisé, A. Demus, Y. Shokh, M. Kepe, J.W. Welburn, K. Holynska, *Rivalry in the Information Sphere: Russian Conceptions of Information Confrontation*, Santa Monica 2022.
151 Convention on the Prohibition of the Development, Production and Stockpiling of Bacteriological (Biological) and Toxin Weapons and on Their Destruction, drawn up in Moscow, London and Washington on April 10, 1972.
152 Letter dated October 24, 2022 from the Permanent Representative of the Russian Federation to the United Nations addressed to the President of the Security Council, S/2022/796, https://undocs.org/Home/Mobile?FinalSymbol=S%2F2022%2F796&Language=E&DeviceType=Desktop&LangRequested=False.
153 Toxic Mosquito Aerial Release System—Patent US-8967029-B1, PubChem, https://pubchem.ncbi.nlm.nih.gov/patent/US-8967029-B1#section=Information-Sources.
154 B. Woodward, *How Much More of Russia's Nonsense do We have to Endure: UK Statement at the Security Council*, GOV.UK, October 27, 2022, https://www.gov.uk/government/speeches/how-much-more-of-russias-nonsense-do-we-have-to-endure-uk-statement-at-the-security-council.
155 *Ukraine—Joint Statement by Foreign Ministers of France, the United Kingdom and the United States*, Ministère de l'Europe et des Affaires étrangères, October 24, 2022, https://www.diplomatie.gouv.fr/en/country-files/ukraine/news/article/ukraine-joint-statement-by-foreign-ministers-of-france-the-united-kingdom-and.

156 Questions of the Russian Federation to the United States and Ukraine regarding the compliance with their obligations under the Convention on the Prohibition of the Development, Production and Stockpiling of Bacteriological (Biological) and Toxin Weapons and on Their Destruction (BTWC) in the context of the activities of biological laboratories in the territory of Ukraine, BWC/CONS/2022/WP.7, https://www.mid.ru/upload/medialibrary/e16/G2248060%20questions%20to%20Ukraine%20(Part%201%20of%20Article%20I)%20ENG.pdf.
157 *Response by the United States of America to the request by the Russian Federation for a consultative meeting under Article V of the Biological and Toxin Weapons Convention (BWC)*, August 22, 2022, https://www.state.gov/wp-content/uploads/2022/09/Response-of-the-United-States-to-Questions-Posed-by-the-Russian-Federation.pdf#page=2.
158 *United Nations not aware of any biological weapons programs in Ukraine, Senior Disarmament Affairs Official Tells Security Council*, UN Press, October 27, 2022, https://press.un.org/en/2022/sc15084.doc.htm.
159 *Security Council rejects text to investigate complaint concerning non-compliance of Biological Weapons Convention by Ukraine, United States*, UN Press, November 2, 2022, https://press.un.org/en/2022/15095.doc.htm.
160 R. Roffey, A.K. Tunemalm, Biological weapons allegations: A Russian propaganda tool to negatively implicate the United States, *The Journal of Slavic Military Studies* 2017, vol. 30, no. 4, pp. 521–542.
161 *The Kremlin's never-ending attempt to spread disinformation about biological weapons*, U.S. Department of State, March 14, 2023, https://www.state.gov/the-kremlins-never-ending-attempt-to-spread-disinformation-about-biological-weapons/.
162 *The Kremlin's never-ending attempt to spread disinformation about biological weapons*, U.S. Department of State, March 14, 2023, https://www.state.gov/the-kremlins-never-ending-attempt-to-spread-disinformation-about-biological-weapons/.
163 T. Kuzio, Old wine in a new bottle: Russia's modernization of traditional Soviet information warfare and active policies against Ukraine and Ukrainians, *The Journal of Slavic Military Studies* 2019, vol. 32, no. 4, pp. 485–506.
164 T. Kuzio, Old wine in a new bottle: Russia's modernization of traditional Soviet information warfare and active policies against Ukraine and Ukrainians, *The Journal of Slavic Military Studies* 2019, vol. 32, no. 4, pp. 485–506.
165 H. Mölder, V. Sazonov, Information warfare as the Hobbesian concept of modern times—the principles, techniques, and tools of Russian information operations in the Donbass, *The Journal of Slavic Military Studies* 2018, vol. 31, no. 3, pp. 308–328.
166 T. Hobbes, *Leviathan*, London 1651, after H. Mölder, V. Sazonov, *Information warfare....*
167 T. Kuzio, *Old wine...*
168 I discuss these issues at length in my book *Philosophy of Cybersecurity (CRC Press, 2023).*
169 V. Putin, *On the historical...*
170 G. Roncone, A. Wahlstrom, A. Revelli, D. Mainor, S. Riddell, B. Readdell, UNC1151 assessed with high confidence to have links to Belarus, Ghostwriter Campaign aligned with Belarusian government interests, *Mandiant*, November 16, 2021, https://www.mandiant.com/resources/blog/unc1151-linked-to-belarus-government.
171 *Analysis of cyber attack on Ukrainian government resources*, CSIRT MON, January 17, 2022, https://csirt-mon.wp.mil.pl/pl/articles/6-aktualnosci/analiza-cyberataku-na-ukrainskie-zasoby-rzadowe/.
172 H. Foy, J. Politi, R. Olearchyk, US accuses Russia of planning 'false-flag operation' in eastern Ukraine, *Financial Times*, January 14, 2022, https://www.ft.com/content/ac431782-62c6-4f3a-a08e-d832fc4ac2a1.
173 H. Foy, J. Politi, R. Olearchyk, US accuses Russia of planning 'false-flag operation' in eastern Ukraine, *Financial Times*, January 14, 2022, https://www.ft.com/content/ac431782-62c6-4f3a-a08e-d832fc4ac2a1.

174 M. Untersinger, *Ukraine: Une cyberattaque contre des sites gouvernementaux n'a provoqué "aucune fuite de données personnelles"*, LeMonde.fr, janvier 14 2022, https://www.lemonde.fr/international/article/2022/01/14/ukraine-une-cyberattaque-touche-de-nombreux-sites-gouvernementaux_6109424_3210.html.
175 G. Myre, *From drone videos to selfies at the front, Ukraine is the most documented war ever*, NPR, August 2, 2023, https://www.npr.org/2023/08/02/1191557426/ukraine-war-news-coverage.
176 G. Myre, *From drone videos to selfies at the front, Ukraine is the most documented war ever*, NPR, August 2, 2023, https://www.npr.org/2023/08/02/1191557426/ukraine-war-news-coverage.
177 M. Zabrodskyi, J. Watling, O.V. Danylyuk, N. Reynolds, *Preliminary lessons in conventional warfighting from Russia's invasion of Ukraine, February–July 2022*, Royal United Services Institute for Defence and Security Studies, November 30, 2022, https://www.rusi.org/explore-our-research/publications/special-resources/preliminary-lessons-conventional-warfighting-russias-invasion-ukraine-february-july-2022.
178 S. Mitzer, J. Oliemans, *Lost in lies: Keeping track of Russian propaganda claims*, Oryx, October 28, 2022, https://web.archive.org/web/20230928080840/https://www.oryxspioenkop.com/2022/10/lost-in-lies-keeping-track-of-russian.html.
179 S. Al-Atrush, M. Seddon, Kremlin Backers Openly Target Russia's Generals for Battlefield Setbacks, *Financial Times*, October 7, 2022, https://www.ft.com/content/41352a44-d723-4d06-abb0-ea41feffe4e.
180 V. Kim, E. Schmitt, Ukraine says it shot down hypersonic Russian missiles over Kyiv, *The New York Times*, May 16, 2023, https://www.nytimes.com/2023/05/16/world/europe/ukraine-russia-hypersonic-kinzhal-patriot.html.
181 T. Lozoventko, China's envoy does not believe US-made patriot shot down Russian hypersonic missiles over Ukraine in May—Financial Times, *Ukrainska Pravda*, July 5, 2023, https://www.pravda.com.ua/eng/news/2023/07/5/7409908/.
182 No country has capability to counter Russian Kinzhal hypersonic missiles—Rostec, *TASS*, July 10, 2023, https://tass.com/defense/1644661.
183 *The guns of August 2008: Russia's war in Georgia*, ed. by S.E. Cornell, S.F. Starr, Armonk 2009.
184 D. Kumar, Media, war, and propaganda: Strategies of information management during the 2003 Iraq war, *Communication and Critical/Cultural Studies* 2006, vol. 3, no. 1, pp. 48–69.
185 M.J. McNerney, B. Connable, S.R. Zimmerman, N. Lander, M.N. Posard, J.J. Castillo, D. Madden, I. Blum, A. Frank, B.J. Fernandes, I.H. Seol, Ch. Paul, A. Parasiliti, *National will to fight: Why some states keep fighting and others don't*, Santa Monica 2019, https://www.rand.org/content/dam/rand/pubs/research_reports/RR2400/RR2477/RAND_RR2477.pdf.
186 M. Shaw, Russia's genocidal war in Ukraine: Radicalization and social destruction, *Journal of Genocide Research*, March 8, 2023, https://www.tandfonline.com/doi/abs/10.1080/14623528.2023.2185372?journalCode=cjgr20.
187 M. Shaw, Russia's genocidal war in Ukraine: Radicalization and social destruction, *Journal of Genocide Research*, March 8, 2023, https://www.tandfonline.com/doi/abs/10.1080/14623528.2023.2185372?journalCode=cjgr20.
188 P. Wehr, Nonviolent resistance to occupation: Norway and Czechoslovakia, *Journal of Social Issues* 1974.
189 R. Ramesh, R.S. Raman, A. Virkud, A. Dirksen, A. Huremagic, D. Fifield, D. Rodenburg, R. Hynes, D. Madory, R. Ensafi, *Network responses to Russia's invasion of Ukraine in 2022: A cautionary tale for Internet freedom*, https://www.usenix.org/conference/usenixsecurity23/presentation/ramesh-network-responses.
190 M. Zabrodskyi, J. Watling, O.V. Danylyuk, N. Reynolds, *Preliminary lessons…*
191 D. Geissler, D. Bär, N. Pröllochs, S. Feuerriegel, Russian propaganda on social media during the 2022 invasion of Ukraine, *EPJ Data Science* 2023, vol. 12, https://epjdatascience.springeropen.com/articles/10.1140/epjds/s13688-023-00414-5.
192 F. Sharevski, B. Kessell, *Fight fire with fire: Hacktivists' take on social media misinformation*, 2023, https://www.usenix.org/conference/soups2023/presentation/sharevski.
193 F. Sharevski, B. Kessell, *Fight fire with fire: Hacktivists' take on social media misinformation*, 2023, https://www.usenix.org/conference/soups2023/presentation/sharevski.
194 F. Sharevski, B. Kessell, *Fight fire with fire: Hacktivists' take on social media misinformation*, 2023, https://www.usenix.org/conference/soups2023/presentation/sharevski.

195 T.P. Gerber, J. Zavisca, Does Russian propaganda work?, *The Washington Quarterly* 2016, vol. 39, no. 2, pp. 79–98.
196 F. Splidsboel Hansen, When Russia wages war in the cognitive domain, *The Journal of Slavic Military Studies* 2021, vol. 34, no. 2, pp. 181–201.
197 T.W. Kleisner, *Tactical TikTok for great power competition applying the lesson of Ukraine's IO Campaign to Future Large-Scale Conventional Operations*, Army University Press, April 2022, https://www.armyupress.army.mil/journals/military-review/online-exclusive/2022-ole/kleisner-and-garmey/.
198 T.W. Kleisner, *Tactical TikTok for great power competition applying the lesson of Ukraine's IO Campaign to Future Large-Scale Conventional Operations*, Army University Press, April 2022, https://www.armyupress.army.mil/journals/military-review/online-exclusive/2022-ole/kleisner-and-garmey/.
199 Military drone from Ukraine war crashes into Croatian capital Zagreb, *The Guardian*, March 11, 2022, https://www.theguardian.com/world/2022/mar/11/ukraine-military-drone-crashes-into-croatian-capital-zagreb.
200 О. Ганюкова, *"Настав час розплати": хакери зламали росТБ і показали ролик із ЗСУ та "Лебедине озеро". Відео*, OBOZ.UA, 13 июля 2023, https://news.obozrevatel.com/ukr/russia/nastav-chas-rozplati-hakeri-zlamali-rostb-i-pokazali-rolik-iz-zsu-ta-lebedine-ozero-video.htm.
201 Из-за хакерской атаки жители Черноземья услышали по радио о *мнимой* угрозе ракетного удара, *Коммерсантъ*, 22 февраля 2023, https://www.kommersant.ru/doc/5841058.
202 D. Black, G. Roncone, *The GRU's disruptive playbook*, Mandian, July 12, 2023, https://www.mandiant.com/resources/blog/gru-disruptive-playbook.
203 D. Black, G. Roncone, *The GRU's disruptive playbook*, Mandian, July 12, 2023, https://www.mandiant.com/resources/blog/gru-disruptive-playbook.
204 D. Kapellmann Zafra, K. Lunden, N. Brubaker, We (did!) start the fire: Hacktivists increasingly claim targeting of OT systems, *Mandiant*, 22 March 2023, https://www.mandiant.com/resources/blog/hacktivists-targeting-ot-systems.
205 J. Greig, *Coverage of killnet DDoS attacks plays into attackers' hands, experts say*, October 11, 2022, https://therecord.media/coverage-of-killnet-ddos-attacks-plays-into-attackers-hands-experts-say.
206 *Кіберполіція Викрила Організаторів Ботоферм, Які Поширювали Ворожу Пропаганду Та Займалися* Інтернет-Шахрайствами, Департамент Кіберполіції, 18 липня 2023, https://cyberpolice.gov.ua/news/kiberpolicziya-vykryla-organizatoriv-botoferm-yaki-poshyryuvaly-vorozhu-propagandu-ta-zajmalysya-internet-shaxrajstvamy-7156/.
207 J. Watling, O.V. Danylyuk, N. Reynolds, *Preliminary lessons from Russia's unconventional operations during the Russo-Ukrainian War, February 2022—February 2023*, RUSI, March 29, 2023, https://rusi.org/explore-our-research/publications/special-resources/preliminary-lessons-russias-unconventional-operations-during-russo-ukrainian-war-february-2022.
208 J. Watling, O.V. Danylyuk, N. Reynolds, *Preliminary lessons from Russia's unconventional operations during the Russo-Ukrainian War, February 2022—February 2023*, RUSI, March 29, 2023, https://rusi.org/explore-our-research/publications/special-resources/preliminary-lessons-russias-unconventional-operations-during-russo-ukrainian-war-february-2022.
209 J. Watling, O.V. Danylyuk, N. Reynolds, *Preliminary lessons from Russia's unconventional operations during the Russo-Ukrainian War, February 2022—February 2023*, RUSI, March 29, 2023, https://rusi.org/explore-our-research/publications/special-resources/preliminary-lessons-russias-unconventional-operations-during-russo-ukrainian-war-february-2022.
210 J. Tomé, D. Belson, Tracking shifts in Internet connectivity in Kherson, Ukraine, *The Cloudflare Blog*, May 4, 2022, http://blog.cloudflare.com/tracking-shifts-in-internet-connectivity-in-kherson-ukraine/.
211 G. De Vynck, R. Lerman, C. Zakrzewski, How Ukraine's internet still works despite Russian bombs, cyberattacks, *Washington Post*, March 29, 2022, https://www.washingtonpost.com/technology/2022/03/29/ukraine-internet-faq/.
212 J. Beck, Ukraine's repair crews dodge bullets and splice cable to keep the country online, *Bloomberg.com*, November 17, 2022, https://www.bloomberg.com/news/features/2022-11-17/ukraine-stays-online-during-war-thanks-to-repair-crews.

213 L. Olejnik, Smartphones blur the line between civilian and combatant, *Wired*, June 6, 2023, https://www.wired.com/story/smartphones-ukraine-civilian-combatant/.
214 Protecting civilians against digital threats during armed conflict, *ICRC*, 19 October 2023, https://www.icrc.org/en/document/protecting-civilians-against-digital-threats-during-armed-conflict.
215 A. Staalesen, Pensioner tried to set fire to military recruitment office in northern Russian town Usinsk, *The Independent Barents Observer*, April 14, 2023, https://thebarentsobserver.com/en/life-and-public/2023/04/pensioner-tried-set-fire-military-recruitment-office-north-russian-town.
216 S. Alinsky, *Rules for radicals: A practical primer for realistic radicals*, New York 1989; J.M. Waller, Weaponizing ridicule, *Military Review* 2017, vol. 97, pp. 49–59.
217 M. Srivastava, Ch. Miller, R. Olearchyk, "Trolling helps show the king has no clothes": How Ukraine's army conquered Twitter, *Financial Times*, October 14, 2022, https://www.ft.com/content/b07224e1-414c-4fbd-8e2f-cfda052f7bb2.
218 SUCHO Meme Wall, https://memes.sucho.org/.
219 A. Rakityanskaya, The SUCHO Ukrainian war memes collection, *Slavic & East European Information Resources* 2023, vol. 24, no. 1, pp. 53–70.
220 S. Budnitsky, Global disengagement: Public diplomacy humor in the Russian-Ukrainian war, *Place Branding and Public Diplomacy* 2023, vol. 19, no. 2, pp. 211–217.
221 Z. Cass, Don't answer that! Russia-aligned TA499 Beleaguers targets with video call requests, *Proofpoint*, March 1, 2023, https://www.proofpoint.com/us/blog/threat-insight/dont-answer-russia-aligned-ta499-beleaguers-targets-video-call-requests.
222 A. Sennett, Film propaganda: Triumph of the Will as a case study, *Framework: The Journal of Cinema and Media* 2014, vol. 55, no. 1, pp. 45–65.
223 *Déclaration de Catherine Colonna—Ingérences numériques étrangères—Détection par la France d'une campagne de manipulation de l'information*, Ministère de l'Europe et des Affaires étrangères, juin 13, 2023, https://www.diplomatie.gouv.fr/fr/politique-etrangere-de-la-france/securite-desarmement-et-non-proliferation/actualites-et-evenements-lies-a-la-securite-au-desarmement-et-a-la-non/2023/article/declaration-de-catherine-colonna-ingerences-numeriques-etrangeres-detection-par.
224 *RRN: Une Campagne Numérique de Manipulation de l'information Complexe et Persistante*, SGDSN, 19 juin 2023, http://www.sgdsn.gouv.fr/publications/maj-19062023-rrn-une-campagne-numerique-de-manipulation-de-linformation-complexe-et.
225 B.J. Auten, Political diasporas and exiles as instruments of statecraft, *Comparative Strategy* 2006, vol. 25, no. 4, pp. 329–341.
226 M. Czarnecka, Aucune trace d'œuvres de street-art anti-Zelensky prétendument apparues dans plusieurs villes du monde, *Factuel*, February 6, 2023, https://factuel.afp.com/doc.afp.com.338B2DL.
227 Jigsaw, Defanging disinformation's threat to Ukrainian refugees, *Medium*, February 14, 2023, https://medium.com/jigsaw/defanging-disinformations-threat-to-ukrainian-refugees-b164dbbc1c60.
228 Jigsaw, Defanging disinformation's threat to Ukrainian refugees, *Medium*, February 14, 2023, https://medium.com/jigsaw/defanging-disinformations-threat-to-ukrainian-refugees-b164dbbc1c60.
229 S. González-Bailón, Y. Lelkes, Do social media undermine social cohesion? A critical review, *Social Issues and Policy Review* 2023, vol. 17, no. 1, pp. 155–180.
230 R.M. Bond, C.J. Fariss, J.J. Jones, A.D. Kramer, C. Marlow, J.E. Settle, J.H. Fowler, A 61-million-person experiment in social influence and political mobilization, *Nature* 2012, vol. 489, no. 7415, pp. 295–298.
231 C. Richards, *Boyd's OODA Loop*, Necesse, 2020, vol. 5, no. 1, https://ooda.de/media/chet_richards_-_boyds_ooda_loop.pdf.
232 J. Ferris, Netcentric warfare, C4ISR and information operations: Towards a revolution in military intelligence?, *Intelligence & National Security* 2004, vol. 19, no. 2, pp. 199–225.
233 J.L. Snyder, The Soviet strategic culture: Implications for limited nuclear operations, September 1977, p. 8, https://www.rand.org/content/dam/rand/pubs/reports/2005/R2154.pdf.
234 P.W. Gray, XII. Why study military history?, *Defense Studies* 2005, vol. 5, no. 1, pp. 151–164.
235 S. Shaheen, The Russia-Ukraine war through the lens of strategic culture, *Journal of International Affairs* 2023, vol. 75, no. 2, pp. 247–264.

Chapter 8

The end is near

We are coming to the end of the journey with propaganda. I realize that the perception of some of the content in this book may vary. It may be seen as controversial, or uncomfortable. Such is the subject matter. Such are the risks involved. This is the challenge of our times.

The understanding of this topic is not only worthwhile—it is even absolutely necessary. Especially in this day and age. Being equipped with this knowledge and information in the information age—in our era—is indispensable and crucial. For my part, I strived to ensure that the presentation of this material is done in an unbiased, objective way, based on sources and references, in academic format, with good quality. As I point out in places, I strived not to impose my views on the Readers. I leave it to each individual to formulate his or her own opinions.

References to historical facts, content, and elements are dictated by necessity, relevance, objective needs, and expert considerations. This is an expert book on security, security studies, strategic studies, and science. By nature of the topic, issues of technology, such as information technology, are critical, but sociology, psychology, and anthropology remain relevant and important; aspects of military, politics, diplomacy, international relations, and others cannot be omitted as well. Hence, for these fields as well, the book is of value.

I prepared this book being aware of the rapid changes. I tried to write it in such a way that it would be as accessible to the reader as possible and that it would stand the test of time. So that it would remain relevant for long, perhaps even 50 years or beyond? While working on this book, I used materials from several hundred years ago, being aware of materials from the 19th and 20th centuries that constitute milestones in this field. I understand how the subject was looked at in the 19th century, and how it evolved into the 1920s or in the 1960s. And how we view propaganda today. Such a broad awareness of the subject allowed me to write this book just so. So if the Readers find reasons to reach for it many years after its publication, I hope they will find valuable insight. Of course, technical issues, like infrastructural aspects, will inevitably change, but the analysis of the means of radio propagation in the 1920s or 1960s still provides analytical value today. I believe similar will be true of the trends captured in this book and the technological moment of the third decade of the 21st century.

The basic principle will remain in force: not everything is as it may appear at first glance.

We started with history from several centuries ago, we even touched on Antiquity. Of course, for the most part, the issues covered are those of the 20th and 21st centuries, times more familiar to us.

I discussed what propaganda is and outlined the profiles of several instrumental figures involved in its development. This shows that … actually, after reading this book, the Reader should already know what it shows. "Propaganda" as a term that is today completely demonized, perceived even pejoratively. This has not always been the case, the word was used to describe ordinary activities such as propagating information, educating, and using methods to steer societies in a direction. This would suggest that propaganda in itself is not necessarily

DOI: 10.1201/9781003499497-8

good, or bad, while the purposes of its use may be. However, there is no escaping the negative connotation of the term. Therefore, today we often utilize other terms: public relations, public affairs, etc., reserving the term "propaganda" for activities more focused on informational influence.

I do not prejudge how the Reader should perceive the term, or the wording. It is an individual decision. But everyone must admit that "propaganda," as a term for spreading information about health, does not sound harmful. Medical doctors thought the same way back in the 20th century. Thus, the phrase can be understood in many ways—as a legal, technical, military, political, or journalistic term.

We function in a world that is rich, complicated, complex, and beautiful, sometimes difficult to grasp. To make the analysis of information processes more efficient, easier, or at all possible—simplifications are introduced: mathematical, physical, and mental models. Such a model is the information environment—a certain system distinguishing elements that have informational influence. Elements of the system influence this environment, in some specific way (e.g., technical), for some specific purpose (intentions), to some extent (effectiveness). When designing, but also analyzing, influence or propaganda campaigns, it is always worth specifying such a model.

Technically, the case is fascinating. It started with poems, stories, and rumors. The invention of the printing press was a revolution. It enabled the creation of books or pamphlets repetitively and on an industrial scale. Print, however, has a limited reach. This changed with radio—the ability to distribute the message universally. Radio technology is at the root of the first major interstate controversies over the direction of propaganda and was used before, during, and after wars—to shape the information environment. Sometimes to simply cause a stir or popularize entertainment (such as music), and other times to promulgate content leading to genocide.

Forms and technical capabilities have developed continuously, with another renaissance brought by newer technologies such as television, the Internet, and social media, including short film or audio creations. An important stage in technical development was microtargeting—reaching small groups of people, perhaps individuals, with precision. Another revolution are information processing methods—computational methods, including machine learning or artificial intelligence techniques. Certainly, the new information techniques will be adapted for information influence, not necessarily just political, military, social, or medical. But also in commercial activities, such as in advertising.

Violating the sovereignty of States is a violation of culture and the principles of international law. This can also be brought about by information methods. States could or may impose restrictions on the exchange and flows of information within their territory. However, censorship is a delicate matter—because it touches the freedom of expression and freedom of speech—some of the basic values on which the functioning of a democratic society is based, protected by strong guarantees in the world of Western States. Undoubtedly, actions in the political and military spheres—such as the kinetic attacks in Ukraine—have also affected the information environment in Europe. Countermeasures have been deployed, isolation has been introduced, and certain information channels have been cut off. This underscores that the information environment is a complex thing, and in order to introduce changes, or interferences, or to defend from such activities, certain well-motivated legal and political conditions are needed.

This is because propaganda and information influence is a state-on-state process, with an impact on real-world events. Conversely, events in the physical world affect the information environment. New technologies in particular offer rich opportunities for influence, even information diversion. Also because they are new. So they are prone to be misunderstood, or underestimated by some parties. In general, however, it is challenging to assess what measure to apply to the effectiveness of propaganda or information operations. The most appropriate measure are the effects achieved.

There is a plethora of information incentives in pluralistic countries. Many people, institutions, entities, and parties—influence the information environment. In a totalitarian state, everything can be subordinated and subjugated to a single goal and message: from means of informing people, to education, advertising, etc. In a pluralist state, it is more difficult to create an effective informational impact for the simple reason—there are many sources of information. There is no obligation to read or listen to only one of them. On the scale of a pluralistic society, it is difficult to assume that everyone becomes "plugged in" to one relay. Here, there is free choice—everyone decides where they get information from. One can try to influence this, but still, everyone has free will and access to multiple sources of information. Another issue entirely is what people actually do with their free will. It is wiser to try to understand the informational and psychological conditions, instead of blaming someone, such as society as a whole, for not being as it should be in someone's view.

Propaganda and psychological operations (PSYOP) have accompanied wars for a long time. These methods are lawful and explicitly provided for as permitted by international law and laws of armed conflict. This "legalization" is an expression of the methodical use of such methods from times immemorial. They were used by Richelieu, Napoleon, Bismarck, Lenin, and many after them. An understanding of the need for information capability exists in the armed forces of all States, and information operations can accompany others, such as kinetic ones.

Is this indeed the end? Of this book—yes, it is the end. As for you, dear Reader, I would like to believe that this is the beginning. I hope that the knowledge in this book and the way it is laid out has appealed to you. Always keep in mind a basic fact: information surrounds us, and it affects us. Even if this information is neutral, we can react to it, and ignoring it is also a reaction—if only a defensive one against information overload. In some situations, the possibility arises that events will be exploited and others will even be created to drive informational influence in some direction. This can apply to the encouragement to buy shoes but also to many other issues, much more serious.

Thus, I wish you successful analyses, but ideally without exaggeration—keep things in the right proportions. Analyzing everything around too deeply and breaking it down into parts or subparticles is tiring and makes life unbearable. This is also why cleverly crafted propaganda can have an effect, but in principle, not much can be done about it. It's important to deal with situations that matter, when the stakes are high. When the impact can be significant.

And this is the point where I leave you.

Appendix

Author's postscript

INVISIBLE DISABILITY IN THE WORLD OF TECHNOLOGY

My name is Lukasz Olejnik. I have been disabled since the end of primary school. In 1999, I underwent a brain tumor surgery in a very difficult location. It goes without saying that the consequences of such a procedure can be very serious; in my case, it resulted *just* in hearing problems that can't be corrected with a hearing aid.

I had to deal with this in school, high school, during college, throughout my PhD, and now in my professional career. My disability has a health and a social dimension. Living with a disability that isn't evident to others poses some unique challenges, and that's what I'd like to focus on in this article. (I have had other challenges in my life, but in this essay I want to focus on disability).

I'm sharing my story and experiences to help others who might be struggling with similar difficulties; I hope it can be helpful for at least one person struggling with difficulties such as disability, lack of self-esteem, or uncertainty about the future. As for those who have been spared this fate, I would like to make them more aware of what others might be going through and encourage them to be open to people who are struggling with disabilities.

Let me start with an example: with my hearing loss, it is really difficult for me to perform two activities at the same time. For instance, I can't listen and take notes at the same time. At university, I coped by photocopying notes from students or professors, but undoubtedly some nuances of lectures eluded me. I looked for more information on the Internet, in books, and in publications. I had to put significantly more time and effort into studying than others. It paid off: my master's thesis resulted in a scientific publication that's cited to this day. I was lucky to do this work under the guidance of an excellent supervisor. In the early stage of my research, it helped that much of the work didn't require collaboration with others. Reading publications and books, or writing, I could do independently. This definitely worked in my favor. My subsequent publications proved to be a continuation of my earlier success and opened many doors. From there began my work in cybersecurity, and fortune led me to places like CERN (The European Organization for Nuclear Research), University College London, and the International Committee of the Red Cross. All of these places aim to challenge their staff. To me, each presented additional, unforeseen obstacles.

I went to France for my doctoral studies. Since 2011, I have worked as a researcher at the French Institute for Research in Computer Science and Automation (INRIA). Learning a foreign language with a hearing impairment is quite a challenge—it's hard to learn correct pronunciation and speech comprehension. I learned the basics of English prior to my fateful surgery, which helped in the future development of this skill, but French came later and proved to be especially difficult, with its phonetics, syntax, and fast speech rate. Around that time, I also discovered an interesting effect: consuming a small amount of wine improved my understanding of speech (of course, going overboard, on the other hand, negatively affects perceptual abilities, as any reader probably understands).

In 2015, I defended my Ph.D. thesis in Computer Science (privacy and security). I studied the privacy of web and online advertising systems and cast a light on a number of serious issues. I demonstrated risks and security weaknesses in web browsers. I believe that my work led to significant real-world improvements in reducing data leaks.

Despite my academic successes, I had an acute sense of my limitations while working on my Ph.D. I realized how great an impact disability has on the lives of everyone who experiences it, including young scientists. My daily work was very individual. My supervisor and other Institute staff supported me very much, and I will always be very grateful for this. Unfortunately, at the same time, I realized how big a problem meetings in larger groups are: both when it comes to work and to social after-work outings, which unfortunately I had to give up for fear of being misunderstood.

I faced similar challenges when attending scientific conferences. Participation, listening, and presenting were never an issue. Even when fielding questions from the audience, I could simply approach the person and ask them to repeat the question or ask the session chair for assistance. But again, my hearing impairment limited my ability to participate in group discussions, including informal networking opportunities, such as those after the presentation, during coffee breaks, lunches, and dinners. This is when others have the opportunity to gain contacts, make friends, or collaborate, increasing their chances of interesting future projects. I've had to limit myself to smaller groups, or individual conversations. Not everyone finds this convenient or acceptable. The effect is that it all depends on where one stands, or with whom in particular one exchanges a few words. In essence, a kind of career lottery.

These days, a lot can be achieved by communicating over the Internet, but even there, hearing still plays a major role. Professional, conference, or even personal meetings are often dynamic and chaotic. For people like me, following the flow of such interactions can be a challenge. One approach is to identify a couple of key participants and focus my full attention on them, but this doesn't always pan out.

It helps to set an agenda and goals for the meeting beforehand, but this requires planning and cooperation from all participants. Limitations on communication due to hearing loss can raise questions and thoughts about how well one can really function in today's educational or scientific system, or even outside of it more broadly in technology or policy communities. There are situations where overcoming these limitations can be very difficult.

Today, automatic transcription applications, like speech-to-text on smartphones, are a great help, although they don't always perform well. For most of my life, however, I didn't have access to such solutions.

With a hearing impairment, you often find yourself an outsider, effectively excluded from the flow of events, with the need for intuitive adoption of goals and priorities, and sometimes, out-of-the-box thinking. Unconventional approaches may not be welcome or acceptable to everyone in academia, in the corporate world, or in office life. And yes, I am such an outsider. Those are the cards I've been dealt. Isolation from others is not my intention, although some people may make this simplistic conclusion.

My disability is *invisible*. You can't see it when looking at me on the street. You can't see it when I appear at a conference, or when I give an interview. Paradoxically, this in itself can be a problem: in fact, because I learned to compensate for it so well, some people who don't know me might doubt I have a hearing impairment when they interact with me. And therein lies the crux of the social dimension of my disability: its invisibility can lead to misunderstanding. People may assume that I heard something; that I know what the conversation was about, what they said to me, what they asked me to do. When I don't respond as they would expect, they may consider me ignorant or arrogant. This, in turn, can lead to untrue or mistaken conclusions and opinions about me. This social dimension of disability in interpersonal relations is much more complex than it might seem.

What can I do? I may ask if I heard something correctly. And if I have the opportunity, I do so to avoid misunderstandings. This can seem weird in various workplace interactions, including watercooler, "at the printer" chats, or at lunchtime. At times, it feels easier not to ask questions, not to speak up, and to accept not knowing what the conversation is about. As if that would happen, that is, if I would even go to a lunch or pub outing with a group. As I explained earlier with the example of balancing listening *or* writing at the same time, a similar challenge occurs with listening *or* eating simultaneously.

So, what can an "outsider" do? I love walking, running, swimming, and reading books. I love culinary culture and local specialties, and I am a bit of a wine aficionado (here, the doctorate in France and work in Switzerland came in handy). My childhood sentiment for agriculture and farming also stayed with me. And I write a lot.

But speaking of foreign countries: moving can be unexpectedly complicated for people with disabilities too. I experienced a lot of support but also confusion and headaches. I did not think that the differences between health care systems would prove so significant. In France, for example, I was able to find a family doctor who was willing to communicate by SMS or e-mail, and it was possible to interact with many specialists in English; this was not so easy in Belgium. In the United Kingdom (London), in my situation, everything worked quite well, due to a system of correspondence between doctors that made sure all health details were written down, making any confusion or mishearing impossible. In Poland, for the most part it was satisfactory, although the antiquated system of making appointments in person or over the phone would get in the way. In the end, it wasn't about the quality of health care as much as the challenges of navigating the bureaucracy.

I'm actually not able to talk over the phone. This proved to be a great challenge when it came to, for example, dealing with the bank or the public services. Sometimes while abroad, there was no one who could make such a phone call on my behalf, so I was left to write and send traditional postal letters. In that scenario, instead of receiving a response the same day, I sometimes had to wait weeks or months. Of course, it's not all doom and gloom. For example, in France, I experienced an uplifting story. I once walked into an office in a small town, 20 minutes before closing time. I explained the problem I had, asking them to contact another office on my behalf, and to help me fill out an official form. Everyone was very helpful and friendly, and the matter was resolved without an issue. Sometimes you have to think outside of the box and bypass systemic problems implemented by bureaucracy, offices, corporate structures, and banks, and sometimes you can count on the help and kindness of wonderful strangers.

I act as an independent researcher and consultant, working on technology, cybersecurity, and privacy. Digital and technology issues are often at the intersection of technology, law, and policy. To develop my skills I completed a law degree (LL.M) at the University of Edinburgh. I can communicate effectively, including with the media. I have developed a standard of activity and have been providing expert commentary to international media (including *Washington Post*, *New York Times*, *Financial Times*, *Le Monde*, and others) for more than a decade. This requires clear and comprehensive communication about often difficult and complex topics. My interactions with journalists have taken place in a variety of ways: written text, and less often by voice or video conference. I can't use the phone, which was sometimes received with surprise, or even doubt; I then tried to explain my situation, even if in the dynamic world of the media not everyone had the patience to listen.

I wrote a book (I'm finishing another one). I author articles, analysis pieces, and op-eds. I analyze and explain complex issues. For communication, e-mail or instant messenger usually suffices, sometimes a video call, and perfect hearing is not usually necessary. However, contrary to what one might think, even in such a line of work, hearing can be extremely important—for example, while researching additional information or trying to listen to audio content.

In the case of my involvement within the World Wide Web Consortium's (W3C) standardization efforts, hearing has been a particular problem. Working group communications are often multi-person teleconferences, without a video feed or captions. The lack of video is a big problem for me, because I can better understand a person when I can see *how* he or she is talking. Luckily, such meetings are usually transcribed, although the full context is not always written down.

In a world where multi-person meetings are the norm, hearing loss can be a significant limitation. Not all of my former employers understood this. Perhaps some didn't want to understand. How did I cope? Today, "live" text captions in video conferencing programs can be helpful, but unfortunately, these features are not always enabled by IT teams. Moreover, such facilities did not exist in the early days of my studies and work. Despite these difficulties, I worked with many people, including in teams. I managed projects, even if communication was sometimes a challenge. My chairing of steering committee meetings at a research and development agency was not a problem. In this case, the situation was clearly improved also by the pandemic, when the video conferencing format became a standard. That's also when it became apparent that many in-person meetings were unnecessary.

Before my hearing loss, I, too, could hear music and birds without having to think about trying to listen. Today, passively experiencing ambient noise is not possible for me, as it is for others. In order to hear these sorts of sounds, I have to concentrate, but then other activities, such as work, may become affected. I perceive too many sounds as distracting noise. This is a big downside of working in an open-plan office environment.

It took me years to learn how to function effectively. In my adult life, I have avoided highlighting my disability: I have kept this detail a secret or asked that no attention be paid to it and that people not inform others of it. Despite my requests, this was sometimes done against my will: I had a particularly bad experience when, after a BBC Radio interview about the privacy of technology, the material portrayed me as "a hearing-impaired security and privacy research engineer," despite the fact that I had previously explicitly asked that they not focus on or highlight this fact. Back then I was devastated to learn about it; today I view this as trivial. However, sometimes my hearing loss was used against me knowingly and deliberately, to propagate falsehoods. I can't help it. Perhaps this risk will diminish now, as I explain everything here openly.

When you're facing a serious health condition, it can come with a lot of problems and doubts about life, including about the future. Understandably, it can be difficult to believe in yourself. It can be unpleasant and uncomfortable at times. It might not be easy to get motivated to act or to live at all. That is why I am writing this. I hope that my story can at least be a motivation, an example, and relatable for someone.

I will also never say "I achieved everything in life by myself." I want to point out that I have received a lot of help, and for everything I am sincerely grateful, appreciate, and remember. I am not mentioning people by name for fear that I will leave someone out or that someone would not want to be mentioned.